D1035721

THE
PSYCHOANALYSIS OF
CULTURE

THE
PSYCHOANALYSIS OF
CULTURE

C. R. Badcock

BASIL BLACKWELL · OXFORD

© C. R. Badcock 1980

First published 1980 by
Basil Blackwell Publisher
5 Alfred Street
Oxford OX1 4HB
England

British Library Cataloguing in Publication Data

Badcock, C R
    The psychoanalysis of culture.
    1. Ethnopsychology

    2. Psychoanalysis

    I. Title
    301.2   GN508

    ISBN 0-631-11701-6

Typeset by Cotswold Typesetting Ltd, Gloucester and
Printed in Great Britain by The Camelot Press Ltd, Southampton.

CONTENTS

'If the development of civilization has such a far-reaching similarity to the development of the individual and if it employs the same methods, may we not be justified in reaching the diagnosis that, under the influence of cultural urges, some civilizations, or some epochs of civilization—possibly the whole of mankind—have become 'neurotic'? An analytic dissection of such neuroses might lead to therapeutic recommendations which could lay claim to great practical interest. I would not say that an attempt of this kind to carry psychoanalysis over to the cultural community was absurd or doomed to be fruitless . . . we may expect that one day someone will venture to embark upon the psychology of cultural communities.'

—Sigmund Freud, *Civilization and Its Discontents*.

I

THE PRIMAL TRAUMA

In the canon of the works of Freud case histories occupy a justly prominent place. This is because they reflect the material out of which psychoanalysis grew and which must always remain its principal foundation. But Freud's most important case history is seldom realized as such, and among the more familiar names of Dora, the Wolfman, and Little Hans, it is seldom, if ever, mentioned. Yet it remains of superordinate importance, for not only did it give rise to many of Freud's most original and influential ideas, it also has the distinction of being the case history of the most prominent subject whom Freud ever analyzed, and has to this day a significance for the mass of the human race which is unparalleled in any other of his works. The case history to which I refer is that contained in Freud's writings on anthropology, sociology, and religion. It is the case history of man and his culture, nothing less than the psychoanalysis of the human race itself.

My aim in this book is not merely to pull together the parts of Freud's analysis and present it as a whole (although this is certainly a subsidiary intention), but rather to systematize and develop his insights into a fully-rounded interpretation of the case-material. This Freud was never able to do. Perhaps he never would have done it; but this would not have been because it was not worth doing. On the contrary, I can think of nothing more worth doing as far as psychoanalysis is concerned because it involves us in what is perhaps the greatest psychological undertaking of which we are collectively capable: I mean the understanding of ourselves as a species and the resolution, through that understanding, of the collective neurosis which we call 'culture' or 'civilization'.

The record of Freud's analysis of man and his neurosis is to be found in *The Future of an Illusion, Civilization and its Discontents, Group Psychology and the Analysis of the Ego, Moses and Monotheism,* and a host of papers.[1] But of all these works the most important, certainly as far as understanding the basic element of Freud's psychoanalytic investigations of humanity at large is concerned, is unquestionably *Totem and Taboo.* It is without doubt the most famous of Freud's writings on anthropology and also, with the possible

---

[1] A list of Freud's writings dealing with this subject is to be found in an appendix to *Totem and Taboo,* XIII, 162. This, and all subsequent references to the works of Freud is to the *Standard Edition of the Complete Psychological Works,* quoting volume and page number.

exception of *Moses and Monotheism*, quite the most notorious. The reason for this notoriety will soon become clear, and we shall see that it is related to the fact that Freud's analysis in *Totem and Taboo* reveals the most strenuously repressed and strongly repudiated part of the case-material—the Oedipus complex, in this instance that of the entire human race.

Before we go on I must pause to say a word or two about the fate of Freud's interpretation. Analysts are, of course, habituated to encountering resistance in their patients; and this not uncommonly takes the form of an irrational refusal to accept the analytic interpretations which the patient's own symptoms demand. So it is hardly surprising to find that the subject of the analysis in this case, humanity at large, has not taken kindly to what Freud has proposed. Those who are most immediately concerned, those whom we might call researchers in the human sciences, have roundly rejected the findings of *Totem and Taboo* as being 'unscientific' and implausible. But, as at least one other writer has pointed out, 'the fact that so many eminent, learned and authoritative social scientists have condemned the theory suggests . . . that there is an even chance of its being right'.[2]

It is my belief that it is right, and so I intend to ignore all that social scientists, psychoanalysts and others have written on the assumption that it is wrong and instead begin again with Freud's theory and propose the reasons why I believe that it should be accepted as the most plausible and powerful explanation we possess of the origin of human society, and of culture in general. In my view, the relative failure of the human sciences to provide convincing and exact explanations of cultural phenomena is in large part to be attributed to their failure to take account of Freud and, in particular, of his analysis of the origin of civilization as propounded in *Totem and Taboo*. We shall see in the course of this book that, once this major defect is remedied, much can be achieved, and many aspects of society and culture that previously defied rational explanation can be satisfactorily accounted for.

In *Totem and Taboo* Freud begins by pointing out that among many of the most primitive men the horror of incest is the greatest horror of all. So great is the fear and abhorrence with which incest is regarded that complicated kinship rules, ritual avoidances and other means are used to avoid it. So great is the outrage that the most severe penalties—often death itself—are reserved for those who succumb to temptation in this way. Incest is, in other words, 'taboo'. Indeed, it is (along with totemic taboos) the principal taboo of these societies. But taboo is a puzzling concept, especially if we go into its finer details, as Freud does in the second essay of the book. Its puzzling, contradictory nature seems to reflect the fact that taboos are closely associated with emotional ambivalence—that is, with a tendency to feel contradictory emotions about the same object. In this respect taboo has a clear parallel in the irrational prohibitions which neurotics sometimes lay upon themselves. Like taboo, the neurotic prohibition seems an arbitrary rule imposed without clear reason and, like it, reflects the fact that it is of an unconscious origin. Indeed, Freud comes to the conclusion that, psychologically speaking, there is no significant difference between the two, and that both the taboo and the neurotic prohibition are unconscious defences against ambivalence. In other words, he begins his analysis of the case of man with the observation that those men who manifest human life at its simplest and most primitive also manifest a high degree of unconscious ambivalence which, like the exactly similar situation in certain neurotics, leads to the formation of compulsive prohibitions in the guise of taboos.

If the taboo is the outcome of ambivalence it follows logically that the most important taboos ought, psychologically speaking, to hide the greatest ambivalences, and so, if our contention above about the severity of incest taboos is correct, we should be justified in affirming that, at least among some primitive peoples, the most extreme case of emotional ambivalence adheres to this aspect of the sexual code. Now, if incest is so energetically repudiated by the taboo we should expect that the exactly contrary purpose hides in the unconscious under its interdict. In other words, the great importance of denying incest in the conscious content of the taboo must be motivated by a correspondingly immense need to affirm it in the unconscious. The taboo therefore owes its very existence to a powerful, but suppressed, desire to break it.

In following Freud's interpretation of taboo we see that he applies exactly the same principles as are used in clinical analysis. He takes a neurotic symptom—taboo, or obsessional prohibition—and subjects it to an analysis which aims to discover its latent, or unconscious basis. Then, having done so, he seeks to relate it systematically to other apparently unrelated or equally arbitrary manifestations. Eventually, a clinical picture emerges in which all the neurotic symptoms become comprehensible as part of a single, coherent and intelligible set of unconscious ideas. As we shall see later, the clinical picture that emerges from the analysis of the incest taboo and its related phenomena corresponds not merely in structure with that obtained by analysis of individuals, but in its content as well.

Incest taboos, like neurotic prohibitions in individuals, do not exist in isolation. On the contrary, in the case of the Australian aborigines, for example, we always find them closely associated with taboos relating to totems.

A totem is an animal, plant, or natural object with which an individual has a special ritual relationship and with which he shares his name.[3] Usually he regards himself as descended from it in some way or another. Totems come into connection with the taboo against incest because individuals of the same clan share a common clan totem. The clan is exogamous, that is, it is a unit into which a man may not marry—on the contrary, all his clan 'sisters' are taboo to him because of the laws forbidding incest. Hence the possession of a

---

[3] G. Róheim, 'Psychoanalysis of Primitive Cultural Types', *International Journal of Psychoanalysis*, XIII, 57.

clan totem in common rules out women in the clan as legitimate sexual partners.

Surprisingly, however, it is not just clan sisters sharing the same totem who are taboo. The totem is itself taboo and members of the clan are subject to complex ritual prohibitions with respect to it. Thus, if what was said above about taboo and emotional ambivalence applies to taboos against incest it should also apply to those affecting the totem. There must, in other words, be a nexus of ambivalent feelings associated with it, quite independent of its connection with incest.

In the last essay in *Totem and Taboo* Freud shows that the taboo prohibitions associated with totem animals correspond to neurotic prohibitions found in individuals suffering from an animal phobia. Analysis of cases of animal phobia show that this neurosis originates in an identification of the animal with the father (and in particular, with the father's penis) and that the fear of the animal is in fact fear of the father arising out of guilt felt in connection with incestuous wishes directed towards the mother. Hence the origin of the taboo relating to the totem is, according to Freud, guilt resulting from the incestuous wishes of the clan brothers. This is why the two phenomena—exogamy and totemism—are so intimately related.

No mere summary like that offered here can possibly do justice to Freud's masterful interpretation as expounded in the pages of *Totem and Taboo*. It must suffice to say that, drawing on all manner of material not reproducible here, he finally comes to the question of the origin of totemism and exogamy and gives the following apparently incredible explanation.

Following a suggestion by Darwin, he proposes that men originally existed in a condition which he calls the 'primal horde'. A single tyrannical father dominated it, enjoying the favours of a number of females and absolutely excluding the sons from it as soon as they achieved sexual maturity. Eventually, these excluded sons, driven on by their frustrated sexual desire for their mothers and sisters, banded together, drove out the primal father, killed him and devoured him. But, having done so, they became—just like some modern individuals who suddenly have their desires gratified by their parent's death—subject to deferred obedience and a sense of guilt. This resulted from the fact that their relation to the primal father was ambivalent. They both hated and loved him because, although he drove them out and enjoyed all that they desired, they nevertheless gave him grudging admiration for what he had done, and in their unconsciouses each desired to be like him. Once their negative, sadistic feelings about the primal father had been satisfied by killing him, only the positive, loving ones remained. These got the upper hand in causing the sons to re-instate the primal father in the guise of the animal totem as the symbolic manifestation of their bad conscience. His prohibition of their access to the mothers and sisters was retrospectively obeyed by instituting the ban on incest so that a form of social organization emerged like that found among the Australian aborigines, in which a band of clan brothers submitted themselves to a tabooed animal and a rule of exogamy.

The events described above are the collective equivalent of the kernel of an individual neurosis. They are, in other words, the Oedipal crisis of the entire human race. Just as individual human beings desire to possess their mothers and murder their fathers, so the forerunners of modern man were motivated by incestuous desires to murder the primal father. And just as modern individuals resolve their Oedipus complexes by submitting to the authority of the father and set him up within them as their super-ego—the force of conscience—so primal man put himself beneath the authority of the primal father he had killed by worshipping him under the forms of totemism. And just as the principal commands of the modern conscience are directed against the very desires which led to it being set up, namely, love of the mother and hatred of the father, so in totemism the principal taboos address themselves to the very temptations whose gratification is their historical basis—incest and parricide. Thus in his first, and perhaps greatest, contribution to the psychoanalysis of man, Freud has succeeded in accomplishing the central task of any analysis—the uncovering of the Oedipus complex of the patient along with the deepest instinctual bases of his ambivalence. It is, as we shall find later, the study to which one returns time and time again as one tries to unravel the subsequent history of the subject and relate it to the primal trauma of mankind.

But why should this be so? Why, if Freud has so manifestly failed to convince any significant proportion of thinking humanity that he is right about its origins, should we waste any more time on his far-fetched constructions? Freud himself considers the possibility that the revolt of the sons against the primal father may never have happened in actuality but only in the phantasies of primal man. But he rejects it with the observation that, just as the neurotic conflicts of modern men are based on the psychological realities underlying their phantasies rather than the phantasies themselves, so the primal conflict of the whole human race must have been based on a reality rather than a mere dream. 'In the beginning,' Freud concludes, 'was the Deed.'[4]

It sometimes happens that a patient who has abandoned a good analyst and gone to other more accommodating ones in the vain hope of finding an easy way out of his unconscious difficulties, suddenly returns to the true path of resolution of his neurosis as the result of some objective and independent corroboration of one of the original analyst's interpretations (perhaps by way of unexpected confirmation of some event from his childhood). The sudden removal of the patina of implausibility which his resistances have deposited on a crucial piece of analytic insight may temporarily rob him of his capacity to maintain his intellectual defences against it. He is forced to re-appraise it and perhaps even to accept its truth.

Approximately the same sort of thing may have begun to happen with regard to the common resistance to the findings of *Totem and Taboo* when,

[4] Freud, *Totem and Taboo*, XIII, 161.

in 1970, the anthropologist Clifford Jolly published an article in which he drew attention to some remarkable adaptive similarities between the gelada baboon and man.[5]

In many ways, this paper marks the most outstanding single advance in our understanding of human evolution since Darwin published his *Descent of Man*. Until 1970, our understanding of man's evolution had merely progressed along the lines already foreseen by Darwin and had vindicated his chief conclusion: namely, that man and the modern great apes share a common ancestor. But, with Jolly's paper, a completely new and startling prospect was opened up, one not in any way suspected by Darwin. This was the possibility that man, although not closely related to the gelada baboon as he was to the apes, might nevertheless share with it common adaptive features which reveal a striking parallelism in the evolution of the two species.

The gelada baboon (*Theropithecus gelada*) is a ground-dwelling monkey found in Ethiopia. Like modern man's hominid ancestors, it inhabits open grassland and shares with them a large number of significant adaptive characteristics. This observation in no way contradicts Darwin's realization that in many respects humans are closely related to today's great apes, the gorilla and chimpanzee, and modern bio-chemical research has proved the close genetic relationship which exists between them and ourselves. But it is significant that it is precisely in those characteristics which most distinguish humans from apes that we most resemble the gelada baboon. For instance, all the pongids are forest dwellers and spend at least part of their time in trees. Hominids and geladas are almost totally terrestrial and are found in open country. Both have hands allowing excellent opposability between thumb and index fingers, and are thus adept at picking up small objects. Both show striking resemblances in the structure of the jaw and teeth (not to mention numerous other more subtle structural resemblances elsewhere). The gelada and man are the only primates to have evolved fat deposits on the buttocks and pectoral secondary sexual characteristics in the female (breasts in the case of human females, a hairless area fringed with polyphs which signal sexual receptivity in the case of the female gelada). Males of both species have evolved impressive displays of hair around the mouth and neck. It is noteworthy that it is precisely these same features which distinguish *T. gelada* from the closely related species *Papio* and *Mandrillus*. In other words, what the gelada baboon and man have in common is the very set of adaptive features which distinguish them both from their nearest relatives. It is on this basis that Jolly concludes, 'There are some grounds, therefore, for assuming the existence of evolutionary parallelism, and perhaps some degree of functional equivalence between the differentiation of *Theropithecus* and that of the basal hominids.'[6]

[5] C. Jolly, 'The Seed-Eaters: A New Model of Hominid Differentiations based on a Baboon Analogy', *Man* 5 (1), 5–26, 1970.

[6] *Ibid.*, p. 12.

His explanation of this 'evolutionary parallelism' is that both the ancestors of modern man and the gelada baboon have evolved to exploit a similar sort of diet in similar habitats. The striking convergence between hominid and gelada dentition may well be the result of the fact that early hominids, like the modern gelada, underwent adaptation to a diet of small, tough objects. This would explain the otherwise quite untypical reduction of the canine in the case of the gelada. Most baboons—like the great apes—have developed large canine teeth in the male as a secondary sexual characteristic and weapon of defence. In the case of the gelada, however, the canine teeth have undergone a relative reduction, a reduction which, according to Jolly, is the result of the need to chew the blades of grass and the rhizomes which typically constitute its diet. Man has gone somewhat beyond the gelada in this respect, almost certainly because he is adapted to exploit not the blades of grasses but the *grains*—a resource which, in domesticated form, still comprises the staple of his diet to this day. Hence the mouth and dentition of hominids and geladas seem to be special adaptations to a grassland diet, a conclusion which also probably applies to their joint evolution of the good opposability of thumb and index finger which would be needed to pick up such small items as grass-blades and seeds. Other features, too, such as the development of buttocks and pectoral sexual characteristics in females, are almost certainly the outcome of an existence in which much time is spent sitting upright while feeding (other ground-dwelling primates like *Papio* usually do this standing on three legs).

But—and this is the reason why I have gone into the evolutionary parallelism between geladas and hominids in some detail—the similarities do not end there. According to Jolly, there is one other respect in which geladas and humans resemble one another. This is their common possession of a 'one-male breeding unit'. For a full understanding of the sociological dimension of gelada and human evolutionary convergence we need to turn to a study of the gelada social structure made by J. H. Crook.[7] He describes it as follows:

The 'one-male group' is the reproductive unit of a gelada population. It consists of a large adult male, a group of females including both mothers and non-maternal animals in all stages of the oestrous cycle, variable numbers of juvenile animals, infants and babies, and an occasional sub-adult male often almost totally grown but not sexually mature. In areas where the population is widely dispersed such social units are the commonest, observed associating inconstantly with small groups consisting wholly of large sub-adult males and mature males (possibly old animals) not possessing 'harems'. These 'all-male groups' likewise move independently from other units and show considerable cohesion over several weeks.[8]

This, then, is what Jolly is referring to when he speaks of a 'one-male breeding unit' in the case of the gelada. Having made the point that a social

[7] J. H. Crook, 'Gelada Baboon Herd Structure and Movement', *Symp. zool. Soc. Lond.*, 18, 237–258, 1966.
[8] *Ibid.*, p. 241.

structure like that of the gelada is also exhibited by the two other true 'open country' monkeys, *Erythrocebus patas* (patas monkey) and *Papio hamadryas* (hamadryas baboon) Jolly concludes:

It would not be unreasonable to expect a similar social organisation, with permanent, monogamous or polygamous one-male groups set within the matrix of a larger society, to be developed by a hominoid adapting to a gelada-like way of life. *The pattern is also, one might add, still distinctive of the vast majority of Homo sapiens.*[9]

In other words, Jolly is arguing that if man and gelada have developed similar adaptations in response to a lengthy period of evolution in a grassland habitat and eating a similar diet, it is not unlikely that they might also manifest convergent social evolution and share common social units. Indeed, he goes further, and in the final italicized sentence from my quotation says that a gelada-type social organization is '*still distinctive of the vast majority of Homo sapiens*'. If we now look back at what Crook says about the gelada social structure, we see that what Jolly must have in mind is the characteristic feature of the mature adult male who exercises exclusive sexual rights over one (which corresponds to the monogamous case mentioned above by Jolly) or a number (corresponding to the polygamous case) of mature females, and from which sexually potent sons are excluded. Understood in this sense, his statement is undoubtedly correct. But it is equally obvious that there are important differences between a gelada and a human social structure, and if the similarities are to be accounted for by the origins of mankind in a gelada-like condition, then the differences must be the result of subsequent development on the part of humans. So it might be worth looking more closely at these differences to see how they can be explained.

The principal difference between the gelada and human 'one-male units' is that, in the case of all existing human societies, the exclusion of sons and the maintenance of the exclusive sexual rights of the adult male are the result of and incest-taboo and a ritual which we call marriage. In the case of the gelada baboon, the adult male's possession of exclusive sexual rights over his females is the outcome of the exercise of aggression by the male in question towards the members of his harem and any male foolish or brave enough to challenge him.

Incest is not a factor at all, and although males as they reach maturity and acquire harems may well not take over females which previously belonged to their fathers and may thus be their mothers and sisters, it is certainly not impossible that they should. Again, the violent means by which male geladas acquire their females through direct competition with existing harem owners has no parallel in human societies. The sons of humans do not have to take on their fathers in combat before they can get a woman. Thus the two distinguishing features of human 'one-male units'—incest-avoidance and the absence of conflict with the paternal generation—must be the result of social

---

[9] Jolly, *op. cit.*, p. 16. My italics.

evolution which has taken place subsequent to our originally acquiring a true gelada-type social structure of the sort described by Crook. Summing up the situation, one might say that although Jolly was correct in saying that the 'one-male unit' is still distinctive of man today, it is dependent for its existence on quite different and completely human institutions, namely, incest-avoidance and the suppression of hostility against the paternal generation. It is precisely these two distinguishing features of hominid social adaptation which any complete theory of human social evolution must attempt to explain.

By now, the reader will be becoming aware of the extreme relevance of all this to *Totem and Taboo*. The social structure described in the quotation from Crook above and which is possessed by the primate with whom man shares most of his distinctive adaptive traits is precisely the same as that which Freud termed the 'primal horde'. We have the same despotic adult male (Freud's 'primal father') who monopolizes a group of females to the exclusion of the younger and less-fit males (Crook's 'all-male group', Freud's 'sons').

We notice that the two most important respects in which present-day human 'one-male units' differ from this gelada prototype is exactly in terms of the phenomena claimed by Freud to be distinctive of the most primitive human societies—an all-important taboo on incest, and a suppression of aggression against the father (expressed in the quasi-animal phobic form of totemism).

I have already briefly alluded to how Freud explained the origin of this taboo and this suppression of hostility in terms of the supposedly unlikely theory of the revolt of primeval 'all-male groups' against the 'one-male group' of the primal father, his murder, consumption by the sons and the emergence of guilt and deferred obedience within them. I believe that a closer consideration of Jolly's discovery can give us a quite new insight into this series of events which will make them seem far from implausible.

We have established that the adaptive convergence between gelada baboon and human beings is the outcome of our distant hominid ancestors having lived in a similar habitat to today's gelada and having subsisted on a similar diet. Yet we know that hominids were not always seed-eaters. Palaeontological evidence shows that the hunting of big-game animals developed in due course of time, and today there are no human beings who live by gelada-like foraging (although seeds still form an important part of our diet in the form of domesticated grain). How could this transition from vegetarian foraging to big-game hunting have come about? Most writers on the subject, such as Jolly in the article referred to above, seem to think that it was made gradually and naturally, without any dramatic changes. My opinion is different, and to see why this is so we need only review what has already been established about foraging hominids.

If such hominids had lived in primal hordes under the domination of a single adult male it is most unlikely that hunting would have been possible. Solitary hunting by night would have been ruled out by the fact that early hominids would themselves have been in great danger of predation from other much more lethal nocturnal hunters like the larger felines and hyenas. By day, individual hunting would have been most unsuccessful for such a relatively ill-equipped pursuer as a hominid. On the open grasslands where they would have been living, solitary hominids would have had little chance to surprise prey at close range and would have had to undertake a long chase. In this event success would have been very difficult. A study quoted by Schaller and Lowther[10] showed that if one jackal pursued a fawn it was successful in only 16 per cent of cases. If two jackals co-operated, 67 per cent success was achieved. If one lion hunted alone it succeeded in capturing 27 per cent of the prey pursued; if two hunted together they brought down 52 per cent. Similar ratios apply to the weight of prey which can be hunted if individuals co-operate. After a careful analysis of the situation Schaller and Lowther conclude: 'An ecological opening exists for a social predator hunting large animals and scavenging during the day, an opening some early hominid may well have filled . . ..'[11]

However, an adult male hominid controlling a primal horde could not possibly have participated in a co-operative hunt. He would have been most unlikely to join up with other males for a chase which might take him far from his jealously guarded harem, and could hardly have hunted with his females who would have been slowed down by their physical inferiority in speed and aggressiveness and the encumbrances of children. The need for permanent watchfulness over the harem, distrust of other males, and the individualistic feeding habits of a full-time forager would have greatly discouraged hunting by the primal fathers. But what of the sons?

By contrast with the 'one-male units', the 'all-male groups' would have been ideally pre-adapted from the sociological point of view to undertake co-operative big-game hunting. They would not have been encumbered with females and young. They—like the young males in the 'all-male groups' of today's gelada baboon—would have been on terms of much greater equality with one another than the primal father would have been with his despotic colleagues. Their social group would have approximated closely in structure to that found in social hunting species today, such as the African wild dog, the lion, spotted hyena, or wolf. All of these species manifest social structures which are much more plastic and egalitarian than the gelada 'one-male unit'. Furthermore, they all show signs of considerable development of altruism and the ability to share food—two features totally lacking in the behaviour of mature gelada baboons. Wild dogs will co-operate to bring down an animal and will share food with pups and adults left to guard them at the den by means of a regurgitation-reflex triggered by a begging behaviour on the part of the recipient animal. Baboons, by contrast, have hardly

[10] G. Schaller & G. Lowther, 'The Relevance of Canivore Behaviour to the Study of Early Hominids', *Southwestern Journal of Anthropology*, 25 (4), 307.
[11] *Ibid.*, p. 329.

ever been seen to share food. Even mothers will not give solid food to their young ones, who are expected to fend for themselves in this respect from the beginning. Significantly enough, the rare cases of food-sharing which have been observed among baboons were in circumstances where they got hold of meat.[12]

This exception to the rule of baboon dietary individualism is suggestive, and prompts me to put forward the following theory of the origin of co-operative hunting among hominids: We may safely assume on the strength of the evidence marshalled by Jolly that originally all early hominids were vegetarian foragers subsisting like today's gelada baboon. We may also assume, with Jolly and Freud, that the social structure was closely comparable to that of the gelada. However, our early seed-eating hominids were living in a habitat where there was an important source of nutritious high-protein food which their primal horde social structure did not allow them to exploit: Big-game.

The 'all-male groups'—Freud's 'sons'—were not subject to the same restriction because they banded together into looser, less rigidly hierarchical groups which were in fact ideally pre-adapted to hunting. Perhaps most important of all they were, unlike today's gelada baboons, possessors of considerable intelligence, which, combined with their youth, gave them a behavioural plasticity and resourcefulness not present in a mere monkey. Some of them (perhaps the more aggressive ones, or those who felt the deprivations enforced on them by the ruling adult males more painfully but who also found their aggressiveness easy to divert onto other recipients) might easily have begun to hunt and rapidly acquired a taste for meat. Such a modification in their behaviour would have been highly gratifying because, quite apart from the outlet for their resentment and aggression that hunting would have provided, it would have brought them a highly-nutrious source of food which would have freed them from the laborious monotony of foraging for seeds, and offered them instead all the thrills and excitement of the chase. But even more importantly, if they had begun to make a real success of co-operative hunting and begun to develop the rudiments of altruistic behaviour, they would have found their individual fitness promoted by the greater security within the group which altruism always procures. Collective action would thus not only have secured success in hunting, but also better protection from predators and generally increased chances of survival now that it was assisted by the cohesion of the group.

However, no matter what the gain in individual fitness from the better diet and conditions of life in a hunting 'all-male group', natural selection would have conferred no benefit as long as such groups did not reproduce themselves. We may assume that, to begin with, most bands of young male

[12] Usually, however, whenever baboons get hold of small game a fight over the spoils ensues in which the dominant male appropriates it all. Cf. H. Kummer, *Primate Societies*.

hunters broke up when their members became sufficiently mature to relinquish the new way of life, challenge existing dominant males for females and start harems of their own. The constraints of the 'one-male group' would have meant a return to the traditional foraging for the rest of the individual's life. But it is also possible that after a time a hunting band emerged which might not have wished to dissolve, but rather to acquire females as it was, without undergoing fission into many independent 'one-male groups'. How would such a band of hunters have obtained females? Only by one method, namely, a concerted attack on some dominant male and the collective rape of his probably considerable harem. And how would this attack have been executed? Why clearly, just as every other such undertaking was executed—as a hunt. Techniques of co-operative aggression fully practiced and perfected in pursuing game animals would have come to hand wonderfully in the situation of having to confront one of the ruling adult males. They would probably have attacked him at first from a distance with stones as Róheim suggests[13] and then at close quarters with bare hands and teeth. That they might even have consumed him in a first grisly act of cannibalism, as Freud suggests, does not seem so unlikely if we recall that these hominids could not have been provided with the inhibitions of modern, civilized men, but would rather have been applying to the primal father a means of satisfying their aggressive instincts against him which they had already most successfully applied in satisfying their need for food. It is most unlikely that a mode of behaviour which was probably established in the traditions of the hunting band was not fully carried through to its conclusion, so that the equivalence between the murder of the primal father and a hunt was exact.

But what would have happened then? Freud, we will recall, argues that the next thing to occur was a feeling of guilt and deferred obedience in the band of parricidal sons who, as a result of their crime, set up taboos on incest and a religion of totemism. Let us take the incest question first.

It is clear that if a group of hunting male hominids attacked a dominant male forager with a harem in order to acquire some females there would be a great danger of the group dissolving in any subsequent sexual rivalry. We can easily imagine that what might have begun as a harmonious and well concerted attack by an 'all-male group' on a hapless lone male and his harem may well have quickly degenerated into a vicious and, in all probability, bloody internecine quarrel. Examples of such conflicts among modern primates are common. Describing a field study of langurs in India, E. O. Wilson tells us that 'a group of seven males attacked and displaced the resident male. Fighting then erupted among the usurpers until six were ousted and only one remained in control.'[14]

If such broadly egalitarian and altruistic groups were to survive they would have to develop some means of dealing with the problem of conflict over

[13] G. Róheim, *The Riddle of the Sphinx*, p. 202.
[14] *Sociobiology*, p. 138.

sharing out the spoils of the rape of the women. Freud shows in *Totem and Taboo* how guilt and deferred obedience would have achieved this. But this would have only been so if the members of the band of hunting brothers had appropriated a group of women who really were their mothers and sisters. If they attacked a 'one-male group' which was unrelated to themselves they might have had no good reason for such guilty consciences, certainly not over the question of incest. As a result, there would have been no effective means of avoiding a conflict for exclusive ownership of the females of the group.[15] Such groups would have dissolved into internecine strife over the females; but the parricidal, incestuous groups would have encountered powerful psychological motivations in the form of guilt and remorse to make them submit to a rule of incest-avoidance which would have resulted in sharing out the females in some way in which a hominid avoided taking his actual mother or sister as a sexual partner. The inhibition of internecine sexual rivalry which this would have produced would have been enough to protect such groups of hunters from the worst effects of their own success, and would have set the scene for the intervention of the most important factor of all—natural selection.

We have already seen what sort of advantages, as far as individual fitness is concerned, the new hunting bands would have bestowed on their members. But such advantages are slight when compared with the immense advantage which such groups would have had in the struggle for survival once they had acquired females. As we have already seen in discussing the question of incest-avoidance, the acquisition of females would have demanded notable increases in altruism and the suppression of internal conflict within the hunting bands. Every one of these reductions in individual aggressiveness would have powerfully reinforced the strength of the group and its capacity to look after all its members. But the need to establish some sort of home base at which the females and young could be left would have conferred an overwhelming advantage on such groups.

The free-ranging gelada baboon has no such home bases, and individuals who fall ill or become immobilized cannot count on being looked after.

[15] It is, of course, true that recent field studies of primates have established that some slight measure of 'natural' incest-avoidance appears to occur, albeit among species with a rather different social structuring to that of the gelada, and, we must suppose, our hominid ancestors. Nevertheless, it is possible that among primates generally (and this must include primal man) incest may be inhibited by the reluctance of females to allow themselves to be mounted by sons or brothers whom they customarily regard as of lower status than themselves. If this was true of our hominid ancestors then the 'natural' incest-avoidance would perhaps have re-inforced the Freudian mechanism invoked here. It would have provided another excellent reason why it was only the incestuous and parricidal groups which could maintain their altruistic and co-operative way of life. Any attempt to show that humans possess an innate or acquired fundamental disinclination for incest must founder on the impressive evidence for the contrary accumulated by psychoanalysts the world over. For an excellent discussion of the primatological evidence see R. Fox (Ed.), *Biosocial Anthropology*, p. 21ff.

Infants will be guarded for a while, but adults and those who cannot move on with the group after a day or so are left to their own devices, which almost always means death. But a group of hunting hominids with a well-hidden home base to which highly nutritious and easily transportable animal flesh could be brought and at which sick or convalescent individuals could be accommodated along with the women and children would have a simply tremendous advantage in terms of survival. If we recall for a moment how many illnesses which affect men cause temporary incapacity but from which an individual can expect to recover given sufficient time and rest, we begin to see how the change-over to a fully-fledged hunting economy must have benefited those hominids capable of it. Even slight injuries like a badly sprained ankle, which might be fatal to a free-ranging, foraging biped, would be only temporary inconveniences to a hunter with a home base to repair to and comrades altruistic enough to take him there.

In short, natural selection would have powerfully and decisively favoured the hunting hominids who managed to maintain the structure of an 'all-male group' even when it succeeded in getting hold of females. Better fed, better able to survive illness, injury, and the rigours of childbirth, with better facilities for bringing up the children and protecting the weak, such groups would have fared better than the foragers in the competitive struggle for existence. In their capacity to fight off predators, to take advantage of weapons and tools (which would have been of only marginal use to full-time foragers but of crucial value to hunters), and in their need to develop means of efficient symbolic communication, such hunters would have started on the upward path which leads to technology, speech, and ultimately to civilization. Had such a change-over to hunting not occurred, gelada-like hominids might even today still be wandering the savanna grasslands of the tropics, eking out a meagre existence grubbing about for grains, totally preoccupied with a way of life which would have contained no possibility of the spectacular development achieved by the human race since it abandoned it.

In decisively acting in favour of the parricidal, potentially incestuous hominids who had begun to hunt, natural selection was effectively handing evolutionary success to those individuals who manifested the greatest ambivalence. Emotional ambivalence is, as Freud noted,[16] an innate constant of human personality. If our speculations above are correct, we can clearly see why. The reason is that the most successful hunters would have been those capable of the greatest resentment against their fathers, but also capable of the greatest love and respect for them. Such individuals would have been powerfully motivated to undertake the essential parricide, but they would also have had to be those who, once the deed was done, were most able to realize the positive side of their ambivalence and obey the father in the form of submission to the interests of the group, both erotically in relinquishing

---

[16] Freud, 'Instincts and their Vicissitudes', XIV, 131.

incest, and altruistically in renouncing some considerable part of their egoism. Hence, natural selection, doubtless operating over hundreds of generations and many thousands of years, must have repeatedly and unerringly selected those who could be most aggressive in the chase (whether or not this included the pursuit of the primal father) but who could also be most submissive to the interests of a group which of necessity must have contained many who could not join in the hunt but had to rely on others for food, protection, and shelter. These quite contradictory requirements—boundless aggression against other species in hunting, but far-reaching inhibitions with regard to one's own—must be the origin of the genetic endowment of modern man which so demonstrably predisposes him to mental conflict and neurosis. In due course we must suppose that the hunting confraternity wiped out the older and more traditional, if less neurotic, foragers, and secured for themselves alone the right to be the progenitors of all subsequent generations of the human race.

But one further difficulty remains: the continuity of the fraternal hunting groups. We have seen that the aggressive and incestuous desires of groups of young male hominid hunters may have led them—indeed, in all probability, *must* have led them—to kill the primal father and acquire his harem. We have also seen that the son's guilt must have prevented them from committing actual incest and that a phobic reaction to the dead primal father—the simplest and most primitive of all neurotic actions—made them set up a religion of totemism as Freud describes. But what of their children? Why should the sons of the original parricides not have committed incest with *their* mothers or sisters? Clearly, my account so far may explain why taboos on incest and an animal totem existed for the perpetrators of the ghastly primal deed, but how can it explain their continued existence in communities who no longer had any need to fear, or even to remember the primal father?

A first, but incomplete answer may be that in the beginning the sons of the original parricides were themselves excluded from the father's group in just the same way as the fathers had been excluded by their foraging forbears. 'All-male groups' made up of the sons of hunters may well have existed alongside similar groups composed of the sons of the more conservative foragers. Indeed, there is every reason to believe that the original parricides, even in their dim and still somewhat sub-human intelligences, perceived the same incestuous and murderous motivations stirring in the minds of their sons as had so conspicuously emerged in their own. They had every reason to behave as the primal fathers had done, and to expel such dangerous rivals the moment they approached sexual maturity. Such a situation may have lasted for thousands of years. Indeed, there is no reason to suppose that even the eventual disappearance of foraging primal hordes should have brought an end to it. Bands of young men expelled from their fathers' groups could still have engaged in violent conflict with them, albeit they had now lost the advantage of being the many attacking the one, the hunters in pursuit of the hunted.

Nevertheless, it is clear that what would have been a simple massacre of one individual in the original situation would now have become one in which opposed bands of hunters, one with women, the other without, fought out a potentially suicidal pitched battle in which the success of the younger men was by no means a foregone conclusion. The dangers of internecine conflict which existed within the original hunting bands would now have disastrously broken out *between* them.

The only way to prevent this was to reproduce for each generation a repetition of the events which had caused the original parricides to suppress their mutual antagonisms and lust for sexual hegemony and so submit to the altruistic renunciations demanded by the incest and totem taboos. Some of the original totemists brought this about by the invention of something which has to this day remained a notable feature of many religions—the initiation ceremony.

The altruism and internal harmony of the original totemic hunting bands was based on the guilt and remorse of the parricides which led them to set up the totem in the place of the dead father as their shared super-ego. The super-ego is, according to Freud, the psychological basis of all social life. The reason for this is that it is the agency of the mind that censors and controls the originally quite egoistic instincts of the individual. Altruism means suppression of these egoistic impulses, and in the case of the original parricides this meant the possession of a super-ego—a purely psychological agency of self-control. As long as parricide remained the only origin of the super-ego and of the altruism which made a co-operative hunting life possible, sons would have to go on being expelled from the paternal groups and would have to go on murdering their fathers if they were themselves to succeed in creating viable hunting bands. The solution to this potentially-disastrous situation for the forbears of the human race was to create some other means of producing a super-ego in the sons, some other source of inhibition of incest and of hostility against the father apart from bloody acts of rape and murder.

The solution to this problem was found in the initiation ritual. In the language of the central Australian aborigines the term applied to such rituals is *kenguma*, which means to 'repeat', 'to follow' or 'to imitate'.[17] Doubtless this refers to the traditional basis of such observances, but it may also reveal something of the fundamental psychological and sociological significance of such events. Opening his classic psychoanalytic study of initiation rituals, Theodor Reik says:

The significance of initiation and puberty rites with their elaborate and impressive ceremonial can hardly be overestimated in the religious life and social organisation of primitive peoples.[18]

[17] G. Róheim, *The Riddle of the Sphinx*, p. 105.
[18] T. Reik, *Ritual: Four Psychoanalytic Studies*, p. 91.

James Frazer, in his *Golden Bough* refers to them as 'the central mystery of primitive society'.[19] We shall see that their importance has not been over-estimated but that, on the contrary, in providing a repetition of the primal trauma of man's psychological evolution they have provided the basis for all subsequent religious and social developments.

Initiation takes place around puberty, and although there are great differ-ences in the ways in which primitive societies undertake the initiations, cer-tain factors seem to be more or less constant. One of these is the separation of the novices from the rest of the society, and especially from their mothers. Among the Pitjentara of Australia, lads who begin to show signs of approach-ing manhood are driven out of the camp, where they live on the fringes until initiated. Alternatively, they are beaten insensible by the men and initiated on the spot.[20] Women are always excluded from the ceremonies, and in some societies have their sons forcibly dragged away from them. Violence, often of the most extreme kind, is a universal feature of the rites. In central Australia they invariably begin with some sort of assault on the boys, usually aimed at making their noses or mouths bleed; the native explanation for this is that it is necessary to make the initiates 'fear and respect the elders'.[21] In New Guinea, boys are dragged off to what all non-initiates and women believe is a mon-ster, whose jaws are actually the overhanging eaves of the ceremonial house and within whose 'belly' they are circumcised.[22] In Africa, between the Niger and Lake Chad, boys are initiated by a man who pounces on them dressed in a leopard skin. He scratches them with artificial claws and proceeds to remove a testicle from each. In the Sudan, uncircumcised boys are ritually beaten with phallus-shaped rods. The Cewa require them to eat and drink excrement, and in other cases a cord is tied to the candidates' genitals and violently pulled.

Circumcision, or some comparable genital mutilation, is usually a central feature of initiation rituals the world over. This, too, is closely connected with aggression against the initiates. Róheim reports that among some tribes of central Australian aborigines the circumcisor and his assistants 'chew their beards' (a sign of anger) and engage in all manner of threatening behaviour while they carry out the operation.[23] 'Among the Bukaua, feigned attacks coupled with a frightful noise are made on the boys . . . Among the Kai . . . after the circumcision the men stand in two rows facing one another, and the youths have to pass down between the men who rain violent blows upon them.'[24] Among the Mandan Indians, Reik reports that the initiates are

[19] J. G. Frazer, *The Golden Bough*, vol. ii, p. 278.
[20] G. Róheim, *The Eternal Ones of the Dream*, p. 74.
[21] G. Róheim, *Psychoanalysis and Anthropology*, p. 76.
[22] T. Reik, *op. cit.*, pp. 93–8 (quoting Frazer).
[23] G. Róheim, *The Eternal Ones of the Dream*, p. 74.
[24] T. Reik, *op. cit.*, p. 103.

covered with wounds and hoisted up on ropes attached to pieces of wood pushed into them.[25]

The ritual mutilations are frequently followed in Australia and elsewhere by the instruction of the young man in the laws and ritual observances of the tribe. When the Murngin youth has been circumcised, the elders read to him from the tablets of Murngin law:

You must not use obscene language. You must never tell a lie. You must not commit adultery, nor go after a woman who does not belong to you. You must always obey your father and respect your elders. You must never betray the secrets you have learned from us to the women or to the boys who have not been circumcised.[26]

Much the same sort of thing happens among the Aranda and many other aboriginal peoples.[27] In the case of the Pitjentara, after the circumcision wound has healed the young man appears before the elders and is called on to make 'an examination of conscience' and a full confession of all his past misdeeds.[28] Among the Nandi of Africa novices must make public confessions of sexual transgressions before they are circumcised.

During this time, the newly-initiated youths are kept in ritual sequestration and often, on return to their families when it is finally all over, are expected to affect complete forgetting of their previous life, even needing to be taught how to eat and drink, and by which door to enter the hut.[29]

What are we to make of these extraordinary practices? Perhaps we could begin with the circumcision, which is such a common, and such a central feature.

Circumcision is understood by psychoanalysis as a substitute for castration. Róheim reports that one of his aboriginal informants told him that prior to his initiation he had had a dream in which his entire penis, and not just the foreskin, had been cut off.[30] According to Aranda traditions, one group of totem-ancestors castrated boys instead of circumcising them.[31]

The threat of castration, whose ritual simulation—circumcision—is such a basic and constant feature of initiations the world over, plays the ceremonial counterpart of the castration fears of children suffering from animal phobias. Analysis shows that their fear of the animal in question is ultimately a fear that it will bite off their penis.[32] This fear of castration is itself the outcome of

[25] T. Reik, *op. cit.*, p. 104.

[26] G. Róheim, *The Eternal Ones of the Dream*, p. 236.

[27] G. Róheim, *Psychoanalysis and Anthropology*, p. 85.

[28] *Ibid*, p. 90.

[29] T. Reik, *op. cit.*, p. 137.

[30] G. Róheim, *The Riddle of the Sphinx*, p. 118.

[31] G. Róheim, 'Dying Gods and Puberty Ceremonies', *J.R.A.I.*, LIX, 188, 1929.

[32] For the classic accounts of animal phobia see Freud, *Analysis of a Phobia in a Five Year Old Boy*, X, 5–149, and Ferenczi, 'A Little Chanticleer', in *Contributions to Psychoanalysis*, p. 204.

incestuous wishes directed towards the mother. The feared animal represents the father who the child fears will carry out this retaliation against him. Similarly, in the initiation rites, the father is the monster who castrates (i.e. circumcises) the boy, as Reik so convincingly shows.[33] In Australia, where there is no house representing a monster to which the boys can be taken, it is the future father-in-law of the young man who carries out the operation.[34] Frequently, he eats the fore-skin of the young man, sometimes it is given to the initiate's mother or sister who carefully preserve it.[35] Here the alternatives —having the penis *eaten* by a father-figure or *preserved* by a mother or sister— are quite transparent, and clearly refer back to the nexus of castration anxiety and incestuous desire which is the root of the animal phobia and the initiation ceremony alike. This makes it easy to understand why the Aranda say that in the beginning circumcision was carried out by *biting*[36] and why they regard castration as the correct punishment for incest.[37] We can also see why the Becwana call the uncircumcised 'bulls and steers', and say that just as castration has a modifying effect upon the animal operated upon, so the circumcision keeps the sexual passion in bonds.[38]

In the animal phobia, as in the initiation rite, jealousy of the father and a desire to remove him are closely intertwined with the incestuous wishes and their attendant castration fears. Reik comes to the following conclusions:

If we understand circumcision as a punishment for incestuous wishes, then the . . . tortures will be punishments for wicked wishes against the father. The rite of being devoured by a monster is a threat of death and psychic reaction to the youth's unconscious intention to murder his father.[39]

This, then, is the reason why the castrators/circumcisors are *angry*. Their anger at the initiates and their maltreatment of them is righteous anger at the death-wishes which the novices harbour against the fathers. The tortures and punishments which go along with the circumcision and which are described above are clearly a mitigation of the real punishment—which ought to be death by virtue of the primitive *lex talionis*, just as circumcision is itself a mitigation of castration. Indeed, as Reik shows, in many instances the natives describe the ritual as one of the death and resurrection of the novices.[40] Róheim points out that, according to the myths of central Australian aborigines, originally all the novices really were put to death.[41] Reik sums up the

---

[33] T. Reik, *op. cit.*, pp. 104–5

[34] G. Róheim, *The Eternal Ones of the Dream*, p. 72.

[35] G. Róheim, *Psychoanalysis and Anthropology*, p. 89.

[36] Spencer & Gillen, *The Arunta*, p. 366.

[37] G. Róheim, *Children of the Desert*, p. 14.

[38] G. Róheim, 'Dying Gods and Puberty Ceremonies', *J.R.A.I.*, LIX, 188, 1929.

[39] T. Reik, *op. cit.*, p. 106.

[40] T. Reik, *op. cit. passim.*

[41] G. Róheim, *The Eternal Ones of the Dream*, p. 75.

situation as follows, 'the circumcision is carried out for the purpose of punishing and preventing incest; the killing for the punishment and prevention of parricide'.[42]

These two things—the avoidance of incest and the suppression of overt aggression against the paternal generation—we have already seen to be the very features which distinguish human from gelada-like 'one-male groups'. Freud showed in *Totem and Taboo* that taboos on incest and on aggression against a totem animal which represented the father were the psychological core of totemism. Clearly, they are also the core of initiation rituals, which must have evolved as a means of transmitting to subsequent generations the inhibitions created in the original parricides by their violent deed.

The other details of initiation ceremonies fit into this picture neatly. The recitation of the tribal decalogue which, as we saw, frequently follows the circumcision, can be readily seen to be a part of this process of constructing an inhibiting super-ego in the novices. After a careful comparative study of such incidents of moral instruction, Reik concludes that 'the most important counsel given to the circumcised youths is of two kinds, namely, to have no incestuous intercourse and to renounce hostile impulses towards the father'.[43] Again, the ritual amnesia which causes the newly-initiated youth to feign forgetfulness of his home and family can be understood as an equivalent of the childhood amnesia which descends on the latent feelings of the Oedipus complex when repression sets in.[44] Róheim sums it up well when he says that such rites are 'the dramatization of super-ego formation'.[45]

T. G. H. Strehlow, an anthropologist who was brought up among the Aranda and developed an incomparable insight into their way of life, comes to similar conclusions, albeit that his standpoint is not an analytic one. I cannot refrain from quoting at some length from his description of one of the ceremonies which follow circumcision itself:

The novices soon learned to respect and even to fear the supreme power wielded by the old men of their clan on the initiation ground. The *rukuta* [initiate] soon had to undergo another torture in most of the Aranda groups. It consisted in having their scalps split open by means of a sharp stick, their heads thereupon being liberally bitten by the old men until their hair and cheeks were dripping with blood. Its alleged purpose was to promote a flourishing growth of hair on the heads of the *rukuta*. Udepatarinja, who gave me a very graphic account of the intense and almost unbearable pain which he suffered at the hands of the old leaders, added proudly:

'I set my teeth and groaned from time to time: I did not actually cry out. My mate Apma could not bear the pain; great tears streamed down his cheeks. My hair afterwards grew vigorously. It fell down past my shoulders in a thick mass.

[42] T. Reik, *op. cit.*, p. 116.
[43] T. Reik, *op. cit.*, p. 136.
[44] *Ibid.*, p. 139.
[45] G. Róheim, *Psychoanalysis and Anthropology*, p. 86.

None of the young men of the present generation could endure such pain. We have had to dismiss them with a lighter payment.'

One or two months after the novice has submitted to circumcision there follows the second principal initiation rite, that of subincision. On this occasion the *rukuta* is allowed to witness further ceremonies. The novice has now undergone all the requisite physical operations which have been designed to make him worthy of a man's estate; and he has learned to obey the commands of the old men implicitly. His newly-found blind obedience stands in striking contrast to the unbridled insolence and general un-ruliness of temper which characterized his behaviour in the days of his childhood. Native children are usually spoiled by their parents. Mothers gratify every whim of their offspring, and fathers do not bother about any disciplinary measures. The deliber-ate cruelty with which the traditional initiation rites are carried out at a later age is carefully calculated to punish insolent and lawless boys for their past impudence and to train them into obedient, dutiful 'citizens' who will obey their elders without a murmur and be fit heirs to the ancient sacred traditions of their clan.[46]

But how did such rites originate? I have attempted to give some account of their psychological function, but clearly, this is not to be confused with a casual explanation of their origin. No one sat down and invented them be-cause they thought that they would serve a useful social function.

We have already seen that the beginnings of an answer may lie in the potentially disastrous consequences of early hunting bands having to rely on the original mechanism of super-ego formation—that is, wholesale rape and murder. We may suppose that after the primeval foraging 'one-male groups' had been wiped out by generations of repeated predation by hunting homi-nids these bands themselves became the subject of attacks from their own adolescents. In place of potentially very damaging set-piece battles, the ten-dency may have grown up over a period of time to mitigate the worst aspects of this conflict by allowing the adolescent groups to kill just one, preferably marginal, member of the paternal band. Echoes of this custom may still linger on in those societies which demand that a man may not be considered fully initiated until he has committed a homicide. In the case of the Kiwai, a warrior will frequently have a young man administer the *coup de grace* to an injured enemy.[47] In Nagir, a warrior traditionally took the eyes and tongue of a man he had killed, mixed them with urine and then gave the potion to a young man who had to sit between his legs and be fed as if from the penis.[48] Róheim draws an instructive analogy between this and the cere-mony of drinking the blood of the clan fathers in Australia. Among the Pitjentara and Karadjieri tribes the culmination of the initiation ritual is reached when the newly-circumcised boys drink the blood which flows from the freshly re-opened subincision wounds of the adult men. According to

---

[46] *Aranda Traditions*, pp. 98–9.
[47] G. Landtman, *The Kiwai Papuans of British New Guinea*, p. 660.
[48] G. Róheim, *War, Crime and the Covenant*, p. 54.

one account[49] 'in former times this blood was obtained from a man who had been killed specially for the purpose, and portions of his body were eaten'.

The initiation rituals therefore seem—if such repulsive practices can really be taken as remnants of earlier rites—to be derived from the primal crime fairly explicitly. And if, following Freud, we are correct in attributing the earliest bonds of altruism and self-restraint to the consequences of a gruesome murder, it should hardly be surprising if the very institutions designed to perpetuate those self-restraints should resemble their prototype so closely. The ritual blood-drinking in Australia, and the ritual homicides and cannibalism of Melanesia and elsewhere are clear derivatives of the original primal canni-balism. We must remember that it was a common struggle to obtain food that united the original hunters. They banded together because co-operative hunting was so much more rewarding. When they attacked the primal father they did so for his women, but to them it was also another hunt. If they ate him once they had killed him, then it is clear that the origins of all sacrificial meals are, as Freud long ago concluded, to be found in the primal crime.[50] Among the Murngin, a ceremonial loaf is baked and eaten by all participants in the initiation ritual. Among the Dua Norra the same rite occurs, with the leader of the elders singing over the sacred bread the names of all the higher totems (i.e. representations of the primal father) who then infuse it. Of the bread, the Murngin say 'this is sacred, and belongs to the totem'. When the natives hear of the Christian communion they conclude, along with Freud,[51] that the two ceremonies are the same. Their interpretation of it is that 'it makes one people'.[52] Nothing could be a more eloquent expression of what held the primal hunting groups together. They were united in the first place by being hunters, by carrying on a co-operative economy in which each relied on the others for help and protection in their hazardous occupation. Then, when they committed the great crime of displacing the dominant males of the old foraging groups, they had another, but closely analogous, reason for feeling that they were 'one people'. This was the murder of the primal father and their joint consumption of his flesh; what they shared above all was their guilt.

As initiation began to evolve, this common guilt and feeling of identity with the group had to be transmitted to future generations. But if, as I suggested above, the damaging effects of unrestrained repetitions of the primal crime threatened to wipe out the hunting communities altogether, then some sort of ritualized replacement for the original event was needed. This, as I have already stated, probably began with putting some sort of limitation on

[49] R. H. Matthews, in *Queensland Geographical Journal*, XV, 70.
[50] Freud, *Totem and Taboo*, XIII, 140.
[51] Freud, *Ibid.*, XIII, 154.
[52] G. Róheim, *The Eternal Ones of the Dream*, p. 226.

the conflict between paternal and fraternal groups, but the drawback with this was that the more the original conflict was mitigated by such restrictions the less effective the experience would have been for the new generation, for the power of conscience and remorse is in direct proportion to the magnitude of the crime. Ritual tends to resemble make-believe more than real life. So if the primal crime tended to become only make-believe, its psychological effects would have been vitiated and would have tended to make it disappear. How then could ritual have developed out of the restriction of such conflicts which probably preceded it?

To understand this, we need to look at one other factor in the situation. This is the attitude of the fathers. Once the original primal hordes of vegetarian foragers disappeared, we may assume that the threat posed to hunting bands by homicidal groups of adolescents produced a change of attitude in the leaders of the bands. They began to see their sons as threats and competitors, just as the original primal father had done; some might even have practised male infanticide, murder, or castration of the sons. But natural selection would soon have dealt with such tendencies. However, other, less draconian measures against the sons would have been a different matter. If the fathers could deal with the potentially-disastrous threat of the sons without resorting to means which would have put them collectively at a disadvantage as far as natural selection was concerned, then hope for the maintenance of their groups existed. Yet the question remained: How was this to be done? Once again, mitigation was the answer. Just as wholesale intergeneration conflict may have been averted by ritual cannibalism and the sort of ceremonial homicide still in force in some parts of the world until quite recently, it is possible that, on the father's side, what contributed to the ritual was the emergence of mitigated acts which likewise reduced all-out conflict but satisfied aggressive drives nearly as well. Thus they allowed the sons to kill and consume some suitable and unimportant victim, but also allowed themselves to 'kill' and 'castrate' the sons in a relatively harmless way, by ritual circumcision and the physical punishments described above. Indeed, as we have seen, these are the two essential ingredients of initiation rituals to this day.

But ritual circumcision and punishment would have been quite ineffective if they had not reflected the same civilizing psychological forces that operated in the original parricides and were the secret of their success.

It is highly likely that, as Róheim suggests,[53] initiation ceremonies originated in acts of mourning carried out for the primal father. Initiation mutilations and punishments would then have been the result of the aggressive impulses of the original parricides turned back against themselves.

To anyone unacquainted with psychoanalytic findings about the unconscious psychology of mourning and depression, such an assertion may sound

53 G. Róheim, *Australian Totemism*, p. 396.

a little far-fetched, to say the least. But there is ample evidence that such aggressive feelings do play a part in mourning and that they do tend to be turned back against the mourner. In one Australian tribe mentioned by Róheim[54] the dead are upbraided for dying and speared as the assailant says, 'Why did you die? Take that for dying!' But much more common than this overt expression of resentment against the loved one for being so inconsiderate as to die is the tendency to avoid expression of aggression against him precisely because he was loved and to turn that aggression instead back against the self. Róheim comments that among all the Australian aborigines self-laceration, cutting of the hair, and fasting are typical expressions of mourning. Sometimes the injuries inflicted are so serious that the mourner himself has been known to die as a result. Among ourselves, self-deprecation, loss of interest in the outside world, depression, and melancholy are all common features of mourning and the results of inner, unconscious punishment of the self.[55]

In the light of considerations like these, it is by no means far-fetched to suppose that after the original murder of the primal father at least some of the groups of hunter-sons experienced just such emotions. Such feelings would have been the natural outcome of their original ambivalence. They harboured powerful aggressive resentments against the primal father, it is true; but they also felt secret admiration and respect for the one who was enjoying all the privileges which they coveted and who ruled his primal group of women and children with such despotic egoism. Thus, when they had succeeded in removing him and were now ready to begin to identify with him and to let the positive side of their ambivalence have the upper hand, those very same feelings of love and admiration caused them to hate themselves for what they had done. This would have been especially true if the sons who attacked their fathers were, as I have supposed, members of groups of adolescent hunters whose ambivalence was enough—or, whose courage was insufficient, which comes to the same thing—to allow any one of them to take on the old man on his own. The very fact that they must have launched a concerted attack reminiscent of, and modelled on, a hunt was itself in all probability the result of ambivalence that was sufficient to deter any individual from confronting the terrifying primal father himself but which could be overcome in the security of the group. And if we further recall that I have argued that the result of the primal parricide was not incestuous indulgence but neurotic inhibition, it is clear that in the general disappointment and frustration which followed the deed, self-reproaches would tend to get the upper hand. After all, no son could have fully realized his secret ambition to overcome and replace the primal father as sole head and ruler of the group if, as I have supposed, natural selection favoured precisely those groups which maintained their fraternal

---

[54] G. Róheim, *War, Crime and the Covenant*, p. 31.
[55] See Freud's *Mourning and Melancholia*, XIV, 219 for a full explanation of this.

structure after the acquisition of the females. Those groups most likely to survive and prosper because they could go on hunting as before would also have been those which had to accept only partial gratification for their incestuous and parricidal wishes.

Thus it is not unlikely that after the Deed, at least in some of the hunting bands, self-reproaches and inwardly-directed aggression typical of mourning would have got the upper hand. If this was the case, then it is not incredible that those masochistic aggressions and self-reproaches should have been directed against the parricides themselves in just the same sort of overt and uncomplicated way that we see manifested among the aborigines today. The sons, unlike Róheim's aborigines, could not have speared the primal father for dying, because they had just killed him. They would have been much more likely to spear themselves as the aborigines also do, and to practise some mutilation against the organ which was responsible for their revolt in the first place—the penis. Perhaps some castrated themselves, a practice which is certainly not unknown among higher forms of father-worship in the subsequent history of world religion, or even among modern neurotics. If they did, natural selection would soon have eliminated them. However, those who practised a mitigated form of castration, say circumcision, would have positively benefited from selective forces, and this for two reasons. First, because intensity of mourning—i.e. self-chastisement—is directly proportional to the amount of ambivalence felt towards the lost object, and we have already seen that the more ambivalent individuals (that is, those more able to inhibit their anti-social tendencies towards committing incest and aggressions against their own fellow men), would have been favoured by selection in the new hunting economy. Secondly, because those who did carry out such self-punishments and milder forms of mutilation of the generative organs would have been favoured by selective pressure because they would have evolved the starting point of the initiation ritual, and therefore the means of ensuring the transmission to future generations of those crucial inhibitions which were to make human societies viable.

Thus having initiated *themselves*—as, incidentally, the ancestors invariably do in Australian aboriginal myths—it was but a small step to initiating the sons, particularly since the mutilations in question would serve as an ideal mitigated form of the inter-generation conflict which had to be resolved. In such conflicts, the original parricides who had maintained altruistic co-operation among themselves by forgoing incest and sexual and social hegemony, were bound to direct their aggression against temptations to violate those very same inhibitions. Hence it was against their sons' incestuous desires for sexual monopoly of all the women in the group and their desire to remove the fathers standing in their way that the fathers had to fight. Initiation rituals must have begun as a mitigated form of such an attempt on the fathers' part.

While the sons' side of the conflict was being reduced in disruptiveness by allowing them to make one symbolic killing, perhaps of a stranger, or someone who did not figure prominently in the paternal group, so the fathers' side of the conflict was being mitigated by gradually replacing it with a purely ritual assault on the boys at the climax of which they were ritually castrated—that is, circumcised.[56]

Once this had happened, all could participate in the final culmination of the rites—the cannibalistic consumption of the murdered victim. This, on the part of both fathers and sons, expressed their unity in the supreme psychological bond, now they were all initiated. This bond was their joint identification with the primal father. To this day cannibalistic consumption of the dead figures in some mourning rites. 'The Tangara carry the remains of the deceased in a bag. Whenever they feel sorrow for the dead they eat of the flesh until nothing remains but the bones.'[57] Cannibalism of the dead, which is far from uncommon among the Australian aborigines, corresponds to the other main ingredient of mourning, the introjection of the lost object. That part of the ego of the mourner which cannot give up its memory of the loved person incorporates the lost one into itself by an act of identification, a process which tends to reinforce the tendency to turn reproaches against the dead inwards because the deceased is now encompassed within the mourner's ego. Eating the body of the dead person is an outward and visible sign of this inward and unconscious process. Both sons and fathers could unite in expressing it in ritual cannibalism because it bore most eloquent testimony to that which made them one and which guaranteed their social structure and economic success. This was the psychological process which underlies the unity of all social groups—the possession of a common super-ego and a narcissitic identification of each with all.[58] That common super-ego was the primal father whose chief injunctions they now obeyed in the form of taboos on incest and aggression against the totem which stood for the primal father and their unity with him as brothers of the totem clan.

It may be wondered just how the super-ego of the sons is established by initiations of this sort. We have already seen how that of the original parri-

---

[56] Such an interpretation would also have to fit all other mutilations suffered by initiates, and I believe it does. The outlandish head-biting mentioned above by Strehlow as being practised by the Aranda may seem difficult to interpret in this way, but this is only so if we fail to notice two things: first, that the head commonly figures in the unconscious as a symbol representing the penis (in which case head-biting is equivalent to penis-biting, which is the archaic form of castration, both in the individual (cf. Freud's Little Hans) and in the race); secondly, that the *chin* is also sometimes bitten. The Aranda claim that this 'makes the hair grow' (Spencer & Gillen, *op. cit.*, p. 206), but it is easy to see that biting hair off a young man's chin clearly represents the exact (and doubtless, unconscious) opposite: that is, *preventing it from growing* which, since growth of the beard is a characteristic of sexual maturity in men, is equivalent to *preventing them from maturing into men*, which is again a form of castration.

[57] A. W. Howitt, *Native Tribes*, quoted by Róheim, *War, Crime and the Covenant*, p. 31.

[58] Freud, *Group Psychology and the Analysis of the Ego*, XVIII, 69.

cides originated in their ambivalence turning into mourning and causing them to acquire a super-ego by identification with the dead primal father. But what of the sons? Mutilations which were the expression of self punishment (i.e. *conscience*) in the original parricides were mutilations received at the hands of the fathers by those initiated in this way. Their mutilation could hardly be the outcome of a force of conscience. A first answer to this objection lies in realizing that nevertheless to some extent they were. When the sons were initiated by the fathers they knew unconsciously that, although what was being done to them might ostensibly be a rite of transition through which they could acquire the status of adult men, it was in fact a punishment for incestuous and aggressive wishes directed against their parents.

At least one side of their ambivalence would have caused them to welcome the punishments meted out to them as wholly-deserved retribution for their anti-social impulses. The other side of their ambivalence—their hatred of their fathers—would have to be strenuously repudiated if they were to undergo initiation and gain access to the ranks of the adult men. Now, experience shows that whenever aggressive feelings against others have to be suppressed they tend, as in mourning, to be turned back against the ego of the subject who feels them. Thus, whereas the original parricides turned their aggressive feelings back against themselves in mourning, the initiates did so because they had to submit, more or less voluntarily, to the violence which was done to them. In these circumstances, encouraged by unconscious feelings of Oedipal guilt, the sons' super-egos were reinforced by the aggressiveness which they felt against the fathers but which they had to suppress.

At the time, this is experienced as depression, both in mourning and any circumstance in which the ego is forced to turn its hatred back against itself. But later, successful gratifications of the sadism of the super-ego tend to be perceived as moral victories (that is, successes of the force of conscience and gratification of the ego-ideal). This comes out strongly in the oldest, but, of course, not necessarily the most primitive, account of circumcision we have. An Egyptian inscription from the 23rd century B.C. records the following facts:

When I was circumcised, together with one hundred and twenty men, there was none thereof who hit out, there was none thereof who was hit, there was none thereof who scratched, there was none thereof who was scratched. I was a commoner of repute . . .[59]

The inscription continues to record the virtues of the man in question, but it is significant that he is so concerned to convince us that he offered no resistance, nor did the others with him, to being circumcised. The basis of his self-righteous satisfaction was that he had successfully accomplished the most

59 J. Pritchard (Ed.), *Ancient Nr. Eastern Texts Relating to The Old Testament*, p. 326.

difficult psychological part of initiation, the suppression of hostility against the initiators.[60]

There is one other difficulty about this interpretation of initiation and its place in totemism that we must face. This is the question of why today's aborigines and other primitive peoples—and, we may safely conjecture, primal man—left the initiation and instilling of the super-ego until so late. Psychoanalysis teaches us that the super-ego is largely formed in modern 'civilized' man in childhood, certainly by the age of 7 or 8. If the suppression of incestuous wishes and parricidal tendencies is so important, why do initiations not take place at the time when these anti-social forces first manifest themselves in childhood?

I think that a large part of the answer lies in the historical circumstances in which initiation evolved. The reader will recall that I suggested that it must have originated in a mitigation of the conflicts between parental and adolescent hunting groups. If young males had been driven out of hunting bands, just as from the original 'one-male groups' (primal hordes), the initiation could only have been performed at the time of reaching full sexual maturity for the simple reason that it was only at this moment that the inter-generation conflict would manifest itself. If initiation was a substitute for that conflict then it would have to be performed at that time. The second reason, and the one which with the first gives what is, I think, a complete explanation of the situation, is the fact that early man had no reason, as we have, to suppress infantile sexuality and aggression.[61] Why should he? Five-year-olds pose no threat to the social structure, however irritating they may be. Weapon-wielding full-grown adolescents are quite a different matter.

There is a great deal of evidence that among today's Australian aborigines infantile sexuality and agressiveness go largely unrepressed. Róheim reports that no mother ever really weans her child, and that children who cannot get milk or even just a nipple to suck from their own mothers will be accommodated by any other woman who is available. No serious attempt is made at toilet-training and even adult aborigines relieve themselves whenever, and wherever, they want to.[62] Mothers sleep lying on top of their sons, and

---

[60] If this analysis, like that of Strehlow above, is correct, here is extensive proof of what all modern and so-called 'enlightened' penology denies exists: the salutary effects of corporal punishment. Let us make no mistake, if such an understanding of the psychology of initiation is justified, then for many millenniums the principal means of social control used by our ancestors was cruel and remorseless corporal punishment of the young. It would be a great mistake to confuse the undesirability of such practices with a belief in their inefficacy.

[61] It is, of course, true that the Aranda do practice a purely symbolic suppression of childhood sexuality immediately after birth (Róheim, *Children of the Desert*, pp. 67–8), but it is unlikely that this has any traumatic effect, as Róheim notes.

[62] G. Róheim, 'Psychoanalysis of Primitive Cultural Types', *International Journal of Psychoanalysis*, XIII, 75, 82.

although they will not tolerate intercourse with them, may well masturbate them. Children are never prevented from masturbating themselves and castration-threats are rare.[63] This does not mean that infantile traumas are totally absent, but the fact that the prohibition against witnessing parental intercourse is the only restriction on infantile sexual curiosity means that in general repression is light. [64]

The result of this is that the Australian aborigines are a notably uninhibited and care-free people, with a total absence of impotence, frigidity, and sado-masochistic perversions.[65] 'They certainly have a super-ego,' declares Róheim, 'but not much of it.'[66] Such a situation is hardly suprising if we realize that the major cultural process of super-ego formation is delayed until the character is almost formed.

The danger in such a situation is that initiation may be insufficient to achieve what it must, namely, a suppression of the incestuous and parricidal tendencies that threaten all human social structures. We might imagine that repetitions of it would be called for, yet initiation seems to be a once-and-for-all event. Actually it is not, and if we look more closely at the religion of the Australian aborigines we find that initiation, or something very like it, is repeated at great length throughout a man's life. This occurs at the ritual dances which take place from time to time, and often go on for weeks. There are two kinds of such celebrations, one at which women are present and which ends in the exchange of wives, and another from which women are rigidly excluded and which begins with mutual masturbation.[67]

Let us take the second case first. The masturbation which begins it is purely customary and is designed to produce the erection necessary to obtain blood from the subincision wound. It is a requirement of etiquette that each man should express admiration for the size of the other man's penis. Blood is extracted from the subincision wound and used to stick on the feathers and down with which the dancers decorate themselves. It is at ceremonies like these that an extension of the original mutilations of initiation is carried out. This is usually in the form of the enlarging of the subincision—a cut in the urethra which may be enlarged to such an extent that it runs from the glans to the scrotum. In exceptional cases a single testicle is also removed. The central feature of the ceremonies is a ritual dance to the accompaniment of a song which describes the wanderings of the ancestors. The principal figure of these dances is a ceremonial trembling called *alknantama*, which the aborigines describe as a stylized version of the trembling associated with erotic excite-

---

[63] *Ibid.*, pp. 87, 93.
[64] For a fuller discussion see G. Róheim, *Riddle of the Sphinx*, p. 30ff.
[65] *Ibid*, p. 237, G. Róheim, *Psychoanalysis and Anthropology*, p. 69ff.
[66] 'Psychoanalysis of Primitive Cultural Types', *International Journal of Psychoanalysis*, XIII, 120.
[67] *Ibid.*, p. 65.

ment. The meaning of many of these dances is obscure, but some are known to represent copulation of the totem animals.[68]

The second type of ceremony is more often associated with multiplication of the totem species, and in the intercourse which follows many of the couplings may be technically incestuous (i.e. with a woman who is a 'clan sister' or in some other forbidden kinship class).[69]

The first type of ceremony is clearly one which resembles initiation quite closely. We have the same mutilations of the penis at the beginning of every dance and the showing of *churungas* (sacred stones associated with the totem ancestors) which is also a feature of Australian initiations. But a major difference is that there is no physical violence. Instead, there is a major homosexual and erotic element which, although not absent in initiation, is relatively less important. This homosexual element manifests itself in the initial mutual masturbation and in the dances, in which, of course, men play the role of the copulating totems. The exclusion of women is also an aspect of this.

Such rituals can only have evolved as a means of constantly reaffirming and reinforcing the trauma of initiation. They serve to strengthen the repression of incestuous wishes by re-opening the ritual castration-wounds and extending them. The homosexual elements of the rites serve to bind a man ever more closely to his fellows, thus suppressing any hostility which might result from rivalry. The identification with the totems which is basic to both types of rite is clearly the manifest content of a latent desire, also seen in childhood animal phobias, namely, the desire to identify with the father.

Those rites which end with incestuous intercourse and at which women are present seem to correspond to a psychological process which we shall have cause to say much more about in the coming chapters, the 'return of the repressed'. Actually, such incestuous unions and suspensions of taboo are by no means unknown in connection with initiations. Reik gives several examples.[70]

The origin of these paradoxical lapses into what totemism is most supposed to abhor may well lie in the original situation out of which they evolved. We have seen that the first type of rite (those from which women are excluded) seems to relate to initiation rituals in so far that they are mitigations of the fathers' original behaviour towards the sons (i.e. circumcision and subincision instead of castration, and homosexual attachments as a counter to parricide). The increase-rites at which women are present are probably based on mitigation of the sons' original behaviour towards the fathers (i.e. ritual sacrifice of the totem instead of the killing of the father, sexual indulgence in contempt of the official rules of exogamy instead of incest with the mothers and sisters). But, whatever their origin, they result in a breakthrough into consciousness

---

[68] For a full description of these ceremonies see Róheim's *Eternal Ones of the Dream* and *Riddle of the Sphinx*.

[69] G. Róheim, *Eternal Ones of the Dream*, p. 92.

[70] T. Reik, *Ritual*, p. 130ff.

of the most powerful and most important of the repressed wishes—that for incest with the mother—for we must not forget that it is this desire which is at the root of all hostility to the paternal generation. It is almost as if the aborigines in their rites were giving recognition to the fact that incestuous eroticism is so deeply rooted in the human race that a more-or-less complete suppression of it—like that practised by most other peoples and ourselves—is just not possible, at least for *them*. Here the relative lack of sexual repression in childhood is probably the decisive factor.

We can conclude that the ritual practices of the Australian aborigines must be the result of the same process which created initiation rites, namely, natural selection in favour of the most efficient hunting groups whose existence was, as we have seen, dependent on defending and reinforcing the two features which made those groups possible, and which caused hunting hominids to become differentiated from their foraging gelada-like ancestors. These two features were the avoidance of incest and the suppression of open conflict with the parental generation.

Of these two, the incest question is the most important, as we have already seen. Now, if this is the case, it ought to be possible to show that all human societies to this day are based on this primal avoidance and that all social structures, no matter how much they might differ otherwise, share this in common. The anthropologist, Claude Lévi-Strauss, has done us the valuable service of demonstrating this to be true, especially in showing that all kinship systems can be understood in terms of sister-exchange between wife-giving and wife-receiving groups of men. This sister-exchange is, of course, the outcome of an incest-avoidance, and Lévi-Strauss shows that all kinship systems, no matter how complex or chaotic, can be understood in terms of this very simple and very Freudian model.[71]

Quite apart from all this, however, there is one last issue raised by Freud's *Totem and Taboo* on which the foregoing theory of human social evolution can cast a lot of light. This is the vexed question of Freud's belief in the inheritance of acquired characteristics. Reverting to my opening remarks for a moment, it is obvious that this has been one of the major points around which resistance to his sociological theories has crystalized. It is only hinted at in the pages of *Totem and Taboo*[72] but in *Moses and Montheism*, his last contribution to the psychoanalysis of man, and apart from *Totem and Taboo* perhaps the most important, it is dealt with much more fully. Freud remarks that 'If we assume the survival of . . . memory traces in the archaic heritage, we have bridged the gulf between individual and group psychology: we can deal with peoples as we do with the individual neurotic . . . If it is not so, we shall not advance a step further along the path we entered on, either in analysis or in

---

[71] It is not my intention to go into the details of this here, but the reader can find Lévi-Strauss' theories of kinship explained briefly in my book, *Lévi-Strauss*.

[72] Freud, *Totem and Taboo*, XIII, 158.

group psychology.'[73] And if we ask just what these memory traces might contain, he replies: 'I have no hesitation in declaring that men have always known (in this special way) that they once possessed a primal father and killed him.'[74]

Freud's entire sociological theory and the justification for his psycho-analysis of humanity as if it were comparable to an individual therefore seems to rest on a discredited biological principle: the inheritance of acquired characteristics.

But does it? Let us look more closely at what he says. Explaining what he means by 'the survival of memory traces in the archaic heritage', he adds:

If any explanation is to be found of what are called the instincts of animals, which allow them to behave from the first in a new situation in life as though it were an old and familiar one—if any explanation at all is to be found of this instinctive life of animals, it can only be that they bring the experiences of their species with them into their own new existence—that is, that they have preserved memories of what was experienced by their ancestors. The position in the human animal would not at bottom be different. His own archaic heritage corresponds to the instincts of animals even though it is different in its compass and contents.[75]

Now, if this is what Freud means, there is no difficulty. True, his phrase 'they have preserved memories of what was experienced by their ancestors' sounds highly Lamarckian but, as a manner of speaking, it is fair enough. What Freud does not appear to appreciate, but what modern biologists do, is that this 'persistence of memory' of the experiences of past generations is not brought about by each individual up-dating the genetic code during its lifetime but, like all other evolutionary change, by mutation.[76] This fact is so well-established that it can now be taken for granted. Edward O. Wilson sums up the situation admirably at the beginning of his monumental *Sociobiology* when he says,

In a Darwinist sense the organism does not live for itself. Its primary function is not even to reproduce other organisms; it reproduces genes, and it serves as their tem-porary carrier. Each organism generated by sexual reproduction is a unique, acci-dental subset of all the genes constituting the species. Natural selection is the process whereby certain genes gain representation in the following generations superior to that of other genes located at the same chromosome positions. When new sex cells are

[73] Freud, *Moses and Monotheism*, XXIII, 100.
[74] *Ibid.*, p. 101.
[75] *Ibid.*, p. 100.
[76] However true this might be, this is clearly a subject about which one should keep an open mind. Experiments on rats summarized by E. O. Wilson in his *Sociobiology* (pp. 152–3) show that 'in a mammal no more complex than a rat, the histories of parents and grandparents can bias the behavioural development of individuals strongly, and with it their future status within societies and even the likelihood that they will survive and reproduce. What is true of rodents is almost certainly true of . . . the higher primates.'

manufactured in each generation, the winning genes are pulled apart and reassembled to manufacture new organisms that, on the average, contain a higher proportion of the same genes. But the individual organism is only their vehicle, part of an elaborate device to preserve and spread them with the least possible biochemical perturbation. Samuel Butler's aphorism, that the chicken is only an egg's way of making another egg, has been modernised: the organism is only DNA's way of making more DNA.[77]

Freud, in his *Introductory Lectures on Psychoanalysis*, echoes this final point and, despite his belief in the inheritance of acquired characteristics, is clearly at one with modern biological science in his insistence that:

... the individual organism, which regards itself as the main thing and its sexuality as a means, like any other, for its satisfaction, is from the point of view of biology only an episode in a succession of generations, a short-lived appendage to a germ-plasm endowed with virtual immortality—like the temporary holder of an entail which will outlast him.[78]

The interpretation of *Totem and Taboo* advanced in these pages enables us to retain Freud's 'memory traces in the archaic heritage' without violating the principles set out above. As long as we understand them as *mutations* in the genetic code rather than *acquisitions* in the organism's lifetime, no Lamarckian overtones remain. Let us take this opportunity to summarize our findings so far in the terminology of modern biology.

I began by drawing attention to the recent discovery by Jolly of the remarkable evolutionary parallelism between the gelada baboon and man. I looked more closely at Jolly's comparison of the similarities of the social structures of the two and argued that what distinguished modern human social systems from that of the gelada was the existence of very considerable altruism expressed in two crucial respects: the inhibition of incest and of conflict for sexual hegemony between dominant males. This is an example of what Wilson calls the 'central theoretical problem of sociobiology': How can altruism evolve when, by definition, it reduces personal fitness? Speaking in general, he says:

In the process of natural selection, any device that can insert a higher proportion of certain genes into subsequent generations will come to characterize the species. One class of such devices promotes individual survival. Another promotes superior mating performance and care of the resulting offspring. As more complex social behaviour by the organism is added to the genes' techniques for replicating themselves, altruism becomes increasingly prevalent and eventually appears in exaggerated forms.[79]

In Freudian psychology the equivalent of 'devices which promote individual survival' is the ego instincts (aggression); the equivalent of those 'promoting

[77] E. O. Wilson, *Sociobiology*, p. 3.
[78] XVI, 413–14.
[79] *Sociobiology*, p. 3.

superior mating performance' is the libido, the instincts of the id; and as we have already seen, what is responsible for altruism is the super-ego. Wilson himself remarks[80] that, as far as man is concerned, the interplay of these devices results in 'ambivalence'.

The reader will recall that I argued that although the grasslands on which our gelada-like ancestors lived were well stocked with game animals, the 'one-male groups' with their jealous overlords would have been unlikely to attempt to exploit such an alternative source of food. It was a different matter where the 'all-male groups' were concerned. Wilson observes that 'success or failure in evolving a particular social mechanism often depends simply on the presence or absence of a particular *pre-adaptation*'.[81] The 'all-male groups' possessed such a pre-adaptation to hunting because they approximated much more closely to the social structures of predatory species and because they were unencumbered with slow-moving females and young. But the success of such hunting ventures depended on co-operation and altruism not selected for in the traditional gelada-like existence where aggressive individualism was at a premium. 'Other than suicide,' says Wilson, 'no behaviour is more clearly altruistic than the surrender of food.'[82] This behaviour had to be acquired by the hunting groups, and, if this were to happen, those capable of inhibiting their erstwhile strongly-reinforced aggressive individualism were at an advantage. Yet, in order to get females and reproduce, such individuals would have had to confront dominant males of the traditional foraging groups. Such behaviour repeated over hundreds or thousands of generations would mean that, given the adaptive advantages of hunting, natural selection would favour individuals motivated by powerful aggressive feelings towards their fathers.

Stresses resulting from the acquisition of females in groups who first evolved co-operative techniques in their absence would have been too great for them to survive as viable entities in most cases. However, in those groups who by chance or design acquired females by the hunting down of their actual fathers, psychological forces producing guilt and resistance to incest on the part of some of the males would have favoured the emergence of a situation where individual members could forgo their desire for sexual and social hegemony and instead distribute the females equally between them. Here, the general ambivalence which Wilson mentions as operating between devices which favour individual survival, sexual success, and altruism, would result in psychological conflict between ego, id, and super-ego. Basic instincts would have motivated an individual to want to kill his rivals and establish his sexual hegemony over the women, but the super-ego would have acted to inhibit those instincts in the interests of his better chances of survival within the group. Freud's theory in *Totem and Taboo* is the explanation of how these

[80] *Ibid.*, p. 4.
[81] *Ibid.*, p. 34.
[82] *Ibid.*, p. 128.

psychological mutations emerged, and what their structure was. Because the male super-ego is produced in large part by introjection of the father, natural selection must have favoured those with the greatest ambivalence towards their fathers, for it was these individuals who had the greatest chance of solving the problems of altruistic behaviour within the group and who would have thus handed on their psychological peculiarities most successfully to their offspring. Genes favouring ambivalence and altruism would rapidly propagate throughout the population. It is in this sense that we can talk of the persistence of memories of the primal father and of his murder. Individuals would have tended to inherit from their parents not just a general proclivity to neurosis, which ambivalence and the capacity to repress it would have given them, but also the specific behaviours which would have caused such neurotic conflicts to flow in the channels serviceable to natural selection. These specifics would have been simultaneous love and hatred of the father expressed in terms of the fundamental behaviours which they sprang from, namely, parricide, and fear of castration coupled with incestuous love for the mother—for as we have seen, it would have been those groups which actually murdered their own fathers and tried to mate with their own mothers who would most likely have survived. Thus, if modern men spontaneously tend to harbour death-wishes against their fathers, incestuous desires towards their mothers, and are haunted by fears of castration, it can only be because natural selection has arranged things that way and has rewarded with the crown of evolutionary success those who inherited the genetic determinants of the Oedipus complex.

Similar comments can be made about the other question we considered in this chapter, the evolution of ritual. This, like the innate predisposition to neurosis, was the result of selective pressures. Wilson sums up the process when he points out that 'Altruistic behaviour might be induced when it results in and increase in inclusive fitness through benefits bestowed on the parents and other relatives.'[83] This, as we saw, is exactly what initiation secured because it reduced conflict and promoted altruism to the benefit of the whole group, fathers, sons, mothers and other relatives included. 'The social pressure' (to such induced altruism in the young) 'need not be conscious,' observes Wilson in a remark which is very apposite to initiation rituals, 'at least not to the extent of explicitly promoting the welfare of the family. Instead, it is likely to be couched in the sanctions of custom and religion.'[84]

Such a mechanism could well throw light on the other main aspect of phylogenetic 'memory' mentioned by Freud—the unconscious basis of symbolism. According to him, the remarkable similarity of symbolism found in individuals from widely differing cultures and found reflected in different

[83] Ibid., p. 343.
[84] Ibid., p. 343.

languages and customs was the result of a phylogenetic inheritance of symbols.[85] It is possible that its origins are to be found in inherited psychological propensities to evolve certain types of symbolism which would have been powerfully selected for, if my speculations on the crucial adaptive role of initiation rites are correct. Clearly, the ability to develop effective rites involved the capacity to substitute symbolic equivalents for the overt behaviours which they replaced, and to relate these symbolisms to the fundamental behavioural and psychological mechanisms of the Oedipus complex. Furthermore, the high adaptive premiums which must have existed in connection with the evolution of speech may well have also involved selection for certain sorts of innate symbolic tendencies.

In short, if modern Darwinian theory can account for the evolution of instinctive behaviours in animals, there is no reason to believe that it cannot do so in the case of man. Freud's Lamarckianism is to be accounted for, in part at least, as a not-unusual tendency in evolutionary theory when the exact selective forces are as yet unclear and when the details of the picture cannot be filled in. Once the basis of selection is understood—and in this case it was the evolution of hunting, a factor which Freud could not have taken into account—characteristics no longer give the impression of having been acquired but are seen to have been provided by random mutation.

Sociobiology has shown us just how problematic and unobvious the evolution of human social behaviour is. In the elaboration of his social structures, the degree of the development of his altruism, and the extent of the specialization of his corporate behaviour, man is only comparable with the social insects. Yet, phylogenetically, man is descended from notably unaltruistic species, and is related to living ones whose level of social development falls far below that found in the insect world. Indeed, if Jolly's hominid gelada theory is correct, man is descended from an ancestor even more sadistically egoistic than the majority of mammals, who in general are not notable for the refinement of their social evolution. The great strength of the theory propounded by Freud in *Totem and Taboo*, and elaborated in these pages, is that it explains the origin of altruism and social co-operation in man by means of typically human (i.e. *psychological*) processes which, although very different from the genetically determined and automatic social responses of the lower animals, are nevertheless in their net effect closely comparable. The soldier ant, which kills itself in defending its nest, and the human soldier who dies on the battle-field for his country are manifesting exactly comparable behaviours. Yet each is motivated quite differently, and it is to the explanation of the peculiarly human in social behaviour that psychoanalysis can most successfully apply itself.

Putting the argument of this chapter into one sentence, one might say that in the case of humans, social behaviour and most acts of altruism are *reactive*.

[85] Freud, *Introductory Lectures on Psychoanalysis*, XV, 199, *Moses and Monotheism*, XXIII, 132–3.

That is, they are the result of inhibiting forces which turn aggression and egosim back upon themselves to produce altruism and co-operation. The more new sciences like sociobiology advance, the more will the fundamental truth of the psychoanalytic theory of human origins be vindicated. It is that man is not a social animal in the sense in which the insects are, one programmed for altruism, genetically pre-destined for self-sacrifice. Man is fundamentally a sadist and an egoist; his altruism and ability to co-operate with other men originate in his characteristically human ability to turn his aggression against himself and discipline himself for the sake of his social existence. What I have tried to explain in this chapter is merely the first and more elemental instance of this. And if what I have said is in large part correct, I am tempted to quote with regard to Freud's much maligned *Totem and Taboo* a remark which he himself made in connection with attacks on the equally much-maligned libido theory: 'He who knows how to wait need make no concessions.'[86]

---

[86] *Group Psychology and the Analysis of the Ego*, XVIII, 91.

THE OMNIPOTENCE OF
THOUGHTS

I OEDIPUS IN EMBRYO

We may sum up the main thesis of the previous chapter by saying that man has an Oedipus complex because he evolved it. This is true in the two different senses in which that remark can be taken. It is true, first of all, of the whole human race: that it collectively experienced a primal, Oedipal trauma as a result of a profound change of behaviour when a species which had evolved originally to the life of vegetarian foragers in arid grasslands suddenly undertook the hunting of big, fast-moving game. Secondly, it is true of every individual human being who has descended from those original parricidal hunters and who carries within him, preserved in his innate behavioural responses and psychological make-up, the proclivities to ambivalence towards the father and incestuous love for the mother, which make the Oedipus complex what it is. We have also seen that man, who is an essentially religious and ritualistic animal, evolved ritual and religion in a way closely related to that in which he acquired the Oedipus complex, and that originally these characteristics of the species were, like everything else which is fundamental to it, produced under the ever-watchful promptings of natural selection, and of that alone. In the second part of this chapter I shall go on to consider later developments arising out of the primal trauma and the fundamental nature of man, but first I want to consider the question of whether there might not be other lessons about human evolution to be learnt from Freud's theory and the corroboration which I have been able to give it. We might ask, for instance, whether these traumatic events have not left any physical mark on man, quite apart from the immense psychological reprecussions which they have had on him.

I believe that they have, and to understand what these physical concomitants of the primal trauma might be we must return for a moment to my opening remarks about human adaptations. The reader will recall that I stated in connection with Jolly's observations on hominid/gelada adaptive parallelisms that, apart from them, man most resembled his ape cousins, the gorilla and chimpanzee. Human evolution might therefore seem a simple process of differentiation of hominids from chimpanzee or gorilla-like ancestors in the direction of gelada-like adaptations to a seed-eating existence. However, it is not that simple. Although biochemical tests show great similarity, even identity, between long stretches of human and chimpanzee genetic codes, it is only correct to say that modern man resembles the chimpanzee closely in his anatomy if we first specify that we are talking about a *foetal* chimpanzee. The resemblance here is quite remarkable. It seems to be the specifically foetal characteristics of the chimpanzee which typify human beings most explicitly, if we put on one side the gelada-like adaptations. Unlike the adult ape, both foetus and human being have thin-walled, globular skulls with an almost vertical plane of the face, and brains which in their proportions and morphology are very similar. Both foetal chimpanzee and man lack the prominent brow-ridges characteristic of the mature ape. The legs of the unborn ape look a trifle short, but the arms are about as long in relation to the body as in man. In adult apes they become much longer. The embryonic hand, in its generalized and immature appearance, closely resembles the hand of man in a way which it will not do later on; and the human foot retains throughout life the simple toes and general structure found in the feet of unborn apes. Both man and foetal chimpanzee are largely without body hair, but do have it on the head and chin. The organs of the lower abdominal region in both foetal ape and man (that is, the rectum, vagina, and urinary tract) point somewhat forward in a manner which is as untypical of adult apes as it is of most other adult mammals, in which these organs lie parallel with the spine. Unlike all adult apes, both male foetal chimpanzee and man lack a penis bone. In the female, the *labia majora* are retained as a permanent feature in humans, but appear only as a stage in the infantile development of the sex organs in female chimpanzees. Again, the hymen, present only in the foetal ape, can be retained indefinitely in human females. A number of other features, such as the shape of the cartilage of the ear and the late closing of the cranial sutures, might also be added to this list.[1]

These characteristics are evidence of what the anatomist Bolk called *foetalization*, but which is also frequently termed *neoteny*. Neoteny, or foetalization, can be defined as the retention in maturity of features which characterized the young of an animal's ancestors or, alternatively—but which comes to the same thing—the premature sexual maturity of an otherwise immature form. Apart from man, a number of other examples of this evolutionary tendency have been found; in particular, one might point out that all vertebrates probably owe their existence to a neotenous form of primitive echinoderms (star-fish, sea-urchins, etc.) known as *chordates*.[2]

If all the anthropologists who have pointed to neoteny as a major factor in human evolution are correct about it, a major problem is raised with regard to Jolly's observations. This problem lies in the fact that there is no

---

[1] For a discussion of neoteny in man see G. De Beer, *Embryoes and Ancestors*, J. B. S. Haldane, *The Causes of Evolution*, M. F. Ashley Montagu, *Introduction to Physical Anthropology*.

[2] De Beer, *Embryoes and Ancestors*, p. 76ff.

way in which such a trend to foetalization—that is, retardation of maturity—can be reconciled with a seed-eating, gelada-like way of life. Let us take as an example of these difficulties the question of retardation of development of the young. Neoteny means that human babies are born far 'earlier'—that is, in a more retarded condition—than are the neonates of the apes. The result of this is that, unlike new-born apes, they are unable to hold on to their mothers even if those mothers had fur to hold on to which, thanks to neoteny, they have not.

This means that human babies must be carried in the mother's arms for all of the first year or so of life, and very frequently for much longer than that. Under conditions where a mother had to support herself by gathering seeds and other small objects, the need to look after such slow-maturing and helpless infants would have caused insurmountable problems. There is just no way in which one can imagine neoteny being adaptively significant to a gelada-like seed-eater. And indeed, if it had been, we should today see the gelada baboon manifesting those very neotenous traits which are so distinctive of man. Yet no other primate, and few other mammals, show such features, so we must conclude that they are the result of evolutionary forces which have been active in man but in no other creature which is closely related to him. The obvious question arises: What could these forces have been?

An answer may lie in a remark made by De Beer in the course of his consideration of neoteny in human evolution:

It may then be safely concluded that the rate of development of the human body has been retarded. On the other hand, the reproductive glands have probably not varied their rate of development, for the human ovary reaches full size at the age of about five, and this is about the time of sexual maturity of the apes, and presumably of man's ancestors.[3]

That this may have something to do with the subject of my first chapter is borne out by a closely similar remark of Freud's made in connection with the phenomenon of the latency period:

In contrast to popular opinion, the sexual life of human beings (or what corresponds to it later on) exhibits an early efflorescence which comes to an end at about the fifth year and is followed by what is known as the period of latency (till puberty) in which there is no further development of sexuality and indeed what has been attained undergoes a retrogression. This theory is confirmed by the anatomical investigation of the growth of the internal genitalia; it leads us to suppose that the human race is descended from a species of animal which reached sexual maturity in five years and rouses a suspicion that the postponement of sexual life and its diphasic onset (in two waves) are intimately connected with the history of hominization.[4]

[3] Ibid., p. 75.
[4] Freud, Moses and Monotheism, XXIII, 74–5.

If we ask to what, in the history of hominization, Freud is referring, we are told in a footnote to his late *Outline of Psychoanalysis* that 'some major external influence was brought to bear on the species and at that point interrupted the straight course of the development of sexuality'. He goes on to add that 'other transformations in the sexual life of man as compared with that of animals might be connected with this, such as the abolition of the periodicity of the libido'.[5] Ferenczi had put forward the improbable idea that the ice ages had been this 'major external influence' and Freud did mention this theory a couple of times in connection with the origin of the latency period,[6] but his original opinion was that it was closely related to the things which he had proposed in *Totem and Taboo*. In *Group Psychology and the Analysis of the Ego* he says:

The repression during the period of latency is an internal obstacle . . . or rather one which has become internal. We may assume that the father of the primal horde owing to his sexual intolerance compelled all his sons to be abstinent, and thus forced them into ties that were inhibited in their aims, while he reserved for himself freedom of sexual enjoyment.[7]

This appears to be another of Freud's unacceptable pieces of inheritance of acquired characteristics, but just as I was able to show how natural selection of random mutants could be shown to lead to the same results as his Lamarckian arguments about innate dispositions to the Oedipus complex, so I believe I can show that the appeal to inheritance of acquired characteristics seen here is only shorthand for a more roundabout process.

We saw in the quotation from De Beer that the retardation of sexual maturity which Freud regards as connected to the phenomenon of latency is itself related to the overall trend to foetalization of the human species. I also argued that among the primates foetalization was unique to man and could not seem to be made to agree with Jolly's gelada/hominid convergence theory. The way out of this difficulty lies in a fuller consideration of Freud's suggestion that the latency period and its associated delay in sexual maturity (and perhaps the whole process of foetalization in man), has something to do with the primal horde hypothesis.

Essentially, neoteny, or foetalization, boils down to the idea of *retardation of maturity*. If we can discover conditions which would have favoured such a retardation we might then be able to construct a simple Darwinian explanation of how such a paradoxical human adaptation could have come about. Freud's original idea was that it had something to do with conditions in the primal horde and with the primal father's monopolization of all the females and his exclusion of the sons. But under gelada-like conditions there appears to

[5] *Totem and Taboo*, XIII, 153n.
[6] *The Ego and the Id*, XIX, 35, and *Inhibitions, Symptoms, and Anxiety*, XX, 155.
[7] XVIII, 139–40.

be no adaptive advantage to retardation of sexual maturity. How could there be? On the contrary, if only those animals who were big and ferocious enough to be able to drive a dominant male away from his harem stood any chance of mating and raising young, it is clear that the faster an individual reached maturity and the quicker he acquired the sexual and physical maturity to undertake such a daunting task the better. Neoteny, as I observed before, could serve no purpose whatever for a gelada-like hominid.

Having said that, one might wonder what, if any, adaptive advantage there is in foetalization. At first sight the situation looks inexplicable. How could an evolutionary trend which increases infantile dependency and vulnerability be favoured by natural selection? Some of the fossil hominids we have found died as the result of violent blows to the head. How then, could evolution have gone about reducing the thickness of the skull as it has done, thanks to neoteny? The answer lies in the fact that foetalization is the key to human intelligence and intellectual development. The crucial factor is the way in which it increases the size of the brain relative to the body and greatly extends the period of learning. In the apes the major part of the growth of the brain is completed by the end of the first year. In the rhesus monkey and gibbon 70 per cent of brain growth has been achieved by birth and the rest is completed in the first six months. In man, however, the major part of brain growth *begins* at birth. In the first year of life it more than doubles in weight and by the age of three has almost reached its adult size, even though it goes on growing slowly right up to adolescence and beyond. Montagu sums up by saying:

It seems reasonably clear that the growth and development of the human brain is a neotenous phenomenon. In other words, man preserves something akin to the rate of growth and developmental characteristics of the foetal brain or preserves and improves upon the rate of growth and development of the infant ape-brain long after the latter has ceased to grow.[8]

The development of high intelligence would have been of little significance to the monotonous life of a seed-eating hominid, but to a hunting hominid, unequipped as he would have been with physical adaptations to predation, the acquisition of high intelligence would have been the adaptive imperative of his hopes of survival. Lacking instinctual behavioural adaptations to hunting, he would have been forced to rely on intelligence and experience alone in going about it. Furthermore, the use of tools and weapons, which were to become of such importance to all subsequent human economies, and must have made the decisive contribution to the success of hunting, was entirely dependent on the acquisition of a level of intelligence sufficiently high for their invention. Finally, we should not forget that the considerable inhibition of instinct and co-ordination of social behaviour which group hunting

[8] Ashley Montagu, *Introduction to Physical Anthropology*, p. 301.

demanded were also synonymous with the development of man's intellectual powers, since intelligent behaviour always demands the inhibition of some other less appropriate instinctual response and the substitution of a more rational one.

Neoteny, in other words, would have favoured hominids who began to hunt, and a reference back to the theory propounded in Chapter one will show how this was associated with the retardation of sexual maturity. We may take it as granted that the evolution of high intelligence could only have adaptive significance for those early hominids who began to rely on hunting for their food. In Chapter one I argued that the first hunters must have been bands of adolescent males who had been expelled from the primal hordes. If success in hunting for an otherwise unadapted primate like man depends on innate intelligence and slowly accumulated experience, it follows that those male hominids who postponed their sexual maturity would have been at an advantage. This is because the primal fathers would have expelled males at the first signs of puberty and thereby left them economically to their own devices. Those who, by the occurrence of some retarding mutation, reached puberty later than the rest, would have been favoured by a longer period of childhood with proportionately greater opportunities for learning. They would also have possessed the anatomical correlate of this—a relatively larger brain. This would lead to higher innate intelligence and better acquisition of skills, given the longer period available for it. Such late-developers would have a marginal advantage in hunting over other less neotenous individuals, and generally superior chances of survival. When they came to command a harem of their own (with the almost certain return to a foraging existence) such superior individuals would pass on their higher intelligence and later maturation to their offspring. (Before the institution of incest-avoidance and totemic inhibitions on inter-generation conflict the social structure would have restricted reproduction to only that minority of males who had acquired harems and so would favour the rapid transmission of their mutant genes through the population.)

Gradually, the development of the cerebral cortex would mean that still higher powers of inhibition of instinct and of enhanced capacity to undertake intelligent behaviour became possible for hunting hominids. Thanks to neoteny, their brains would eventually reach a level of sophistication where characteristically human psychological processes would begin to occur, and the unconscious foundations of the guilt and ambivalence which was to produce totemic society would gradually emerge. Once the psychological rubicon had been crossed and men had begun to forgo incest and had renounced their instinct for sexual hegemony within the group, the final constraints on neoteny would have been removed when women became fed and protected by the rest of the group. Freed from the necessity of foraging all the time and provided with a secure home base where they could nurse slow-maturing babies, women would have found themselves in conditions where helplessness and long parental dependency in the young were not maladaptive to any serious extent.

Now neoteny would have powerfully reinforced trends towards greater cerebral complexity and psychological development because from here on all the great advances in human adaptation (like the invention of initiation ceremonies) would have been based on intellectual and inhibitory mechanisms. We may surmise that the most recent addition to the brain of man—the frontal lobes—would have come to prominence during this phase of human evolution because of their important connections with higher mental functions of self-constraint and intellectual synthesis.

All this means that the reason why man is the only primate to show important signs of foetalization, despite his undoubted evolutionary parallelisms with the gelada baboon, is that man is the only one of the higher primates who has become a hunter. He has done so, what is more, by dint of psychological and sociological adaptations that necessitated acquisition of the high intelligence, great powers of self-restraint, and capacity to learn from experience, which only neoteny could give him. The inhibition of sexual maturity at the age of about five is therefore, just as Freud imagined, the outcome of circumstances within the primal horde and has only become part of the phylogenetic inheritance of mankind because of the great turning point in man's history described in the pages of *Totem and Taboo*. The sons of the primal father inhibited their sexual maturity, just as Freud said, because they were forced to do so by the tyrant. Neoteny is the factor which enables us to explain how this came about and how natural selection undertook that inhibition on their behalf.

But one or two doubts may perhaps still remain in the reader's mind. Why, he may pertinently ask, was foetalization not limited to the male sex alone? There would appear to be no advantage in slow maturation in the case of females.

A first but almost certainly not very convincing answer might be that the mutant genes in question just did not happen to be sex-specific and so foetalized the whole human race irrespective of sex. This is unconvincing because great evolutionary changes are seldom the result of such arbitrary factors. It would be much better if we could find some positive adaptive reason why the females of the human race should have become foetalized along with the males. What is certain is that whatever the reason, it could not have been the same one that was operative in the case of men. Young female hominids had no reason to be expelled from the primal hordes, and hence no reason to find a delay in maturity adaptively advantageous. Nevertheless, having said this, it is still possible that, although the specific cause was not there, the general trend was still in evidence and that the female of the species became subject to neoteny for the same reason as the male, namely, to promote intellectual ability. Even if we grant that women did not need to become intelligent for exactly the same reason—that is, to hunt—it is nevertheless possible that there was an adaptive trend favouring greater intelligence and capacity to learn among the females because of the general intellectual advance into culture represented by the hunting economy of the men and the attendant need to evolve complex symbolic systems such as speech and ritual as a means of better adaptation. Such is, I am sure, the case; but this explanation is still too generalized and unscientific to meet the objection.

We must be more rigorous. Let us start again on a different line of inquiry. Where in evolution an adaptive change only affects one sex of a species or can be shown to affect both sexes in different ways as neoteny—if I am correct in what I said above—manifestly does, then the operative principle must be *sexual* rather than natural selection. Neoteny, in other words, must have conferred some advantage on female hominids in sexual terms. Here, the rather loose and impressionistic explanation above might fit. Hunters who were themselves responding to the effects of foetalization, and consequently increasing their intellectual powers in the course of many generations, may have tended to mate with females whose cerebral development fell into a range similar to their own. But however that may be, I believe that there is another and much more important respect in which neoteny was sexually selective as far as women were concerned.

This is in connection with the absence of periodicity in the sexual response cycle of the human female. In the case of all other female primates an estrous cycle is present in which the female in question regularly comes 'on heat' at a certain period. Receptivity to conception is usually signalled by the alteration in appearance of some secondary sexual characteristic. In the case of the female gelada baboon, this is the polyp-like adornments on the chest which undergo a change in colour, in that of the chimpanzee it is a large perineal swelling which appears at peak estrous. Studies of the physiology of human females show that although they have the same periodic cycle of hormone secretion, they do not manifest any very obvious peak of sexual receptivity, but remain sexually receptive all the time. This difference, which is not the outcome of the suppression of the hormonal stimulus to estrous, is accounted for by the development of the cerebral cortex which has the effect of reducing behavioural responsiveness to internal chemical signals and of increasing responsiveness to intellectual and sensory stimuli from the outside. Such a development is doubtless, as Freud realized,[9] the outcome of the general primate trend towards less reliance on the sense of smell and increased use of sight and sound. But in man this trend has reached unprecedented development, and there can be little doubt that neotenous mutations retarding the onset of sexual maturity and promoting the development of the cerebral cortex are mainly responsible. In short, as far as human females are concerned, foetalization has meant not just intellectual advance in general but the disappearance of periodicity in the sexual cycle.

[9] Freud, *Civilization and its Discontents*, XXI, 99n.

The connection of all this to what has gone before may seem a little nebulous until I point out that the presence of periodicity in females would have been adaptively most disadvantageous to hunting hominids practising incest-avoidance. The reason for this is obvious. In the traditional foraging primal hordes periodicity of sexual responsiveness would have been no more maladaptive than it is to today's gelada baboon. It simply would have meant that the dominant male would mate with whatever female was on heat at the time and would ignore those who were not (but being careful all the while, one must point out, to make sure that other males did not try to appropriate them even so). In bands of hunting hominids who could only maintain the unity of the group by sharing females out among themselves, sexual periodicity would have been most disruptive. It would have meant that males who were permanently sexually active were paired off with females who were only sexually desirable for a few days each month. Interest in other females who were on heat when one's own female or females were not would have been a major temptation to return to the traditional social structure in which one male had total sexual hegemony.

Permanent sexual receptivity, on the other hand, would mean that women were as sexually active throughout the cycle as men, and would have greatly promoted the chances of incest-avoidance and its resultant social arrangements being a success. It would also have had the useful corollary of ensuring that female intellectual development followed a path similar to that of the men, since we must recall that they were living in groups of hunters which were coming increasingly to rely on intelligence as a major adaptive ploy in the struggle for existence. Hence neotenous mutations that may have begun as sexually specific would soon have become operative in both sexes because of the selective pressure affecting the maintenance of hunting bands in which the evolution of non-periodicity in the sexual response cycle of the females had removed a major cause of disintegration of the groups.

Thus, in essence, the effects of neoteny were the same for both sexes because the underlying cause was the same. In both men and women the principal effect of neoteny was to greatly expand the neocortex and thereby to facilitate a vast increase in the extent of intelligent control over what had previously been largely instinctive behaviour. The suppression of sexual periodicity in women because of cortical immunity to hormonal stimulation was thus only another example of the increasing hold which the higher mental functions of the cerebral cortex were taking over every aspect of human behaviour.

Before we leave the question of man's physical adaptations and their relation to the theme of *Totem and Taboo*, there is one further issue which I would like to raise. I want to raise it because I think that it is interesting and throws light on one of Freud's most controversial—or perhaps it would be more accurate to say, most *resisted*—ideas.

I pointed out in Chapter One that the human female, like the gelada baboon, carries her principal secondary sexual characteristic on her chest. But we have just seen that, unlike the gelada baboon, the human female does not have secondary sexual characteristics which signal that she is in a state of receptivity for conception. (It is true that slight swelling of the breasts may occur as menstruation approaches, but this is hardly significant when compared with the very obvious and dramatic changes which affect the secondary sexual characteristics of apes and monkeys.) Remarkable as it may seem, there is considerable evidence to support the contention that this function may have been transferred to the primary sex organ of the male.

One of the apparent paradoxes of foetalization is that it does not seem to have resulted in a diminution in the size of the sex organs in males. While it may arguably be the reason why man is the only large primate to lack a penis bone,[10] it cannot possibly be the reason why he has the largest penis, both relatively and absolutely, of any primate. Foetalization ought to have foetalized the sex organs—that is, made them smaller and more like those of the opposite sex. In fact, the reverse has occurred, and man, who is considerably smaller than the average gorilla, has a penis approximately twice as long in erection and much more thick. Such a large organ cannot have been evolved in order to make it more efficient in copulation since the other primates get by quite well with much smaller ones. Its significance must be that in the case of humans the penis has taken on the secondary sexual characteristic of indicating sexual arousal and receptivity of the male in the unique circumstance of the female being permanently receptive. This accounts for its impressive size, which would have been positively favoured by sexual selection in a species where the male was the usual initiator of sexual activity. With the acquisition of a bipedal mode of locomotion, the sexual organs of the male would have come into prominence and undergone an increase in size if success in mating depended on a man being able to arouse the sexual interest of women through the sight of his erect penis.

Such a development, like the suppression of sexual periodicity in females which it accompanied, must have occurred after the transition to hunting began and must have contradicted the neotenous trends in human evolution which were foetalizing the male generative organs by removing the penisbone.[11] If this is correct, then the notable hypertrophy of the penis in men must have been accompanied by a corresponding instinctual response in women. If erection of a prominent penis became the principal sexual cue of the species, then sexual selection would see to it that those females who responded to it most readily would tend to bear the most offspring. In other

[10] Because this is one of the last parts of the foetal ape skeleton to be formed.

[11] This process may be part of the explanation of why the penis became much thicker as well as longer, since the loss of internal support of the erect organ which resulted from the atrophying of the penis bone had to be compensated for by increasing the thickness of the supportive tissues.

words, selection would favour responsiveness to the erect penis as a sexual signal. Consequently, we should expect to find a desire to see the penis as an innate instinctual disposition in women, just as our earlier considerations led us to expect to find ambivalence and incestuous desire as part of the genetic endowment of men. Such an innate tendency is doubtless there, but it is worth pointing out that it may be the basis of Freud's findings regarding penis-envy.

The reality of penis-envy in women was something which Freud never doubted, and its existence has recently proved measurable in the laboratory situation.[12] Freud, in his last formulations of psychoanalytic theory, says of the girl that 'from the very first she envies boys . . . her whole development may be said to take place under the colours of envy for the penis'.[13] He defines penis-envy as a 'positive striving to possess a male genital'.[14]

Clearly, this desire to possess a male genital is closely akin to straightforward desire for sexual intercourse but, in the little girl as in the adult woman, it retains a more primitive aim—a desire for a penis of her own.

That this tendency to penis-envy may have an instinctual basis explicable by reference to hypertrophy of the penis in males can be understood if we recall what Freud said about instincts in *Beyond the Pleasure Principle*: '*An instinct is an urge inherent in organic life to restore an earlier state of things* which the living entity has been obliged to abandon under the pressure of external disturbing forces; that is, it is a kind of organic elasticity, or, to put it another way, the expression of the inertia inherent in organic life.'[15]

Now, if Freud is right about instincts being 'the expression of the inertia inherent in organic life', then it is possible that penis-envy in women may be an expression of just such biological conservatism. This would be because the secondary function of the penis in males—signalling sexual receptivity and readiness to mate—had been acquired by it relatively late in evolution and had previously been exercised by the organs of the female. The instinctual basis of her penis-envy would therefore be an innate conservatism which manifested itself in an unconscious desire to go on doing what females of the species had once been able to do, but which they could do no more and which had instead become the privilege of the penis. Her penis-envy would be the psychological expression of a deep instinctual trend that went back to the foundations of female sexuality in the primates as a whole and to a period

[12] See Freud, *New Introductory Lectures on Psychoanalysis*, XXII, 125–9, 'Some Psychical Consequences of the Anatomical Distinction between the Sexes', XIX, 252–6, 'On the Transformations of Instinct as Exemplified in Anal Erotism', XVII, 129–32. For laboratory tests see R. B. Levin, 'An Empirical Test of the Female Castration Complex', *Journal of Abnormal Psychology*, 71, 1966, and C. S. Ellman, unpublished doctoral dissertation reported in S. Fisher and R. Greenberg, *The Scientific Credibility of Freud's Theories and Therapy*, p. 200ff.

[13] *An Outline of Psychoanalysis*, XXIII, 193.

[14] *Ibid.*, XXIII, 250.

[15] XVIII, 36 (author's italics).

before foetalization had suppressed sexual periodicity in the female and the changes in her secondary or primary sexual characteristics which accompanied it. Foetalization may well have overlaid such primitive sexual urges with the higher developments of intelligence, but there is no reason to suppose that fundamentally—that is, *unconsciously*—anything has changed. If this is the case, then penis-envy is the expression of an instinct for sexual periodicity which has had to be renounced by the species in the interests of safeguarding its elaborate social structures. Here again, as in so much else of this material, the history of the race and of the individual seem to be perfectly complementary, for just as the realization that she lacks a penis comes as a major set-back for the little girl and a powerful reinforcement to the forces of instinctual renunciation, so in the case of the species as a whole the suppression of sexual periodicity in females strongly supported the trend towards renunciation of the anti-social egoistic and libidinal instincts which threatened to undermine it. By making marriage more possible for man, foetalization of the female promoted the cause of instinctual renunciation on which the whole of human culture always has been, and always will be, based.

Before I leave altogether the consideration of man's anatomy and physiology and turn exclusively to history and religion, it is worth pointing out that there is one last aspect of neoteny, or foetalization, which deserves to be mentioned. I remarked at the beginning of this chapter that one possible way of expressing the principle was to call it *the precocious sexual maturity of an otherwise immature form*. In other words, man, as well as being a developmentally retarded animal, might be loosely termed a sexually precocious child. This means that behaviourally he manifests in his maturity all the plasticity and playfulness which is otherwise only found in the young of other animals. Indeed, as we saw, this is related to the key element of neoteny in man— intellectual advancement. But this playfulness and plasticity also applies to his sexual life and so, whereas most animals confine their sexual activity to straightforward instinctual behaviour governed by internal instinctual and chemical controls, man is much more childlike and innovative in his sexual responses. Indeed, neoteny has meant that of all creatures he is the most infantilized in his sexual activity because—and this is the essence of psychoanalysis—his entire adult sexual and psychological life is built on the foundation of an early efflorescence of childhood sexuality which, thanks to foetalization regarded as a retarding mechanism, he is forced to renounce temporarily during the period of latency. Here, once again, the history of the species and of the individual run in parallel, and what is true of the one and so unmistakably represented in its neotenous anatomy is also true of the other where it insistently reveals itself in the infantilisms which live on preserved for ever in the depths of the unconscious mind.[16]

[16] The relevance of this aspect of neoteny to psychoanalysis was first expressed by Géza Róheim in his *The Riddle of The Sphinx*. It was independently rediscovered by myself some years ago, and as summarized in this book owes little or nothing to his work.

The foetalization of man must have taken a considerable amount of time. Such far-reaching behavioural and physical changes cannot happen overnight. As we have seen, I have suggested that they must have occurred sometime after the beginnings of hunting among hominid 'all-male groups', and they may have continued well into the period when culture came more and more to take over man's major adaptive tasks. None of the evolutionary changes suggested in these pages could have been a simple or straightforward affair. There must have been many falterings and failures, and the whole process of human physical and psychological evolution must have exhibited to the full the desultory and random character typical of all phylogenetic change. There must have been many hominids who started out on lines of development which led nowhere. Some must have regressed along paths which led others to greater adaptive success, and the vast majority must simply have been unsuccessful in securing the privilege of being genetically represented in the future. The vast majority of all animal and plant species are, we must not forget, extinct.

If man's neotenous characteristics began to be acquired during the period of evolutionary development which covered the events outlined in the last chapter—in other words, the murder of the primal fathers and the emergence of fraternal hunting bands provided with females—it is worth enquiring whether such a lengthy period of human development may not have left psychological traces comparable to those left by the primal parricide. In the latter case, we saw that the traces left were principally of two kinds. First, there were rituals and religious institutions—those of totemism—which can still be found in many parts of the world. Secondly, we saw that there were innate and genetically-transmitted predispositions to ambivalence and neurosis which natural selection determined were to be conserved as adaptively advantageous to man—or at least, to the maintenance of the altruistic behaviours on which man's adaptive success as a hunter was based. If a pre-totemic phase existed it would be interesting to know whether comparable rituals and psychological pre-dispositions could be found left over from it.

A clue to what we might be looking for could perhaps be found in pursuing the analogy between the individual and the species. If we ask ourselves what, in the individual, precedes the equivalent of the totemic phase—that is, the Oedipus complex—we find that, broadly speaking, it is what may be called 'primal narcissism'. Long before the child is even aware of the persons of the parents as distinct entities, and when there is as yet no inkling of the ambivalences to come, it experiences only a flux of sensation in which its own self—the baby's ego—is not as yet in any way distinguished from its surroundings. Such a state of beatific oneness with the world is the origin of the 'oceanic feeling' experienced by some people[17] and is, as we shall see later, not unrelated to religious feelings as such. In early childhood, however, the

[17] Freud, *Civilization and its Discontents*, XXI, 64ff.

period of primal narcissism does not last long. It begins at birth—indeed, perhaps before birth, when the child really is a unity in the limited world of the womb—but it starts to come to an end as the child's awareness of itself and its distinct existence gradually emerges.

One of the major causes of the emergence of this realization of being an entity not continuous with the rest of the world lies in early experiences of frustration. It is the periodic absence of things which the baby desires—such as the mother's breast—which lead it to realize that such things are not a part of itself. Another major factor, and one which becomes more important as time goes on, is the development of intellectual powers which lead the young child to perceive the differences between itself and its surroundings. But primal narcissism is tenacious and only disappears slowly. In many neurotics it persists as a belief in what one of Freud's patients called the 'omnipotence of thoughts'. Thought is only omnipotent if it can treat the rest of the world as it can treat itself—that is, if it can indulge in fantasy and wish-fulfilment unfettered by reality. Such a process presupposes that the world and the ego are a unity, or, in other words, that one has retained something of one's primal narcissism.

Frustration and primal narcissism may not seem to have much to do with human evolution or foetalization, but the 'omnipotence of thoughts' might be seen to do so by virtue of the fact that the main effect of neoteny was to promote human intelligence, itself the necessary condition for any such belief in the overwhelming power of thought. A phase of unfettered indulgence in the belief in the omnipotence of thought may perhaps have gone along with neotenous evolution of the human species, and certainly corresponds to what Freud called animism.[18] This was the term he applied to the system of thought which preceded the appearance of totemism and religion proper. Basic to all systems of animistic thinking is the belief that man can bring about the fulfilment of his wishes by some ritual means or other. As such, it can be seen as a generalized application, or perhaps one should say, an *over*-application of something which neoteny had provided for man in the interests of the new hunting adaptation of the young males. (We are talking about the period immediately preceding the primal crime and totemism.) This, of course, was intelligence, and intelligence essentially consists in an ability to think out rational responses to situations for which an innate behavioural repertoire has not prepared one. Hunting was the most important of these new responses and required men to substitute for the innate predatory skills that they lacked, intelligent techniques of hunting which neoteny did enable them to acquire. What could be more natural than to apply such intellectual responses in every situation in which one's innate behaviour was insufficient to secure what was desired? The result of such

[18] For Freud's writings on animism see *Totem and Taboo*, XIII, 64–5, 75–99, *The 'Uncanny'*, XVII, 240–50, *New Introductory Lectures*, XXII, 164–7.

inappropriate application of thought to the satisfaction of what were perhaps often unrealizable ends is the essence of animism. In fact, of course, man *has* dominated nature by the 'omnipotence' of his thoughts, but we can hardly assume that in the beginning it was appreciated that these thoughts could only be truly omnipotent if they were also rational. But let us return to the question of what traces, if any, animism could have left behind.

If there ever was an animistic stage preceding totemism in the development of the psychology of the human race its only traces existing now are what we commonly call 'magic'. All magical practices rest on the implicit belief that an individual or group of individuals who follow the correct procedures can in some way or another control or determine the outcome of some event. In love magic this is often represented by symbolism which is especially transparent. Róheim mentions that among the Vends a girl would sleep with an apple on her genitals and then give it to the young man whom she wanted to fall in love with her.[19] In Hungary it was believed that a woman could regain the affections of a disenchanted husband if she fed him bread which she had kneaded between her thighs. Similar examples could be multiplied almost without limit. Most primitive peoples have elaborate systems of magical practices by means of which they think they can influence the weather, their enemies, their animals, the outcome of hunting expeditions, the success of legal proceedings and political negotiations, the growth of crops, and an almost limitless list of other things whose only common feature is that most of them are in one way or another totally independent of individual human control. And this is, of course, precisely the reason why magic is applied to them. Things that are important to man but also outside his control are an offence to his narcissism. He would like to believe himself omnipotent, but knows that in reality he is not, so just as love magic panders to the narcissism of the person practising it by making him believe that he really can make himself irresistible to the object of his love, magic in general secures the desires of man's bruised narcissism by making him believe that he is in control of his destiny when in reality he is not.

If narcissistic over-valuation of the power of thought is the essence of magic and animism, and if such wish-fulfilments are applied to matters which frustrate man's narcissism, it would be interesting to know just what, in the case of the species as a whole, this narcissism consisted of and to what frustrations the remedies of magic were applied. In the case of the individual, we have already seen that the narcissism in question is that of the very young ego, as yet undifferentiated from the world and applying to it assumptions of mental control which in reality only belong to its own self. Róheim reports that one of his patients who had developed a private system of magic said that the magical process consisted 'in the removal of boundaries' and in her capacity to project herself into other people.[20]

[19] G. Róheim, *Magic and Schizophrenia*, p. 14.
[20] G. Róheim, *The Riddle of the Sphinx*, p. 82.

In the case of the species as a whole, magical and animistic thinking go back to the period when it occupied with regard to nature a position exactly analogous to that of the individual in the first months of life. The primal narcissism of the human race was the stage of its existence in which it was barely differentiated from the rest of nature, and had not yet acquired the altruism which brought the period of unmitigated egoism to an end. It was the era during which the principal organ of its emergent self-consciousness and capacity for altruistic behaviour was evolving. That organ was, of course, the brain, or, more accurately, the advanced cerebral cortex which covers the brain and is the site of its higher mental operations, among which self-consciousness is one of the most notable. We have already seen that this highly-developed cerebral cortex was the product of foetalization and the delaying of maturity in which it resulted. Thus in the early stages of foetal-ization, when man was only just beginning to develop his outstanding mental powers, the condition of the species as a whole must have been very like that of the new-born child in whom we can see the same process of gradual cere-bral development combined with slowly emerging consciousness of itself out of a previously undifferentiated narcissism. It was the evolution of intelli-gence and consciousness which robbed man of his primal animal narcissism in which he had lacked consciousness of himself as a separate being and had been totally immersed in the unity of living beings.

Even today, much of the charm of wild animals lies in their evident nar-cissism, self-contentment, and lack of concern for us—a phenomenon which also has much to do with the appeal of young children.[21] From the behavioural point of view, early foraging hominids who had not yet had to undergo the trauma which led to the emergence of altruism in the interests of a hunting economy must have manifested a very considerable degree of egoism, rather as the gelada baboon does today. We have already seen that a foraging economy does not demand the sharing of food or the other co-operative activities demanded by hunting. On the contrary, the nature of gelada-like societies rewards brutal egoism with reproductive success and allows dominant males to pursue their own desires without hindrance. In short, we can say that both in terms of the non-differentiation of the ego and the self-centred nature of their existence the new-born individual and the early foraging hominids were much alike.

Another parallel arising out of this is what we might call the *oral* character of magic. Róheim is undoubtedly correct when he says that 'the almost universal cure-all of primitive medicine is sucking.'[22] Associated with this is the curative reputation of spittle attested to in the New Testament by Christ's miraculous use of it.[23] A 25-year-old patient of Róheim's asserted that she had the power of making anyone she wanted fall in love with her merely by

[21] Freud, *On Narcissism*, XIV, 89.
[22] G. Róheim, *Magic and Schizophrenia*, p. 8.
[23] *Ibid.*, p. 7.

making a sucking action with her lips in their direction. This sucking action she associated with sucking milk from her mother's breast.[24] Bychowski reports a case in which a patient was subject to delusions of being 'eaten up' by other people, and identified himself with his mother's breast.[25] In central Australia the people believe that one becomes ill as a result of a demon entering the body by means of biting, sucking, or boring.[26]

The relationship between the oral region and magic results from the fact that in the period of primal narcissism of both the individual and the species the oral zone is all-important. In the case of the child this is because this period is one of total nutritional dependence on the mother's breast. Indeed, because of the non-differentiation of the child from its surroundings, it originally regards the breast as a part of itself, and its pleasure in absorbing its contents is a supreme narcissistic gratification. As a result, the oral region becomes associated with intense sensations of pleasure which make it an erotogenous zone for the rest of the individual's life. In the species, we must recall that a corresponding period of primal narcissism preceded that of totemism and was associated with a foraging existence and with the beginnings of hunting. In the case of foraging, where the creatures in question are reliant on a diet of seeds and tubers like the gelada baboon of modern times, nearly all the waking life must be devoted to feeding.

A food resource which is dispersed in arid regions and comes in such small and numerous particles demands a great deal of time to be devoted in harvesting it and almost constant action of the mouth, especially if, as in the case of grains, the particles are hard and require a great deal of chewing. We have already seen what important physical adaptations such a diet led to, and it seems by no means unreasonable to conclude that behaviourally and psychologically, foraging hominids in whom foetalization had not begun at all or had only progressed slightly might be dominated by an oral character comparable to that of new-born babies. This is all the more so if we recall that the cause of neoteny in the species—the beginnings of hunting by groups of unmated young males—would also have powerfully featured the element of oral aggression that is inseparable from hunting before recourse can be made to weapons and tools. Neoteny would provide these in time in the form of the intellectual talent to invent them, but, to begin with, hominid hunters must have had to rely on the only weapons nature had given them, hands and, above all, *teeth*. Considerations such as these, along with the individual associations of the oral zone with the 'omnipotence of thoughts' are the reasons why magic uses such evident oral symbolism.

So much for the narcissism of the species, but what frustrations of it could animism have remedied?

[24] *Ibid.*, p. 97 and *Riddle of the Sphinx*, p. 81.
[25] Quoted by Róheim, *Ibid.*, pp. 65–6.   [26] *Ibid.*, p. 65.

A classic study of the oral character by Abraham[27] shows that in modern individuals it is often associated with the character trait of *envy*. Persons in whom envious feelings play a prominent part can usually be shown to have oral personality types in which the resentment felt against a younger sibling whose arrival brought about their abrupt weaning has become the basis of all subsequent resentment and envy. At bottom, what they really envy is their younger brother's or sister's possession of the mother's breast.

It would be tempting to see a similar situation existing in the primal hordes of the early foraging hominids. Here, envy would have been the major psychological response of the sons to the dominant position of the father or to any one of themselves who succeeded in replacing him as sole leader of the group. Indeed, we can go further and say that only those sub-dominant males who envied the position of a ruling dominant male would have had the motivation to try to unseat him. The sons, in seeing the primal father enjoying his opportunities for unfettered indulgences of all his egoistic and erotic desires, would have been eaten up with envy of all the things that he possessed.

Such an observation may well explain another of the most notable features of magic. Notwithstanding all that I have said about its oral nature, there can be no doubt that there are manifest *phallic* aspects to it as well. Among the Aranda, black magic intended to cause harm to others invariably uses sticks, cords, or bones which, by means of magical spells, are transformed into snakes or lethal darts which enter the body of the enemy. Correspondingly, if an Aranda falls sick and suspects foul play, a magic bone will be treated with semen and excrement in a rite which is supposed to turn the evil sorcery back against whoever sent it.[28] The Pitchentara and Mularatara believe that one can magically 'sing' the scrotum and testicles of an enemy and make them rot. The Nambutji believe that the magic bone used in black magic enters the enemy's penis. The demons who may also cause disease and who have already been mentioned as biting and sucking their way into a person's body are chiefly characterized by huge, ever-erect penises.

So far I have not had occasion to refer to belief in spirits or demons, but the association above between the phallic aspect of magic and the persons of the demons suggests that such a connection may exist and may be important. Róheim reports that among the Aranda the storm-demons are both male and female and are locked together in copulation like dogs.[29] This is also true of the Matuntara who call the male dog *Mamara* ('like father') and the female *Jakura* ('like mother').

One of his aboriginal informants told Róheim that he had a devil inside his leg who went around cutting off people's testicles when they were asleep, as

---

[27] K. Abraham, 'The First Pre-genital Stage of the Libido' in *Selected Papers*.

[28] G. Róheim, *The Riddle of the Sphinx*, p. 58, 'The Pointing Bone', *J.R.A.I.*, 45, 90, 1925.

[29] *The Riddle of the Sphinx*, p. 28.

well as urinating in their faces and sleeping with their women.[30] The behaviour of the demons reveals some remarkable contradictions: if they are far away they can come immediately, but if they are near they take a very long time to arrive; they can only set fire to wet grass; they cannot get over a trickle of water, but great rivers hold no difficulties for them, and so on.[31] Phallic attributes are also the characteristic of female demons in central Australia. The chief class of these are called *alknarintja* ('eyes-turn-away'). According to the Aranda, these spirits are women who actually existed in mythological times and had three penises which they subsequently cut off, leaving only the clitoris. They come up to men at night and have intercourse with them by sitting on top of them, and in dreams they appear as women with whom sexual relations would be incestuous.[32]

A clue to the meaning of this may lie in another of Róheim's observations: 'According to the . . . Western Aranda, if the young men were not subjected to the discipline of initiation they would become demons, would fly up into the sky and would kill and eat all the old men.'[33] In a dream, one of his informants who had lost a testicle at his initiation saw a devil come up to him and cut off the remaining one.[34] This connection between initiation and the devils is the key to understanding the phallic aspects of magic, and will enable us to relate it to the subject of the previous chapter. The first thing which the quotation above tells us is that a demon is equivalent to an uninitiated man.

In the first chapter we saw that initiation was a process whereby the super-ego was formed by subjecting the initiate to punishments and mutilations which served to bring about the repression of his incestuous and parricidal desires. The only meaning in the statement that uninitiated men would become demons must be that a demon is like a man who has not repressed those antisocial desires; indeed, we see that the behaviour which is attributed to the demons—killing and eating the old men—is exactly what initiation is intended to prevent. But the dream recounted by the informant who had lost his testicle also reveals another aspect of the demon because it shows that he is the person who does the initiating—the father. This should not surprise us in the least if we recall that in the last chapter I argued that what the fathers did to the sons at initiation was merely a mitigated form of what the primal father had originally tried to do to them, namely, to kill and castrate them. Hence the man who is uninitiated (that is, who has no super-ego) behaves just as the primal father did—he murders and castrates at will, and, we must also suppose, commits incest. Hence the female demons, who represent the incestuous desires of those who dream about them as women in forbidden categories of relationship, are represented as having been *castrated*.

[30] *Ibid.*, p. 77.
[31] *Ibid.*, p. 153.
[32] G. Róheim, *Psychoanalysis and Anthropology*, pp. 68–9.
[33] *The Eternal Ones of the Dream*, p. 75.
[34] *The Riddle of the Sphinx*, p. 38.

The loss which they have suffered is the very loss which the sleeper fears he may suffer if he allows himself to succumb to temptation to commit incest.

Thus, it is the demon woman who has intercourse with the man, rather than the other way around, so that by this means he can unconsciously deny all responsibility for what has occurred. The male demons really are 'like father' because they represent the primal father in his enjoyment of the mothers (to whom he is stuck like a dog during copulation). Their paradoxical behaviour in being far but coming soon, or being near and never arriving, reflects the fact they *they represent the exact opposite* of the actual state of affairs. In reality, in a totemic society men do not behave like the primal fathers did—on the contrary, by means of the taboos on incest and the totem they seek to deny such wishes—but in presenting the demons as doing the contrary of what men actually do they affirm that the demons are doing what men would have done if they lacked those inhibitions.

The phallic aspects of magic therefore originate in association with the demons who are the primal father in the guise of his more negative and threatening aspects. The demons are castrators and evil-doers, murderers and tempters to incest because these are the very elements of the primal narcissism of the sons that had to be suppressed by the totemic religion. They live on in magic because magic, by means of the 'omnipotence of thoughts', seeks to gratify those very aspects of man's narcissism which reality forces him to realize he cannot satisfy. The phallic symbolism of magic corresponds to the oral by referring back to the most important respects in which the original narcissism of man has had to be frustrated by human altruism. It refers back to the incest and parricide which the envy of the sons led them to want to perpetuate but which, once the primal truama of the co-operative killing of the father and the institution of totemism had occurred, were denied to them forever by the taboos on which the new religion was founded. It is not to be wondered at that in those parts of the world where totemism still exists magic and the 'omnipotence of thoughts' should provide men with the gratifications which human society inevitably forbids them.

II OEDIPUS REX

I think that the time has come to pause for a moment and to reflect on our progress so far. Putting the matter into the terms of an analogy with an individual analysis, one might say that we have now dealt with both the Oedipal and pre-Oedipal phases of the patient's history. We have been able to go right back to the earliest period of his existence and reconstruct it with a considerable amount of detail. We have explored the primal narcissism of man and related it to his evolution as a species. We have uncovered the oral character of that distant epoch and found it preserved, like some sort of psychological fossil, in present-day systems of magic, and found it still active in the phantasies of modern neurotics. We have seen how the Oedipal crisis developed out of this period of animism, and what its adaptive and economic concomitants were. We saw that the adaptively most desirable transition to an economy of co-operative hunting produced a trauma in human history unparalleled by any other, and that the results of that trauma still remain of the first importance for the maintenance of human society and personality today.

But should we continue? After all, the reader may feel that what has been achieved so far has hardly been worth the effort expended on it. He may, with some justice, argue that all that I have done is to fill in some minor details in the interpretation of the origins of human society put forward by Freud and that now, having dealt with periods of human history about which our knowledge is, to say the least, sketchy, I can hardly hope to have anything more to say of any value, particularly if it has to do with subsequent historical developments which will inevitably be found in epochs less remote and therefore known in more troublesome detail. He will probably feel that the interpretations so far put forward, while perhaps applicable to historical periods about which we know little and thus can speculate much, might be quite insufficient to explain more reliably recorded events that are open to the full range of critical and archaeological scrutiny. He will probably want to know how I can possibly hope to establish historical interpretations based on such a broadly-painted theory of human development as that advanced so far and expect them to stand up against rival theories which appear to have so much more to recommend them. And if he has been able to read some of the works of those who have been before me in this undertaking he will probably conclude that he is about to see me abandon all pretence at a rational and scientific approach to the material and instead, begin to indulge in an exercise in unrestrained fantasy.

For the last reaction I am afraid he could not be blamed, but any other misgivings the reader may have are, I think, mistaken. Even if we grant that all I have achieved so far is an expansion of Freud's analysis, we should note that we have not yet finished with it and that important aspects of it, such as his interpretation of the origins of Jewish monotheism, still remain to be mentioned. This in itself is probably a good enough reason for proceeding with our investigation. Furthermore, I have a feeling that the reader will find that we have just reached a crucial stage, and that failure to proceed now would be most unfortunate. We may well have reached one of those landmarks in analysis after which a sudden, unexpected and rapid progress is possible. It is by no means uncommon in an individual analysis that once a major piece of important material has been successfully worked through, all sorts of other things quickly and easily fall into place. We shall find that such is the case from here on, and that having dealt with the central issue of the patient's neurosis—the Oedipus complex—we can now expect quick and rewarding progress through a great deal of other material. As for the criticism that the sort of ambitious interpretation of world history which I am about to offer is in some way or another not compatible with a critical and rational approach to history, I can only reply that such prohibitions on the attempt to find a general theory of historical evolution sound to me like the resistances frequently revealed in individuals when they deny that their lives are anything more than the outcome of chance and haphazard events, are lacking in an inner meaning, and cannot be held up to analytic scrutiny. Invariably one finds that once the core of the neurosis has been successfully resolved details of the analysand's life which previously seemed so accidental and unintelligible suddenly fall into a meaningful pattern and become explicable in terms of the latent constants in his personality. Such is also the case where the psychoanalysis of man—in other words, the study of culture—is concerned.

It would be wrong to think that the present study can be anything other than fragmentary or provisional. The detailed psychoanalysis of human history is a vast and daunting undertaking which no single person could attempt in one lifetime, let alone one book. It is not my intention to try, however sketchily, to provide it. Instead, I wish merely to follow through some lines of enquiry already embarked upon in the earlier pages of this book and to indicate succinctly what I believe to be the main conclusions with regard to subsequent history that we can draw from what has already been said. In short, I want to follow through the implications of Freud's *Totem and Taboo* and other works for subsequent religious and economic developments in rather the same way that I followed them through in the opening chapter, filling out his theory where possible with new insights, and developing its logic, so that its ultimate conclusions can be drawn. In doing this, the reader will find me being highly selective with the material at which I shall be looking. Because time and space do not allow—indeed, could not allow—an exhaustive presentation, he must be content with something that falls short of any sort of completeness. He will find in the remainder of this chapter, for instance, that I limit myself to a consideration only of ancient Egyptian and ancient Greek polytheism. This is not because I consider these to be the only polytheisms to which the theory to be expounded applies. Rather, it is the outcome of the fact that selectivity forces us to limit our analysis to clear, well-known, and relatively simple cases, and because later chapters will demand that it is precisely these two particular polytheisms that should be considered. Again, in the next chapter where we shall be considering monotheism, I shall limit myself to just two examples of the form of religion concerned, a choice dictated by the unusual quality of the material in the cases in question and the clarity with which it reveals its characteristics. Later in the book I shall confine myself entirely to a consideration of the evolution of Christianity in the West; again, not because the interpretation offered here will not apply elsewhere, but because of the relevance of the material to my final point and because of the natural precedence which Western religion assumes in Western minds. As a result of these and other considerations, the reader will find no mention of Oriental or Indian religions, despite the fact that I suspect that these could provide excellent material against which the validity of my conclusions could be tested. But this is the subject for another study. For the present let us continue undeterred, and turn our attention to the next phase in the development of religion after animism and totemism, to what it is convenient to call polytheism.

E. Wallis Budge remarks in one of his books[1] that it is incomprehensible to him why the ancient Egyptians gave their animal gods human *bodies* rather than heads. This is doubtless because a human head on an animal body would suggest that the animal in question had been made into a human divinity, which is what Wallis Budge's interpretation of Egyptian deities leads him to expect. But if we suppose, as the foregoing consideration of totemism suggests, that animal deities represent a human being—the primal father—then the fact that Egyptian theriomorphic gods have human bodies but animal heads is easily comprehensible and exactly what we should expect. A notable apparent exception to this rule, the Sphinx (an animal body with a human head), will be considered shortly.

The totemic prehistory which underlies Egyptian polytheism is so obvious that it cannot be mistaken.[2] It is reflected in the fact that each of the nomes of Egypt was associated with one particular animal god rather as totemic clans are associated with particular totems.[3] Animal cults flourished. At Mendes a sacred ram was kept and when it died was buried with great pomp at public expense.[4] A sacred cat was kept in the temple of Neith at Sais; and scores of mummified cats, crocodiles and other animals have been found throughout Egypt.[5] According to one account, the primeval gods were four male frogs and four female snakes.[6] The chief god, Amun, was represented with the head of a ram; Thoth, the Egyptian Hermes, had the head of an ibis; Horus was a falcon god.[7] Bast was a cat; Shu and Tefnut were lionesses.[8] The Apis bull was worshipped as the incarnation of Ptah, the Mnevis bull as that of Ra, the Buchis bull as that of Montu.[9] According to Reik[10], the sphinx was a vestige of totemism; and ritual copulation with sacred rams was reported by Strabo (quoting Pindar).[11] Wallis Budge says that he saw women having intercourse with donkeys and ganders during peasant plays in Egypt, and

---

[1] *From Fetish to God in Ancient Egypt*, p. 101.
[2] H. Frankfort, *Kingship and the Gods*, p. 16.
[3] E. Wallis Budge, *op. cit.*, p. 111.
[4] *Ibid.*, p. 76.
[5] *Ibid.*, p. 81.
[6] J. Manchip White, *Ancient Egypt*, p. 24.
[7] *Ibid.*, p. 25.
[8] E. Wallis Budge, *op. cit.*, p. 143.
[9] J. Manchip White, *op. cit.*, p. 34.
[10] *Dogma and Compulsion.*
[11] E. Wallis Budge, *op. cit.* p. 75.

affirms that similar things used to occur in antiquity.[12] The pig was ritually unclean and highly taboo. However, it was consumed at an annual sacred feast reminiscent of the totem sacrament as described by Freud, and, long before Freud, was associated by the Egyptians with an incident in the legend of Osiris, symbolizing his castration at the hands of Seth, who incestuously desired his sister, Isis, wife of Osiris.[13]

Far from being peculiar to Egypt, totemic elements can be found in nearly all polytheisms, even that of ancient Greece. 'Since there is no member of the Olympian pantheon who is not associated in all sorts of ways with animals and plants,' says Thomson, 'it is a legitimate presumption that Greek religion in general rests on a totemic foundation.[14] He goes on to cite the evidence of the numerous snake cults in ancient Greece and the association between certain cultic practices and certain clans. According to Reinach,[15] Marsyas and Apollo were originally divine asses or mules, Orpheus was worshipped as a fox, and Dionysus as a bull or goat. In early times, the cult of Zeus was associated with snake-worship,[16] and Pan, the inventor of masturbation, was a phallic goat. 'Centaurs are rough-haired, animal-like beings who live in mountain forests. They eat raw meat and rape women.'[17] They are also, along with satyrs and other half-human creatures, clearly derived from ideas which originally must have been totemic.[18] Speaking of the origins of Greek polytheism, Nilsson says, 'One thing is clear: it was supposed that the gods appeared in the shape of birds.'[19] He expresses the opinion that Athena is the descendant of a Minoan snake goddess.[20]

E. O. James, in describing the Cretan fore-runners of much of Greek religion, numbers among the 'emblems and adjuncts' of the Mother Goddess cult the following: 'snake, dove, double axes, horns of consecration, phalli, obese female figurines, sacred trees and pillars, and mountains on which she is often depicted as accompanied by wild and fantastic beasts and horned sacrificial victims'.[21] In particular, the Minoan goddess is usually shown holding three snakes; and the snake was undoubtedly worshipped as a deity in its own right.[22] When represented as 'Mistress of Animals' the Mother Goddess is 'surrounded with real and monstrous creatures, among whom lions, doves, bulls, griffons and sphinxes predominated', there were also 'demons

---

[12] Ibid., p. 431n.
[13] Plutarch, De Iside et Osiride, 354A. See below p. 76–7.
[14] G. Thomson, Studies in Ancient Greek Society, p. 123.
[15] Cited by T. Reik, Ritual, p. 292.
[16] J. Harrison, Prolegomena to a Study of Greek Religion, ch. 1.
[17] Mannhardt, cited by Róheim, Riddle of the Sphinx, p. 48.
[18] Ibid., pp. 46–9.
[19] M. Nilsson, A History of Greek Religion, pp. 17–18.
[20] Ibid., p. 26.
[21] The Cult of the Mother Goddess, p. 128.
[22] Ibid., pp. 129–30.

with the head of a horse and the body of a lion'.[23] So comparable are Greek and Egyptian religion in this and many other respects that Herodotus thought that the Greek gods derived originally from Egypt.[24] Even scenes of copulation with animals were not unknown in Greek drama and, according to Licht,[25] 'were put on the stage *in puris naturalibus*'. Such rituals, like cases of intercourse with animals in modern neurotics, can be shown to be based on unconscious forces identical to those operative in totemism.[26]

In short, there can be little doubt that animal cults, which must themselves have been derived from totemism, are closely associated with the earlier and more primitive forms of Greek[27] and Egyptian polytheism. Yet the question of the origin of polytheism and the way in which it might have evolved out of totemism remains to be answered.

Freud suggest that the origin of polytheism lay in a partial breakdown in the original totemic fraternities and the emergence of sons who identified with the primal father more closely than had previously been possible.[28] This in turn was the outcome of a deeper cause, namely, the longing for the father which, according to Freud, is the root of all religious feeling. So far we have not had occasion to look at this aspect of Freud's theory of religion, but we shall see that a consideration of it is essential if we are to understand the psychological basis of polytheism. It will involve us in pausing for a moment to consider his book, *The Future of Illusion*.

Although *The Future of An Illusion* was written many years after *Totem and Taboo* it deals with something which is logically anterior to it, namely, the origin of religious feelings in general. *Totem and Taboo* was about the origin of religion in the particular and most elemental instance. *The Future of an Illusion* and the opening pages of *Civilization and its Discontents* approaches the problem from another angle. In these works Freud argues that the origin of the predisposition to religious feelings about the world—that is, the feeling that one is subject to the will and inscrutable workings of God, or Providence, or Destiny, or whatever—is to be found in the infantile situation in which the young child is totally reliant on the care and protection of the parents. If this is so, then it is clear that religion is based on a mental infantilism which seems to be a psychological parallel to foetalization in man's physiological evolution. Just as immature anatomical features have been preserved in the adult because of neoteny, so infantile attitudes to reality have been preserved in religion. Indeed, so arresting is this parallelism that one is tempted to

[23] *Ibid.*, p. 138.

[24] Nilsson, *op. cit.*, p. 277.

[25] H. Licht, *Sexual Life in Ancient Greece*, p. 158.

[26] K. A. Menninger, 'Totemic Aspects of Contemporary Attitudes towards Animals' in Wilbur & Muensterberger, *Psychoanalysis and Culture*.

[27] For a fuller account of the totemic origins of Greek polytheism see J. Harrison, *Themis*, especially p. 118ff.

[28] *Totem and Taboo*, XIII, pp. 146–53.

wonder whether there might not be some deeper connection. I believe that there is, and to see what this is we must think back for a moment to our earlier consideration of the psychological effect of foetalization.

It is clear that the first and major psychological effect, apart from raising intelligence to the threshold of conceptual thought, would have been the instilling in the child of an important feeling of dependency on the parents. Any animal which commits itself to a neotenous retardation of maturity must face the problem of a greatly increased period of infantile dependency and all the responsibilities and inconveniences which that brings for the parents, and especially the mother. Indeed, as we saw earlier, these disadvantages are so considerable that they would have been enough to rule neoteny out alto-gether if the compensating adaptive advantage, increased intelligence, had not outweighed it. In the young, a greatly extended period of infantile dependency combined with huge cerebral and intellectual advances must produce important feelings of need for protection from the parents. It is quite probable that in such a situation natural selection would positively favour those young who elicited the most protective and supporting behaviour from the parents, so that one can well imagine that those individuals who most adopted an attitude of dependency on the parents might have procured the best parental care and the resulting higher chances of survival. Indeed, in an environment in which the interests of the young to delay maturity and those of the adults to speed it came into direct conflict, one can suppose that selection would produce some sort of behaviour on the part of the young which would promote their chances of securing the attention they needed. A psychological attitude of positive reliance on the parents would be inevitable in the case of a hominid rapidly evolving intelligence. And furthermore, it is clear that throughout its lengthy childhood a young hominid would readily develop a feeling of need for the protection of adults, especially in an exis-tence where danger in the form of predators was ever near and in which it was essential that the young should stay close to the adults as they wandered incessantly in search of food.

Such may well have been the origin of the human need for protection by the parents which in the individual, as in the race, results from the long period of infantile dependence upon them. In time, says Freud, the father becomes of chief importance in this respect to the individual, and so, we may conclude, he must have done for the race. The way in which this basic reli-gious attitude corresponds to the subject matter of my first chapter Freud himself explains as follows: 'The child's attitude to its father is coloured by a peculiar ambivalence. The father himself constitutes a danger for the child, perhaps because of its earlier relation to its mother. Thus it fears him no less than it longs for him and admires him. The indications of this ambivalence in the attitude to the father are deeply imprinted in every religion as was shown in *Totem and Taboo*.'[29]

[29] Freud, *The Future of an Illusion*, XXI, 24.

In other words, the hatred of the father which was the motivation for the primal deed was not unrelated to love for the father which is the other aspect of the primary ambivalence out of which all that is religious—both generally and specifically, emotionally and ritualistically—proceeds. In totemism, the ambivalence was expressed by the murder of the primal father, but also by the worship of him in the guise of the totem. In polytheism, Freud suggests that the primal father returned in a new guise, and with different manifestations of the basic ambivalence.

Expressed succinctly, one might sum up Freud's explanation of the appearance of anthropomorphic deities in polytheism as an example of *the return of the repressed*, and in particular of the return of the primal father. We have already seen that in the course of the transition to an economy based on co-operative hunting the social structure appropriate to open-country terrestrial primates was suppressed, and egalitarian and altruistic totemic clans emerged. Lacking physical adaptations to the new mode of subsistence, hominids adjusted to it by means of psychological and behavioural changes which hinged on the neurotic processes described by Freud in *Totem and Taboo*. All men now become subject to the two great laws of the hunting economy: those forbidding incest, and the killing of the totem which, in a quasi-animal phobic form, represented the old dominant primal fathers who had been eliminated in the transition. Their permanent elimination depended on the maintenance in each generation of the inhibitory mechanism which had operated in the original hunting groups. We have seen that this was effected by the institution of initiation rituals whose psychological function it was to hold the parricidal and incestuous desires of each new generation firmly under control. Any breakdown in this process would have led to a return to the pre-totemic *status quo* and to the primal horde, along with its economic corollary, the abandonment of co-operative hunting.

At first sight, such a 'return of the repressed' as suggested by Freud as the origin of polytheism looks impossible because it implies a return to be a pre-civilized, non-altruistic existence. That this is not the whole story will appear in due course. But for the time being, let us examine the evidence for believing that in polytheism there was a return of the primal father, albeit perhaps to a limited extent.

I have already said something about Egyptian religion, and it is to one of the earliest written accounts of Egyptian religious belief that I want to turn in attempting to find evidence for what Freud proposed. A really good theory should be able to explain not just what other theories explain in a different way, but also what they cannot. This is the case with Freud's 'return of the primal father' hypothesis in the context of the most archaic elements of Egyptian religion. A literary relic of these is preserved in the so-called Pyramid Texts found in tomb inscriptions of the Vth and VIth dynasties (about 2400 B.C.). These inscriptions are not merely very old in themselves. They also contain material which is much older and which was copied out by scribes who no longer understood the meaning of many of the passages they transcribed.[30] The texts were associated with the mortuary rituals of the dead Pharaoh, who throughout is treated as a god. Yet some of the attributes of the deified Pharaoh have puzzled all previous commentators. 'Why the Egyptian priests who had reached such a high state of civilization under the Vth Dynasty wished to represent a great king like Unas as a brutal, cruel, licentious and cannibalistic despot is not easily understood,' Wallis Budge observed. Some of the passages to which he refers run as follows:

The messengers run about distractedly, when they see Unas who appears . . . who lives on his fathers and eats his mothers. King Unas is one who eats men and lives on the gods. King Unas is the Mighty One who overpowers the Mighty Ones. His limit is everlastingness in this his dignity of 'If-he-wishes-he-does' and 'If-he-wishes-not-he-does-not'. (He is the one who) takes women from their husbands whether he will and when his heart desires it.'[31]

I believe it would be hard to imagine a more lively and exact portrait of the Pharaoh-as-primal-father. Here is a perfect representation of the ways of the old despotic dominant male of the gelada-like primal horde who exercises his tyranny by means of complete and untrammelled indulgence of his egoism, aggressiveness and lust. Indeed, the Pyramid Texts themselves seem to insist on this interpretation when they say:

This Unas is the god who is older than the old gods . . . the father of the gods has given him authority as the Great Power . . . Unas has risen up again as king in the heavens . . .[32]

Even incest is not disallowed to him, for, as the primal father, he is above morality: 'the King is he who will unite himself with his mother, the great wild cow'.[33]

Wallis Budge expresses the opinion that these quotations are from one of the oldest sections of the Pyramid Texts,[34] and the passage in question is notable for its frequent references to cannibalism and oral aggression:

He tears out whatever is in their bellies . . . He cooks parts of them in his cauldrons . . . This Unas eats their magic and swallows their noble powers. The great ones are for his meal of the following day . . . He whom he finds on his way he devours immediately

---

[30] E. Wallis Budge, *op. cit.*, p. 322.

[31] J. Breasted, *The Development of Religion and Thought in Ancient Egypt*, p. 127ff., also Wallis Budge, *op. cit.*, p. 322, both slightly modified to make English redactions compatible. See also R. O. Faulkner (Ed.), *The Ancient Egyptian Pyramid Texts*, pp. 81–2.

[32] Wallis Budge, *op. cit.*, p. 325.

[33] Pyr, 388c, cited by J. G. Griffiths, *The Conflict of Horus and Seth*, p. 50.

[34] Wallis Budge, *op. cit.*, p. 323.

. . . He has eaten the Red Crown, he has swallowed the Green Crown. Unas has devoured the lungs of the wise, he is replete for he is living in the hearts of the gods and likewise on their magical powers.[35]

But such oral-sadistic overtones should not surprise us if we recall that the era of the primal fathers corresponds to the oral phase of individual development, and the animism and magic are based on narcissistic and oral elements. Clearly, the other aspect of magic which I referred to above—that of the primal father as demon—is also present if we notice that in the Pyramid Texts Pharaoh is doing everything that the evil spirits do among the Aranda and other peoples. Even among the much less primitively polytheistic Greeks, traces of the primal father can still be seen in the behaviour of the gods. Nilsson remarks that 'In spite of their detestation of the tyrants, the Greeks could not help admiring them as the equals of the gods who, like the gods, could permit themselves to do whatever they pleased.'[36] Perhaps this is why it was said that in early antiquity kings were called 'zeuses'.[37]

In short, the suspicion begins to grow on us that these texts do indeed represent just such a 'return of the repressed', and that in Egyptian religion the divine Pharoah is seen as the re-embodiment of the primal father. It is a fact that Pharaoh was addressed as 'Embodiment of the Lord of All'; furthermore, the Egyptian word usually rendered 'Majesty' carries the connotation of embodiment or incarnation of a deity.[38] Frankfort states simply that 'Pharaoh was divine',[39] and observes that the epithet of Horus, 'the Great God', appears associated with names of the kings of the IVth and Vth Dynasties.[40] The Pyramid Texts constantly emphasize the megalomania and divinity of Pharaoh:

The King sits with those who row the bark of Re, the King commands what is good and he does it, for the King is the great god . . . Make salutation, you gods, to the King, who is older than the Great One, to whom belongs power on his throne; the King assumes authority, eternity is brought to him and understanding is established at his feet. Rejoice at the King, for he has taken possession of the horizon . . . The King is omnipotent, and his arms do not fail, this King is pre-eminent . . . The King is a master of wisdom . . . For the King is a great Power who has power over the Powers . . . The King's place is at the head of all the august ones who are in the Horizon, for the King is a god, older than the oldest . . ..[41]

We might sum up by saying that *incarnation* is the attribute of Pharaoh,

[35] *Ibid.*, pp. 324–6 (modified).
[36] Nilsson, *op. cit.*, pp. 198–9.
[37] J. Harrison, *Epilegomena to a Study of Greek Religion*, p. 18.
[38] H. Frankfort, *Kingship and the Gods*, p. 45.
[39] *Ibid.*, p. 6.
[40] *Ibid.*, p. 39.
[41] Utt. 252, 257, 268, 273–4, translation by Faulkner, *op. cit.*

and of all divine kings. The Shilluk of the Sudan say that each of their divine kings is a re-embodiment of *Nyakang*, the immortal founder of Shilluk kingship.[42] The ancient Egyptians saw each Pharaoh as Horus in his lifetime and as Osiris after his death. (Osiris was the first king of Egypt, Horus was his posthumous son.) The Pyramid Texts seem to insist on this interpretation when they say:

> The King is a sacred image,
> The most sacred image of the sacred images of the Great One.[43]

This insight explains the apparently anomalous character of the Sphinx, which, as I pointed out earlier, is not represented as a human being with an animal head as are most other Egyptian deities, but rather is an animal with a human head. Traditionally, the Sphinx was closely associated with the Pharaoh (and, interestingly enough, with an 'Ethiopian ape' which may well have been the gelada baboon),[44] and particular Pharaohs were on occasions portrayed as Sphinxes. If the divine king is the reincarnation of the primal father who, in the totemism which underlies polytheism was worshipped as the totem animal, we immediately see why Pharaoh has theriomorphic, that is, *totemic*, attributes. He is the totem incarnate, and the elaborate taboos that surround his person and office are the equivalent in divine kingship of the taboos that habitually surround the totem species. He becomes a god among men because he is a man among gods, one whose pre-eminent role in a grain-eating economy is equivalent to that of the primal father in the foraging societies of our hominid ancestors.

But even if we grant that Egyptian and possibly Greek and other polytheisms were the outcome of the return of the primal father in the guise of divine kings, we are still left with the problem of having to explain why these individuals appeared and how they came to resemble the primal father. Freud suggested that this may have had something to do with agriculture, and it is to a consideration of this that we must now turn.

Let us begin by reviewing the part which economic factors have played in the story so far. We have seen that the decisive adaptive advantage of big-game hunting was in large part economic, that hunting was so much more effective a way of getting food compared with foraging. But it would be quite wrong to imagine that material forces operate in some occult way, as proposed by Marx, and that economic systems and the technology that go with them have any other origin than the mind of man. When the Wright brothers invented the aeroplane they did not do so because of any crude materialistic determinism, they did so because flight provided those two

[42] C. G. & B. Z. Seligman, *Pagan Tribes of the Nilotic Sudan*, p. 77.
[43] Utt. 273–4.
[44] T. Reik (quoting Agatharchides), *Dogma and Compulsion*.

notably celibate young men with one of the most obvious of all sexual sub-limations. And if Marxists will rejoin that they could only have secured the technological and material wherewithal to undertake such a sublimation in the context of capitalism, I will reply that such is undoubtedly the case but that capitalism, as we shall see in a later chapter, is itself just such a product of psychology and of a religious ethic which is based on it. And what is true of the Wright brothers is equally true of the origins of stone technology and of all other inventions and discoveries in the economic sphere. A short con-sideration of this will not be out of place here because it will serve as an introduction to the more important question of the technological origins of agriculture and the domestication of plants.

Stone technology undoubtedly grew out of the use of natural stones as missiles in the early days of hunting. But if used in hunting they would also have been used in those frequently repeated acts of parricide by means of which countless generations of hunting hominids confronted and destroyed the dominant males of the foraging groups. Indeed, as I pointed out before, Róheim may well be correct when he states his opinion that the use of stones originated in the need of the sons to find a compromise between their con-tradictory desires to kill the primal father with their bare hands, but also to keep a respectful distance from the feared master of the horde.[45] In any event, it is clear that stones, because of their association with the murder of the primal father and their pre-eminent place in the economy which was based on totemism, took on important psychological and religious characteristics. Some of these have survived into historical times. Plato asserts that if any man has killed someone in his own family he should be killed himself and his corpse left at the cross-roads where the leaders of the people should cast stones on it. Throughout the world stone heaps are associated with murder. In Sweden, cairns accumulated where two men killed each other; and in West Prussia every passer-by was supposed to cast a stone on the spot where a suicide was buried. In Brandenburg this was done for the grave of anyone who met a violent end. Similar customs are reported among the Bushmen, and on the Zambezi stone cairns are built up on the scene of rapes. Róheim multiplies examples throughout the world, most of which seem to establish a connection between violent death and stones.[46]

Among the Australian aborigines sacred stones, the *churungas*, are of the greatest importance in the religion. These objects are highly taboo and must never be seen by women or the uninitiated. They are responsible for pro-creation and, according to the Aranda, the first ancestor to be turned into a churunga had an ever-erect penis. Originally, this churunga was his penis and he used it to drive his sons away.[47] In the totemic ceremonies the sacred stones are decorated with blood from the penis and with feathers—just like

[45] G. Róheim, *The Riddle of the Sphinx*, p. 202.

[46] G. Róheim, *Australian Totemism*, pp. 358–67.

[47] G. Róheim, *The Riddle of the Sphinx*, p. 121.

the performers—and leave us in little doubt that, psychologically speaking, they are closely associated with the central element of the totemic animal phobia, fear of, and love for, the penis of the primal father. Hence stone technology developed using a material which in all probability had deep religious and psychological significance for the men of the old stone age. If this is so, there is every reason to suspect that those deep unconscious forces of ambivalence which underlay the social order and the religion also under-pinned the technological process of the palaeolithic era. Hunting and stone technology were adaptively advantageous—that is, economically successful—but their origins were unconscious and instinctual.

What is true of stone technology is even more true of agriculture, or *cultivation* as I would prefer to call it, since I mean to indicate by that term the domestic culture of *plants* rather than animals. Throughout the world the usages of languages and religions leave no doubt about its deep erotic signi-ficance. According to Licht, 'Sowing and begetting children are identical among the Greeks in conception and linguistic usage.'[48] A member of the clan which was thought to have first invented ploughing was called upon to ritually repeat the act with a plough in the shape of a huge phallus. According to Plato,[49] the earth has not imitated women, but women the earth in their manner of generation. In classical Greek the words for 'garden', 'meadow', and 'field', were slang for the female genitals.[50] In Hebrew the expressions for 'male' and 'female' are 'drill' and 'hollow'.[51] In India the furrow was identified with the vulva and the seed with semen; and an Anglo-Saxon spell used on barren land ran 'Hail Earth, Mother of men, be fertile in the god's embrace, be filled with fruits for man's use!'[52] Róheim draws attention to the erotic nature of gardening in Melanesia: 'When in the month of Karakonakona, the natives of Boasitorba make a hole in the ground for the new yams, they rub, stroke and pat the new yams in a *loving, petting* manner.'[53] The growth of the yam is associated with the erect penis ozzing semen, 'defloration' refers to the breaking of the ground, and 'a big vulva' means deep planting.[54]

Such examples can be multiplied limitlessly and make intelligible Freud's assertion that agriculture provided new albeit symbolic, satisfactions for man's, incestuous libido.[55] In other words, just as stone technology must have been associated with early man's aggressive and parricidal instincts and must have

[48] H. Licht, *Sexual Life in Ancient Greece*, p. 110.

[49] In his dialogue *Menexenes*.

[50] W. Weisskopf, *The Psychology of Economics*, p. 123.

[51] *Ibid.*, p. 144.

[52] E. O. James, *op. cit.*, p. 248.

[53] G. Róheim, *The Origin and Function of Culture*, p. 54.

[54] *Ibid.*, pp. 55–7.

[55] *Totem and Taboo*, XIII, 152. For a brilliant analysis of eroticism in agriculture as reflected in the works of Jean Francois Millet see S. Dali, *Le Mythe Tragique de l'Angelus de Millet*.

constituted a sublimation and continuation of them when they became socially and consciously unavowable, so cultivation, when it was invented, must have arisen as a sublimation and extension of the other principal instinct, incestuous libido. Once men began to plough and plant the land they began to satisfy the principal urge in them which was forbidden by totemism and held under more or less strict suppression in the hunting economy. Meanwhile, the economic, social, and political effects of the beginnings of cultivation would have been of the first importance.

The social structure of the hunting economy was based on the need for high mobility and a considerable degree of co-operation and altruism. With the appearance of cultivation, however, sedentary communities became possible—indeed, necessary—and provided the possibility for much greater economic and social individualism. A man and his family could become largely, if not entirely, self-supporting in an agricultural economy and in no way necessarily dependent on their fellows. Sowing and reaping and all the other tasks of cultivation were types of work in which women and even children could be employed, unlike hunting which was a pursuit only for men who were fit and vigorous. Hence, small local family groups could come into being and maintain themselves more or less independently of the rest. Furthermore, the possibility of political domination became much more real. In nomadic hunting communities rough egalitarianism and independence of groups is the rule; chiefs and kings are not a feature of such economies. Almost invariably, as among the Australian aborigines, political authority is vested in the assembly of all mature men and in the elders; no individual has anything like absolute power. But among settled agriculturalists the situation is quite different. Here it is quite possible, indeed it is the rule, that more centralized forms of political domination emerge and that local chieftains, kings, and emperors can come to exercise wide powers over considerable areas.

Thus the emergence of an economy which involved a return to a grain-eating diet comparable to that of man's gelada-like ancestors was accompanied by psychological and social changes which were something of a return to the original situation. A man could now become self-subsistent once again and keep his women and children permanently around him while, like his foraging ancestors, he harvested grains from the land. Now that man had returned to seed-eating he also found that he had returned to satisfaction of his incestuous desires—not, it is true, as the primal father had done, but in the symbolic sense provided by cultivating the land. His egoism and aggressiveness could not be fully gratified in the way in which that of the old tyrannical dominant males had been, but it could be satisfied in terms of the new institutions of chieftainship and kingship. Now kings could lord it over their subjects just as the primal father had done, and aspire to procure in grandeur and magnificence what they lacked of his vicious and immediate tyranny. In this way the reappearance of the primal father in polytheistic religions as the new anthropomorphic deities was the result of the coming of a new economy which recreated something like him in the agricultural communities. With the coming of cultivation, strenuously-repressed incestuous and aggressive instincts found an opportunity for re-expression and were strongly rewarded by the economic success of the new mode of subsistence.

If this was the case, and if the primal father really did return with the agricultural economy, then there is every reason to believe that the corresponding feelings in his subjects would also have made a reappearance and that an outbreak of hostility between the kings and their subjects (who were the equivalent of the original 'sons') would have taken place. Faint echoes of such events may perhaps still be heard in the Greek myths of the revolt of the Olympians against Zeus, and in those of the insurrections of the Titans and the Aloeids. It is interesting that in the latter case the war was only ended by the giants being made to kill one another, and that in the former the gods could only be saved by a single lion-skinned mortal. Pharaoh always wore such a lion skin in his ritual functions and it doubtless symbolizes in both Greek myth and Egyptian rites the fact that the gods were totems reincarnated as divine kings. Further echoes of this primal conflict between kings and their subjects may be detectable in the traditions which hold that in Africa kings seldom met a natural death. It is said that the divine kings of the Southern Bantu and the Balobedu were regularly murdered, and those of the Unyoro and Banyankole committed suicide before their powers failed.[56] Significantly, we are told that the Mashona chief was liable to have his throat cut if he became enfeebled, impotent, or suffered any genital mutilation[57]—a fate exactly analogous to that of the failing primal father or, for that matter, any enfeebled dominant male gelada. The Shilluk are said to have believed that at any time a member of the royal house might kill the king and succeed him.[58] Having done so, a revealing ritual follows which further emphasizes the parallels with the subject matter of my first chapter. The new king heads an army which does mock battle with that of *Nyikang*, the founder of Shilluk divine kingship whom I mentioned earlier. *Nyikang* wins and is enthroned, but is then displaced by the king-elect, into whom the spirit of the ancestral founder of the kingship enters. A girl (who is in fact a wife of the new king) is said to be the wife of *Nyikang*, but is claimed by the king-elect, who fights a second mock battle and succeeds in capturing her. With this, *Nyikang* concedes defeat and ceases to contest the right of the new king to rule.[59] In the case of the Igala, the Oedipal symbolism of succession to the divine kingship is even more obviously revealed when the new incumbent of the throne is obliged to have intercourse with the chief wife of his predecessor.[60] Even the

[56] C. G. Seligman, *Egypt and Negro Africa, A Study in Divine Kingship*, pp. 30, 33.
[57] *Ibid.*, p. 30.
[58] *Ibid.*, p. 33.
[59] 'The Divine Kingship of the Shilluk of the Nilotic Sudan', E. Evans-Pritchard, *Essays in Social Anthropology*, p. 79.
[60] C. G. Seligman, *Egypt and Negro Africa*, p. 44.

murderous tyranny of the primal father over the sons is not neglected among
the Baganda, whose king killed young men in order that he might 'live
longer than his fore-fathers' (i.e. so that he might evade the fate of the primal
father by killing the sons).[61]

If the primal father had come back because the conditions which produced
him originally had returned, then it is by no means impossible that the sons
of the primal father might also stage a reappearance in the guise of marauding
'all-male groups'. Indeed, one can easily imagine that when the change-over
to the new agricultural economy took place a head-on confrontation between
it and the preceding hunting economy was inevitable. Bands of hunters
would have preyed on settled cultivators just as the sons of the primal father
had preyed on the grain-eating primal hordes. Selective forces in such a
situation would have favoured the better organized and better defended
agricultural communities and this would inevitably have meant the emergence of warrior-kings who could appropriate the surpluses of the economy
for purposes of defence and self-aggrandisement.

Yet such measures would not fully have met the demands of the situation.
If local landlords emerged who had no reason to respect the laws of altruism
that governed the old hunting bands and practised incest and the indulgence
of their aggressive and egoistic desires (as we have seen Pharaoh doing in the
Pyramid Texts), then their own sons and those not fortunate to be in their
position would have had no reason to restrain the impulses to parricide,
which the abandonment of totemism and its rituals would have produced in
them. The result, in short, must have been a return to the original parricidal
conflicts and the recommencement of the inter-generational war from which
totemism and its rituals had secured a temporary truce. But such outbreaks of
all-round hostility would have been as adaptively undesirable as the original
conflict between the sons and the primal father. Something would have had
to emerge to remedy this, and, once it had, selective forces would ensure that
those groups that could resolve the situation would flourish and survive to
transmit their genes and traditions to new generations.

In the case of the original conflict between the primal father and the sons,
we have seen that it was those groups which evolved religious and ritual
means of dealing with these conflicts that were successful. Much the same
must have occurred in relation to the conflicts sparked off by the coming of
cultivation. It is clear that those groups who managed to maintain some of
the original totemic inhibitions in spite of the transition to a new economy
might have been selectively at an advantage. In fact, there is no reason why
they should not have done so since it is clear that the psychological root of the
conflicts present in the new situation was exactly the same as that in the
original one, and religious institutions that had been evolved to meet it
originally might be able to meet it again. I believe this is the reason why all

[61] *Ibid.*, p. 53.

forms of polytheism, not just the Greek and Egyptian forms examined here, show strong evidence of the presence of aspects of totemism. They do so because the maintenance of at least the main outlines of totemism was adaptively most advantageous in the new situation. Thus, it is not surprising that among the ancient Egyptians (who were the most conservative of all the peoples of antiquity) totemic elements continued to play such a large part, and that vestiges of initiation rituals in the form of circumcision lived on as an important part of the religion. Part of the reason why polytheisms are so complex is that they exist as some sort of compromise between different religious systems and different gods, both those of totemism, partly humanized, and the new primal father gods associated with cultivation. And we can be certain that the two principal psychological realities which the vestiges of totemism in polytheism were meant to maintain were the principal prohibitions of the totemic religion, namely, those forbidding incest and parricide.

We saw in Chapter one that such anti-social forces were countered by initiation ceremonies and by the whole ritual tradition of aboriginal society. The ancient Egyptians practised circumcision and, as we saw earlier, something resembling a totem sacrament (the eating of pigs). In Greece, an arresting parallel with totemic rituals is found in the mystery religions, especially in the mysteries associated with Demeter at Eleusis.

The mysteries appear to have begun as an open-air fertility festival and were supposed to have been founded by Demeter herself during the time when she was in search of Persephone. They were mystical initiations which were preceded by elaborate ritual lustrations and a long series of preparatory rites. According to E. O. James:

On the 22nd day of Boedromion, which coincided with the autumnal sowing, after a nocturnal vigil the neophytes repaired to the *telesterion*, . . . Veiled in darkness, and in complete silence . . . the *mystae* beheld the sacred sights in the . . . inner shrine of the Goddess . . . in which her relics were deposited and the mystic rites were performed . . . It seems that they may have included certain mystic and symbolic utterances, and the revealing to the neophytes of cult objects, as well as the enactment of . . . dramatic performances depicting the abduction of Kore (Persephone), episodes in the wanderings of Demeter, her experiences at Eleusis, and her reunion with her daughter.[62]

He adds that the initiates probably partook of a ritual meal and, according to J. E. Harrison, the hierophant and a priestess consummated a ritual marriage after which the birth of a divine child was proclaimed.[63] Initiates had to observe taboos on certain foods and believed that by undergoing the rites they achieved mystical union with the god.[64]

In many respects such mysteries show remarkable similarities with totemic ceremonies in Australia and elsewhere, a fact already noticed by such scholars

---

[62] *Op. cit.*, pp. 154–9.
[63] *Prolegomena to a Study of Greek Religion*, p. 564.
[64] *Ibid.*, p. 509.

as Van Gennep,[65] Harrison,[66], Lang,[67] and Webster.[68] The silence and darkness recall the rites of initiation, where initiates are secluded in much the same way. The revealing of cult-objects recalls the showing of the sacred *churungas*, which are a feature of all totemic rituals in Australia, and the 'mystic and symbolic utterances' remind one of the esoteric cult songs sung by the aborigines at their corroborees. At some of the mysteries bull-roarers were swung as in Australia.[69] The dramatic performances depicting the wandering of the god or goddess are exactly like the ritual enactments which are the central feature of all totemic rituals and which are meant to re-enact the journeyings of the totem ancestors. The ritual copulation of the mysteries resembles the mimicked copulation of the totems reproduced in the aboriginal rites.

If we look further into mystery religions we find even more striking resemblances. The rites of Demeter at Eleusis were relatively formalized and were highly assimilated to Greek culture which, as we shall see later, was particularly emancipated from the more primitive aspects of religion. But the mysteries of Dionysus or Orpheus were a different matter. Just like the Australian aborigines, the devotees of Orpheus daubed themselves with white mud or clay.[70] Like them, they observed strict taboos on certain foods following initiation, and worship of quasi-totemic divinities was practised and expressed in the *symbolon*, an esoteric formula which ran, 'The bull is the son of the snake, and the snake is the father of the bull.'[71] Both snake and bull were associated with the mysteries. In the case of the Dionysian mysteries, a veritable 'return of the repressed' seems to have occurred in which female devotees heard the bellowings of bulls and tore to pieces and consumed raw the animals in whom they saw their god.[72] A meal of raw meat by means of which the initiate became mystically identified with his god was also probably a feature of Orphism. Such rites closely resemble the totem meals described in Chapter one and approximate closely to the events of the primal trauma.

The only feature of Australian aboriginal rites which seems to be missing from Greek mystery-religions is self-mutilation. However, we have already seen that the ancient Egyptians practised circumcision, and devotees of the Syrian goddess Astarte

lacerated their arms and scourged one another to the accompaniment of the beating of drums, playing on pipes and deafening cries. Many of the young men were caught

---

[65] *The Rites of Passage*, p. 89ff.

[66] *Themis, Epilegomena.*

[67] *Myth, Ritual and Religion*, II, 294.

[68] H. Webster, *Primitive Secret Societies*, p. 189.

[69] R. Graves *The Greek Myths*, p. 31. Harrison, *Themis*, p. 61.

[70] Harrison, *Prolegomena*, p. 492.

[71] *Ibid.*, p. 496. C. Kerenyi, *Dionysos*, p. 117.

[72] Nilsson, *op. cit.*, p. 206.

up in the frenzy, stripped off their clothes and emasculated themselves, running through the city with their severed organs and throwing them into any house.[73]

Self-mutilation accompanied the rites of Attis celebrated at the *Hilaria* by Asian immigrants in Rome. In Syria, priests of the goddess Atargates castrated themselves and those of Ma Bellona were given to ecstatic self-mutilation.[74]

The Eleusian and other mysteries are clear evidence of the continuation of totemic rituals into polytheism, which I suggested was likely if the new agricultural societies were to survive the transition. Like the most sacred rituals of the aborigines at which only initiated men are present, we can see beneath the surface of the rites the same psychological processes of identification with the collective super-ego in the form of the totem or the god, and the same reinforcements of the shared values of the initiates.

But this in itself does not tell us a great deal. It may explain why totemism lived on in some form or other, but it cannot explain why the new religious practices of polytheism emerged. It is obvious that it was the inadequacy of totemism in the face of the new situation that was the important factor in conditioning the rise of new religious systems.

In the case of totemism, we found that the problem of transmitting to new generations the inhibitions produced in the original parricides by the primal crime was solved by the invention of initiation rituals which allowed new generations to acquire super-egos comparable to those of their murderous forebears. This was done by subjecting young men to treatment at the hands of the fathers that was a mitigated form of the violence which they would have done them had the original Oedipal conflicts been allowed to run unchecked. Similarly, we saw that the young men, by drinking blood, eating the totem sacrament, and in some cases actually killing a victim, equally acted out in mitigated form their side of the conflict. I believe that if we look into the primitive rituals of polytheism we shall find a similar pattern emerging.

Freud, following Frazer, puts forward:

the view that the earliest kings of the Latin tribes were foreigners who played the part of a god and were solemnly executed at a particular festival. The annual sacrifice, (or, as a variant self-sacrifice) of a god seems to have been an essential element in the Semitic religions. The ceremonial of human sacrifice, performed in the most different parts of the inhabited globe, leaves very little doubt that the victims met their end as representatives of the deity.[75]

In Mesopotamia the king represented the god Tammuz who, in sacred rituals, married his mother, the goddess Ishtar. After this marriage Tammuz was supposed to die and be reborn with the spring. In Egypt, the slaying of the divine king was commemorated at the annual 'Sed' festival. The legend of

---

[73] E. O. James, *op. cit.*, p. 167.   [74] *Ibid.*, pp. 173, 180–1.
[75] *Totem and Taboo*, XIII, 151.

Osiris follows much the same pattern. So illuminating is it that it is worth recounting it in some detail: Osiris was king of Egypt and married to his sister Isis. His younger brother, Seth, fell in love with Isis and plotted to kill Osiris. This was effected by shutting him up in a lead coffin which was cast into the Nile. Eventually it came to rest, and a tree grew round it. The king of the place in which the coffin had come to rest admired the tree and had it cut down and made into a column of his palace. Isis came in search of Osiris and became nurse to the king's son. By night, she burned away the mortal part of the prince's body and eventually she revealed herself and took away the column, and the coffin. But Seth discovered it and hacked the body of Osiris into pieces. Isis succeeded in finding all of it again, except the phallus. When he came of age Osiris' son Horus did battle with Seth during which he lost his eye, but hacked off his uncle's testicles. At an attempted reconciliation, Seth tried to have homosexual intercourse with Horus, who foiled him by making him ejaculate into his hand. Isis cut off the polluted hand and fashioned a new one for him. Then she masturbated her son and made him ejaculate into an urn. She poured this emission onto plants which were eaten by Seth, who conceived as a result. Seth pleaded before the nine great gods that he should succeed Osiris because he had violated Horus. Horus disputed this and challenged the gods to call on Seth's seed for proof. They did so, and it answered from the swamp where Isis had thrown Horus' polluted hand. The semen of Horus emerged from Seth's head and became the solar disk.[76]

An analysis of the myth will show that it contains mythological equivalents of the very situation which we are looking for, and which can also be found in the stories of Tammuz, Adonis, Marduk, Baal, and many other gods. Seth is clearly acting out the son's role in the primal trauma; he is a successful parricide who kills his father out of incestuous lust for his mother. Significantly though, he kills Osiris by locking him up in a chest or coffin. Now, in dreams containers of this sort always represent the female genitals,[77] and when they are associated with water, as here where the coffin is flung into the Nile, there is a suggestion of rebirth. The nature of this death and rebirth in the womb are explained by the subsequent fate of Osiris. A tree grows where the coffin comes to rest, but it is cut down by a king. There follows an incident identical with one in the myth of Demeter among the Greeks in which the goddess becomes a nurse to royal children and makes the young prince partially divine.[78] In the case of the Demeter legend, these events are associated with the abduction of Persephone to the nether regions, her return in the Spring, and with the invention of agriculture. The Osiris legend also seems to refer to agricultural symbolism. We know that in rituals associated

---

[76] Adapted from Plutarch, *De Iside et Osiride*, 356B–358E, Manchip White, *op. cit.*, pp. 29–31. Wallis Budge, *op. cit.*, pp. 178–81, 333–66, *Osiris and the Egyptian Resurrection*, *passim*.

[77] Freud, *Introductory Lectures on Psychoanalysis*, XV, 156.

[78] E. O. James, *op. cit.*, pp. 154–6.

with the Osiris cult wooden figures of the god were filled with earth and planted with seeds whose subsequent sprouting were taken to represent his resurrection. Julius Firmicus Maternus, writing in the fourth century A.D., held that Egyptians equated grain with the seed of Osiris, and Isis with the earth.[79] In the myth, the body of Osiris lodges in the earth and causes a tree to grow over it which is harvested by a king. The *partial* acquisition of divinity by the son of this king perhaps refers to the partial reappearance of the divine primal father in the new agricultural kingdoms. The fact that Osiris's body is later broken up and scattered over the land strongly supports the contention that in the myth the murder of Osiris is closely associated with the idea of copulation with Mother Earth which, as we have already seen, is unconsciously present in ploughing and planting. In this second violence done to Osiris by Seth, the symbolism of castration is particular obvious since Isis manages to find all the pieces *except the phallus*. However, her son Horus avenges his father, first by castrating Seth (and being himself mutilated—but we should expect this, since Horus plays the part of the good son, that is, the one who is concerned to avenge his father and who renounces his incestuous love for his mother). Later, he secures his right to rule in place of the parricidal Seth by means of clear agricultural symbolism. As a good son, he does not copulate with his mother, but instead he places his seed in the earth. Seth eats the plants which grow from it and is thus cast in the subordinate feminine role (because this makes him the one who is copulated with). His crime is that of actually committing parricide from motives of incest, whereas Horus's virtue rests on his having established his right to rule by a purely symbolic and mitigated form of incest—the placing of his seed in the earth. The myth skilfully uses this detail to bring about the downfall of Seth and the victory of Horus. In this way the new agricultural kings proclaim that they are the legitimate re-embodiments of the greatest authority known to man and the source of all later domination—the primal father, the dominant male who ruled the society of the first hominids to harvest grains.

Just as the ritual practices of totemism originated in a mitigated form of the primal conflict between fathers and sons, so the rites of polytheism probably developed as mitigated forms of Oedipal conflicts like that between Seth and Osiris, mitigated first in the sacrificial murder of the king and then later in even more attenuated forms such as that found in Babylon, where the king, as the incarnation of the god Marduk, had to undergo merely a ritual humiliation at the hands of a priest. This was followed by a ritual marriage to a priestess which would ensure the fertility of the land. Here the two symbolic acts, a ritual slap across the face and intercourse with a priestess, correspond to the original murder of the king following his incestuous mating with his mother. But the original situation had to be maintained, at least symbolically, because the very existence of an agricultural economy depended upon the

[79] E. Wallis Budge, *Osiris and the Egyptian Resurrection*, p. 15.

symbolic incest involved in ploughing the land. This in turn meant that the new god of the agricultural economy had to play the role of the old totem gods—that is, he had to prevent incest and parricide—but had also to legitimize the new social order in which kings exercised much of the authority of the old primal fathers within the agricultural communities. To do this, the male gods of polytheism represented the primal father in his new guise as divine king and supreme landlord, and the rituals of polytheism served the psychological purpose of securing the position of the newly returned primal fathers against the incestuous and parricidal impulses of the masses. By worshipping the primal-father-as-divine-king, rulers and people alike maintained the super-ego structures on which all social life is based.

One or two other ritual practices of polytheistic peoples that I have so far failed to mention can be shown to serve the same social and psychological function. In Egypt one of the most notable of these is mummification and the elaborate mortuary rites which accompanied it. The origin of these was supposed to lie in the story of Osiris, mummified by Isis, who appointed priests to carry out the mortuary ritual for evermore.[80] At his death, every Pharaoh became identified with Osiris, and later, when the habit of mummification spread to commoners, every man aspired to be with Osiris in the kingdom of the dead. To some extent the practice of mummification was part of the powerful narcissism of the ancient Egyptians who abhorred death as the greatest injury administered by nature to their great self-regard. But whatever the psychological basis of mummification—and we shall see in a moment that narcissism is not the only one—it is undeniable that its major aim was to preserve the appearance of life in the bodies of the dead. As such, the practice seems to have arisen from motives similar to those detectable in the extraordinary passages in the Pyramid Texts which deal with the death of the Pharaoh. The most outstanding feature of these is the way in which they seem to obsessively deny the fact of death and corruption. Breasted speaks of these insistent denials as 'building up a bulwark against death' by means of endless repetition. Here are some typical examples:

O King Unis, thou hast not departed dead, thou hast departed living . . . He lives, this King Unis lives. He does not die—this King Unis does not die. He does not perish—this King Unis does not perish. He is not judged—this King Unis is not judged.[81] King Teti has not died the death. This King Pepi does not die. Live! You shall live! If you die, you live![82]

When, in the psychoanalysis of individuals, we come across similar repetitions and obsessive denials of self-evident facts we suspect that such excessive reactions hide feelings of an exactly opposite nature. Indeed, they invariably

[80] E. Wallis Budge, *From Fetish to God in Ancient Egypt*, p. 181.
[81] J. B. Pritchard, *op. cit.*, pp. 32–3.   [82] J. Breasted, *op. cit.*, pp. 91–126.

turn out to be reaction-formations designed to stave off powerful contradictory desires which have been repudiated in consciousness—they are a
'bulwark' in Breasted's terms. Such excessive denials of the fact of Pharaoh's
death prompt one to wonder whether they may not have been just such a
reaction-formation against the exactly-opposite feelings—a desire to kill him.
If our conclusions about Pharaoh being the re-embodiment of the primal
father are correct, Egyptian funerary ritual might be seen as performing the
function of a reaction-formation, that of preventing the return of the repressed (in this case the repressed reactions of the sons to the primal father).
This supposition is made overwhelmingly likely when we recall that burial
and mummification were by and large the responsibility of a son to his
dead father.[83] Indeed, Gardiner goes so far as to say 'that a son should piously
attend to the funerary needs of his parents was the thought underlying the
entire ritual of the temples, where the Pharaoh . . . typified Horus in the act
of supply the material needs of his father Osiris'.[84] And this was in a culture
where, according to Breasted, 'the most common virtue discernible . . . is
filial piety'.[85] In the funeral rituals this piety was expressed in having a sculp-
ted image made of the dead father (the Egyptian word for sculptor means
'he who makes to live'). It was 'brought to life' by an elaborate ritual process
of restoring the bodily functions and attributes one by one[86] In the case of a
Pharaoh it was his son and successor who performed the ceremony himself.
It ended with the eating of a sacred, quasi-totemic meal.[87]

During the 'opening-of-the-mouth' ceremony, another cult practice for a
dead king, a priest persistently repeated the words, 'Do not strike my father!'[88]
The mouthpiece of the super-ego could hardly be more explicit. In the
Pyramid Texts equivalent prohibitions are expressed as spells: 'May you not
come against the King . . . You knife of the castrator!'[89] They go on to
give eloquent expression to the filial piety of the son of the dead Pharaoh:

O my father the King, arise! Take this first cold water of yours which came from
Chemmis! Arise, you who are in your tombs! Cast off your bonds, throw off the sand
which is on your face, raise yourself upon your left side, support yourself upon your
right side, lift up your face that you may see this which I have done for you; I am your
son, I am your heir, I have hoed emmer for you, I have cultivated barley for you,
barley and emmer for your yearly sustenance; O lord of the House, your hand be on
your goods![90]

[83] Ibid., p. 63.
[84] A. H. Gardiner, The Attitude of the Ancient Egyptians to Death and the Dead, p. 8.
[85] Breasted, op. cit., p. 167.
[86] E. O. James, Prehistoric Religion, p. 112.
[87] Ibid., p. 113.
[88] H. Frankfort, op. cit., p. 134.
[89] Utt. 375 (Faulkner).
[90] The Ancient Egyptian Pyramid Texts, trans. R. Faulkner, utt. 262, p. 272.

Finally, it is worth noting that the constant references in the Pyramid Texts to the king being given the Eye of Horus are easily intelligible if we recall my earlier interpretation of the Osiris myth. If the dead king is Osiris, and if his son is Horus, then the presentation by Horus of his eye to Osiris is an ultimate act of filial homage. This is because Horus's loss of his eye must be understood as a genital mutilation exactly like that inflicted on himself by Oedipus who, we will recall, *puts out his eyes* in remorse at his incest and parricide. By giving his eye—that is, his mutilated genital—to his father Osiris, Horus, the good son, is making the greatest possible affirmation of his piety, the greatest imaginable denial of his Oedipal temptations.

Egyptian mortuary ritual and that large part of Egyptian religion which was concerned with the fate of the body and soul after death was therefore a huge reaction-formation against the return of the repressed incestuous and parricidal motivations of 'the sons'. Its chief aim was to deny death-wishes against the father by denying the fact of death itself. This is why mummification and protracted funerary rituals played such a large part in Egyptian religion and why such huge expense was lavished on it. Egyptian mortuary practices were not intended so much to provide for the dead in some other life in the hereafter as to suggest that they were still continuing to live here below. The names of dead persons in inscriptions of the XVIIIth Dynasty are followed by a phrase which literally means 'repeating life'; this is why tombs are modelled on living apartments, and in some cases were even equipped with privies.[91] Denial of death is unquestionably the major motivation. This is further reflected in the euphemisms and circumlocutions used to refer to the fact of death. Pharaoh, as Meyerowitz points out,[92] did not die. He was 'ill', or 'tired', 'he departs' or 'he has gone to join his *ka*'; it could never be admitted that he could die as other men do.

Budge points out that the daily service performed for the dead kings of the early dynasties consisted of a series of 'acts of service such as the servant of a king . . . would perform for his master each day'.[93] Van Gennep states that 'the funeral rites both (1) revived the deceased and made him a god by mummification and various rites, and (2) prevented a real and final death by a reconstitution and nocturnal rebirth . . . All these rites of rebirth prevented the deceased from dying again each day.'[94]

Whereas the more primitive divine kingships mentioned above actually institutionalized regicide, or, at the very least, acknowledged it as a tradition of their antiquity, Egyptian civilization strenuously denied it to the point where the very obsessiveness of the denial revealed its existence as a latent constant of divine monarchy. Fundamentally, what was reappearing was the primeval ambivalence which had been responsible for the collective neurosis

[91] A. H. Gardiner, *op. cit.*, pp. 13, 11.
[92] E. L. A. Meyerowitz, *The Divine Kingship in Ghana and Ancient Egypt*, p. 204.
[93] *Osiris and the Egyptian Resurrection*, p. 252.
[94] *The Rites of Passage*, pp. 159–60.

that we call 'culture' in the first and most elemental instance. Love for, and hatred of, the primal father—of all fathers—precipitated the original religion of men and continues to precipitate religions to this day. In ancient Egyptian polytheism this ineradicable ambivalence created one of the greatest divine monarchies the world has ever seen. It also produced one of the world's greatest traditions of mortuary ritual for the simple and adequate reason that the supremacy of the father represented by the divine kingship of the Pharaohs inevitably gave rise to an unconscious, parricidal hostility whose only remedy was insistent and elaborate denial.

The principal shortcoming of my treatment of polytheism so far is that I have left out of account the female deities. The reason for this neglect is obvious. If we follow Freud and argue that polytheism is essentially a return of the repressed primal father under the stimulus of the psychological, economic, and social forces that we have already discussed, it seems highly surprising that female deities should appear on the scene and that, what is more, they may have some claim to precede the father-gods. Freud, with his usual candour, recognizes this explicitly. In the closing pages of *Totem and Taboo* he admits that he 'cannot suggest at what point in this process of development a place is to be found for the great mother-goddesses, who may perhaps in general have preceded the father-gods'.[95]

Even if Dionysus is arguably another Osiris/Adonis/Tammuz/Marduk in that he begins as a totem-god who is torn to pieces by the Titans but reborn from his blood which impregnates the soil, and which therefore suggests that he is, like these other gods, the primal father who returns with the agricultural economy, it is still difficult to understand why his devotees are *women*—the Maenads. Surely, it should be bands of young men, the sons of the primal father, who are going about tearing totem animals to pieces and consuming them in grisly feasts. Surely Orpheus, who is clearly the primal father of the Orphic mysteries, should have died at the hands of men, not female Bessarids. However much we may grant the persuasiveness of Freud's characterization of the gods of polytheism as the primal father returned, it is still incumbent on us to explain why he seems to have returned in such a different form, why he is accompanied by female deities, and why polytheism differs in so many respects from totemism.

I believe that Freud's failure to deal with this question was the result of his neglect of an important part of the process of religious and psychological evolution which led to polytheism. However, in his studies of the origin of monotheism he gave it full prominence and called it the *renunciation of instinct*.[96] Let us now try to see how, in complementing the other principal process in the evolution of religion—the 'return of the repressed'—the remaining difficulties in our discussion of polytheism can be cleared up.

Until now I have argued that polytheism was the concomitant of a return

[95] XIII, p. 149. [96] *Moses and Monotheism*, XXIII, p. 116ff.

of mankind to a seed-eating existence which also brought about something of a regression in social and religious terms. Because the old hunting confraternities were no longer necessary, totemic religion fell into eclipse and men's desires for incest and sexual hegemony found new gratifications in the ways I have suggested. Cultivation and polytheism therefore seem to be very closely related. But how did cultivation begin? If we could answer this question we might also find out much more about the beginnings of polytheism, and in particular about the mother-goddesses who may have preceded the appearance of the gods.

All those who examine the problem of the origins of cultivation, or agriculture, face some difficulties which cannot be easily surmounted. The first of these is that cultivation, or rather the domestication of plants which occasioned it, could not have been discovered overnight. It must have taken generations to obtain even partly-useful yields, let alone those necessary to make the cultivation of plants a going concern. Any theory attempting to explain the origins of cultivation must also explain the origins of the experimentation which must have preceded it. But when this difficulty has been cleared up even greater ones remain. Perhaps the most formidable is that of explaining why communities of hunters, who need work for only an hour or two each day and can obtain their food in a manner which is instinctually so highly gratifying that it has been made into a sport by most other societies, should abandon that way of life for one which demands back-breaking labour all day long and which can afford none of the quick and relatively easy spoils of hunting. If we imagine that we can explain this by recourse to an argument based on the commonsense and foresight of hunters in times when food is scarce we shall be disappointed by the facts. Róheim reports that when Australian aborigines are hungry their first response is to tighten their belts, their second to practice infanticide, and their third to starve to death. The first difficulty mentioned above is enough to dispose of such a theory even lacking evidence such as this. If the domestication of plants took some considerable time to accomplish, then cultivation could not be resorted to in event of famine, and if there were no famine there would be no motivation to undertake the task of domestication in the first place. Faced with difficulties like this, let us abandon any attempt at such a naive type of explanation and look at the problem from the point of view of psychoanalysis.

There can be little doubt that cultivation evolved out of what must always have been an important complementary activity to hunting, namely *gathering*. Among modern hunters like the Australian aborigines anything up to 70 per cent of the food eaten may in fact be vegetable food collected by the women and children. Although it is probable that in the not-so-distant past game was much more plentiful throughout the world, it is still certain that the gathering of vegetable foodstuffs was always important. In the case of *Homo erectus*, who was probably the first big-game hunting hominid (and, incidentally, the first cannibal), large quantities of fruits like the hagberry were eaten and were a vital source of vitamin C.[97] Among modern hunters and gatherers, most of the gathering is done by women. Such gathering activities are very like the foraging done by the gelada baboon and, we may safely assume, by man's pre-hunting ancestors. If throughout the period when man was a hunter, women were continuing to forage for edible vegetable matter, we begin to see how the 'return of the repressed' in polytheism must have come about. For man's original foraging way of life never entirely died out; on the contrary, it always existed side by side with hunting as an important part of the economy but one which, unlike the exclusively-male pursuit of hunting, was largely in female hands. In these terms, totemism was a largely male institution because it addressed itself to social and psychological restraints which affected only males. This is because the fraternal alliance which totemism made possible was a necessity for the chief male activity in economic life—the carrying on of co-operative hunting. As far as women were concerned, totemism was something which affected them in many important ways (for instance, in determining whom they might marry) but in which they did not really need to participate. They had no need to castrate themselves like the men—they were castrated already (the Aranda children's word for the vagina is *mama*, which means 'wound');[98] and even if female 'circumcision' was practised in some societies as it is today, female totemic rites still must have remained of much less significance than those of the men. This must have meant that when conditions analogous to those which had existed before totemism staged a return they found a ready-made avenue for them existing among the women, who had never wholly given them up, at least from the economic point of view. Thus it is not unlikely that cultivation was invented by women, and that even if it was not, there can be no doubt that whoever did invent it was operating in what had been up to that time a province of female endeavour.

Yet it is most important not to lose sight of what makes cultivation different from foraging. From the psychological and instinctual point of view, by far the most important difference lies in the fact that cultivation demands a *postponement of gratification*. When man originally adapted to eating seeds he acquired a mode of subsistence which simply meant him having to learn to look for the right sort of food, pick it up with all the manual dexterity natural selection had obligingly given him, and put it in his mouth. When he invented cultivation he returned to this instinctive way of gathering food, except that a new stage was introduced into the process. Now he still had to look for the food, pick it up, but—and this is the crucial point—he had then to resist the temptation to eat it right away, and instead he had to return it to the ground and wait. Then, when the crops had grown, he could at last consume them—or at least that part of them not needed for sowing the next year. Such a great renunciation of immediate instinctual gratification and

[97] F. E. Poirier, *Fossil Man*, p. 141.
[98] G. Róheim, *The Eternal Ones of the Dream*, p. 174.

deferment of pleasure is not easy to acquire, especially in a world where it has not yet become customary and in which the vast benefits which were to accrue to mankind because of it were by no means obvious.

A capacity to renounce pleasure and defer gratification is not one of the features which is well developed among hunters like the Australian aborigines. We have already alluded to the way in which the aborigines will satisfy their excremental needs whenever and wherever they happen to be, and Róheim reports that he often saw aboriginal women standing talking to his wife in their kitchen with urine trickling down their legs.[99] Similar lack of self-consciousness applies to defecation, although a small concession is made to modesty by the provision that one should at least turn one's back to those in whose presence one is relieving oneself.[100] According to Róheim, the individual Aranda:

has absolutely no notion of time, one day is as good as another. He will let the flies cover his face or other dirt collect anywhere on his body and never trouble to wipe it off. He loves water: a swim and a good cool drink mean happiness. But he has never thought of washing . . . You can tell your Aranda boy or girl as often as you like that he is to warn you when new supplies of flour have to be ordered; they will never do it; *they cannot understand anybody wanting to do anything else than satisfy his immediate hunger.* Wandering about the bush, one often picks up a perfectly good boomerang. The owner has simply thrown it away because he is tired of it. He will then make a new one and the loss of time and labour will not trouble him in the least.[101]

Róheim's words speak for themselves, but apart from making the aborigines a remarkably happy and contented people, such personality norms mean that they are incapable of agriculture and the deferment of gratification on which it is based.

Not so the people of Normanby Island in Melanesia. These are agriculturalists, and according to Róheim notable for their stinginess, hypocrisy, and fastidiousness.[102] As I remarked earlier, in Australia, children are never really weaned even when new babies come along; and the death of a younger sibling is not uncommonly caused by an older one refusing to let it replace it at the breast (this is why envy is largely unknown to the aborigines). In Normanby Island however, children are weaned at one year old. There is a strict and early emphasis on toilet-training and the need to use the village latrine. Great importance is attached to personal cleanliness, and the people are ashamed of nakedness. Purgatives are commonly used and sado-masochism is a marked trait in their love-making. Generally they are very cruel. In

[99] G. Róheim, 'Psychoanalysis of Primitive Cultural Types', *International Journal o, Psychoanalysis*, XIII, 82.

[100] *Ibid.*, p. 83.

[101] *Ibid.*, pp. 84–5.

[102] In other words, they sound very like ourselves.

Australia, by contrast, sado-masochistic perversions are unknown.[103] Róheim sums up by saying that 'Agriculture necessitates a postponement of pleasure which seems to suggest a strengthening of the sphincter function and an increased capacity for constraint.'[104]

It is clear, then, that whoever invented agriculture or cultivation, as I would prefer to call it, did so by virtue of two distinct psychological processes which, as we shall see, can be shown to underlie every breakthrough in economic life and world-religion. The first of these is the 'return of the repressed'. This occurred in the invention of cultivation to the extent that it provided substitute-gratification for the powerful instinctual drives which had been repressed by totemism. One of these was the incestuous libido which found expression, as we have seen, in the universal unconscious symbolism which sees the earth as the body of the mother and sowing seeds in it as the equivalent of sexual intercourse. The other instinct that came to be fulfilled was that which desired to overcome the primal father once again and which was satisfied by means of the overthrow of the religion which enshrined his authority—totemism—and the emergence of divine kings who claimed something of the prerogatives of the original tyrannical fathers. The second psychological process was that of the 'renunciation of instinct'.[105] This renunciation was that of immediate gratification of the desire for food; and it went along with the establishment of inhibitions which enabled seeds to be stored for future use, planted in the ground, patiently waited for, and eventually harvested.

I believe that women invented cultivation and were its first practitioners because only in women did these two contradictory processes operate at first. Later, they undoubtedly were taken over by men and probably greatly developed, but originally I am quite certain that women were responsible, and, as we shall see, I think that this provides the best possible basis for a theory which can explain the origins of the mother-goddesses in psychoanalytic terms.

The first reason for supposing that cultivation was invented by women is the realization that it could not have begun suddenly, but must have evolved slowly, and in a desultory and unsystematic fashion. Since women were the main work-force employed in the traditional gathering, and since cultivation must have begun as a simple extension of that activity, it is by no means unlikely that the first, primitive phases of its evolution were carried out at the hands of women and that they made the crucial early discoveries. Habituated as they were to gathering seeds and fruits, tubers and berries, it is not far-fetched to assume that they were the first to observe the facts of plant germination and growth and that they were the initiators of early experiments in

[103] G. Róheim, *Psychoanalysis and Anthropology*, p. 160. *The Riddle of the Sphinx*, p. 276ff.
[104] *Ibid.*, p. 276.
[105] *Moses and Monotheism*, XXIII, 113.

domestication. Since agricultural produce could not have suddenly taken over as the main source of sustenance, men would have had to continue to hunt and procure game while women stayed at home and tended the first, poor, and probably quite unreliable crops. These would have been grown in any case in conjunction with the harvesting of wild vegetable food; and so a lengthy period of overlap must have elapsed during which early agriculture was practised side-by-side with gathering. So much for the 'return of the repressed' as far as the economy was concerned. Effectively it boiled down to being a continuation of a mode of economic life which had been over-shadowed by hunting but never extinguished.

The second reason for believing that women must have initiated cultivation lies in that aspect of it which shows it to be a renunciation of instinct. In this respect, it seems that women must once again have been the originators of the advance because only women can induce in children that instinctual renuncia-tion which will make possible similar renunciations in adult life connected with an agricultural economy. The reason the Australian aborigines are such carefree individuals and so incapable of renunciation is that in their youth, as we have already seen, they are subject to practically no inhibitions. Wit-nessing of parental intercourse is forbidden, but that is about all. In the all-important matter of infantile and adolescent masturbation they are not restricted in any way.[106] The people of Normanby Island are fastidious and inhibited because they are peremptorily weaned at one year and subjected to strict parental discipline during childhood. It is clear that if groups of culti-vators were to emerge they would have to do so as a result of the sort of childhood discipline exercised in Normanby Island. The key personnel in such a situation would have been the mothers rather than the fathers. So it must have happened that women who subjected their children to strict discipline, for whatever reason that may have occurred, and who also were beginning to experiment with the domestication of cereals and fruits, would have been laying the psychological and historical basis for the great step for-ward which cultivation was to bring. Until their great initiative began to suc-ceed and reveal to their menfolk clear and effective ways of sublimating their repressed incestuous and parricidal desires it must have been the women of the human race alone who carried out the major part of the psychological and technological work on which the agricultural economy was based. Only they were connected by their gathering activities to the origins of human society and economy in the primal hordes; and only they, by virtue of their strategic position as rearers of future generations, could influence the mental life of man in the direction of greater instinctual renunciation and the advance into the more rational mode of economic life which cultivation represented.[107]

[106] G. Róheim, *Psychoanalysis and Anthropology*, p. 69ff.

[107] For a non-psychoanalytic cross-cultural study of the relation between child-rearing and economy see H. Barry, *et. al.*, 'Relations of Child Training to Subsistence Economy', *American Anthropologist*, 61, 1959.

In this process natural conditions obviously played an important part. In the warm period which followed the end of the last glaciation conditions were ideal for the emergence of agricultural communities in the lands of the Fertile Crescent. Even if Australian aborigines did begin to discipline their children and experiment with domestication of plants their efforts would be in vain since it is clear that in the Australian desert nothing of any significance can be made to grow. In this, as in all other developments in human affairs, natural selection played the decisive role. The psychological factors in the process—in this case the repression of instinct in children and the instilling of the ability to defer gratification—can be regarded as random cultural mutations which arise by chance, since even among the aborigines neurosis is not unknown (although it is rare), and mothers might begin to bring up children in ways not identical to the norm.

Nevertheless, having said that psychological developments can be seen to play the part of random mutations in allowing novel cultural phenomena to appear, it is desirable that we should be able to give some sort of explanation of their origin. It is certainly not immediately self-evident why psychological factors fostering cultivation should appear in a hunting society, even if natural conditions are highly favourable to it.

I believe that a clue to this problem may lie in what has already been said about the psychological significance of agriculture. We saw above that there is a vast amount of evidence to support the contention that agricultural work provides men with one of the more obvious means of sublimating their sexuality. But what of women? Why should not the same be true of them? At first sight, the idea of women gratifying their sexuality by agricultural labour seems a little odd, especially if we recall that in the unconscious the earth is the mother and planting is equivalent to insemination. This is undeniably true, but all it means is that if women were motivated to undertake agricultural labour it may have been because they had a similar motivation to that of men. This would imply that the women in question must have been playing a masculine role as far as the earth was concerned and were sublimating sexual instincts closely comparable to those of males.

However strange such an idea may seem to those ignorant of psychoanalysis, to those who have some acquaintance with it such a proposition will by no means seem absurd. We know that initially the psycho-sexual development of both sexes is identical. For both the baby boy and the baby girl the mother is the first love-object; and it is only later, when the awareness of differences between the sexes dawns, that the paths of development of boys and girls begin to diverge. Of course, this early love for the mother does not become associated with genital eroticism for the little girl because she has not got a penis, but the phenomenon of penis-envy, whose phylogenetic basis I discussed earlier in this chapter, can play a decisive part. In the case of the boy, the possession of a penis leads to the development of a straightforward Oedipus complex; but in that of a girl early love for the mother can become associated with a reaction to penis-envy which makes the girl in question formulate an overriding wish that she should have a penis, and thus become much more like her father. Such an outcome can lead to a situation in adult life in which a woman does everything she can to act like a man, even in some cases going as far as overtly loving other women. At the very least, it can lead to an attitude of envy and resentment of men, and a desire to compete with them in the vain attempt to prove that she really is as good as any man—in other words, that she has a penis too.

If this is the case in individual psychology, it seems to me not unlikely that it may also be true of social psychology, and may provide the key to an understanding of circumstances like those surrounding the invention of agriculture, in which women initially at least played the part of men in psycho-sexual terms. In other words, penis-envy may have been the unconscious origin of agriculture, just as envy of the primal father and the desire to supplant him was the unconscious origin of the hunting economy. If my earlier suggestions about the evolutionary origins of penis-envy in women are correct, we begin to see the outlines of a theory of the origins of human economic and social systems which is elegant indeed: In the beginning, man is a gelada-like forager, eating seeds and berries and living in primal horde groups like modern open-country primates. The hunting specialization of groups of unmated males leads to an evolutionary trend favouring the acquisition of high intelligence by means of general foetalization of the species. The gradual emergence of high intelligence and the extensive powers of inhibition which go with it make possible the psychological basis of totemism, and gradually men evolve organized hunting communities of both sexes which are based on considerable altruism maintained by the emergence of the first collective super-ego in the form of the totem. Foetalization of the female reduces sexual periodicity and transfers the function of signalling sexual receptivity to the penis of the male. This leaves an instinctual predisposition in women to envy the penis and unconsciously to want to go on performing the function which cerebral development has caused them to lose to the male. But the continuation of foraging in the form of gathering to complement the meat diet procured by the hunters causes women to maintain their contact with the original economic base of the primal horde. Eventually, their repressed desire for the penis, conditioned both phylogenetically and through purely individual factors like those uncovered in analysis today, lead them to find a substitute gratification in agriculture. This they exploit to good effect, precisely because it provides such an excellent satisfaction of the one thing which the evolution of hunting and totemism has made them repress.

The beauty of this theory is that it explains the other crucial factor: why new modes of child-rearing emerged in which a capacity for instinctual renunciation and postponement of pleasure was one of the major features. Women whose penis-envy leads them to behave in a masculine way (in other words, as if they had a penis) tend to be less feminine as a result. 'Being feminine' is a term which covers a wide range of behaviours and attitudes some of which, like a tendency to coyness, seem to be almost universal.[108] But clearly, maternal behaviour is one of its most important constituents, and it is noticeable that in women who develop a more masculine attitude to life it is the maternal side of their character which undergoes the greatest reduction. This is obviously because close identification with the father, which is the psychological basis of masculinity in either sex, is incompatible with a simultaneously close identification with the mother, which is the source from which maternal behaviour flows. So it is not unlikely that women who, in the early days of agricultural development, sublimated their masculinity and penis-envy in working on the earth also showed a marked reduction in their maternal behaviour and were consequently much less tolerant of their role than would have been normal at the time. Quicker termination of breast-feeding, less tolerance of soiling and long dependency would have tended to mean that the children of such women would be subject to treatment which would curtail their previously more or less unlimited access to their mothers and make them experience frustrations which would lay the foundation for adult character-types in which the capacity to tolerate delayed and reduced gratification was accentuated. Thus in gratifying their penis-envy by inventing agriculture, early women cultivators would also have been unconsciously promoting methods of child-rearing which would ensure that the personality-type which would make a success of cultivation became much more common.

Throughout this process another contributing factor was probably the subordinate position of women in the totemic societies and their reaction to it. Speaking of the Australian aborigines, Róheim says, 'The whole culture is built on the repression of women.'[109] The reason for this is easy to see. It is because, as I remarked earlier, totemism is mainly a religion for the men, and is concerned to maintain a system of inhibitions which makes possible an economy only practised by men, namely, hunting. Women, as we know, are excluded from all the more important totemic ceremonies. Advancing the sound psychoanalytic principle that 'with our children we satisfy the libidinal impulses which we have not otherwise fulfilled',[110] Róheim shows how this excessive masculinity of aboriginal society and its suppression of the feminine leads to a reaction in which women tend to play a more dominant sexual role with regard to their children. This finds expression in their habit of sleeping on top of their sons in a position which resembles that of a man when copulating with a woman.[111] This in turn leads to a traumatic reaction on the part of the sons who see the mother as phallic and aggressive and compensate for this by exaggerated shows of masculinity in adolescence and

[108] See Edward O. Wilson's interesting comments on the biological basis of coyness in female animals in his *Sociobiology*, p. 320.
[109] G. Róheim, *The Riddle of the Sphinx*, p. 165.
[110] *Ibid.*, p. 170.
[111] *Ibid.*, p. 170ff.

adult life. This in its turn causes the women to manifest their behaviour, and so we have a self-perpetuating cycle which maintains the masculine nature of aboriginal society against the possibility of change. If such exaggerated masculinity was typical of earlier totemic societies, we can see that it might be an important factor which would exacerbate the penis-envy of women and cause them to seek satisfaction of their ungratified masculinity not only in symbolic acts of copulation with their sons, but by means of the substitute gratification of masculine genital eroticism which we call cultivation.

The time has come to consider what bearing all this may have on the origin of the great mother-goddesses. My hypothesis that it was women and not men who must have invented agriculture may explain why, in Greek mythology, Athene is credited with having invented the plough.[112] It may also explain one of the most surprising features of the mother-goddesses. This is the fact that some of the more primitive of them, like the Egyptian Mut, are represented with an erect phallus. Freud pointed out that they are a religious equivalent of the 'phallic mother' of every individual's early childhood, that is, that period during which he imagines that his mother must have a penis like himself.[113] This is undoubtedly the individual basis of the ithyphallic mother-goddesses, but their historical and collective basis must lie in the period of human history when cultivation had only just been invented and when it was the women and not the men who sowed their seed in Mother Earth.

Yet such an explanation does not take us far. Even if we grant that this might just be true, I have not yet explained why the phallic, agricultural mother became *divine*; and clearly, as far as religion is concerned, that is the important thing. We think that we know why the male divinities of polytheism emerged: they were the primal father returned in the era when men took over agricultural work from women and when powerful local chieftains or kings appeared. But what of female deities? Were they the primal father come back as well? I hardly think so; yet a difficulty exists if we claim that the mother-goddesses are the primal *mother* returned, because there is no apparent reason for believing that she ever went away. She was not exterminated like the primal father and enshrined in a cult object like a totem. Among the central Australian aborigines there is not the slightest trace of any goddess, only of female demons, and these, as we have seen, have a different origin. We seem to be in a position where psychoanalysis insists that divinities are the wish-fulfilments of man's frustrated desire to retain the parents as protective and all-powerful benevolent agencies, and yet cannot for the moment see how those desires, at least with regard to the mother, could ever have been frustrated.

Certainly, the mother of the primal horde was not dealt with like the father; and hence there is no possibility of religion treating her in quite the

---

[112] R. Graves, *op. cit.*, p. 96.   [113] *Leonardo da Vinci*, XI, 88, 94, 97–8.

same way. Yet I think that I have already explain how the mother was lost, albeit in a less violent way, when I accounted for the origins of the psychological inhibitions necessary for the agricultural economy. In fact, the coming of agriculture *did* mean the loss of the mother, if by that we understand the disappearance of the totally maternal and unrestrictive mother of totemism. The mother who, as we have seen among the Australian aborigines of modern times, lets the child come to the breast whenever it wishes, who makes no attempt to enforce discipline or to carry out toilet-training, who tolerates masturbation and anything short of copulation with herself, is the all-loving, perfect mother who is lost with the coming of agriculture. The frustrations of the child's egoism and eroticism now have to look for phantasy fulfilments, and the ever-provident and ever-seductive mother-goddesses appear. Just as the primal father reappeared in the guise of the totem after his actual disappearance from society, so the mother is seen again in heaven once she is lost on earth. Her position becomes further idealized and developed when she is identified not merely with her human prototype, but, thanks to the very thing which robbed men of her, with the earth itself and with the providence of nature upon which the agricultural economy depends. Hence she becomes the phallic mother who fecundates the earth and therefore herself, she is the 'Magna Mater . . . the goddess of many names, the queen of heaven, mother of the stars, first-born of all ages, parent of nature, patroness of sailors, star of the sea, Mater Dolorosa . . . and . . . redemptrix.'[114] In her many guises the goddess represents all the aspects which a mother shows to her child. She is the protector of the weak, helper of the needy, provider of sustenance, seductress, paragon of virtue, advocate and intercessor with the father-god, embodiment of beauty, origin of all things.

Her rise to power and influence goes hand-in-hand with the decline of totemism because the ritual and psychological basis of the totem cult—initiation—gradually becomes unnecessary as the mother limits her maternal role and, by way of compensation, becomes enthroned in heaven. This is because the main function of the initiation ceremony, which is the instilling of the super-ego and its inhibitions on the instincts, is now fulfilled by the more rigorous pattern of child-rearing. The genital mutilations of adolescence are now replaced by the castration-threats of childhood as a principal means of suppressing incestuous libido, and parental discipline over toilet-training and other aspects of infantile conduct come to make the punishments of initiation unnecessary. Long before puberty arrives, the super-ego is secure. Róheim illustrates this process among the Melanesians of Dobu by revealing how fathers will play a 'game' with their children by way of which they customarily take the child's genitals into the mouth and threaten to castrate it saying, 'I bite, I eat it!'[115] Needless to say, the Dobuans are agriculturalists and notable for the way in which they inherit seeds through the female line.

[114] E. O. James, *The Cult of the Mother Goddess*, p. 180.
[115] *The Riddle of the Sphinx*, p. 163.

Not surprisingly he says they have a puritanical and hypocritical attitude towards sex. In Australia on the other hand, Róheim never once heard any sort of castration-threat. Far from being peculiar to the societies mentioned, it is almost certainly generally true that *the extent and importance of adolescent initiation ceremonies is inversely proportional to the extent and importance of discipline in early childhood.*

The existence of systems of matrilineal descent like that of Dobu has been taken to be evidence of the fact that once upon a time matriarchy must have existed and must have preceded the existence of patriarchal authority. It is possible that the rise of agriculture also meant the ascendancy of women in a political as well as a religious sense, and that in the beginning the primal father did, in a sense, come back as a woman. Presumably the argument would run something like this: Once women had mastered the technique of cultivation they became powerful and prestigious for that reason and approximated to the status of the primal father by being able to rule over local groups with considerable agricultural surpluses. Kings would originally have ruled only as adjuncts to the divine queens, useful for pleasure and procreation, but ritually sacrificed at the end of the agricultural year. They would only have established their ascendancy gradually by lengthening their reigns and beginning to usurp the ritual functions of the queen.[116] Such a pattern of evolution may find an echo in Hesiod's account of the five ages of man, in the course of which he alleges that there first came a golden race 'who lived without cares or labour, eating only acorns, wild fruit and honey . . . never growing old and laughing much'. These were followed by 'the silver race, eaters of bread . . . The men were utterly subject to their mothers and dared not disobey them'.[117] If the golden race corresponds to hunters like the aborigines who have such a carefree, uninhibited life, the silver race may be the subjects of the matriarchs who succeeded them and who were eaters of bread—that is, dependent on agriculture. In Egyptian mythology echoes of something similar may exist in an episode in the Contendings of Horus and Seth which recounts that after the battle Isis released Seth and that Horus in anger snatched the crown from her head (according to an older version, he decapitated her).[118] The obvious interpretation which suggests itself is that Isis releases Seth because women, by inventing agriculture, unleash the incestuous and parricidal motivations of men; but that she is in her turn robbed of divinity by kings who, as the primal father returned, succeeded in re-establishing the old political and psychological order of the primal horde. It is certainly true that in Africa the evidence suggests that there were two phases of hoe-cultivation: an earlier one associated with root crops and 'dominantly

[116] A modern version of this theory is found in the works of Robert Graves, and in particular in his *White Goddess* and *Greek Myths*.

[117] R. Graves, *The Greek Myths*, p. 36.

[118] Plutarch, *De Iside et Osirde*, 358A.

female', and a later one associated with cereals and male predominance.[119]

As far as the interpretation of why it is that the totem-gods Dionysus and Orpheus are torn to death by *female* devotees is concerned, the actual existence of a matriarchy does not seem important. What these traditions obviously assert is that it was women and new female deities who supplanted totemism and who, in bringing agriculture, destroyed the old totem-gods. Later, of course, the father gods supervened when divine kings emerged (doubtless partly as a response to the military threat of hunters competing for land with the new agricultural communities). In New Guinea, where one finds a particularly primitive state of agricultural society, the Maenads and Bessarids may have parallels in the behaviour of women among the Iatmul, a people who live on the headwaters of the Sepik river. Here a ritual called 'Naven' is celebrated during which a general transvesticism occurs, but in which women put on all the men's most impressive trappings while the men don old rags and the clothes worn by women who are menstruating. With the men bemoaning the hard lot of women and submitting to ritualized copulation in the female role (which they decry as highly unpleasurable and inferior), the women enter the usually highly-taboo men's house, handle the tabooed ancestral skulls and generally give themselves up to riotous enjoyment. Such a reversal of role would be unthinkable to the Australian aborigines, who despite their easy-going way of life, are strict about taboos and not letting women or the uninitiated see the *churungas* or sacred dances. The Iatmul practice crude forms of agriculture, and the cause of their extraordinary ritual may lie in the transition which agriculture implies from totemism—many vestiges of which they still retain—to something more akin to polytheism.[120] Certainly, there can be no doubt that the Iatmul women, like the Maenads and Bessarids of ancient Greece, are ritually usurping the role of men, and in the latter case at least, manifesting behaviour which reproduces the parricidal side of the ambivalence of the totem sons. If women really did invent cultivation because of envy of the penis and of men, such behaviour on their part becomes immediately and unmistakably intelligible.

I cannot, of course, hope to give an exhaustive explanation of every aspect of polytheism even if I limit myself, as I am doing, to Greece and Egypt. Such an attempt would carry us far beyond the scope of this book, which is principally concerned to show how the study of the history of world religion is relevant to an understanding of the psychological development of man. But one important aspect does remain which cannot be passed over in silence. On the contrary, it is one of the most illuminating insights that our study can give us, and it is one to which in concluding this chapter I now want to turn.

Cultivation did not only bring with it the female deities and the return of the primal father in his new form of divine king. It also brought with it a

[119] D. Forde, *Habitat, Economy and Society*, p. 172.
[120] For a description of Naven see G. Bateson, *Naven*.

return of the mode of thought typical of the regime of the original primal
father, a return of what, in the first part of this chapter I called 'animism'. In
Egyptian religion the animistic, magical elements are so obvious that they
hardly need any emphasis on my part. All commentators on Egyptian polytheism have pointed out that it went along with a vast confusion of spells,
magical amulets, divinations, soothsayings, charms, ritual incantations, and
occult signs and practices of all sorts.[121] The ancient Egyptians were notori-
ously superstitious, and every aspect of their religion was surrounded by
complex magical ritual, whose principal aim was to influence the gods.[122]
Rather like the demons and spirits of animism who were thought to control
the world, but who could themselves be controlled with the correct spells
and ritual performances, the many gods of ancient Egypt were thought to be
under magical control and subject to ritual manipulation. Judging by mortuary observances, although a clear conscience was thought of as necessary
for happiness in the next world, the right spells and amulets were deemed
more important still. Pharaoh himself was designated 'Lord of Ritual' and
had animistic control over the destinies of the kingdom and the order of the
cosmos. Only he could perform the vital ceremonies, such as that of the
Morning Worship, which ensured the fertility of the land and the maintenance of world order. If disaster befell, it was because the right magic or the
right ceremonial had not been used, and attempts were made to counter it by
further ritual means. Indeed, so pervasive is the magical aspect of ancient
Egyptian religion that if one removed the pantheon of human and theriomorphic deities from it what remained would be barely distinguishable from
animism.

So much for Egypt. 'If,' says Nilsson, 'we examine the Greek sacred customs . . . we . . . find a great number of . . . pre-deistic magical practices. They
are particularly associated with agriculture.'[123] In rites connected with
Demeter, figs, pine-cones, and phalli were placed in chasms in the earth.[124]
An animistic attitude to religion, albeit a very intelligent one, is reflected in
Plato's dialogue *Euthyphron* in which Socrates remarks that 'Holiness is . . . an
art in which gods and men do business with one another.'[125] Nevertheless,
there can be no denying that magical and animistic elements are much less
obtrusive in Greek polytheism than in that of Egypt. Part of the reason for
this lies doubtless in the extreme conservatism of the ancient Egyptians and
the fact that their civilization remained free of major foreign influence for
upwards of three thousand years. As implied by Nilsson in the quotation
above, animistic elements in polytheism seem to be among the more primitive aspects, and hence it is no surprise that they were retained rather more
by the more conservative Egyptians. But there may be another reason.

[121] See especially E. Wallis Budge, *Egyptian Magic*.   [122] *Ibid.*, p. 28.
[123] Nilsson, *op. cit.*, p. 98.   [124] *Ibid.*, p. 91.
[125] Harrison, *Prolegomena to a Study of Greek Religion*, p. 3.

Animistic characteristics in polytheism are associated with the phenomenon of the 'return of the repressed' and, as we have seen, they are connected with the return of the mode of thought typical of humanity before totemism and the fall of the primal hordes. With the return of the primal father, it is logical to expect a return of animism; and indeed, we might go further and predict a positive correlation between the two, and rule that the extent of the return of the repressed as represented in the institution of divine kingship would be reflected in the degree of animism in the polytheism in question. This correlation holds in the two cases under review, and I suspect in all others.

In the case of ancient Egypt, Pharaoh seems to have approximated rather closely to the original primal father. He was a supreme despot, he may on occasions have married incestuously, and was accorded divine honours. His position rested on the fact that Egypt was not merely an agricultural economy but an irrigated one. Wittfogel has advanced the thesis that despotisms of the pharaonic sort are dependent on irrigated agriculture;[126] and it is clear that in terms of the Freudian theory a modified version of this hypothesis is plausible. This would hold that where agriculture was of the irrigated variety and centralized control and distribution of water was practicable, the primal father would return even more completely, and one could expect him to approximate even more closely to his pre-palaeolithic prototype. Such is obviously the case in Egypt. Hence the particularly clear return of the repressed in the Pyramid Texts, and the absolutism of Pharaoh's despotism.

In Greece, however, irrigated agriculture of the Egyptian sort did not exist. Here, cultivation was more or less wholly dependent of rainfall rather than irrigation, and so the ruthless centralized control of the entire economy was for purely geographical and meteorological reasons impracticable. On the contrary, the hills and valleys of Greece favoured the existence of autonomous smallholders who could co-operate for defence within their small cities, which must have begun as *citadels*. As a result, the return of the primal father, although clearly observable, is attenuated in Greece, and, instead, the other factor to which I have drawn the reader's attention, the renunciation of instinct, comes to the fore.

In the pages of *Moses and Monotheism* Freud points out that a renunciation of instinct can produce what he terms *an advance in intellectuality*.[127] This occurs when the renunciation of the gratification of some instinctual drives reduces the scope of the 'omnipotence of thoughts' and instead promotes progress of rational intellectuality. In the case just quoted, Freud only discusses the phenomenon in the context of Judaism, but there is no reason to suppose that it cannot be recognized in other cultures. In Classical Greece the 'advance in intellectuality' and the triumph of rationality over the omnipotence of thoughts seems especially marked and to have had far-reaching consequences of Greek culture as a whole.

[126] K. Wittfogel, *Oriental Despotism*.
[127] XXIII, 113.

To begin with, let us limit ourselves to the religious sphere. According to Nilsson, 'Hermes' is 'etymologically transparent' and means 'he from the stone-heap'.[128] We have already seen what the significance of stone is, and the way in which it is associated with the economic and technological advances which followed man's transition to hunting and totemism. Throughout Greece stone-heaps were associated with a *daimon* or *herme* who was a protector of passers-by.[129] 'A god is a daimon which has acquired importance and a fixed form through the cult,' says Nilsson[130] and, anticipating my point about the return of animism in polytheism remarks, 'Animism implants in the gods human will and feeling, passions and caprices.'[131] In other words, the primal father returns in the *daimon*, but, thanks to animistic elements which return with him, is made into an anthropomorphic entity who is pictured as endowed with human psychological qualities. Just as the demon of animism represented the primal father who was regarded as the origin of all natural events and supernatural happenings, so the *daimon* or god now becomes the paternal agency behind the appearance of things. Soon he becomes the thoroughly anthromorphic god of the epics. Anthromorphism turns protection from supernatural spirits into favouritism of the gods. So rapidly does Greek polytheism stride towards rationalism that soon the gods come to resemble very closely what they ultimately stand for: the parents of the individual and of the race. The reason for this is that rationality is ultimately a question of correspondence with reality. (This is why it also implies instinctual renunciation. In the individual, as in groups and nations, instinctual renunciation is carried out at the behest of the ego (individual or collective as the case may be) and usually in the interests of coping with conflicts which arise between the unconscious and the outside world.)

So advanced in intellectuality do the Greeks become that they begin to emancipate themselves from the more irrational and superstitious aspects of their religion. Excepting the more sectarian and primitive cults like those of Dionysus and Orpheus, it is true to say that Greek religion advanced very far down the road towards complete exorcism of the supernatural. They despised strict adherence to primitive taboos as superstitious, and speaking of the function of the oracle of Apollo at Delphi Nilsson says that its 'task was not to arouse consciences, . . . but to calm them'.[132] In general, Greek religion did not emphasize moral goodness, but *justice*—which is a supremely rational approach to ethics. Anthropomorphization of the gods led to increasing scepticism and rationalism because the elements which impart impressiveness and the uncanny to the religion had been removed. The Olympians were so

---

[128] Nilsson, *op. cit.*, p. 109.
[129] *Ibid.*, p. 110.
[130] *Ibid.*, p. 112.
[131] *Ibid.*, p. 152.
[132] *Ibid.*, p. 199.

human and natural that they ceased to seem divine at all. This soon led to a tendency to see natural causes as underlying divine phenomena. In the fifth century, Hippocrates believed that the 'sacred disease' of epilepsy had a natural cause. Heraclitus seems to have been a sceptic, perhaps even an atheist. Protagoras was prosecuted for atheism, and Xenophenes and Antisthenes (one of Socrates' pupils) were inclined to monotheism. Ultimately, Greek religion declined to the point where living men could be 'deified' (not for the same reasons that caused the Egyptians to deify Pharaoh, but rather the opposite ones; that is, because gods had become men rather than vice-versa), and where only the mysteries and the cult of Asklepios at Epidaurus (a sort of Greek Lourdes) remained.

As religion declined, an attempt at a rational understanding of things developed. Animism, which had begun as the 'omnipotence of thoughts', now developed into the first rational philosophies and the beginnings of science. Where thought once had recourse to fantasy in the face of the frustrations of nature, it now turned to reason and began to lay the foundations of a rational understanding of the forces of nature, and in place of magical conjurings began to discover the basis of technology. Animistic and magical habits of thought, which had returned from the repressed with the coming of agriculture, underwent a huge advance in rationality at the hands of the Greeks, and reminded one of the great progress which a child makes in his intellectual apprehension of the world after the resolution of the Oedipus conflict. Certainly, in no other period of philosophical and scientific development do we find the same childlike mixture of naivete and lucidity of insight as is seen, for instance, in the paradoxes of Zeno or the speculations of Heraclitus. What Greek philosophy, at least in its early stages, has in common with the awakening reason of a young child is its concentration on absolutely fundamental issues and its ever-present sense of wonder at the world. It is a system of thought which is slowly giving up its claims to omnipotence through fantasy, and is slowly substituting a faith in reality as the final arbiter of what is possible.

As explained earlier in this chapter, animism is only a part of the extreme narcissism which characterizes the first years of life of the individual and of the primal foraging existence of mankind. If animism returns in polytheism as magic, or, in the exceptional case of Greeks, as the beginnings of philosophy and science, we ought to expect to find very strong elements of narcissism present in polytheistic cultures. There is little doubt that this is true of the ancient Egyptians. Gardiner concludes that the 'ancient records display the Egyptian as an exceptionally light-hearted and individualistic race, singularly little troubled with regard for their fellows'. In a note he defines what he means by 'individualistic' as 'prone to self-aggrandisement'—in other words, what the psychoanalyst would call 'narcissistic'.[133] That a tendency to

[133] A. H. Gardiner, *op. cit.*, p. 16.

rationalism is not absent among the Egyptians and that it is linked to their narcissism is suggested when he refers to 'their amazingly logical . . . and self-centered outlook'.[134] Notwithstanding my earlier analysis of Egyptian funerary ritual, there can be no doubt that, to the extent that mummification and the provision of elaborate tombs was planned by individuals for themselves, such a concern to deny the fact of one's own death has a narcissistic origin.

The capacity to think logically is above all an attribute of the ego, and rational conceptual thought is its most distinctive mode of operation, at least on the conscious level. Here, a tendency to rationalism is psychologically linked to narcissism which is, of course, the ego's love of itself. This arises from its managerial responsibilities in acting as a mediating agency between the inner, instinctual demands of the organism and the external exigencies of reality. Compromise is unknown to the unconscious instinctual id and foreign to the censorious nature of the super-ego, but to the ego it is often its greatest hope and principal means of responding to the demands made upon it. If we understand this, the Delphic aphorisms of 'Nothing overmuch' and 'Know thyself' become completely intelligible. They both refer to maxims which are appropriate above all to the ego, which is charged, as we have seen, both with the responsibility of self-consciousness and with that of judging between the often conflicting demands of instinctual need and external necessity. Nilsson remarks that 'Moderation is best' is a proverb which expresses a distinctive trait in the Greek character.'[135]

But narcissism, rationalism, and a commitment to self-knowledge and compromise are not only detectable in Greek religion and philosophy. In Greek art, narcissism finds its greatest expression in the depiction of nude bodies which are considered as beautiful in themselves rather than, as had traditionally been the case, being considered beautiful only if they depicted some divine or supernatural essence. Understood as a love of one's own body, narcissism became sublimated as the cultural aesthetic ideal of the Greeks by painters and sculptors, whose main interest lay in representing the body as realistically as was compatible with a desire for perfection in its proportions. Spengler has brilliantly shown how Greek mathematics is essentially a mathematic of whole, rational numbers based on the geometry of solid bodies. It abhorred irrationals and incommensurables, and this appears to have been the origin of the Greek mathematical passion for 'squaring the circle'.[136]

Narcissism is also the basis of another of the most notable features of Greek civilization, namely, individual athletics. Competitive athletic contests arise out of narcissism because they presuppose a narcissistic concern with one's body and with being 'fit', and a desire to gain the egoistic gratifications of winning. So much was achievement in the games appreciated that according

[134] *Ibid.*, p. 24.
[135] *Op. cit.*, p. 224.
[136] *The Decline of the West*, pp. 66–9.

to Pindar, 'an Olympian victory was almost more highly thought of by the Hellenes than a triumph by a Roman General'.[137] Narcissistic pleasure in being 'fit' and beautiful to look at, and individualistic satisfaction in athletic endeavour, make Greek sports quite unlike those of the modern Olympiads which, like everything else in recent Western civilization, are dominated by the quite different and anal-sadistic values of self-punishment, the acquisition of money, and a quite anti-individualistic emphasis on nationalism. Needless to say, the state of nudity in which such athletic contests were carried on was another major manifestation of Greek narcissism and quite unlike the prudery of today. Their toleration of masturbation—obviously a narcissistic practice —and perhaps even the Greek passion for young, beautiful, and slightly effeminate men may have its roots in the narcissism of their culture. Certainly, a powerful impression of the self-assertion which is an indivisible part of narcissism comes over strongly in Thucydides' famous words to the effect that:

of the gods we believe, and of men we know, that by a law of their nature wherever they can rule they will. This law was not made by us, and we are not the first to have acted upon it; we did but inherit it, and bequeath it to all time, and we know that you and all mankind, if you were but as strong as we are, would do as we do.[138]

As Father Copleston remarks, one could hardly wish for a more unashamed avowal of the will to power, that will to power which, both in Nietzsche and the ancient Greeks, is the primal egoism of mankind partially returned from the repression which civilization enforces on it. It seems to me that a great deal of our admiration for the Greeks stems from the fact that we are not as strong as they were and that we see in them an enjoyment of the narcissism which Calvin and Luther and their successors have denied us. But this is a subject for a later chapter. Suffice it to say for the moment that Nietzsche's enthusiasm for the Dionysian aspect of Greek culture was not accidental and was not unconnected with the latent narcissism which we have uncovered in Greek polytheism.

In summing up the findings of this chapter, one might say that neoteny not only enabled man to acquire high intelligence by retarding his development but, by an anologous psychological process of lengthening the period of dependency on the parents, caused him to retain mental infantilisms which predisposed him to religion. These religious predispositions turned chiefly on a desire to retain into adult life the feeling that one was being cared for and protected by the parents, and in particular that the primal father, who was loved as much as he was hated, was ever near and ever-watchfully protecting his own. This need for the father itself grew out of the deep frustration to which man's primal, animal narcissism was subjected by his acquisition of

[137] F. Copleston, *A History of Philosophy*, p. 34.
[138] *Ibid.*, p. 34.

intelligence and the altruistic renunciations of the hunting economy. The primal narcissism with which animism was associated consisted essentially in a lack of awareness of being a separate entity in nature and being barely able to distinguish human wishes from the causal determinants of the external world. Animism returned with the primal father in polytheism, and primal narcissism to some extent reappeared in the cultures of the polytheistic peoples. To the extent that foetalization of the species meant infantilism in its psychology and a retention into adult life of childish attitudes which perpetuate animism and the longing for the father, it can also be held responsible for the genetic basis on which the glories of classical culture were raised; and if neoteny was responsible for making man intelligent in the beginning, it was also responsible, through the psychological and religious processes explained in this chapter, for making him acquire the foundations of his critical philosophy and scientific method. For both the individual and the race, biology is destiny.

3

THE OBSESSIONAL NEUROSIS

One of the most notable features of polytheism is the way in which the gods of the different pantheons arrange themselves into groups which, like geological strata, seem to correspond to the superimposed residues of successive epochs in the evolution of religion. The nature sprites of ancient Greece, and spirits of rivers, mountains, and woods throughout polytheism look -like residues of primal animism; the animal-headed gods of Egypt and the Greek Satyrs, Centaurs, and Sileni seem to be vestiges of totemism; the great mother-goddesses like Isis, Demeter, and Athene correspond to the next period, that of cultivation; finally, we have the perpetually reborn male gods like Osiris and Adonis. But however appealing this arrangement may seem, it does appear to have one grave shortcoming. This is the fact that it leaves no room for what is one of the most important classes of deity in all polytheistic pantheons. My discussion so far has totally failed to take account of what are in most cases the principal gods of polytheism, namely, thunder-gods like Zeus, sun-gods like Re, and that whole class of polytheistic deities whose common characteristics seems to be that they are sky-gods invested with a divine paternal authority which overrides most others. They are also outstanding in their tendency to be the focus of monotheistic trends in the polytheisms concerned.

The sceptical reader may feel that this omission will completely undermine the plausability of the theory so far advanced to account for the evolution of polytheistic religion and that the great celestial father-gods cannot be prevailed upon to fit themselves into the evolutionary schema advanced in these pages. However, another possibility exists. This is that such gods do not appear to fit into the Animism-Totemism-Polytheism sequence because they represent one more stage in the process and that, in terms of my geological metaphor, they are the most recent stratum in the polytheistic pantheons. It is to an exploration of this possibility that I now want to turn.

Historical evidence suggests that 'the Indo-Europeans, living originally in nomadic pastoral communities in a steppe country, unlike settled agriculturalists, had always worshipped the Sky-Father rather than the Earth-Mother as supreme god'.[1] According to James,[2] Zeus had been the supreme god of the pastoralists who entered Greece in prehistoric times.

[1] E. O James, *Prehistoric Religion*, p. 225.
[2] *Op. cit.*

A connection between sky-gods, monotheism, and pastoralism seems to be far from unknown in the modern world. According to Lenski and Lenski, there is a powerful positive correlation between pastoralism and monotheism in recent societies, as the following table shows:

TABLE I

Religious beliefs of agrarian societies,
by percentage of subsistence derived from herding

Percentage of subsistence from herding	Percentage believing in active, moral creator God	Number of societies
36–45	92	13
26–35	82	28
16–25	40	20
6–15	20	5

'Why this relationship developed,' they say, 'is far from clear, but the fact is undeniable.'[3] The only suggestion they can make as to why it may exist is to say that the shepherd's pastoral relationship to his flock in some way or another predisposes men to a monotheistic religion.[4] Certainly, it is undeniable that in the Biblical texts God is sometimes described as a shepherd and his people as his sheep. As it stands, the Lenskis' suggestion sounds like a looser and more impressionistic version of Freud's explanation of the male gods of polytheism; it seems to suggest that because shepherds emerged in society shepherd-gods appeared in heaven. But clearly, it also leaves a great deal to be explained. We would like to know why a herding economy predisposes men to conceive of a single shepherd-god rather than a number; why these sole gods are associated with the sky; why they are so moralistic and so much less anthropomorphic than the deities of polytheism; and why, as in the Greek case, they appear within the polytheistic pantheons despite their alleged monotheistic characteristics. Even more pertinently, we would like to know how such deities fit into the psychoanalytic theory of the evolution of religions, and how they relate to the themes of the first two chapters of this book.

A first line of enquiry might be to look into the origins of pastoralism. In dealing with the initially difficult problem of the mother-goddesses we found that researches into the origins of cultivation were what gave us the clue.

[3] G. and J. Lenski, *Human Societies*, p. 298.
[4] *Ibid.*, p. 299.

Perhaps we might find the same with regard to the sky-gods if we begin by looking into the question of how herding economies began.

Excepting the case of the dog and the use of tame reindeer as game-baits (which is strictly speaking a case of social parasitism),[5] the domestication of animals almost certainly began after the initial stages in the development of cultivation. Zeuner remarks that, as far as taming is concerned,

It is extremely difficult to visualize this happening prior to the beginnings of agriculture, because the initial social contact between man and animal in question would have been an unfriendly one.[6]

Furthermore, it was probably the fallow land left by shifting cultivation which provided the first pastures and the initial opportunity for contact and experiment with species which were to become fully domesticated in the course of time.[7]

We have already seen that cultivation was in all probability begun by women, and it is by no means unlikely that the same is true of the domestication of animals. Men, who in the early days of cultivation would still have been engaged in hunting, would have been most unlikely to accomplish the complete reversal of attitude necessary to domesticate the beasts they were preying upon. Women, on the other hand, would have had no such difficulty and would have been the ones who were coming into contact with the first species to be domesticated as they went about their agricultural tasks. It is even thought by some that the dog, which is known to have been domesticated well before the coming of agriculture and was associated with hunting and with men, was also first tamed and nurtured by women. Scott[8] proposes that dogs came to be domesticated as a result of hunters bringing home wolf puppies which were put to the breast by women who might have lost their babies and were suffering the discomfort of persistent lactation. Róheim puts forward the same suggestion:

The economic basis of our civilization is agriculture and the domestication of animals. Man's first companion is the dog and in Central Australia we can study the process of domestication *in statu nascendi*. If we walk into a Pitchentara camp we see the women sitting at the fire with their babies and puppies. A baby may be feeding at one breast and a puppy at the other. How did they get the puppy? They have been hunting and have speared the old dingoes both male and female. The little ones are brought into the camp and fed by human mothers. A dog that has been nourished by human milk is very '*aknara*' (daring, cheeky). It will bite the strangers and it is a valuable helper in hunting . . . If a dog dies they will cut themselves and cover their head with wounds just as if it had been a human being (Pindupi tribe). Young men have a dog of their own; *i.e.*, several boys are joint owners of a dog. If it is a good dog they call it 'Nyitiyara'

[5] F. E. Zeuner, *A History of Domesticated Animals*, p. 46ff.
[6] *Ibid.*, p. 54.   [7] *Ibid.*, pp. 30, 43.
[8] Quoted by Wilson, *Sociobiology*, p. 509.

('young man') and they mourn for it excessively if it dies. They cut their head till their whole body is covered with blood. Sometimes they bring in too many puppies so that they cannot keep them all. Some of them are knocked on the head in this case, but they are buried and mourned for like human beings. The Nambutji make a tree grave for their dogs just as they do for themselves. The women knock a hole in their skull with their digging sticks, the men cry and cut themselves with their knives. If they lose a dog the Pindupi and the Yumu will thrust a spear into their leg . . .According to Basedow the dog in an Australian society is kept for purely emotional reasons with no economic advantage whatsoever.[9]

Here the emotional aspects of the domestication of dogs come over very clearly indeed, and one is tempted to put forward the suggestion that just as women invented cultivation because of a latent penis-envy which found expression in agricultural work, so they may have begun to domesticate animals as a result of another closely related desire—namely, for children. This would explain why in Melanesia it is customary for women to suckle pigs and nurse them as they would their own children when they are ill, and why experience has shown that it is childless women who take the best care of newly-introduced domestic animals.

Apart from suggesting the psychological motivation for protecting and taming wild animals, this hypothesis also explains how the necessary renunciation of instinct which is associated with it may have come about. We saw that in order to make a success of cultivation new psychological possibilities of renunciation of instinct and postponement of gratification had to be realized. Similarly with herding: if it did develop out of cultivation as seems likely, pastoralism would have been served, at least initially, by the very same tendencies in child-rearing which would have favoured agriculture; for in both cultivation and herding an ability to wait before one eats is essential. Thus the very same psychological conditions which I suggested for the emergence of cultivating economies would have laid the foundations for pastoralism, and, along with the desire of women to nurse young animals, would have led directly to full domestication. Finally, it is worth pointing out that the deterioration of the soil which early cultivation may have produced in some regions would also have favoured the development of pastoralism as an alternative economy; land which was too poor for cultivation might still make excellent pasturage.

Whatever the facts about who invented domestication and for what reason, there can be little doubt that, like cultivation but certainly more so, herding soon became a pursuit of men. As such, it obviously had a lot in common with hunting. This observation prompts me to propose another interesting parallel. Just as cultivation represented a 'return of the repressed' in the sense that it was a return to grain-eating, so pastoralism represented a

---

[9] *The Origin and Function of Culture*, pp. 62–3.

return to the meat-eating economy which had preceded cultivation. And just as cultivation had evolved out of the gathering which women tradition-ally continued to do in the hunting economy, so herding must have developed out of the hunting activity of men who, while cultivation was developing, and probably right up to the time of the first true domestication, still ob-tained meat in the traditional way. When pastoralism became fully estab-lished they must have given up their hunting altogether, since it would have been unnecessary; but it is likely that there was a long period of overlap between the two.

The psychological and religious significance of this must have been as profound as that of the transition to cultivation. If the theoretical approach which I have adopted in this book is correct we should expect that as pas-toralism developed out of cultivation and the hunting sideline of the economy was transformed into fully-fledged herding a process analogous to that which I claimed took place in polytheism might be expected. Just as animism re-turned along with the primal father in a new guise as a polytheistic deity, so totemism might be expected to return with pastoralism, and the primal father might be expected to manifest himself in some appropriate fashion. Both of these processes occur, along with some others of great interest, but it is to the former that I first want to draw the reader's attention.

The Nuer and the Dinka are pastoral peoples of the Sudan about whose religions we have two excellent accounts.[10] Both approximate to the typical monotheism of pastoralists suggested by the table on page 102. As we shall see in a moment, both the Nuer and the Dinka have a good claim to be con-sidered as monotheists who worship a morally exacting and authoritarian sky-god. But equally, both show marked evidence of totemism. The Nuer believe that clans have animal spirits with whom the members share some-thing special and whom, as animal species, they must not eat.[11] Those in the clan have some sort of control over the species in question.[12] The same is true of the Dinka.[13] However, in their case something quite extraordinary seems to have happened. So transparent is the totemism of the Dinka, and so vividly does it seem to portray the psychological realities underlying it that the ethnographer is caused to allude to Freud's *Totem and Taboo* with some respect for what it says.[14] I believe that the reason for this is that in Dinka religion totemism has staged such a dramatic and forceful return from the repressed that in many ways it seems more primitive than that of the Austra-lian aborigines among whom, we must not forget, totemism has only been preserved as the result of a very long process of partial loss and reacquisition according to the flux of time and events over many millenia. Certain aspects

[10] E. Evans-Pritchard, *Nuer Religion*, and G. Lienhardt, *Divinity and Experience*.
[11] E. Evans-Pritchard, *op. cit.*, p. 64.
[12] *Ibid.*, p. 67.
[13] G. Lienhardt, *op. cit.*, p. 104ff.
[14] *Ibid.*, p. 131.

of Dinka totemism have a freshness and immediacy which only the phenomenon of the 'return from the repressed' can explain.

The chief ritual practitioners in Dinka society—the priests, in other words
—are called 'masters of the fishing spear'. The totem of their clans is called
'Flesh'. Unlike the Divinity, which is what the ethnographer of the Dinka,
Lienhardt, calls their supreme, monotheistic god, Flesh is spoken of in sub-
dued tones and in words which would make a fitting motto to the first
chapter of this book:

Flesh is one word.[15] Our ancestors knew about it, but none knew everything about it.
Some say they have seen it. It is a single word, it is of the furthest past, what has always
been.[16]

Flesh is the one totem which is eaten by those to whom it is taboo. It is eaten
raw and in great solemnity at night-time feasts. According to one of Lienhardt's informants, what the masters of the fishing-spear eat is *three raw pieces
of flesh from the thigh of a sacrificial ox*.[17] Participants are said by the Dinka to
be 'afraid' when they eat it.[18] Blood is taboo to spear-masters, who may
neither see nor touch it; and having the blood of one's totem on one's body is
thought to be evidence of incest. Myths of the origin of the masters of the
fishing spear connect their appearance on the earth with an act of incest.[19] In
a hymn quoted by Lienhardt, Flesh is referred to as 'Flesh of my father'.[20] It
manifests itself as a red snake, a baby,[21] or a light. When the spirit of Flesh
takes possession of a master of the fishing spear—who, incidently, wears
around his neck the dried pizzle of a bull sacrificed to his totem—it causes him
to tremble, first in the thighs and knees, then all over. This hysterical trembling call by Lienhardt 'the most solemn religious act of the Dinka',[22] is
identical to the stylized version of the trembling associated with erotic excitement which is the principal movement in the ritual dances of the Australian
aborigines.[23] Despite this, Flesh is said to make people 'cool', that is, to make
them the opposite of hot-tempered and violent. It is supposed to make men
righteous, and may bring the gift of prophecy.[24] Flesh is the most powerful
of all the clan divinities (totems) and, according to the Dinka, in the beginning
there existed only Divinity and Flesh. In the beginning was the flesh, and the
flesh was with God, and the flesh was God.

[15] I.e., it is the truth.
[16] *Ibid.*, p. 138.
[17] For the symbolic significance of '3', the phallic number, see Freud, *Introductory
Lectures on Psychoanalysis*, XV, 163.
[18] Lienhardt, *op. cit.*, p. 144.
[19] *Ibid.*, pp. 145, 128, 131.
[20] *Ibid.*, p. 142.
[21] For the symbolic equation baby = penis, see Freud, XVII, 128ff.
[22] *Ibid.*, p. 138.
[23] See above, p. 29.
[24] *Ibid.*, p. 139.

I will not bore the reader by elaborating on the obvious analytical meaning of all this; that it bears out everything Freud said about totemism is clear. However, there are one or two interesting details which are worth discussing further. One of these is the question of the trembling which takes hold of masters of the fishing spear during sacrifices. Unlike the Australian equivalent, which the Aranda call '*alknantama*', this trembling is not a ritualized dance-movement, but an involuntary hysterical seizure. It is evidence of 'possession' by the spirit of Flesh, and many other kinds of spirit-possession are found among both the Nuer and the Dinka. Those who are possessed by spirits are called 'prophets', the Dinka word being '*aciek*' which means 'monster' or 'monstrous birth'. Common explanations of spirit-possession among the Dinka attribute the phenomenon to a person taken over by the clan totem, his father's or grandfather's ghost, or some other spiritual force. From the psychoanalytic point of view such cases of spirit-possession are seen as the result of a change in the ego and its identification of itself with the super-ego.[25] In the case of the masters of the fishing spear, this identification with the totem, that is, the super-ego, takes the startling form of a hysterical trembling. The Dinkas' own explanation of this is that it is a manifestation in the clansmen of the twitching which is observable in the flesh of an animal just after it has been flayed. But the parallel with *alknantama* is too close to ignore, and the trembling of the thighs and knees has without doubt another, albeit latent, origin. This is borne out by a further observation. A Dinka told Lienhardt that *if one dreams of one's totem the dream is accompanied by a nocturnal emission*.[26] There can be no doubt about the significance of emissions, and if in dreams totems are associated with sexual excitement I see no reason why, in the light of the Australian counterpart, we should not conclude that the hysterical attacks which seize masters of the fishing spear are clear expressions of sexual arousal. They tremble because of hysterical identification with the victim of the sacrifice whose flesh continues to move after it has been killed. But they also tremble because the sacrificial victim is equivalent to the totem to whom it has been dedicated, and because the killing of the totem arouses within the spear-masters intense sexual excitement, just as it must have done among the original parricides millenia before and for precisely the same reason—namely, that the killing of the father is the prelude to incestuous intercourse with the mother. This is why women are never possessed by Flesh in this way; and this is why the effect on the Dinka spear-masters is so profound. A Christian Dinka of a fishing spear clan told Lienhardt that despite his conversion, he dared not come near a sacrifice of an animal dedicated to Flesh for fear of being seized by uncontrollable trembling and fainting away.[27] There can be no doubt that intense hysterical reactions can only

[25] For studies of spirit-possession, see Freud, *A Seventeenth Century Demonological Neurosis*, XIX, 73ff., and Ernest Jones, *The Nightmare*.

[26] Lienhardt, *op. cit.*, p. 130n. 2.

[27] *Ibid.*, p. 138.

arise from instinctual forces which have been long repressed but which under some stimulus or another have returned, albeit in a distorted and incomplete form, to proclaim their undying strength and permanence. In the most solemn religious act of the Dinka, as in ordinary hysteria, the symptom is always produced by the return of the repressed.

But we have seen that there is another side to the picture. The killing of the primal father, acted out in this case in the ox sacrifices of the Dinka, led to his return as the conscience of the sons—their crime was the occasion for their remorse and guilt and the origin of all altruism and self-restraint in man. So it is perfectly intelligible that Flesh makes people 'cool' and righteous, why it may even give the gift of prophecy. The prophet is the mouthpiece of the divinity, the re-embodiment of the father, the voice of the super-ego; his prophecy is founded on righteous indignation and the moral authority which his identification gives him. When the masters of the fishing spear have eaten of the raw flesh of their divinity they—like the original parricidal sons —acquire a super-ego by introjection of the dead father and identification of themselves with him as his successors. No wonder they insist on the primacy of Flesh and Divinity, and doubtless in their unconscious make a complete identification between the two.

This analysis of Dinka religious practice makes many other features of their culture immediately intelligible. We will not be surprised to learn that animals, too, can become famous prophets, or that when they do they are addressed with the title of 'Master'.[28] Nor should we be surprised to learn that Dinka men identify themselves closely with their cattle, especially the bulls, and that at dances young men imitate the motions of the ox, or that cattle are the principal topic of conversation.

Nevertheless, the Dinka and Nuer are not genuine totemists. On the contrary, they have a good claim to be considered primitive monotheists; and it is important that we should not lose sight of what makes them different from the Australian aborigines. The very identification of men with animals which I have just mentioned is a case in point. Róheim reports that among the aborigines he never once saw a child, let alone an adult, imitate an animal in any way.[29] The reason for this perhaps surprising fact is that genuine, primary totemism of the type found among the Australian aborigines is dominated by a phobic reaction to the totem exactly parallel to the phobic reactions of young children; and although in childhood animal phobias identification by the child with the animal does occur, in totemism such identifications are wholly absorbed into the religious rites and are not expressed on an individual level. In the secondary totemism of the Dinka and Nuer however, fear of the totem has been greatly reduced and separate super-ego structures exist, as we shall see in a moment. The result is that individual identification with the

---

[28] *Ibid.*, p. 49.
[29] *The Riddle of the Sphinx*, p. 157.

totem outside of the religious sphere is possible—indeed, as we have already seen, such individual and hysterical identification is the root cause of the trembling fits of the spear-masters.

The reason for this changed state of affairs is undoubtedly to be found in the fact of domestication. In primary totemism of the Australian variety the totem is a wild animal with whom the contacts of the clan brothers are few and mainly ritualized. In pastoral economies however, contact with the totem is much more intimate. Even if such societies maintain totem clans whose totems are wild animals as do the Nuer and Dinka, an inevitable tendency exists for the positive side of the ambivalence towards the totem to become attached to the domesticated species. There is a tendency to see the domesticated animal as the father in his loved and respected, rather than feared and hated form; and in those clans which, like the Dinka masters of the fishing spear, have a totem which is identified with a domestic animal, we should not be at all surprised to find such powerful ambivalences expressed at the moment of sacrifice. Because in Dinka eyes the bull is the loved and revered father sacrifice becomes an act of unbearable emotional impact which finds expression in the hysterical symptom already discussed. Whereas in primary totemism taboo is what is most closely associated with the totem, in secondary, pastoral totemism it is love and sympathy which is most intimately felt for the animal in question.

This positive attitude to the animal is obviously the result of domestication and the tendency to make pets of domesticated species. Evans-Pritchard gives a vivid picture of the affectionate care with which the Nuer herdsman tends his ox: 'When he has tethered it in the kraal for the night he may pet it, removing ticks from its belly and scrotum and picking out adherent dung from its anus.'[30] Speaking of primitive pastoralists, Róheim says:

Cattle-breeding tribes are cattle-loving tribes. The Dinka never slaughter their cows (like the Egyptians) but when sick they are carefully tended till they die a natural death. In this case they are eaten but even then the owner is too sad to partake of the flesh. Cattle are dearer to the Dinka than wife or child ... The Bari have a special word for boasting with these favorite animals in such a way as to taunt others. The Nandi tell us that they love their cattle more than anything in the world, they talk to them, pet or coax them and their grief is great when a favorite sickens or dies. According to Beech: 'The Suk lives for his cattle and everything is done to make them an object of reverence.' The Oromo regard their cattle as forming a part of their soul. The respect the Batussi pay their cattle far exceeds even their realistic value as stock or capital the interest of which (milk) they live on. The whole psychic and social life turns on the question of cattle; they are the very fiber of the social order and the objects of a mystic cult.[31]

Quoting Seligman, Evans-Pritchard says that between a man and his beasts

[30] Op. cit., p. 251.
[31] The Origin and Function of Culture, pp. 65–6.

there is what psychologists would call a close identification.[32] Karl Menninger, in an article dealing with totemic attitudes in the modern world,[33] describes a number of cases of men who had bestial relations with domestic animals and who petted and fondled them in a way which is strongly reminiscent of the way in which pastoral peoples express their affection for their animals. However, the fact that the Nuer strongly disapprove of bestiality suggest that although the positive, loving side of the ambivalence of the son towards the father has been transferred onto the cattle, the negative, revengeful side still exists. Evans-Pritchard tells of an elder who committed an act of bestiality with one of his cows, confessed without being suspected, made restitution by sacrifice, and also cut off one of his fingers in remorse.[34]

There can be no doubt that reactions like this show the presence of a sense of sin and also of a powerful super-ego which can utilize to the full the individual's sadism and aggressiveness once it is turned back against himself as a strict and punitive conscience. Domestication may have made pastoralists like the Nuer and Dinka manifest an affectionate identification with animals unknown among genuine totemists, but it has not robbed their super-ego of any of its power. If the totem has become in some sense domesticated, the power of the father still wreaks dreadful vengeance on those who offend against it. If we want to discover what has been the fate of this negative aspect of the father we should perhaps turn our attention to the question of the origin of moral authority among the Nuer and Dinka.

The transfer of the affectionate side of the ambivalence felt towards the father onto domestic animals is almost certainly why the Neur and Dinka practise what Lienhardt calls 'personal totemism'.[35] Among the Australian aborigines individuals have private totems, but their origins are quite unlike those of the Nuer and Dinka personal totems. Among the latter a man may make a totem of anything which has injured him or subjected him to any sort of suffering. Hence diseases frequently become totems of this sort, as do spears which have been involved in accidents, stones which injured persons who trod on them, and so on. In these cases it is clear that the negative side of the ambivalence has been embodied in the personal totem which is always something which has hurt, inconvenienced, or troubled someone. In psychoanalytic terms, it can be said to be playing the punitive role of the super-ego as pain of conscience and injurer of narcissism. But it does so in a retrospective sense. Prospectively, the punitive force of conscience is symbolized by God.

Before we go any further, let us justify the use of the term. Evans-Pritchard uses 'God' as the best translation of the Nuer word 'kwoth' which also means 'spirit'. Although spirits also exist, for instance as totems, spirit—'kwoth'—

---

[32] Op. cit., p. 249.
[33] 'Totemic aspects of contemporary attitudes towards animals', in Wilbur & Muensterberger, Psychoanalysis and Culture.
[34] Op. cit., p. 281n.   [35] Op cit., p. 151.

is used in the singular in place of a proper name for the single, supreme deity.[36] Lienhardt calls this deity 'Divinity'; and says that 'all Dinka assert that Divinity is one'.[37] Leaving aside for a moment the slightly academic question of whether one is justified in calling these peoples 'monotheists', let us look at the characteristics of their God.

He turns out to be exactly what we are looking for. Evans-Pritchard quotes Seligman to the effect that among the Nuer 'the missionary feels as if he were living in Old Testament times, and in a way it is true'.[38] The God of the Nuer, like that of much of the Old Testament, is cruel, vengeful, and jealous. Each and every misfortune, discomfort, or injury that a Nuer sustains is attributed directly to God and to his justice. All misfortune is punishment for sin. All suffering entails guilt and restless examination of conscience in an attempt to find what sin the subject has committed to warrant his trouble. 'Nuer,' says Evans-Pritchard, 'show a humbleness in respect to God which contrasts with their proud, almost provocative and . . . even insulting bearing to men.'[39] Of them the Seligmans say:

The Nuer bear the loss of cattle or children with the utmost resignation, saying that it is the will of God and that he is ruler of the world. The cattle are his, not man's, and if he cares to take a cow a man must not complain or show great sorrow, lest God be angry . . . Even when a child dies and the women mourn aloud, the men are mostly silent. God has taken his own and they must be resigned . . .[40]

Lienhardt characterized Divinity among the Dinka as being a moral force persecuting evil. Everything that happens is a revelation of divine justice. The first appearance of an aeroplane resulted in fifty piacular sacrifices and one confession of a murder which had occurred years before. So wary are the people of God and his retribution that men will not boast of their possessions or good luck. Evans-Pritchard says that 'Nuer show great uneasiness if their good fortune is so much as mentioned.'[41] God always punishes sin, and none can escape him.

We may sum up the situation by saying that for the Nuer and Dinka God is the force of conscience and the embodiment of the super-ego. The supreme deity in these societies has been invested with all the negative attributes of the totem; he is the Father as he is feared rather than loved, the source of repression rather than consolation. For pastoralists like the Nuer and Dinka all the intimate, affectionate, and mundane aspects of the Father have been transferred to their herds, while all that remains has been handed over to God. True, personal totemism competes with the Deity to some extent in this respect, but totemism cannot work as a viable religious form for a people who

[36] *Op. cit.*, pp. 1, 49–50.
[37] *Op. cit.*, p. 56.
[38] *Op. cit.*, p. vii.
[39] *Ibid.*, p. 12.
[40] C. & B. Seligman, *Pagan Tribes of the Nilotic Sudan*, p. 229.   [41] *Op. cit.*, p. 14.

have overcome their hostility to animals and have had to love their cattle in order to domesticate them. Personal totemism, like personal Christianity today, remains merely a vestige of a once-great religion which psychological evolution has swept away. However much it may have returned from the repressed in the case of the masters of the fishing spear, the very one-sidedness of its return means that monotheism, the essential religious trait of all pastoral societies, is the true religion of the Nuer and Dinka.

The correctness of this conclusion can be tested against the theory of religion advanced in these pages by seeing to what sins the sanctions of the Divinity are particularly applied.

If the essential psychological function of religion is to provide men with a shared super-ego and to prevent the gratification of their fundamental parricidal and incestuous wishes, it follows logically that the worst offences against the god of the monotheists should be precisely these. As we have already seen, the more important of the two is incest because it is temptation to this which is the occasion for impulses to parricide. Among the Nuer, Evans-Pritchard reports that the sin most frequently referred to is incest;[42] and Lienhardt says of the Dinka that their ethical ideal is filial piety.[43] A revealing practice of the Nuer is for a man to call out his ox-name or a kinship term which means 'my mother's sister' when he hurls his spear in a fight or a hunt. These cries, which Evans-Pritchard says are exultant assertions of the self,[44] link parricide with incest in an unmistakable way, since a man's ox-name is an identification of himself with an animal which is a father-surrogate, and his mother's sisters are, of course, a kin group to which his own mother belongs and with whom intercourse is highly incestuous. A Dinka myth tells of attempted parricide and its punishment:

It is reported that the young men of one sub-tribe, fat with milk and spoiling for a display of their strength, once decided that only Divinity himself was a great enough adversary for them. They therefore attacked the rain . . . All were killed except one man who . . . was left with a hole pierced through his thigh.[45]

So much for the psychology of God, but what of his forms? How can this interpretation of God as vengeful super-ego answer the questions about the monotheistic deity which I set out at the beginning?

Let us start with the easiest thing. If God is the punitive super-ego, God is the *Father*. Among the Nuer he is called '*gwandang*', which means 'old father' (or, as Freudians might say, 'ur-father'). He is also called the 'Father of men'.[46] In the case of the Dinka, Lienhardt says that the most frequently mentioned attribute of Divinity is fatherhood:

[42] *Ibid.*, p. 183.
[43] *Op. cit.*, p. 42.
[44] *Op. cit.*, p. 252.
[45] Lienhardt, *op. cit.*, p. 43.
[46] Evans-Pritchard, *op. cit.*, p. 7.

... what the son accepts ... is the authority of the Father—of all fathers—an authority associated with Divinity ... the transcendant fatherhood represented by Divinity reinforces the position and authority of the human father.[47]

But, because he is the father as moral censor and super-ego:

Divinity ... also represents truth, justice, honesty, uprightness, and such-like conditions of order and peace in human relations.[48]

In other words, the first attribute of the god of monotheism is that he is a father-god, and one whose paternal authority is exercised in the interests of morality—that is, in the interests of repression of egoism, narcissism, and instinctual gratification in general. This is why Lenski's table shows pastoralism to correlate strongly with a 'moral, creator God'.[49] Creativity is a generalization of his paternal aspect, morality a generalization of his repressive, punitive, and censorious qualities.

These characteristics of the god of monotheism are closely related to another important attribute. Despite the fact that God is a father, Evans-Pritchard says that he 'never heard the Nuer suggest that he has a human form'.[50] This is by no means a peculiarity of Nuer religious belief; on the contrary, all monotheisms picture God in a remarkably non-anthropomorphic form, and as such stand in stark contrast to polytheism. The reason for this is obvious. We have seen that in polytheism male gods are anthropomorphic because they represent a return of the primal father in human form—that is, as the chiefs, kings, and Pharaohs of the agricultural communities. In monotheism however, God is the primal father as moral conscience and as vengeful super-ego. This is why he is so much more abstract and less anthropomorphic; he is not modelled on any human being but represents instead a *psychological* reality, an attribute of the god of totemism made into a metaphysical principle. In particular, this explains why the god of monotheism is sole god and without competitors or pantheon. Unlike the gods of polytheism who tend to be associated with local cults of deification of the primal-father-as-hero-of-agriculture, the god of the monotheists is the universal force of conscience, that force of conscience which, like the father in the eyes of the young child and the primal father in the eyes of the sons of the horde, is omnipotent, omnipresent, and omniscient. His universality is a function of his abstraction and idealization. He brooks no rivals because, in the unconscious, the Father is unique and almighty. His duplication would be an absurdity. There is only one source of guilt and conscience, and only one power is manifested in the

[47] *Op. cit.*, p. 42.
[48] *Ibid.*, p. 158.
[49] See above, p. 102.
[50] *Op. cit.*, p. 7.

force which makes men see in all misfortunes which befall them the judgement of a cruel and exacting God. That force is simple and indivisible: it is a part of the subject's own ego turned back against himself. If the God of the monotheists is one, it is because the ego originally perceived itself as one and recognizes in the punitive super-ego an alienated aspect of itself.

This insight explains another common characteristic of pastoral monotheisms. Evans-Pritchard comments on the almost total lack of eschatology among the Nuer; and Lienhardt makes a similar observation in the case of the Dinka. Lack of eschatology is also one of the most notable features of Judaism and the monotheism of the Pharaoh Akhenaten (which, as we shall see in a moment, is in fact the same religion). All the polytheisms have highly developed doctrines and cults associated with the after-life; and we have seen that these originate from closely related sources. In the clearest case of all, that of the ancient Egyptians, these two sources were narcissistic intent on the part of the ego to utilize animistic means to escape its own death, and obsessional denial of death-wishes against the father which found their expression in elaborate rituals of affirmation of the continued existence of the dead. In Egyptian eschatology judgement by the gods (i.e. the super-ego exercising its punitive functions) was postponed until after death because their moral influence was ignored during life, principally because the gods were seen as agents of the ego's wish-fulfilments rather than as moral censors. Among monotheists however, we have seen that this punitive function of the super-ego is performed in each and every experience of misfortune that an individual has, so that punishment after death is hardly necessary. Furthermore, the narcissism of monotheists is so mutilated by the oppression of their God that a narcissistic denial of their own death is a grave sin. Death must be accepted as the last and greatest punishment of God and the final proof of his power and of the inevitability of his justice. Hence speculation about the future life of the soul must be denied either as idle dreaming or as sinful resistance to the ineluctable will of God. Perhaps this is why the masters of the fishing spear were traditionally buried while still alive. Their intimate contact with Flesh and the Divinity made ordinary Dinka regard them as partly divine; and those who are a part of God should not suffer his greatest punishment.[51]

Similar considerations explain the much-discussed lack of magic among pastoral monotheists such as the Nuer and Dinka. Such peoples are notably deficient in magical practices when compared with most other primitive societies. From the psychoanalytic point of view, the reason for this is clear. Magic is, as we have seen, basically wish-fulfilment; a question of gratifying the egoistic interests of individuals by means of indulging the 'omnipotence of thoughts', itself a remnant of 'primal narcissism', the infantile state of mind which cannot distinguish an objective reality from itself and consequently identifies a wish with its fulfilment. The principal task of the super-ego is to

[51] Ibid., pp. 298–319.

limit such narcissistic self-indulgence; and so we would expect that a people who had a vengeful and censorious super-ego figure for a God would show correspondingly less magic and correspondingly more true religion. In the case of the Nuer and Dinka this is precisely what we do find.

Another common characteristic of monotheistic gods is their association with the sky. Evans-Pritchard says that the Nuer word '*kwoth*' has the same respiratory connotations as the word 'spirit' in English. Breath, which is the sign of life in man, becomes associated with God, who is the creator of life. Breath, like spirit, is invisible and, like air, permeates all things. This, presumably, is how a highly-abstract universal principle comes to be associated with meteorological phenomena: 'He [*kwoth*] is in the sky, falls in the rain, shines in the sun and moon, and blows in the wind.'[52] Most especially, he is associated with lightning; those who die by lightning—an occurrence less infrequent in Nuerland than one might think—are not buried in the normal way. They have been taken to God directly. Much the same is true of the Dinka. Zeus is without doubt a storm god who hurls his thunderbolts at those who anger him. Yahweh, the God of the ancient Hebrews, is also associated with storms as Psalm 18 suggests:

> The Lord also thundered in the heavens,
> and the Most High uttered his voice,
> hailstones and coals of fire.
> And he sent out his arrows, and scattered them;
> he flashed forth lightnings, and routed them.[53]

I have already suggested a partial explanation of this meteorological symbolism by means of its connection with the idea of the 'Spirit blowing where it listeth'. Since thunder and lightning are only the more spectacular meteorological conditions associated with high winds and storms, we might be tempted to see the thunder-gods as merely an extension of spirit into its more dramatic manifestations. Such is no doubt the case; but there may be another determinant revealed in the fact that Nuer and Dinka also see God as manifested in the rain. This again might be simple association of ideas, since rain is another concomitant of high winds and stormy conditions, especially in the Sudan. But rain is also of vital economic significance to nomadic or transhumance pastoralists.[54] In either case, it is rain which makes the grass grow and determines the fortunes of the economy as a whole. The withholding of rain is just about the worst punishment which God can visit on a pastoral people and, because of its direct association with the other divine attributes of thunder, storms, and wind, is an unmistakable expression of his disfavour. It is doubtless because what agriculture there is in pastoral societies tends to be dependent on surface water supplies and on the labours of women that in the

52 Evans-Pritchard, *op. cit.*, p. 2.
53 vv. 13–14. RSV (Catholic Ed.).
54 Lienhardt, *op. cit.*, p. 161.

cases of both the Nuer and the Dinka the female divinities are associated with rivers and streams.[55]

So much for the attributes of God; but what of the attributes of men? Although theology treats God as a being separate from men and not necessarily interdependent with them, psychology knows better. If the monotheistic God of the pastoralists is who he is because of his psychological attributes, we may pertinently ask what are the psychological concomitants as far as the lives of men are concerned. The answer to this question is that men in monotheistic religions become notably obsessional. I do not merely mean by this observation that they are excessively prone to repetitive religious rituals, to ablutions and lustrations and other such stereotyped acts normally found in association with obsessional neurosis.[56] This is often the case, but here I use the term in the strict psychoanalytical sense, meaning a predisposition of character which shows the signs of a powerful super-ego:

People of this type are dominated by fear of their conscience instead of fear of losing love. They exhibit, as it were, an internal instead of an external dependence. They develop a high degree of self-reliance.[57]

In the case of the Nuer and Dinka fear of conscience is manifested in their fear of the retribution of God and their uneasiness about any good fortune they may have. The obessional basis of their culture is revealed in the commonest form of greeting which is 'Are you at peace?' understood in the sense of 'Are you at peace with yourself?' (i.e. 'with your conscience?').[58] Here the 'internal dependence' of the obsessional character-type is clearly shown in a formal enquiry which presupposes that inner psychological peace is more important to a man than health or worldly success (as implied in 'How do you do?', 'Comment allez-vous?' or ¿Cómo está Vd.?). Unfortunately, Róheim never visited a pastoral people and so we have little information about the things that most matter—namely, sexual life, child-rearing, neurotic symptoms, dreams, and so on. But from the little that anthropologists like Evans-Pritchard and Lienhardt tell us it is clear that the Nuer and Dinka show other revealing traits of the obsessional character-type. Lienhardt reports that to find excrement in the homestead is evidence of witchcraft and is highly offensive to the Dinka.[59] In the case of the Mursi, a pastoral people of Ethiopia who are closely comparable to the Nuer and Dinka, the fouling of the hut by children is highly disapproved of. There is also a marked avoidance of the mention of excrement in the hearing of the opposite sex so that, for

---

[55] *Ibid.*, p. 90, Evans-Pritchard, *op. cit.*, p. 31. Needless to say, such female divinities are of only marginal significance.

[56] Freud, 'Obsessive Actions and Religious Practices', IX, 115ff.

[57] Freud, 'Libidinal Types', XXI, 215.

[58] Evans–Pritchard, *op. cit.*, p. 24.   [59] *Op. cit.*, p. 111.

example, a man would never say in the presence of a woman that he had a stomach-ache because of the connection between this and diarrhoea. The Mursi are addicted to purgatives, and this again is evidence of an obsessional attitude to excretion.[60] We have only to recall what I said about Australian aborigine habits of excretion to see how different the pastoralists are. In fact, a concern with cleanliness and fastidiousness about the excretory function is one of the most common symptoms of obsessional neurosis and, as we shall find when I come to speak about the origins of Protestantism and capitalism, it is a factor by no means without sginificance in world history. The self-reliance to which Freud alludes in the quotation above is also very clearly seen among the Nuer and Dinka; indeed, among all the pastoral peoples the self-sufficiency of men is intimately related to the very factor which deter-mines their obsessional form of religion—their cattle. As long as a man has herds he may wander as he will; as long as he is dependent on cattle he will tend to shift onto them all his 'totemic' affection and reserve for the rain-bearing Deity alone all the punitive functions of his super-ego and the foundations of his obsessional character. His independence and sense of self-possession produce a proud detachment which not infrequently shades over into downright arrogance. The proud, haughty nomad is a common enough figure in anthropological literature, and his sense of moral superiority is exactly like that often found in persons of obsessional character. It originates in the sense of self-congratulation which the ego achieves when it satisfies the stringent demands of the super-ego and lives up to the self-righteousness of conscience.

Such characterizations as these are, I hope the reader will agree, not without their significance or interest; but he may easily object that they are open to the suspicion that there is nothing to prevent a writer finding characteristics which he feels illustrate his point while ignoring those which contradict it. Our estimation of the character of individuals is frequently strongly biased by subjective factors, and the reader may understandably think that a char-acterization of nomadic pastoralists as typically obsessional is just as open to subjective bias as any other. I think that he would be wrong about this, and fortunately I am able to turn to an admirably objective and independent source for further validation of my point.

The most thorough and wide-ranging psychological study of the personality structure of pastoralists which can currently be found is the Culture and Ecology Project,[61] which studied four East African peoples, the Sebei, the Pokot, the Hehe, and the Kamba. In the case of each one of these tribes some groups had taken up settled agriculture, some migratory pastoralism. Sample populations were chosen, standardized for all other variables except economy,

---

[60] Personal communication from Dr David Turton, to whom the author is indebted for this information.
[61] Published in R. B. Edgerton, *The Individual in Cultural Adaptation*.

giving eight groups in all: a pastoral and farming group in each tribe. The members of each group were subjected to an impressive array of personality and psychological measures, including Rorschach Ink Blot, Thematic Apperception Test, and extensive interview schedules of various sorts. The results were given sophisticated statistical treatment and correlation coefficients were obtained for connections between all the measured variables. 'Internal, psychological restraint', or 'self-control' is a dimension of personality measured by the project which is obviously very close to what Freud, in the quotation above, meant by dominance of the super-ego. A coefficient of .782 was obtained for this measure of personality when correlated with the Index of Cattle Concentration (a measure of the extent of reliance on pastoralism).[62] Freud's comment that persons of obsessional character-type 'exhibit, as it were, an internal instead of an external dependence' reproduces exactly what the Culture and Ecology Project has to say about the pastoralists they studied. But by far the highest correlation was obtained for the variable which Freud regarded as the most obvious of all in the obsessional personality, namely, self-reliance. This, the Culture and Ecology Project terms 'independence'. It correlates at the very high and significant value of .921 with an index of pastoralism, and the study says that of the variables studied it 'is one of the most important, for, perhaps more than any other, it serves to characterize pastoral values and personality'.[63] It is what is termed 'an excellent pastoral, diagnostic',[64] and, we might add, an excellent 'obsessional' one as well.

Another characteristic of obsessional tendencies in the personality, and one which we have already examined, is guilt and depression. This, as I argued, results from the introjection of aggression originally directed at others, and, in the case of pastoralists, specifically from the diversion onto the self of Oedipal aggression directed in the first place against the cattle who, as we have seen, are 'Flesh of my father'. The Culture and Ecology Project, quite unprepared for this finding, and totally at a loss to explain it reports:

In all four tribes, pastoralists more often express gloom, despair, pessimism and a strongly depressive feeling-tone . . . Frequently . . . it was a generalized sadness or hopelessness, one without specific referent or antecedent.[65]

The reason for the lack of 'specific referent or antecedent', for this 'strongly depressive feeling-tone' lies in the fact that its origins are unconscious and irrational. In other words, its origins lie in the collective obsessional neurosis which typifies pastoral monotheists. Obsessional neurotics are often typified as suffering from an unconscious sense of guilt (this being the cause of their domination by the super-ego), and so it will not surprise us in the least to

[62] *Ibid.*, p. 267.
[63] *Ibid.*, pp. 266, 194.
[64] p. 266.
[65] *Ibid.*, pp. 192, 194.

learn that the Culture and Ecology Project's personality measure 'guilt-shame' correlated quite strongly with pastoralism.[66]

To those not familiar with the symptomatology of obsessional neurosis it may come as some surprise to learn that the study found 'a heightening of sexuality among Pastoralists . . . When sex was mentioned, there was a profound qualitative difference between the farming and pastoral responses. The pastoralists more often delighted in seeing sex; they revelled in it, grinned and chortled at the very thought of it, and, in short, thoroughly enjoyed themselves'.[67] This, again, is typical of obsessionals. Very often (although by no means always), the obsessional neurotic will not manifest any very obvious abnormality in his sexual life as far as relations with the opposite sex is concerned. On the contrary, this aspect of sexual life is usually quite unimpaired by his neurosis because repression in these cases operates against perverse and passive inclinations of the libido, rather than against normal and active ones. In short, the study's characterization of pastoralists as more self-controlled (without being sexually inhibited), more prone to depression, guilt and shame, and above all, much more independent than farmers, is an exact and revealing picture of what Freud called the obsessional personality-type and which he thought resulted from the ascendency of the super-ego in the personality.

Before we leave our consideration of the Culture and Ecology Project there is one last observation which I would like to make. This concerns what the study has to say about the farmers. In the previous chapter I argued that there were good reasons for supposing that both the ancient Greeks and ancient Egyptians showed evidence of narcissistic cultural personality-types. Both these civilizations were agricultural, and we have just seen that an alternative mode of economic life, pastoralism, correlates with another cultural personality-type, the obsessional. It would be interesting to see whether there was something which connects cultivation, polytheism, and a narcissistic personality-type in a way similar to that in which we have just seen pastoralism, monotheism, and obsessional character traits to be connected. I suggested above[68] that the strong element of narcissistic wish-fulfilment in polytheism, not to mention the supreme egoism of the god-kings, might predispose polytheists to such a narcissistic personality-type. We have already examined the relation between polytheism and agriculture and have seen that the narcissistic wish-fulfilment of its more animistic aspects reflects the new egoism and self-sufficiency which cultivation made possible, at least when compared with hunting. The Sebei, Pokot, Hehe, and Kamba agriculturalists do not qualify as primal cultivators of course, but they are settled agriculturalists and it is perhaps worth examining the findings of the Culture and Ecology Project to see if they show any characteristics which might betray

[66] *Ibid.*, p. 265.
[67] *Ibid.*, pp. 185–6.
[68] p. 97–8.

evidence of a narcissistic personality-type, if only by way of contrast with their pastoral and obsessional co-tribalists.

The narcissistic personality-type is, according to Freud:

> mainly to be described in negative terms. There is no tension between ego and super-ego. . . . The subject's main interest is directed to self-preservation . . . His ego has a large amount of aggressiveness at its disposal.[69]

Unfortunately, the Culture and Ecology Project measured few personality variables which are relevant to this personality-type, perhaps a consequence of the fact that, as Freud points out above, it is mainly to be described in terms of the absence of other traits. Nevertheless, there are one or two pointers. According to the study, 'the quintessential farming diagnostic' is 'disrespect for authority'.[70] Pastoralists, on the other hand, manifest a great deal of respect for authority.[71] This is, again, a characteristic of the obsessional, who respects authority and tends to be markedly conservative for the simple reason that the super-ego which dominates his psyche is the introjected image of the parental authority, not just as it is represented by the father, but by authority-figures of all kinds. The narcissistic type, by contrast, has a very weak super-ego, but a much more aggressive and self-seeking ego. Consequently, he rejects authority and restraint as intolerable limitations of his self-interest and allows his aggressive feelings much more rein than can the person with the well-developed super-ego who, as we have seen, tends to turn those aggressive feelings back against himself. The Project found that 'hatred' (i.e. aggressive feelings directed against others) correlated significantly with certain farming scales.[72] Other measures, such as 'fear of poverty', 'jealousy of wealth', 'litigiousness', 'desire for friends', 'impulsive aggression', etc., seem to reflect personality-traits related to the narcissistic type and are all preponderantly associated with the farmers.

We may sum up our analysis of the relation between character, economy, and religion in the case of pastoralists by saying that in these societies the obsessional proclivities of the people derive from the punitive aspects of the super-ego which are enshrined in the sole God. The loved aspects of the father are retained in quasi-totemic form as an attachment to animals. The monotheistic god of the pastoralists has so much more fear and vengefulness associated with him than the supreme father-gods of polytheism because of the totemic attitude of the pastoralists to their herds. The return of totemism in pastoralism, understood as economic and psychological dependence on animals, also means a return of aggressive attitudes to them which the economy of primal totemism—hunting—entailed. Pastoralists love their herds so much because they are forced to suppress their aggression against

---

[69] Freud, 'Libidinal Types', XXI, 218.
[70] Edgerton, *op. cit.*, p. 265.
[71] *Ibid.*, p. 176.　　[72] *Ibid.*, p. 266.

them so comprehensively. As far as their basic instincts are concerned, there could be no greater satisfaction than to kill all the animals and consume them in an orgy of quasi-parricidal blood-lust. This is exactly what did occur when domesticated reindeer were introduced among the Alaskan Eskimo. Lacking the requisite obsessional religious and personality characteristics, there was nothing to inhibit the Eskimo's hunting instincts and protect the animals from those who wanted to kill them. Yet the true pastoralist cannot kill his animals at will. The whole future of his economy rests on the resistance to such temptations. In the case of the Masai pastoralists, no member of the tribe is allowed to kill an animal; instead Wandorobo serfs are employed to do it for them. The Nuer greatly despise men who kill animals because of hunger. Only sacrifice—that is, obligation to the collective super-ego—is a legitimate excuse to slaughter an animal. All the suppressed hostility and aggression of the id, all the individual's unconscious blood-lust evolved millenniums before in the world of the first hunters, must be suppressed and in a thoroughly typical way turned back against himself. In the individual, as in the group, the vengefulness and aggressiveness of the super-ego is in fact the aggressive instincts of the id turned back against the ego and experienced as guilt and depression. This is why among pastoralists the punitive aspects of the Deity are so much more obvious than among cultivators. In the case of the first cultivators, there was no blood-lust to deny, no hunting atavism to be stimulated by the presence of docile and defenceless beasts. On the contrary, their super-egos could be relatively weak and they could give themselves up to the substitute gratifications of ploughing and planting Mother Earth, while some of them could even aspire to the place of the ancient primal father, marry their sisters and live like gods. Only with the domestication of animals and the coming of true agriculture did pastoral sky-gods appear in their pantheons and monotheistic elements mix with their religion. But for the true pastoral monotheists the gratifications of the agriculturalists did not exist. In their case, preservation of the herds and resistance to the temptation to kill the animals who in the unconscious stand for the father are of prime importance in the maintenance of their social life and the future of their economy. For them, the acquisition of a punitive Deity is the unavoidable necessity on which their culture depends.

We seem to have succeeded in answering the questions set out at the beginning of this chapter that were prompted by the frequently-observed correspondence between pastoralism and monotheism. We now know why pastoralists are monotheists and why their God has the attributes which are typically his. As to the question of the place of the sky-gods in the polytheistic pantheons and the monotheistic tendencies associated with them, we can now see that they are indeed the most recent stratum in the superimposed classes of deities which compose polytheism. Gods like Zeus and Re are the original monotheistic gods of herding peoples which managed to maintain some of their attributes in the polytheistic pantheons into which they were finally absorbed. When monotheistic tendencies re-emerged in due course these gods, originally constituted on the model of God among the Nuer and Divinity among the Dinka, naturally acted as the focus for the new theological trend.

Nevertheless, a number of difficulties remain that I very much fear will so weaken and damage my case that the reader may feel that he must reject it altogether. The first of these proceeds immediately out of what I have just said. We saw in the last chapter that monotheistic tendencies did in fact re-emerge in due course in Greece, but they did so in a way which had nothing to do with pastoralism. It is all very well explaining monotheism as the result of a partial return of totemism in pastoral economies and an association of all the punitive attributes of the father with a single, spiritual God of the sky. But how can such an explanation possibly cover monotheistic tendencies in fifth-century Athens? Those who inclined to monotheism in the ancient world were not primitive herders in every case; some were sophisticated members of the urban intelligentsia. True, such monotheistic trends in Greek religion might be explained away as the aberrations of untypical intellectuals; but even if we accept this, perhaps, too-easy answer, another and much more formidable difficulty remains: that posed by the two great monotheistic religions, Islam and Judaism.[73]

The problem in both these cases is that monotheistic tendencies in the religions in question cannot be shown to correlate exactly with pastoralism. True, the peoples among whom both religions grew up were originally in large part nomadic herders, but they were not always so. Islam can perhaps be explained away with some conviction as merely a copy—and not a very good copy—of Judaism; but Judaism itself still remains. Let us look more closely into the contradictions. If monotheism is, as I have alleged, the outcome of psychological forces employed in creating and maintaining a pastoral economy, then we would expect the Jews to have been more consistent monotheists when they were the most consistent pastoralists. But the facts do not support this. For a start, this would mean that with the diaspora, and the tendency for Jews to become an urban people, monotheism should have tended to disappear among them. There is no evidence that this is true. Perhaps we could get around this by saying that a 'ghetto-mentality' makes a people conservative and means that religiously they live in the past. There is doubtless an element of truth in this, but it will not get us out of trouble. We know that the Jews, particularly in post-exilic times, became more settled and less nomadic than they had been originally when the centre of their faith had been a seasonal encampment at Shiloh. This should mean that the pre-exilic Jews were more monotheistic than those of the post-exilic period; but this is the reverse of the case, and there is no shortage of evidence to prove the

[73] I ignore Christianity for a moment because, as will be argued below, it is far from being a consistent or straightforward monotheism.

opposite. Something must be wrong with the theory of monotheism so far advanced if discrepancies of such huge proportions can arise out of it. We begin to be tempted to doubt the whole thing and revert to the opinion of previous commentators that, while a statistical correlation between pastoralism and monotheism is undeniable, the causal connection defies explanation.

We appear to have reached one of those *impasses* which are so familiar in analytic work. At the very moment when we have got hold of an interpretation which seems to carry us a very long way and which makes so much fall so rapidly into place we suddenly come to a halt and seem incapable of further progress. The Nuer and Dinka corresponded beautifully to my interpretation. Indeed, the 'Flesh-totemism' of the Dinka and the monotheism of the Nuer seem designed to prove my analytic point; one could hardly have wished for better material. Yet with the Jews we have come unstuck. While we might be able to explain an early and partial tendency to monotheism on their part, their austere and authentic later monotheism seems inexplicable. And perhaps even the Nuer and Dinka were not all they seemed to be. After all, although they both undeniably believe in single deities, which they *say* are monotheistic, it is clear that the presence of totem and other spirits confuses the picture and makes them far from being cases of a monotheism which is pure. On the other hand, the Jews, who do not fit my causal analysis so neatly, nevertheless exhibit a pure form of monotheism. One begins to suspect that some other factor must be relevant and that something on which we have so far not touched must be present.

When in an individual analysis progress comes to an abrupt halt after rapid advances have been made and much effective analytic work has been done, experience shows that the reason for the failure to proceed lies in the analysis having come up against a set of new and unexpected resistances. Our analysis, which has worked through the Dinka and Nuer material with such gratifying smoothness, has suddenly struck an obstacle whose nature we cannot for the moment determine. In this situation the mind of the analyst tends to run back over all the material of the case in an attempt to find something which might let him discover what the obstacle submerged in his patient's unconscious might be. Denials and repudiations are often a good indication of what it really is, and so he turns to the most-hotly-denied interpretations which he has put to the patient in the sure knowledge that what is most vehemently repudiated is often what is most analytically correct.

Perhaps the reader thinks that I have indulged my analogy too far. I think not. On the contrary, I am afraid that it is an analogy which is going to be pushed much further in the chapters to come. But for the time being, let us pursue the parallel with the temporarily-stalled analysis and allow our minds to run back over whatever might be relevant, and especially over what has been most repudiated. The sort of thing which I have in mind is something like Freud's only extensive contribution to our subject, his *Moses and Monotheism*.

One of the most notable things about this book is the hysterical and often quite unreasonable criticism to which it has been subjected, particularly by Jews.[74] Its central idea, that Moses was an Egyptian, might be expected to annoy the Chosen People, who have always regarded him as one of their own; but I cannot help feeling that this does not entirely explain the reaction to it. A writer such as Roback, who is objective enough to concede that Freud might have been right about Moses' nationality, betrays all the symptoms of an irrational and unconscious rejection. He expresses admiration for:

Freud's architectonic style of thinking . . . Most authors write down their view. He builds up his thesis like an edifice. There are the pillars and the facade. Here the nave, the arch, the transept . . . Freud's structure reminds one of a cathedral. It possesses the attribute of magnificence, which grows on one as it is beheld again and again.[75]

Apart from an understandable objection to Freud's Lamarckianism, Roback's principal criticism is on the well-nigh incredible grounds that he failed to take account of collections of Jewish fairy-tales about Moses. One begins to suspect that what he is really trying to imply is that Freud should have taken more notice of fairy-tales because his book on Moses *is* a fairy-tale. But he could have said that simply and rationally and could have produced evidence —if there is any—to support it. Alas, Roback is not alone, even among the psychoanalytic confraternity, and so the suspicion begins to grow that the denunciations and repudiations of Freud's book hide something of significance, something still active in the modern world—or at least in those who still retain some connection with Jewish monotheism—and that this something might be what we are looking for. So let us end this brief digression and, like an analyst who has noticed a symptomatic denial in his temporarily-interrupted analysis, turn to a consideration of what is being denied.

I have no intention of giving a detailed résumé of Freud's unique and extraordinary work. The reader should accept no substitute for reading it himself. Consequently, I shall omit most of Freud's frequently-complex argumentation and present his conclusions in a way which will hardly do justice to his masterly analysis of the material but which will reveal what the real issues are.

His first, and perhaps most, important conclusion is that Moses must have been an Egyptian and not a Jew. Apart from the evidence of his name, which is undeniably Egyptian in origin, Freud's main argument rests on an analysis of the myth of his birth. To those unfamiliar with psychoanalysis his approach may seem unconvincing, but to those who appreciate the role which the unconscious plays in the construction of myths Freud's demonstration carries a very high degree of conviction. This is because the myth reveals an altogether untypical and unique feature which Freud shows to be the result of

[74] Some of the more prominent of these are mentioned in Ernest Jones' *Sigmund Freud*, Vol. III, p. 396.

[75] A. A. Roback, *Psychorama*, p. 150.

tendentious revision of the basic birth-of-the-hero myth which can only be explained by the hypothesis that Moses must have been an Egyptian.

Secondly, Freud proposes that Moses not only was an Egyptian, but that he was a follower of the monotheistic Pharaoh Akhenaten, who reigned in the fourteenth century B.C., and within a century or so of the exodus. This explains the origin of Jewish monotheism and also the rite of circumcision which, as we have already seen, was practised by the Egyptians from time immemorial.

Finally, Freud, following a suggestion by Sellin, concludes that Moses was murdered by his adoptive people and thereby provided a repetition of the primal trauma of the human race which had deep and long-lasting effects on the Jewish people from that time onwards.

Such a bald synopsis hardly does justice to Freud's last and most provocative book, but let us leave it there for the time being and consider what its significance may be for our problem.

Essentially, the difficulty lies in making my hypothesis linking pastoralism with monotheism fit the case of the most austere and perfected monotheism we know. Freud's findings regarding the Egyptian origin of Jewish monotheism may help us out of the problem by enabling us to find another determination of it. Let us begin by considering the alleged Egyptian origin of Judaism in more detail.

Monotheistic tendencies begin to be prominent in Egyptian religion during the 'Augustan' epoch of Amenhotep III (1405–1370 B.C.).[76] Breasted calls this Pharaoh 'the most splendid of all Egyptian emperors',[77] and he was heir to the vast empire conquered by the Napoleon of Egyptian history, Thutmosis III. Breasted attributes the monotheistic tendency to this imperialism:

. . . after 1600 B.C. the Pharoah became lord of the civilized world. The conqueror Thutmose III was the first character of universal aspects in human history, the first world-hero. The idea of universal power, of a world-empire, was visibly and tangibly bodied forth in his career. There is a touch of universalism now discernible in the theology of the Empire which is directly due to such impressions as he and his successors made.[78]

Freud accepts this explanation of the monotheistic tendencies of this period of Egyptian history,[79] but without elaborating on its psychoanalytic background. However, we can see clearly how the universalism of Pharaoh came to be reflected in theology. If the male anthropomorphic gods of polytheism are the primal father returned in the agricultural economy as I argued in the last chapter, it is clear that if any one re-embodiment of the primal father

[76] J. E. Manchip White, *Ancient Egypt*, p. 169.
[77] J. Breasted, *The Dawn of Conscience*, p. 275.
[78] *Ibid.*, p. 274.
[79] *Moses and Monotheism*, XXIII, 21.

should become supreme over all others as Pharaoh did in acquiring his world-empire, then the gods, who are deified versions of the earthly kings, should also become subject to one chief god who claims absolute priority in divinity. Under Amenhotep III, father of the Pharaoh Akhenaten (alias Amenhotep IV), this one god was called 'Atum' or 'Aten', an ancient name of the solar deity. Now that Pharaoh was emperor and king of kings, the primal father, whose embodiment he was, appeared in heaven as the splendour of the sun's disk, one God above all. In the words of a hymn of about 1400 he is called:

> Sole lord taking captive all lands every day
> As one beholding them that walk therein;
> Shining in the sky, a being as the sun.[80]

It was in honour of this new deity that Amenhotep IV, successor to Amenhotep III, changed his name to Akhenaten.

In his excellent modern account of Akhenaten and his reign, Aldred concludes by saying that in the religious sphere 'the progress of his [Akhenaten's] thought, in so far as it can be mapped, is all in the direction of greater abstraction and monotheism', and he concludes that 'there was one aspect in which he was wholly original, and that was in his insistence on a true monotheism'.[81] So single-mindedly did Akhenaten set about extirpating polytheism and substituting his new monotheism that he had all references to the name of Amun, the king of the gods and head of the polytheistic pantheon, removed from monuments, and even went so far as to proscribe the word 'god' in the plural. A new capital was built at the modern Tell el-Amarna, well away from Thebes and its traditional priesthood of Amun, and was called *Akhetaten* ('Horizon of the Aten'). Numerous other Aten sanctuaries were built elsewhere throughout Egypt and the empire.[82]

As far as the belief and theological content of the new Atenist faith is concerned, we rely mainly on inscriptions found in the tombs near the city of Akhetaten. Among these, one stands out especially; it is a great hymn addressed to the Aten, and believed to have been composed by the Pharaoh himself. It begins by praising the greatness, power, and beauty of the sun-god:

Thou dawnest beautifully in the horizon of the sky,
O living Aten, who wast the Beginning of life!
When thou didst rise in the eastern horizon,
Thou didst fill every land with thy beauty.
Thou art beautiful, great, glittering, high over every land,
Thy rays, they encompass the lands, even to the end of all that thou has made.

[80] Breasted, *op. cit.*, p. 276.
[81] C. Aldred, *Akhenaten*, pp. 195, 260.
[82] Breasted, *op. cit.*, p. 280.

It goes on to associate sunlight with life, and night with death. The Aten is also the creator of man:

> Creator of the germ in woman,
> Who makest seed in men,
> Making alive the son in the body of the mother,
> Soothing him that he may not weep,
> Nurse even in the womb,
> Giver of breath to sustain alive every one that he maketh!
> When he descendeth from the body (of his mother) on the day of his birth,
> Thou openest his mouth altogether,
> Thou suppliest his necessities.

The theme of the Aten's providence and care for man and creation is mentioned frequently:

> Thou settest every man into his place,
> Thou suppliest their necessities,
> Every one has his food,
> And his days are reckoned.
> The tongues are divers in speech,
> Their forms likewise and their skins are distinguished,
> For thou makest different the strangers.
>
> How benevolent are thy designs, O lord of eternity!
> There is a Nile in the sky for the strangers
> And for the antelopes of all the highlands that go about upon their feet.
> But the Nile, it cometh from the Nether World of Egypt.
>
> Thy rays nourish every garden;
> When thou risest they live,
> They grow by thee.
> Thou makest the seasons
> In order to make develop all that thou hast made.
> Winter to bring them coolness,
> And heat that they may taste thee.[83]

This, and many other inscriptions of similar tone, lead us to the conclusion that the monotheism of Akhenaten, despite a number of superficial similarities, is very different from the monotheism of primitive pastoralists like the Nuer and the Dinka. In their case, the monotheistic sky-god had all the attributes of the father as punitive super-ego. The Nuer God and the Dinka Divinity were vengeful hurlers of thunderbolts; jealous, ever-watchful, and vindictive gods, gods who were so ready to punish a man that he dare not mention, let alone boast, of his good fortune. The god of Akhenaten is also a

[83] Quoted from Breasted, *op. cit.*, pp. 281–5.

monotheistic sky-god, but he is beneficient, provident, kindly disposed to man; he is the life-giving solar disk, the light of day; he has no thunder-bolts, no interest in chastising man, only in preserving him. As Wallis Budge remarks, 'No consciousness of sin is expressed in any Aten text now known.'[84] We immediately begin to see that whereas in pastoral economies the transference of love for the father onto cattle leaves only fear of the father to be represented in the Deity, in other monotheisms, such as that of Akhenaten, it is only the positive attributes of the father which are possessed by the Deity, and it is only love of him that his worship reflects. This is why Akhenaten's Hymn to the Aten bears such a close similarity to earlier hymns to Pharaoh which likewise depict him as a loving father, and even identify him with the sun:

> He is Re, by whose beams one sees,
> He is one who illumines the Two Lands more than the sun disk.
> He is one who makes the land greener than does a high Nile,
> For he has filled the Two Lands with strength and life.
> . . .
> He gives food to them who are in his service,
> And he supplies them who tread his path.[85]

The reason why the God of the monotheist pastoralists is vengeful is that their love of the father has been subtracted from the Deity and vested in their cattle. Similarly, the reason why the Aten is pictured as being such a benevolent god is that he is merely a highly rationalized and abstracted version of the primal-father-as-Pharaoh. We have seen that all along in Egyptian and other forms of polytheism longing for the father and a desire to love and admire him had been at the root of religious feeling, at least as far as the male gods were concerned. When the primal father reappeared in the earthly trappings of kingship the psychological longing of men to see in him the all-provident and all-powerful father of childhood led them to make him divine in his own lifetime and to raise him up to heaven after his death. When a supreme re-embodiment of the primal father appeared on Earth in the guise of world-emperors like Thutmosis III, a supreme counterpart seemed to be called for in heaven, a new collective super-ego needed to be created, and so the cult of 'Father Aten' arose.[86]

Such an analysis as this undoubtedly has much to be said for it, but it nevertheless fails to take account of what all students of the subject agree to be a most important factor, namely, the contribution of Akhenaten himself. The reason for this is clear to see: Atenist monotheism in XVIIIth Dynasty

---

[84] E. Wallis Budge, *Tutankamen*, p. 115.

[85] J. B. Pritchard, *Ancient Near Eastern Texts Relating to the Old Testament*. The quotation is from the stela of Sehetep-ib-Re, Chief Treasurer of Amenemhet III (1840–1790 B.C.).

[86] C. Aldred, *Cambridge Ancient History* (3rd Ed.), Vol. II, Pt. 2, p. 55.

Egypt was very much the creation of this extraordinary man, and, with his death, it, too, soon disappeared. If we are to have any deeper understanding of his monotheism (and, what is perhaps even more important for our purposes, its later repercussions) we must examine the man and his reasons for so drastically departing from the traditional polytheism of ancient Egypt.

A number of psychoanalysts apart from Freud have discussed the problem of Akhenaten, but none has done so more perceptively and with more knowledge of the facts than James Strachey. His researches started from a number of colossal nude statues of the king which represented him:

> with prominent breasts, a narrow waist, wide hips, a protruding abdomen and no sign whatever of any genital organs.[87]

These characteristics have been explained, almost certainly correctly, as symptomatic of Fröhlich's Syndrome (dystrophia adiposo-genitalis), a condition which produces corpulence, slender lower limbs, excessive growth of the jaw, and, in males, a feminine fat distribution and reduced genitals. Every one of these features is found in statues of Akhenaten, who seems to have been at pains to have himself portrayed realistically by his sculptors.[88]

Strachey relates these feminine physical traits to what has been taken as evidence of a homosexual disposition in Akhenaten. An unfinished stela from Amarna shows Akhenaten embracing his successor and co-regent, Smenkh-ka-re, in a way which suggests a possible homosexual relationship. The phrase 'beloved of Akhenaten' was incorporated in Smenkh-ka-re's cartouches, and when Akhenaten's wife died Smenkh-ka-re assumed her name and, by all appearances, her place in the king's affections.

Strachey suggests that Akhenaten shows evidence of a negative Oedipal orientation, one which predisposes men to homosexuality and femininity. In the normal course of events, Oedipal rivalry with the father results in the son abandoning his mother as an incestuous love-object and instead identifying with his father and accepting the latter's prohibitions and moral standards. In this way he obtains his super-ego and masculine ego-identity. But another possibility exists. When the father is inadequate, absent, or when some other disturbing factor intervenes, the son may achieve a negative resolution to his Oedipus complex and identify, not with his father, but with his mother. This inevitably produces a passive, feminine relationship with his father, which may lead to overt homosexuality or to paranoia. Such a negative resolution of the Oedipus complex seems to be present in Akhenaten, doubtless strongly influenced by his pituitary disorder and its resultant tendency to physical feminization.

---

[87] James Strachey, 'Preliminary Notes Upon The Problem of Akhenaten', *International Journal of Psychoanalysis*, XX, p. 34.
[88] Aldred, *Akhenaten*, p. 135.

Akhenaten's negative, homosexual Oedipal orientation has great significance for our understanding of his monotheism. Strachey, in the paper already referred to, draws one of the most obvious conclusions, namely, that Akhenaten's concept of the Aten reflects paranoid tendencies in his thinking. The psychoanalysis of cases of paranoia reveals this disease to relate to a negative Oedipus complex and its most characteristic symptom—delusions of persecution—to be a defence against homosexual libidinal trends, a conclusion which recent laboratory tests have tended to confirm.[89] The most famous of all cases of paranoia in psychoanalytic literature is that of Senatspräsident Schreber, analyzed by Freud from the subject's own account of his illness.[90] Like Akhenaten, Schreber has a special relationship with the sun, who for Schreber, as for Akhenaten, represented God. In his analysis Freud shows how the sun stood for the father in Schreber's delusional system. Strachey comes to the same conclusion regarding Akhenaten's Aten:

Its paternal attributes are, of course, not in doubt; it is explicitly the procreator of the world in general and of Akhenaten in particular. And, although it is carefully de-anthropomorphized, traces of its real identity emerge in various ways. It is treated more clearly as a king of Egypt than any of the other gods ever were: it always wears a Uræus and its titulary is inscribed within two royal cartouches. Thus the universal power of the Aten and the monotheistic nature of his cult are partly at least a representation of the supreme imperial world dominion wielded by the Pharaohs of the Eighteenth Dynasty, though no doubt on a deeper level they are a projection of Akhenaten's infantile phantasies of omnipotence and uniqueness. But the Aten's intimate relations with Akhenaten are not merely paternal. It has not only procreated him; it enters into him and there creates ideas, thoughts, knowledge, which he then hands on to the rest of the world. The vehicle of the Aten's inspiration are its rays, each of which terminates in a hand, usually holding the Ankh (the hieroglyph meaning 'life')—the crux ansata which, in later times at all events, is an acknowledged phallic symbol. This celebrated picture of the 'raying Aten,' seen in countless drawings and reliefs, is to my mind the pathognomic symptom of Akhenaten's case. These rays are the prototype of the various kinds of irradiations which have troubled paranoics through all the centuries and which trouble them today.[91]

Schreber, too, attached great importance to the 'rays of God', which he thought would gradually transform him into a woman so that he could redeem the world—a situation also closely paralleled in the case of Akhenaten. Strachey argues that the Aten was the recipient of all Akhenaten's positive ambivalence—that is, his love for, and dependence on, his father—but that his negative ambivalence, his hatred of his father, was displaced onto Amun, the chief god of traditional Egyptian polytheism, whose name and cult he

---

[89] S. Fisher & R. Greenberg, The Scientific Validity of Freud's Theories and Therapy.

[90] 'Psychoanalytic Notes on an Autobiographical Account of a Case of Paranoia', XII, 1–88.

[91] Strachey, op. cit., pp. 40–1.

attempted to extirpate. This extirpation, it might be added, included the obliteration of the name of his own father, Amenhotep III.

The significance of Akhenaten's psychology for our understanding of his monotheism lies in the fact that his personal delusional system, unlike that of Schreber, became public property and was invested with the dignity of a state religion. Thus whereas Schreber was insane, Akhenaten was inspired; where the former was rejected as deluded, the latter was accepted as a prophet.

If we now compare the psychology of Akhenaten's monotheism with that of pastoral monotheists, we find some interesting correspondences and contrasts. In both cases we find a splitting-up and redirection of primal ambivalence. In the case of pastoral monotheism we find the positive ambivalence (love of the father) separated out from the negative feelings which usually accompany it and disposed so that positive feelings are directed towards the cattle, while the negative side of the ambivalence is reflected back against the self as the force of conscience. In Akhenaten's solar monotheism the positive ambivalence flows, not towards animals, but towards God, and as a result the Deity does not manifest a vindictive aspect, but a beneficent one. Negative ambivalence, which in pastoral monotheism returns to burden the ego in which it originates, is diverted outwards in Akhenaten's monotheism so that it injures others, rather than the self. The result of this situation is that the Oedipus complex among pastoralists tends to have a positive resolution. The pastoralist identifies with the father in so far as he makes the paternal authority his force of conscience, and he acquires a masculine super-ego which forbids incestuous fixation on the mother. Consequently, as the Culture and Ecology Project showed us, the sexual life of pastoralists is notably normal and their masculine sexual inclinations are fully developed. This is the opposite of the situation in Akhenaten's monotheism. In this case, the Oedipal orientation is negative. What in pastoral monotheism is essentially *the sadism of the super-ego*, becomes, because there is no such sadistic super-ego in Akhenaten's monotheism, a form of feminine *masochism*,[92] and a passive relation to the Deity supervenes (which, by virtue of its providence and beneficence plays something of a maternal role). Hence Akhenaten is homosexual and his psychopathology is paranoid psychosis, as opposed to the pastoral monotheist, who is sexually normal and has a psychopathology which is neurotic and obsessional. Perhaps it is not surprising that ancient polytheism which, as I have shown, probably originated in the agricultural experiments of women with negative Oedipal orientations, should culminate in a form of monotheism which also reflects negative Oedipal trends, whereas pastoralism, which depended on the domestication of animals by women with positive Oedipus complexes should have produced a monotheism which was also wholly positive in its orientation. The two monotheisms are therefore in most

[92] Akhenaten, we will recall was at pains to have himself represented in sculptures with *feminine* attributes, and thus, like all true masochists, seems to have taken pleasure in having himself emasculated.

respects opposites of one another: whereas pastoral monotheism is the out-come of positive Oeidipal trends and has a vindictive, punitive, and stormy sky-god, Atenist monotheism is negative in Oedipal orientation and displays a benevolent, providential sun-god; whereas one developed out of pas-toralism, the other developed out of agriculture; whereas one went with nomadic independence, the other went with a settled existence under the domination of divine kings; whereas one produced depression and self-punishment, the other produced unparalleled narcissistic and megalomanic gratifications, at least for its founder and chief practitioner.

In his discussion of libidinal types, to which I have already referred when discussing the cultural character-type of pastoralists and cultivators, Freud remarks that, just as persons of obsessional type will tend, if they fall ill, to develop an obsessional neurosis, so

People of the narcissistic type . . . are peculiarly disposed to psychosis; and they also present essential preconditions for criminality.[93]

After the fall of his religion, Akhenaten was referred to as 'the criminal of Akhetaten'; and there seems to be a real sense in which his monotheism can be seen to play the equivalent role in mass psychology of a psychosis in that of the individual. The narcissistic propensities which we have detected in ancient Egyptian polytheism seem to have come to their climax in Akhena-ten's paranoid monotheism.

The reader will readily appreciate the point of the foregoing discussion. It is intended to show that in certain exceptional circumstances monotheism can emerge out of polytheism in a manner *not* in any way associated with pas-toralism. If I am right in my explanation of this phenomenon, it is clear what the next step must be. We must re-examine Jewish monotheism and try to see whether there are signs of the provident, paranoid monotheism which we associate with erstwhile polytheists like Akhenaten, as well as signs of the punitive and pastoral monotheism which one would expect of nomadic herders.

In his version of the Hymn of the Aten, Breasted prints alongside Akhena-ten's text verses from Psalm 104, which he feels may be based on it. Following are some examples:

> How manifold are thy works!
> They are hidden before men
> O sole God, beside whom there is no other.
> Thou didst create the earth according to thy heart.   (Hymn)

> O lord, how manifold are thy works!
> In wisdom hast thou made them all:
> The earth is full of thy riches.   (Psalm 104:24.)

[93] 'Libidinal Types', XXI, 220.

When thou settest in the western horizon of the sky,
The earth is in darkness like death.
They sleep in their chambers,
Their heads are wrapped up,
Their nostrils are stopped,
And none seeth the other,
While all their things are stolen,
Which are under their heads,
And they know it not.   (Hymn)

Thou makest darkness, and it is night,
Wherein all the beasts of the forest creep forth.   (Psalm 104:20.)

Every lion cometh forth from his den,
All serpents, they sting.
Darkness broods,
The world is in silence,
He that made them resteth in his horizon.   (Hymn)

The young lions roar after their prey,
And seek their food from God.   (Psalm 104:21.)

Bright is the earth when thou risest in the horizon;
When thou shinest as Aton by day
Thou drivest away the darkness.
When thou sendest forth thy rays,
The Two Lands (Egypt) are in daily festivity.
Men waken and stand upon their feet
When thou hast raised them up.
Their limbs bathed, they take their clothing,
Their arms uplifting in adoration to thy dawning.
Then in all the world they do their work.   (Hymn)

The sun ariseth, they get them away,
And lay them down in their dens.
Man goeth forth unto his work
And to his labour until the evening.   (Psalm 104:22–23.)[94]

If we were lacking other evidence, the 104th Psalm alone would be enough to prove that there is in Jewish monotheism something totally lacking in the monotheism of primitive pastoralists like the Nuer and the Dinka. In the accounts of Evans-Pritchard and Lienhardt we find no hint of the sunny, optimistic trust in the goodness of the Deity which is conveyed in the Atenist hymns and in many of the Hebrew Psalms. We now understand the reason: it is simply that Jewish monotheism does not reflect the simple punitive characteristics of the god of primitive pastoralists whose herds were the

94 Breasted, *op. cit.*, pp. 281–2.

recipients of the love which Akhenaten and his followers bestowed on their god; on the contrary, all the evidence of the Psalms, Canticles, and many other books of the Jewish Bible points to the presence within Judaism of a monotheism identical in type with that of Akhenaten—a regal, imperialistic, providential monotheism totally inaccessible to nomadic pastoralists preoccupied with the negative qualities of God. They share with the Jews a highly rationalized and abstract Divinity who lives in the sky and whose worship is not encumbered with elaborate eschatology. But the Jewish God is like Pharaoh in the golden age of the XVIIIth Dynasty, a primal father such as the pastoralist could not conceive:

> The Lord reigns; let the people tremble!
> He sits enthroned upon the cherubim; let the earth quake!
> The Lord is great in Zion; he is exalted above all the peoples.
> Let them praise thy great and terrible name!
> Holy is he!
> Mighty King, lover of justice, thou hast established equity,
> Thou hast executed justice and righteousness in Jacob.
> Extol the Lord our God; worship at his footstool!
> Holy is he!

Moses and Aaron were among his priests . . .[95]

To conclude: Jewish monotheism poses no problem for the theory of religion advanced in these pages if we realize that the failure of monotheism to correlate with nomadic pastoralism in Jewish history is the result of the presence of another type of monotheism, derived from different sources and, if Moses really was an Egyptian as well as a priest, the continuation in Judaism of the religion of Akhenaten.

Thus Freud's much-maligned *Moses and Monotheism* finds a new basis for support comparable to that demonstrated for *Totem and Taboo* in Chapter one. One might add that, quite apart from the evidence marshalled by Freud to underpin his hypothesis concerning the Egyptian origins of Moses, there is the observation by Wallis Budge that Moses closely followed Egyptian precedent in his prescriptions for the design of the tabernacle, regulations for sacrifice, dress for priests, and so on.[96] Had Moses been merely the transmitter to the Jews of an existing monotheism quite opposed to the polytheism of Egypt such imitations of the hated oppressors and their religion would be unintelligible. If Moses was an Egyptian, and if his monotheism was Egyptian in origin, such observations as those of Budge pose no problem at all. Nor would St Stephen's boast that 'Moses was instructed in all the wisdom of the Egyptians' be at all surprising, or that as Budge says, 'there are numerous features in the life of this remarkable man which show that he was acquainted

[95] Psalm 99, vv. 1–6, RSV (Catholic Ed.).
[96] *From Fetish to God in Ancient Egypt*, p. 9.

with many of the practices of Egyptian magic'.[97] One of Moses' most notable magical achievements, his dividing of the Red Sea, is shown by Budge to have an ancient prototype in a comparable feat of a famous magician of the Early Empire.[98] Concerning the Book of Proverbs, Breasted makes the following interesting observation regarding its connection with The Wisdom of Amenemope, an ancient Egyptian text:

All Old Testament scholars of any weight or standing now recognise the fact that . . . about a chapter and a half of the Book of Proverbs is largely drawn *verbatim* from the Wisdom of Amenemope; that is, the Hebrew version is practically a literal translation from the Egyptian. It is likewise obvious that in numerous other places in the Old Testament not only in the Book of Proverbs, but also in Hebrew law, in Job and . . . in Samuel and Jeremiah, Amenemope's wisdom is the source of ideas, figures, moral standards, and especially of a certain warm and humane spirit of kindness.[99]

This 'certain warm and humane spirit of kindness' we understand to be that of the Aten religion rather than that of any pastoral monotheism, to which such a spirit is quite foreign. So it should not surprise us to find Breasted saying that 'Recent excavations in Samaria have revealed the fact that . . . Egyptian conceptions of the righteous Sun-god were common in Palestinian life', and that 'The winged Sun-god of the Nile was not only known to the Hebrews as a God of righteousness, but also as the beneficent protector of his worshippers.'[100] According to Ezekiel:

at the door of the temple of the Lord, between the porch and the altar, were about twenty-five men, with their backs to the temple of the Lord and their faces towards the east, worshipping the sun.[101]

That the temple of Solomon had a solar orientation there can be little doubt;[102] such a connection between a providential monotheism and sun-worship is exactly what one would expect if the Egyptian origin of Jewish monotheism is accepted. It would also explain why the relatively-modest imperial aspirations of the Jewish monarchy were linked with a theological imperialism typical of the Egyptian XVIIIth Dynasty. The following quotation from Albright makes an interesting parallel with the one from Breasted on page 125 above:

. . . in the time of David and especially of Solomon there was no longer room for any doubt as to the universal character of Yahweh's dominion. For a good sixty years

[97] *Egyptian Magic*, p. 4.
[98] *Ibid.*, p. 10.
[99] Breasted, *op. cit.*, p. 371.
[100] *Ibid.*, p. 360.
[101] Ezekiel, VIII, v. 16. RSV (Catholic Ed.).
[102] W. Albright, *Archaeology and the Religion of Israel*, p. 167.

Israel was a state with imperial pretentions . . . David and Solomon controlled virtually all Palestine and Syria . . .; all the deities of the conquered lands were therewith eliminated from serious competition with Yahweh. In the temple Yahweh was enthroned as sole ruler of the cosmos.[103]

In other words, we find not only the providential and loving aspects of Akhenaten's Deity, but also his political and religious imperialism, and even his solar symbolism. One could hardly wish for better illustrations of the remnants of Atenism in Israel.

If we reconsider *Moses and Monotheism* in the light of these observations I believe that we shall see it as a much less unlikely hypothesis than might have been once imagined. In terms of the theory of the dual origins of monotheism set out in these pages, by far the weightiest consideration in judging the plausibility of Freud's theory of the Egyptian origin of Judaism is that regarding the supreme unlikelihood of there being any other possible source of the sun-worshipping, regal monotheism which is so demonstrably present within it. What one might call the pastoral monotheism contained in Judaism is another matter, as we shall see in a moment, but the positive aspects of the Jewish God, those which portray him as a loving and all-powerful father, can hardly have any other origin than in the religion of Akhenaten. We know that Judaism took on its distinctive form with Moses, who is the single most important figure in Jewish history. We know the approximate date of the exodus and we know that it falls within a century or so of the reign of Akhenaten. The recent finding that the religious counter-revolution which followed the death of Akhenaten and restored all the old gods of Egypt did not begin in earnest with his successor Tutankhamun but with the Ramessid dynasty fifty years later allows more leeway for Freud's hypothesis as far as chronology is concerned.[104] Finally, when we recall that according to the explanation of monotheism advanced here it is only out of the imperialistic aspirations of polytheistic agriculturalists and not out of nomadic pastoralism that the typically-Jewish idea of a loving father-god can develop, there seems no possible alternative to Freud's view that Judaism must owe quite a lot to Akhenaten's monotheism. Certainly, my own researches would contradict *Moses and Monotheism* on a number of points, an obvious instance being Freud's belief that the punitive attributes of the Jewish God were unique. We now know that they were not, that on the contrary, they are typical of pastoral monotheists. Nevertheless, as the reader will by now have realized, had not Freud already put forward the view that Judaism is derived from the religion of Akhenaten, I would have felt obliged to advance it myself.

Nevertheless, there can be no doubt that whatever the contribution of Akhenaten to Judaism, pastoral monotheism has always remained an important constituent of the religion. It is even possible that it was not an incon-

[103] *Ibid.*, p. 154.   [104] Aldred, *op. cit.*, p. 152.

siderable element in the origins of Atenism itself, and that Semitic pastoral monotheists had some influence in Egypt during the XVIIIth Dynasty. However that may be, it is certain that the Hebrew tribes that Moses led out of Egypt at the time of the exodus were at least in part ass-nomads,[105] predisposed to monotheism by the psychological and economic mechanism described earlier in this chapter in the context of the Nuer and Dinka. Throughout their history and up to the point where the religion took on something of a fixed form in the definitive redaction of the Pentateuch and other key scriptures, the Hebrews were a people embracing many nomadic and semi-nomadic pastoralists. These elements always retained a predisposition to the gloomier monotheism that worships the father as a predominantly punitive being. This aspect of Judaism finds a perfect illustration in the shrines of Yahweh set up by Jeroboam I at Bethel and Dan where, in the words of Albright, 'Yahweh was represented as an invisible Presence standing on a young bull.'[106] Here the two aspects of God—positive and negative, vengeful and benevolent—find expression as the unseen spirit, the force of conscience, and the loved and admired domestic animal. Broadly speaking, the books of the prophets of ancient Israel seem to have embodied the pastoral monotheism of Judaism, as opposed to the Psalms and Canticles, which are associated with the monarchy.[107] This division is what one would expect if one sees Judaism as a fusion and compromise between two types of monotheism which did not co-exist in the same way in any previous religion. The centralized monarchy always ran the risk of regressing to the polytheism out of which its monotheism had originally evolved in Egypt and, particularly under Solomon, did in fact succumb to that temptation.[108] But visionary prophets could always be found who would recall the people to the 'nomadic ideal' which Max Weber found echoing throughout the books of prophecy:

. . . the desert times remained to the prophets the truly pious epoch. In the end, Israel will again be reduced to a desert and the Messiah king as well as the survivors will eat the nourishment of the steppes: honey and cream.[109]

Even the political fortunes of ancient Israel seem to have been influenced by this fact. Max Weber also noted that many prophets and religious leaders came from the ranks of the herdsmen, and pointed out that the political tension surrounding the existence of the monarchy in Israel was in large part the tension between settled agriculturalists and pastoral tribes.[110] For while we have already seen that centralized monarchy is a social structure which

[105] Albright, *op. cit.*, p. 97ff.
[106] *Op. cit.*, p. 156.
[107] A. R. Johnson, 'Hebrew Conceptions of Kingship', in S. H. Hooke, *Myth, Ritual and Kingship.*
[108] Albright, *op. cit.*, p. 155.
[109] *Ancient Judaism*, p. 285.
[110] *Ibid.*, p. 42ff.

goes with polytheism and the imperialistic monotheism which can in exceptional circumstances develop out of it, the patrilineal, patriarchal tribe is the typical social structure of pastoral monotheists. The Nuer and Dinka have such patrilineages; and Israel with its twelve patrilineal tribes always maintained the fiction, if not the fact, that it was such a society. The reason why pastoralism goes with patrilineal tribal organization is easy to see: it is the outcome of a return to a quasi-totemic social structure in which exogamous clans once again become the basic constituent of the kinship system but in which inheritance through the male line becomes all-important because of the need to transmit rights to cattle, and as a result of which eponymous ancestors replace eponymous totems. Agriculture, on the other hand, because it is a return to something like the primal horde, predisposes men to centralized forms of organization grouped round primal father surrogates like kings and emperors. In ancient Israel the religious tension between the two forms of monotheism present in Judaism was bound to be reflected in social and political tensions originating in the differing social structures which the different monotheisms implied.

It is not my intention to go into any further detail in examining Judaism as a case in this short study of the psychological aspects of monotheism. I hope that what I have already said will be enough to convince the reader that there is nothing in Jewish monotheism which cannot be explained as long as we realize that it is a religion that contains within it a more-or-less unique fusion of two different monotheisms, one very common and associated with pastoral peoples, the other very rare and associated with particular episodes in the evolution of polytheism; but both of which when fused together resulted in one of the most impressive religions which the world has ever seen. Freud ascribed the depth of Jewish religion to the fact that the Jews murdered Moses and thereby created in their religion a repetition of the primal trauma, with all the consequences of that in terms of guilt and remorse. He may well be right about that; indeed, it is my opinion that only Freud's interpretation of Judaism can make sense of its unique characteristics: namely the Covenant, and the consciousness of being the Chosen People. There are no parallels to these features in any other monotheism, or in any other original religion of any kind, and consequently it seems sensible to conclude that Freud is correct in attributing them to events in history which were unique to the Jews and which, like traumas in individual psychologies, happened early on and left indelible traces. I leave the reader who is interested in these peculiar features of Jewish monotheism to consider his own reaction to Freud's explanation of them. For our purposes, it is necessary that we should consider one final issue relating to Judaism. This is the question of which of the two monotheisms, and which of the two distinct psychopathologies on which they were based, predominated in it.

Let us first examine the problem from the point of view of individual psychology. We know that individuals reach either a positive or a negative resolution to their Oedipus complex; but it would be wrong to believe that this was a situation in which a person's Oedipal psychology was either wholly positive or wholly negative. In most cases the position is more complex, with one alternative undoubtedly predominating, but with the other nevertheless present, if only in vestigial form. Exactly the same situation occurs in Judaism. We do not find a perfectly-poised synthesis with both alternatives equally asserting themselves. In group psychology, as in that of the individual, this is a most unstable condition, and is tantamount to a totally-unresolved Oedipus complex. Judaism is the collective equivalent of an at-least-partly resolved Oedipus complex, and so we should expect to find that one of the alternatives predominates. However, as we have already seen, we shall also find evidence of the other and be able to point to the presence, albeit the unequal presence, of both.

If we examine Judaism from this point of view, we find that, on the whole, it was the pastoral monotheism of the Hebrew nomads which seems to have predominated—or, more accurately—it was their obsessional form of religion which predominated over the paranoid, Atenist form. My reasons for saying this are several. First, we must notice that although we have found evidence of solar-worship in early Judaism, it is nevertheless a fact that it was progressively suppressed as time went by, and that the God we find in the Old Testament resembles that of pastoralists like the Nuer and Dinka much more than he does that of Akhenaten, at least in his meteorological aspects. In the Old Testament, as among the Nuer, God is a hurler of thunderbolts rather than the resplendent solar disk. In psychological terms what this means is that God took on a progressively obsessional, rather than paranoid, form in the evolution of Judaism.

There is another reason for supposing that it was the obsessional religion of the pastoralists rather than the paranoid religion of Akhenaten that predominated in Judaism. It is that, excepting the brief and modest imperialistic aspirations to which I have already referred, we find no evidence of a royal cult of unlimited megalomania that comes to see the king as the supreme earthly representation of the Deity and which focuses on him the religious significance which adhered to Akhenaten. Neither David nor Solomon acquired the prophetic charisma of Akhenaten, and neither they, nor any other Jewish king, show evidence of the pathological megalomania and paranoia that was the driving force of Atenism. On the contrary, what paranoid charismatics do appear seem to have been prophets who, as we have already seen, adhered to the punitive, nomadic ideal of God rather than to the solar megalomania of the Aten.

But what is probably the most important consideration of all is the differing conditions and characteristics of the two monotheisms. Of the two, pastoral monotheism was by far the more common, the more 'normal' and the more pervasive. Atenist monotheism was a brief, exceptional, dazzling, and pathological product of a civilization that was otherwise steadfastly polytheistic and in no way fundamentally predisposed to a consistent and austere mono-theism. Pastoral monotheism, on the other hand, tends, as we have seen, to emerge wherever there is nomadic herding, and is the essential psychological structure on which such economies are built. Consequently, we find many excellent examples of it from many different periods and from widely scat-tered geographical locations. Not so Atenism. Its negative, abnormal, and severely pathological unconscious orientation, and the exceptional historical, psychological, and political circumstances which are necessary to produce it mean that examples, although not non-existent, are much more rare. In Judaism the nomads—or, what is perhaps more important, *the nomadic ideal*—always existed to reinvigorate and reinforce punitive tendencies in the com-posite monotheism which characterizes that religion. Atenist elements, on the other hand, seem to have received little in the way of continued support; and, if Freud's speculations about the fate of Moses are true, the blanket repression which seems to have affected the peculiarly Egyptian elements in Judaism inevitably greatly reduced the scope and significance of the Atenist mono-theism which, in the beginning at least, must have been much more import-ant than it was to be later.

If we examine the psychology of the composite monotheism which con-stitutes Judaism we shall find that, despite the many ways in which pastoral and Atenist monotheism appear to be opposites of one another, there is one profound respect in which they are compatible and complementary. We have seen that in obsessional, pastoral monotheism the hating side of the ambivalent feelings for the father are turned back against the self, while the loving side is directed towards the cattle. In Atenist monotheism, on the other hand, the loving side of the ambivalence is directed towards God, who is perceived as being eminently lovable and good, and the hating side of it is directed, not against the self, but against others. Now, these contrasting attitudes towards God—feared and punitive, loved and beneficent—are not incompatible. God can be, and is, in the case of Judaism, both loved *and* feared, punitive *and* provident. What has happened is that the two sides of the basic ambivalence, which both in pastoral monotheism and Atenism were divorced from one another and directed to different recipients, are, in Jewish monotheism, reunited and directed to one and the same recipient, namely, God.

The practical effect of this was to limit the reliance of obsessional mono-theism on pastoralism, and to greatly reinforce the place of the punitive super-ego in the monotheism of a people who became progressively less pastoral. In the case of pastoralists, we have seen that it was economic and adaptive necessity which drove them to love their fathers in their herds and to have their fathers punish them in their religion. With the loss of reliance on pastoralism, punitive monotheism would necessarily be weakened, since the cattle, both as temptations to aggression, and as reasons for its introjection, would have disappeared. But with the appearance of a loved, provident

Deity, who was also feared and could punish, a substitute was found for cattle which, on a religious and psychological plane, worked just as well. If God demanded love, and could do good as well as evil, then his goodness could inhibit hatred of him, and his vengeance could inhibit love of self. In short, the moral sadism of obessional monotheism was reinforced with the moral masochism of paranoia: now one loved God for punishing one, and one punished oneself for hating him.

Because the super-ego now claimed both sides of the ambivalence, love and fear, capacity to reward and capacity to punish, it became enormously developed, and Judaism evolved in a markedly obsessional direction as a result. Although elements of Atenist paranoia and megalomania lived on in the Messianic tradition and in the more hallucinatory visions of the prophets, its principal contribution to Judaism—the image of a good and benevolent God—became compounded with the vindictive God of pastoral monotheism to produce an enhanced and more comprehensive theological equivalent of the super-ego. In pastoral monotheism, the father had been represented by two agencies, the loved cattle and the feared thunder God. In Judaism one agency sufficed—a single God, who was both loved and feared, just like the real father. In this respect, Judaism represents something closer to the situation as we find it in individuals. If we ignore its Atenist, paranoid undertones, and see its image of a good God as wholly absorbed into its obsessional tendencies as a further justification for moral masochism—for, if God is good, his punishment is good also—then we can see that Judaism represents a fully developed and rounded-out obsessional neurosis. It is, in the individual and the group alike, a condition in which the super-ego has the upper hand, and in which pathological conflicts originate in its demands for obedience and its skilful use of ambivalence for its own ends. In the individual psyche, as in the collective cult, passive and loving feelings for the father are fully exploited to enhance the influence of the super-ego, while aggressive, hateful insurrections against it are made the occasion for guilt and punishment of the ego unworthy enough to give rise to them.[111]

We may sum up this chapter and the last by saying that we have successfully followed the course of the development of the basic neurosis of our patient from the immediate post-Oedipal period far into the period of latency. In Chapter one we saw man in the Oedipal crisis, when the sons rose up in rebellion against the primal father and overthrew him. At this time the super-ego was expressed in the animal-phobic form typical of the Oedipal

[111] A possibility which should not be overlooked is that analysis of mass-psychology may give, on occasions, better insights than can usually be gleaned from individual analyses. If this is the case here, then we might conclude that in severe obsessional neurosis (private Judaisms) there might be present a subsidiary paranoia ready to break out if the obsessional psychopathology is cured. This is exactly what seems to have befallen the most famous case of obsessional neurosis in history, Freud's 'Wolf Man'. (See Gardiner (Ed.), *The Wolf-man and Sigmund Freud.*

period. In the polytheistic phase which follows totemism, we see the super-ego beginning to develop as a more effective agency and demanding greater renunciation of instinct through the invention of agriculture. In the individual the mother is the first of the parents to become incorporated into the ego in the form of the 'phallic mother'—the mother-figure who is believed to have a penis.

This phallic mother is soon replaced within the ego by the person of the father when it is realized that the mother actually does not have a penis and appears to have been castrated. The castration-fear associated with this discovery leads to the formation of the super-ego, identification with the father, and turning back against the self of all the aggression and hatred directed towards the father in the Oedipal period. In world-history this phase of development of the super-ego is reflected in the initial appearance of ithyphallic mother-goddesses, who are then replaced by father-gods in the way described in the last chapter. Eventually, as latency progresses in the individual and the super-ego becomes more firmly established and based on the father, the positive feelings which the ego harbours towards him and which consist mainly in a desire for his love and protection flow unimpeded by the other side of the ambivalent feelings—hatred and fear of the father that have now been entirely turned back against the self. Now, instead of hating the father, the individual hates himself for hating him, and so punishes himself with the aggressions which initially he felt only against his father. In the human race as a whole this definitive phase of the development of the super-ego—that is, God—occurs when the invention of the domestication of animals causes some men to take up nomadic pastoralism. This detaches the punitive aspects of the super-ego in the way described in this chapter and creates the reservoir of aggressive feelings against the self associated with the need to conserve herds and resist the temptation to indiscriminate killing which I have mentioned. But whereas in the individual the positive, loving side of the son's ambivalence is always present and becomes strongly reinforced with the successful suppression of the Oedipal conflicts and the setting-up of a strict super-ego, in the race as a whole the psychological evolution associated with the different sides of the basic ambivalence took place in association with different forms of economic and political life: nomadic pastoralism on the one hand, and imperialistic polytheism on the other. What takes place within one mind in the individual needed at least two social structures and modes of economic life in the history of the race. The overwhelming importance and historical uniqueness of the events described by Freud in *Moses and Monotheism* springs from the fact that an event of great intrinsic unlikelihood but vast historical significance took place when an Egyptian follower of Akhenaten became the leader of a tribe of Semitic nomads, and perhaps underwent at their hands a fate which stamped on their national and religious consciousness an impression of their importance in world-history which has not diminished appreciably today. Doubtless much of the resistance to Freud's hypothesis lies in the fact it pertains to the most essential religious formulation of obsessional neurosis we know of, and to realities which have been strongly repressed in the people in whose midst these crucial events took place.

The importance and uniqueness of Judaism lies in the fact that within it both sides of the ambivalence felt towards the father are more or less perfectly fused. This is why it is so much more single mindedly monotheistic than the religions of primitive pastoralists such as the Nuer and the Dinka. They retain vestiges of totemism and other religious forms because both sides of the ambivalence which is fundamental to religion have not been comprehensively taken up into their monotheism. In Judaism however, punitive monotheism is fused with a trust in a benign father-god derived ultimately from the religious configurations of polytheism. The two monotheisms became fused so successfully in Judaism because in the long run they rested on entirely complementary psychological processes. If the father became a vengeful and punishing figure, then he could also become loved once the sinful wishes which he persecuted had been repressed. If the father was loved as the bountiful provider of man's needs, he should be served and obeyed and had every justification to punish those who abused him. With Judaism, the obsessional phase of the development of the human race reaches its culmination and, just as in a child who is passing through the period of latency love of the father and fear of the super-ego will cause him to abandon conscious resistance to the father's wishes and to repudiate temptations to sin against him, so in the history of humanity the Jewish people represent that contingent which underwent the definitive religious experience which created the super-ego in its purest and psychologically most exact form. We shall see below that although few in numbers and, at least from the exile to 1945, of no political significance to the world at large, the Jewish people have by virtue of their place in the development of world-religion had immense significance for all men and have been involved in a process of psychological evolution which was eventually to change the entire world.

As for Islam, my opinion is exactly that of Freud's: that the 'Mohammedan religion seems to me like an abbreviated repetition of the Jewish one, of which it emerged as an imitation'.[112] It was an imitation which succeeded because it was taken over by peoples who were already nomadic pastoralists in some part; and it is interesting to see the way in which the imperialistic Atenist elements in the pseudo-Judaism of Islam soon inspired the followers of the Prophet to establish a vast empire. Their success in doing so ensured that Islam would remain something of a fusion of the two monotheisms for ever more, and very much another version of Judaism. As such, it shares much of the impressiveness and austerity of its forerunner. Certainly, in terms of sheer numerical strength and geographical extent it is far more significant, and no worthwhile account of monotheism can pass over it in silence.

[112] *Moses and Monotheism*, XXIII, 92.

Yet it remains psychologically more or less identical with Judaism, with this difference: that whereas Judaism was the first of the great comprehensive monotheisms, Islam is very much a derivative. In this respect it stands in relation to its Jewish original rather as an adult obsessional neurosis stands in relation to a childhood one. When I said that Judaism represented a fully-developed obsessional neurosis perhaps what I should have said was that it represented a fully-developed *childhood* obsessional neurosis, in the sense that it was the first complete and perfected monotheism to have existed. As such, it corresponds to the first complete coalescence of the super-ego in the individual and, as we have seen, is the historical parallel of processes of super-ego formation that occur in children during latency (between the ages of about six and eight). Islam then becomes the equivalent of an adult obsessional neurosis because, while undeniably an obsessional form in itself, it is one wholly derived from an earlier experience, and one which, in its exaggerated emphasis on scrupulous observance of ritual details, cleanliness, and obsessive forms of piety, corresponds exactly to what one finds in the obsessional neuroses of adults. Such considerations as these would lead us to expect that Judaism, being the original, seminal form would give rise to further developments (as it in fact did), while Islam, being the finalized form of the obsessional neurosis that we call monotheism, would be unlikely to produce significant new departures in religion. Furthermore, it would lead us to expect that while Judaism would become something of a fossil and decline in significance, Islam, by virtue of being the definitive form of a collective obsessional neurosis, would go on growing in significance until it became the most pervasive and successful monotheism. Finally, if we were to take this characterization of Islam seriously we would have to suppose that the two thousand years separating the exodus from the hegira represented the interval between the appearance of a childhood obsessional neurosis during latency and the formation of an adult obsessional neurosis during adolescence. In the course of the next two chapters we shall see that this is exactly the situation and that Christianity, which precedes Islam by about six hundred years, does in fact correspond to the beginning of a period analogous to adolescence, if we take Judaism to mark the phenomenon of latency in the religious history of the human race.

4

THE RETURN OF THE REPRESSED

I À LA RECHERCHE DES DIEUX PERDUS

Thus far I have been talking in the main about forms of religious life in general and only alluding to specific religions as examples of the basic types. In the last chapter the religions of the Nuer and Dinka were such examples, and I could have added many more. If I did not, it was because I was aware of the need to avoid making excessive demands on the reader in the matter of the length and readability of the book and because I did not want to allow consideration of the details and peculiarities of the many pastoral mono-theisms to confuse the basic issue. My reasons for mentioning Judaism were, however, different. The reader will recall that my motivation here lay in answering the obvious objections to my thesis to which the religion of ancient Israel gave rise. In this chapter I want to be more specific and limit myself to the consideration of one religion, not as an example but as the only instance of what we need to examine. This religion is Christianity, and my examina-tion of its origins will provide us with another reason for carefully considering Judaism as a very special case of monotheism.

I have argued that Judaism was a mixture, a compromise. It contained within it two rather different monotheisms which originated in quite different circumstances and which correlated with two different forms of economic life. As such, it was an unstable synthesis, a threatened compromise. At any moment it ran the risk of breaking down in many different ways. But in particular, it ran the risk of springing apart along the main seam in its con-struction—that which linked the paranoid, providential and supra-poly-theistic monotheism of Akhenaten with the obsessional, pastoral mono-theism of the Semitic nomads, who in large part composed the Hebrew tribes at the time of the exodus. If this happened, there was a risk that the whole evolutionary process which led Judasim to become the religion it was, might be unravelled and the reappearance of its original elements might result. In terms of my analogy with individual psychology, the danger was that Atenist elements in Judaism might reappear in their original form and produce some-thing much more like a case of paranoia than one of obsessional neurosis.

I argued that the psychological elements of the two monotheisms which make up Judaism were by no means incompatible. On the contrary, we saw that they were complementary; love and admiration of the father was not incompatible with fear and obedience regarding him. Nevertheless, the very compatibility of these attitudes hides important inner tensions. In terms of my individual analogy, Judaism is an obsessional condition which corresponds to the state of affairs which is potentially present in all human beings during the middle and later part of the latency period. Early rivalry with the father for the love of the mother has been overcome by way of renunciation and repression of incestuous wishes because of fear of castration at the hand of the father. Now the ego implicitly adopts the 'if-you-can't-beat-them-join-them' tactic and identifies with the father. The identification with the mother, which dates from the early period of primal narcissism and which attributes a penis to her now becomes transformed into an identification with the phallic father, and a negative Oedipal orientation is supplanted by a positive one. The boy gives up his sexual interest in his own penis (at least in part) and establishes within him the person of the father as everything he would most wish to be (which of course includes being the lover of the mother). At the same time, more complex negative feelings about the father undergo repression. In this way the super-ego is formed and the Oedipus complex is resolved. Analogous processes occur in girls.

In Judaism a parallel development occurs on the religious level—that is, in group psychology. God, as we have seen, becomes the religious equivalent of the super-ego in a thoroughly typical way. But, in a much less usual fashion the punitive God of pastoralism is fused with the loving God of the more highly-rationalized and imperialistic polytheisms. Here both sides of the ambivalence which surrounds the father are fused; and here the possibility of future conflicts most clearly manifests itself. Exactly the same occurs in individuals. In the individual, as in the group, the two aspects of the super-ego—loving father and feared persecutor—are only kept out of conflict with one another by an expenditure of psychic energy and a vigorous repression of any tension between them. Fundamentally, what is being avoided is an outbreak of hostility between the individual's narcissism and masochism.

The narcissistic—which, in terms of my theory of world-religion, means animistic-polytheistic—attributes of the Hebrew God are very clear. They are his manifestation as loving Father and providential king. As such, the God of Israel is only another version of all the male gods of polytheism; he corresponds to a return of the lost primal father. Similarly, in the individual, the super-ego, in its admired and cherished aspects, corresponds to the protective father to whom the child's neotenous development causes him to remain attached long after early childhood is passed. And we have already seen that this loved father is in turn a substitute for the frustrated narcissism which the process of growing up inevitably produces. The father is loved because he can protect the child from the worst injuries to his self-love, and because he becomes the fulfiller of at least some of the child's frustrated narcissistic wishes. What the 'omnipotence of thoughts' cannot achieve when the child is old enough to appreciate the hard facts of reality, the all-powerful and all-knowing father *can* achieve. Hence a part of the individual's primal narcissism becomes invested in the super-ego; it is from this source that the emotional tone of the super-ego in part derives. The ego, which in accepting the super-ego as its ideal and as an internalization of something which it must not oppose but must rely on to assist it in the struggle to survive, passes over to it some of the attributes which it once thought that it alone possessed. As the ego develops and realizes that its thoughts are not omnipotent it tends to invest in the super-ego—that is, in the psychic image of the father—a transferred and now-alienated omnipotence, and begins to imagine that the father is all-powerful. Indeed, in the very act of accepting the super-ego as a part of itself, the ego is admitting that the father is omnipotent, at least as far as itself is concerned; and in so far as it humbly obeys the dictates of the super-ego it is proclaiming the irresistible power of the father imago over itself. Furthermore, because the super-ego is a part of itself, because it is a part of the managerial and decision-making agency of the mind (or, at the very least, has a most important say in its deliberations), the super-ego becomes not only omnipotent by virtue of its inheritance of the ego's narcissistic omnipotence and the latter's recognition of its incontrovertible authority, it also becomes *omniscient* because, as part of the ego and by virtue of having access to its functions, it really is in a position to know as much as the ego does. Indeed, because the roots of the super-ego reach deep into the unconscious it can often be aware of things which the conscious ego cannot divine. Finally, the superego becomes *omnipresent* by exactly the same considerations.

Here, in individual terms, is the psychological basis of the chief attributes of the Jewish God, the attributes of omnipotence, omnipresence, and omniscience, which he shares with all monotheistic deities but which in him are especially developed by virtue of the complete absorption of the narcissistic omnipotence of thoughts (which in religious terms means the suprapolytheistic megalomania of the Akhenaten religion) into the masochistic attributes of the super-ego (which correspond to pastoral monotheism). The result of this process is chronic obsessional neurosis. The ego gives up all, or practically all, of its narcissistic wish-fulfilments to the super-ego, and becomes its willing slave. Hence the demands of the super-ego rapidly become more and more exacting. What began as repression of incestuous eroticism in totemism becomes the strict code of sexual ethics familiar to us from Judaism. Now a man must not only renounce incestuous love, he must renounce all love that is not legitimated by marriage, and even then he must observe elaborate ritual restrictions on his right to sexual gratification with his wife. Under totemism a man had to swear to obey the elders of the tribe but seldom did so unless it was really important. In Judaism filial piety becomes excessively developed, and a man is expected to be totally subservient to his father in all things great and small. Here the danger of rebellion because of excessive restraint is obviously acute; and because of the extent to which the ego's narcissism has been handed over to the super-ego there is always a possibility that the ego, bereft of what is psychologically speaking its own, might rebel against the authority of the super-ego, question its omnipotence, omniscience, and omnipresence, and begin to reacquire its alienated attributes. The compatibility of love for the father with fear of him is therefore based on distortion of the ego, which costs it dearly in effort in repression, and always contains the possibility of breakdown, or, at the very least, of immense conflict. If my analogy between an individual obsessional neurosis and Judaism is correct, we may expect to see Christianity, which is a development of it, showing signs of inner conflicts comparable to those of obsessional neurosis, and on the historical level perhaps manifesting a breakdown of the uneasy synthesis which characterizes Judaism and even the complete disintegration of the religion into its constituent parts. If this were to happen, the paranoid megalomania of Akhenaten might be expected to reappear, and its benevolent image of God might supervene over the punitive one of the Hebrew pastoralists. Inevitably, obsessional tendencies to self-punishment would be greatly lessened and narcissistic gratifications might be able to stage a counter-attack to the point where they became megalomanic—that is, where the ego reacquired the omnipotence lost to the super-ego in Judaism. With this would go the reappearance of unbridled indulgence in magical and superstitious wish-fulfilments which in pastoral monotheism are kept within some sort of bounds. The hateful ambivalence, turned back against the self in Judaism, could now be freely turned against others, and there would be nothing to stop a reappearance of the paranoid hatred of Atenism for all religions not like itself. In short, just as Judaism was the social equivalent of an obsessional neurosis, so the disintegration of Judaism could produce the equivalent of megalomanic paranoia. As we shall now see, this is precisely what happens.

The most notable feature of the God of the New Testament, as compared with that of the Old, is that he is a loving, providential and regal deity. The God who is portrayed in the parable of the Prodigal Son is most certainly not the vengeful, jealous, and recriminating God so familiar to us from much of the Hebrew scriptures and from the pastoral monotheisms of the Nuer and Dinka. On the contrary, he seems to resemble the Aten much more closely, and the recommendation to 'consider the lilies of the field'[1] is very close in spirit to the attitude of child-like trust in the goodness and power of God that is so eloquently revealed in Akhenaten's hymn to the solar deity. The petitions of the Lord's Prayer are notable in their emphasis on the two principal characteristics of the Atenist God: he is the provident father-figure ('Give us this day our daily bread; and forgive us our sins . . . and lead us not into temptation, but deliver us from evil'), but also the King of Glory ('Thy

[1] Luke XII, v. 27.

kingdom come, thy will be done on earth as it is in heaven.').

True, this coming of the heavenly kingdom is bound up in the teachings of Jesus of Nazareth with a Messianic expectation, but this in itself is derived from the regal monotheism of the Atenist tradition in Judaism. Traditionally, the Messiah was identified with the Israelite kings;[2] and this identification in its turn derives from the essentially polytheistic identification of the king with the god (that is, with the primal father). We know how important the identification between Pharaoh and Horus-Osiris and Re-Amun had been, and in Akhenaten's cult the Pharaoh became 'the beautiful child of the Aten', a divine intermediary between God and man.[3] He replaced the old gods as patron of the dead and hope of the living.

Christ, in claiming to be the Messiah, was implicitly affirming a principle derived from the paranoid megalomanic monotheism of Egypt; one which compounded the figures of earthly kings and supreme deities in a way quite foreign to the punitive monotheism of the pastoralists. This led to a complete revision of traditional Jewish ideas of divine judgement and to a quite new eschatology. Whereas in the past God had chastised the people rather as 'kwoth' does the Nuer, now Jesus proclaims that he makes his rain to fall on both the just and the unjust. The catastrophes of life no longer are signs of divine wrath; instead, judgement is postponed until the coming of the kingdom, until the heavenly king—evidently Jesus himself—comes to establish justice on the earth. Then, one feels that judgement is more a matter of weeding out the undesirables from the utopia rather than of punishing every little sin against the Father. Presumably this is why the treatment of the damned is so drastic—they are grass thrown into the oven, an eschatological detritus whose disposal is more important than any considerations of natural or supernatural justice. While there does seem to be some notion of divine retribution in some of Jesus' teachings, it is clear that the very fact of postponing it until after death, while at the same time putting a great emphasis on God's forgiveness and slowness to anger, greatly reduces the impact of the Deity as moral censor and punitive conscience. In fact, we have already met a similar situation in Egyptian polytheism where, as we saw, the role of the deities as agencies for the enforcement of morals was greatly attenuated when compared with the situation among pastoral monotheists like the Nuer or Dinka.

Christ's identification of himself with the Messiah or, as it is frequently rendered, 'the anointed one', is the key to understanding what is undoubtedly his most important attribute in Christian theology—that of being the Son of God. He is not the Son, or the Messiah, merely because he will come again to judge the quick and the dead; rather, he is judge by virtue of his filial relationship with the supreme Deity. This was a relationship that long before had been claimed by Akhenaten. In the Hymn to the Aten the Pharaoh refers to

[2] A. R. Johnson, 'Hebrew Conceptions of Kingship' in S. H. Crooke, Myth, Ritual and Kingship, p. 207.

[3] C. Aldred, Cambridge Ancient History (3rd Ed.), Vol. II, Pt. 2, p. 51.

himself as the Deity's 'beloved son'.[4] Psalm 2 says of the Messiah, the Lord's anointed:

> The kings of the earth set themselves,
>   and the rulers took counsel together,
>   against the Lord and his anointed, saying,
> Let us burst their bonds asunder
>   and cast their cords from us.
>
> He who sits in the heavens laughs;
>   the Lord has them in derision,
> Then he will speak to them in his wrath,
>   and terrify them with his fury saying,
> I have set my king
>   on Zion, my holy hill.
>
> I will tell of the decree of the Lord:
>   He said to me, 'You are my son,
>   today I have begotten you.'[5]

The last verse of this quotation has been regarded by exegetes from St Paul onwards[6] as a prophecy of the coming of Christ; but rational scriptural critics today mostly follow Gunkel and see it as a poem composed for the enthronement of a Hebrew king. God appears to have quoted from this psalm (or perhaps from the Hymn to the Aten) on the occasion of Christ's baptism by St John.[7] Róheim pointed out that the rite of baptism seems to have been of Egyptian origin, and was associated with rituals connected with the inundation of the Nile. God's words, he further observed, are based on Egyptian royal formulas.[8] This seems to close a circle of associations whose exact interrelations are doubtless complex, but whose drift seems to be clear: Christ's filial relationship to the Deity is a version of a much older idea, an idea which actually originated in the polytheistic notion of the earthly kings being surrogates of the immortal divinities, and which in Egypt during the imperialistic XVIIIth Dynasty culminated in a conception of a sole Divinity whose earthly counterpart was called his son. In declaring himself to be the Son of God, Christ was only repeating a claim which had beenimplicit in the status of all the Pharaohs, but which in the reign of the heretic Akhenaten had become fully articulated in the context of a conception of the Divinity which was extremely close to that of the Nazarene.

Psychologically speaking, what this means is that Christ, in claiming to be the Son of God was (quite literally, in view of the dogma of the Incarnation)

---

[4] Breasted, *The Dawn of Conscience*, p. 281.
[5] RSV (Catholic Ed.).
[6] Acts XIII, v. 33.
[7] Matthew III, v. 17
[8] *Animism, Magic and the Divine King*, p. 157.

re-embodying the megalomania of Akhenaten's solar monotheism. His emphasis on a good and forbearing God had produced such a marked reduction in the punitive subjugation of the ego (self) by the super-ego (God) that the ego—or, at least, *his* ego—could now reclaim its lost, infantile omnipotence, and love itself as ineffable and divine. Christ, like Akhenaten centuries before him, and like countless other paranoid megalomanics down the ages, proclaimed that he was the Son of God because, unconsciously, he was undergoing a regression to that stage of psychological development which precedes the emergence of an omnipotent and punishing super-ego and in which the child's ego still retains much of its primal narcissism and omnipotence.

Megalomania—for what other name can we give to the claim of a mere man to be the Son of God?—is the narcissistic equivalent of the over-valuation normally seen when a person is in love. If the object of the love is another person, that person becomes, by being loved, valued beyond all others, often quite beyond the limits of sober objectivity. If the loved object is one's own self, the same effect occurs, except that the over-valuation expresses itself as a megalomanic exaggeration of one's own worth and significance. Unlike Akhenaten, whose megalomania had a foundation in reality—indeed, *was* the reality since Pharaoh at that time was the single most powerful being on earth—Christ's megalomanic over-valuation of himself had no objective basis. Perhaps this is why it is found associated with another characteristic of paranoia, namely, fantasies about the End of the World. 'At the climax of his illness, under the influence of visions which were partly of a terrifying character, but partly, too, of an indescribable grandeur, Schreber became convinced of the imminence of a great catastrophe, the end of the world.'[9] So did Christ. Following in the tradition of the more paranoid prophets before him, Christ foresaw the imminent end of the world, the Last Judgement and the Second Coming. None of these elements are found in Atenism (although the fact that we know nothing of them does not prove that they did not exist). Nevertheless, it seems likely that the fact that Akhenaten's paranoid megalomania was successful and founded in objectivity restrained him from the more pathological excesses that these end-of-the-world-fantasies connote. Essentially, they represent a further stage in narcissistic regression and withdrawal from reality. Because the paranoid megalomanic is adopting his own ego as his love-object and investing it with all the grandeur and significance which erotic over-valuation gives to it, he progressively detaches his libido from the world around him, concentrates it on himself, and then formulates delusions that the world is about to end because, unconsciously, it no longer exists for him. As Freud remarks in the case of Schreber:

The patient has withdrawn from the people in his environment and from the external world generally the libidinal cathexis which he has hitherto directed on to them. Thus

9 Freud, 'Psychoanalytic Notes upon an Autobiographical Account of Paranoia', XII, 68.

everything has become indifferent and irrelevant to him . . . The end of the world is the projection of this internal catastrophe; his subjective world has come to an end since his withdrawal of his love from it.[10]

But such catastrophic withdrawal from the world seldom occurs without some countervailing unconscious trend, albeit an unsuccessful one, towards recovery of what is being lost. In paranoia, and again as in the case of Schreber, this counter-trend can often express itself as a *delusion of world reconstruction*. After the end of the world—that is, after the abolition of the objective reality which is not pleasing to the regressive ego—the world can be reconstructed on the basis of egoistic phantasy and the 'omnipotence of thoughts'. Hence the paranoiac builds up phantasies of 'a new heaven and a new earth', and Christ preaches the Second Coming and the Kingdom of God, where, evidently, everything will be arranged as he would like it.

Considerations such as these established beyond any reasonable doubt that Christianity represents a previously unparalleled return of the paranoid and megalomanic monotheism of Akhenaten. Yet how can we account for the phenomenon, and why did it occur when and where it did? Christ's psychopathology—evidently closely comparable to Schreber's—is obviously one part of the answer, but it cannot be a complete one, since, as events were to show, one man's paranoid delusions became shared among a sufficiently large number of persons to justify our use of the term traditionally given to mass psychopathology of this kind and call it, not an individual psychosis, but a *religion*. Answers to these questions may lie in a consideration of the political and social conditions of the times.

I have already established that Judaism contained within it the seeds of the Christian notion of God and of his Messiah simply by virtue of being a synthesis between Atenism and the pastoral monotheism of the Hebrew tribes. Once established in the cultural and religious tradition, Atenism could reappear at any time. Only a shift of emphasis would be required which would push it into prominence while simultaneously suppressing the punitive monotheism of the pastoralists. But this still leaves us with the problem of explaining why it was that Atenism, or its Jewish derivative, made such a notable reappearance when and where it did. Its most likely manifestation in Jewish history might have been expected to have been some nine hundred years previously, in the reigns of David and Solomon. But at the time of Christ there appears to be no parallel flowering of Jewish monarchy, and certainly no imperial expansion. At that time, the Jews did, it is true, have a king, but he was a puppet of the Romans, and the Jewish homeland was only another province within the wider Empire. Clearly, Jewish imperialism and regalism could have had nothing to do with it. Nevertheless, and notwithstanding this, one is tempted to wonder whether perhaps the Roman imperialism

[10] *Ibid.*, XII, 70.

could. Christ, we must recall, was born according to legend in an uncomfortable stable because a decree had gone out from Caesar Augustus that all the world should be taxed.[11] Augustus had assumed the imperial authority in 29 B.C. and he held it until A.D. 9. Christ was born and grew to maturity under him and his successor. Thus, although there are no grounds for believing that events within Judea could have predisposed anyone to imperialistic, paranoid monotheism of the Atenist type, it is clear that its reappearance with the establishment of one of the greatest imperial dominations the world has ever known can hardly be accidental. The reader will recall that in the last chapter, when examining the origins of Atenism itself, we noticed that it emerged in what a number of authors have called the 'Augustan' epoch of Egyptian history, the reign of Amenhotep III.[12] This Pharaoh had been the heir to a vast empire conquered by his predecessor, Thutmosis III, in rather the same way that Augustus succeeded to the empire largely established by the efforts of Julius Caesar. Amenhotep III had been the father of Akhenaten (Amenhotep IV) as we have already seen, and it is remarkable that Atenist monotheism appears in Egyptian history at exactly the same moment in terms of this comparison as Christianity appears in the Roman Empire—that is, immediately after the death of the Augustan emperors and only a few years after the establishment of their world-empires.

The coincidence in Christian and Atenist conceptions of God and of his earthly representative, as well as in the historical circumstances of their first appearance, seems too strong to put down to chance. Yet there are a number of important differences. One of the most obvious of these is that whereas Atenism had been the religion of the élite—indeed, of Pharaoh himself—Christianity was founded by an insignificant Jewish carpenter who lived in a place that could prompt the immortal and true observation that no good ever came out of it.[13] If my explanation of the origins of Christianity and Atenism holds any water at all it should have been one of the emperors who followed Augustus who recreated the religion of Akhenaten, not some obscure artisan of a conquered and despised race. And indeed, if we examine the history of the Roman Empire we find that our expectation is in large part fulfilled, at least to the extent that there is a clearly perceptible trend towards imperialistic solar monotheism. The very first of the Roman emperors adopted Apollo, who was identified with the sun, as his patron deity and dedicated the Pantheon to the sun and the stars. Caracalla had himself portrayed as Pharaoh, and his successor, Elagabalus—or Heliogabalus, to give his name its full solar flavour—was in his youth a priest of the sun and continued his worship of the solar deity on becoming emperor by, among other things, building a great temple to the sun on the Palatine. Finally, in A.D. 274 the

[11] Luke II, v. 1.
[12] See above p. 183.
[13] John I, v. 46.

emperor Aurelian instituted the cult of *Sol Invictus* as the official religion of the empire. He wore a solar diadem, reigned with oriental magnificence and styled himself 'Lord' and 'God'. Julian the Apostate revived Aurelian's solar monotheism and composed a *Prayer to the Sun* which some have compared to Akhenaten's *Hymn to the Aten*.

That revival followed, of course, Constantine's adoption of Christianity as the state religion, but it is perhaps not without significance that the event which precipitated the emperor's conversion was a fiery sign, the *labarum*, seen in the sky at midday. Our expectation of the re-appearance of solar monotheism in the religion of the Roman Empire is as fully justified after Christianity became the imperial religion as we have seen it to be before that event. It is by no means accidental that the birth of Christ coincided with the winter solstice, the moment when, reaching its lowest point in the sky, the sun is reborn to begin the new solar year, or that Easter follows the Vernal Equinox. Again, the fact that it is Sunday, rather than the Jewish Sabbath which is the Christian holy day cannot be coincidental, especially when we find Christ called in the anitphons of the Catholic Church 'Day-spring, Brightness of Light Eternal, and Sun of Justice', or invoked by St Ambrose with the words, 'O Sol Salutis', or portrayed at his Transfiguration with his face shining as the sun and his raiment white with light. Such identifications of Christ with the sun are commonplace, and one of the most famous instances of this is seen in the application to Christ of the words of the prophet Malachi picturing him as the Ancient Egyptian winged solar disc, the Aten, the sun of righteousness, risen with healing in his wings. Early church fathers preached against those who simple-mindedly confused Christianity with sun-worship, and even in modern times Armenian Christians are said to have addressed prayers to the rising sun. The halo, or nimbus of the Christian saint has, notwithstanding its regal connotations, solar attributes as well, and these shine out particuarly clearly in the golden rays which surround the consecrated host in the monstrance in which it is held for exhibition to the people. Such raying glories are again commonly seen in church architecture, and a particularly spectacular example forms the culmination of the interior design of St Peter's Rome.

Such observations as these will suffice to demonstrate the fact that religious developments comparable to those of XVIIIth Dynasty Egypt did occur in the Roman Empire and that comparable instances of solar monotheism appeared both before and after Christianity emerged as the official religion of the empire. As for tendencies towards monotheism apart from the pagan solar cult we have only to recall Max Weber's observation that during the first century A.D. large numbers of uncircumcised proselytes were attracted to the austerity of Jewish monotheism to realize that the parallels with XVIIIth Dynasty Egypt are by no means lacking.[14]

[14] *Op. cit.*, p. 418.

Yet the question remains: Why was the successful Christian monotheism of the Roman Empire founded by a Nazarene? Why a Jewish monotheist rather than a Graeco-Roman polytheist?

A first answer might be that the Romans had no significant tradition of monotheism. I have already mentioned the fact that there is some evidence that some form of pastoral monotheism prepared the ground for Atenism in XVIIIth-Dynasty Egypt: but it is clear that, excepting Judaism itself, there is no parallel in Rome. Yet that very admission arouses our interest. Perhaps there is a parallel after all. Perhaps we should regard Jesus of Nazareth, and the Jews in general, as equivalents of whatever monotheistic influences there were in the courts of XVIIIth-Dynasty Egypt, and look to subsequent developments of Christianity as parallels to the subsequent history of Atenism.

Such is, no doubt, the case; but the difficulty still remains, for we can still ask why it was that conditions in the first century A.D. called for a new monotheism—Christianity—rather than an existing one, such as Judaism. I believe that an answer can be given to this question, but it is one that will involve us in a fresh consideration of the psychology of paranoia and its cultural corollary, the Atenist tradition in Judaism and Christianity.

Commenting on the possible cause of the onset of his illness, Freud remarks that psychoanalysis is habituated to finding the origins of such wishful phantasies as Schreber's delusional system in some *frustration*.[15] In Schreber's case, this frustration was probably his inability to have sons who could perpetuate his name and act as recipients for the homosexual component of his libido. If we are to take the parallels between Christianity and cases of paranoia such as that of Schreber seriously we might do worse than to ask ourselves whether some comparable frustration can be established as the precipitating cause of Christ's, and Christianity's, wishful delusions of grandeur and world-redemption. We might be especially encouraged to do this by the observation that an unmistakably paranoid phenomenon in the modern world, namely, *socialism*, can be easily demonstrated to be the outcome of collective frustration: the defeat and humiliation of an entire nation in the case of National Socialism (Nazism), and the dispossession of an entire class in the case of Communism (Marxist-Leninism).[16] If we ask ourselves what the corresponding frustration could have been in the case of the origins of Christianity, the answer seems clear enough. We shall recall that the Atenist tradition in Judaism had always enshrined the megalomanic monotheism which believed in one imperial domination in heaven and on earth. The Messianic prophecies were the expression of that idea, no matter what pastoral accretions they may have acquired. At the time of Christ the Jews had suffered a humiliation to that ideal comparable in extent to that experienced by the German people

---

[15] *Ibid.*, XII, 57.
[16] For a further consideration of socialism and paranoia see below, p. 237ff.

after World War I or by the working class during the Industrial Revolution. They had seen themselves become an enslaved people and their country a mere province in the greatest imperial domination ever seen in the world up to that time. The empire which should have been that of God's Anointed was rendered unto Caesar, and history, rather than seeing the culmination of the increasingly insistent Messianic expectations of the prophets, had instead seen the almost universal ascendency of Rome. When a decree went out from Caesar Augustus that all the world should be taxed, the fact that the Jews obeyed and were taxed was the clearest possible proof of the frustration of their aspirations and the clearest possible incitement to their rebellion. And we know that eventually they did rebel, and were put down, so effectively that it took nearly nineteen hundred years for the Jewish state to re-emerge. But another, silent, unseen rebellion was taking place. It was like the equally quiet and invisible rebellion which occurred in the mind of Senatspräsident Schreber when he realized that he would never have the sons he coveted. It was the insurrection of the unconscious, known as megalomanic paranoia which, both in the case of Schreber and of Christianity, was triggered by the fact that reality could not provide the gratifications demanded, and which in both cases resulted in the flight into phantasy and the regression to narcissism which typifies the symptomatology of the disease in its cultural as well as its individual manifestations. Compared with the impotent failure of the armed rebellion of the Jews, the insurrection which occurred in the unconscious of Christ was by far the more effective and significant in terms of its final outcome. It may not have brought about the realization of the Messianic hope as far as the Jews were concerned, but for the Gentiles the Messiah had come, once and for all. It is now necessary that we should turn to a consideration of the man who, more than anyone else, was instrumental in bringing this state of affairs about. I refer to Saul of Tarsus, known to us as St Paul.

The first thing we should notice about this man is that, besides being a Jew, he was a Roman citizen, and was the creator of Gentile Christianity. The Acts of the Apostles and other early sources leave us in no doubt that Christ's original Jewish followers continued to regard themselves as Jews after his death and continued to frequent the temple. They demanded of their converts circumcision and adherence to the law. St Paul is important because he fell out with them early on, and in the course of his missionary journeys and epistolary efforts created a Christian church of non-circumcised Gentiles which, after the destruction of Jerusalem in 70 A.D., became the sole surviving wing of the followers of the Sage of Nazareth.[17] The circumstances of his own conversion to Christianity are interesting and worthy of our consideration.

Paul began life as a fanatical Pharisee—in other words, a member of the sect of Judaism which was most opposed to Christianity because it practised a strict and obsessional form of religion, one closer to the punitive monothe-

[17] H. Lietzmann, *A History of the Early Church*, p. 104ff.

ism typical of pastoralists than to the paranoia monotheism of Akhenaten. He is recorded as being present at the first martyrdom of a Christian saint, that of St Stephen,[18] and he was notorious as a ruthless persecutor of the heretical followers of the Nazarene. Yet, in the famous incident on the road to Damascus, where he was going intent on more persecution, he was suddenly converted to the very heresy he had up till then been so bent on extirpating. This remarkable reversal in attitude calls for comment, and a number of psychoanalysts have advanced theories about it.[19] All seem to be in broad agreement that the events on the road to Damascus were not unconnected with Paul's previous life or with his fanatical persecution of the Christians. Fanaticism—or, in other words, an intellectual obsession—springs, like all obsessional behaviour, from neurotic conflicts within the mind. Many obsessional behaviours—and this most certainly includes fanaticism—are *reaction-formations*, that is, neurotic defences designed to prevent the return of the repressed. Freud, in a paper on obsessional acts and religious practices,[20] shows how the compulsive acts carried out by obsessional neurotics always serve as defence-measures against the repressed desires. Often these measures take the form of ceremonial routines that must be carried out with a punctilious attention to detail. Those associated with washing and excessive cleanliness, for instance, can often be shown to be related to anal eroticism (that is, libidinal pleasure in dirt) and act as repudiations of it. One of the most amusing and psychologically-instructive examples of an obsessional reaction-formation which I have ever encountered was provided by an acquaintance who told me that when he joined the navy during the last war the swearing which he heard going on all around him caused him much disquiet. He came from a strict and puritanical home in which no blasphemies or obscenities were ever heard, and so the language of the senior service came as a great shock to him. He found that the swearing which he heard around him during the day kept him awake at night, and that the only way he could get to sleep was to repeat to himself under his breath each and every blasphemy and obscenity he had heard that day. Having done this, he could go to sleep; but if he ever forgot to go through this ritual, sleep was impossible until he had performed it. Eventually, a day came when he dropped a very large naval shell on his toe and let out a stream of abuse in the agony of his pain. From that moment onward he was cured, and never again had to resort to saying his late-night litany of expletives. The words mumbled in bed were, in short, an obsessional defence-measure. He wanted to swear in the daytime like everyone else, and the desire to do so would not let him sleep until he had provided it with a substitute-gratification in the form of swearing addressed to himself. This

[18] Acts VIII, v. 1.
[19] Among the more notable are Hans Sachs in *Masks of Love and Life*, and Theodor Reik in *Myth and Guilt*.
[20] Freud, 'Obsessive Actions and Religious Practices', IX, 117ff.

story nicely illustrates another fact about obsessive practices, which is that they become in due course (even if they do not start out as such) a substitute-gratification and an alternative expression of the repressed wish. The obsessional concern with cleanliness and tidiness common in neurotic reactions against anal eroticism inevitably leads to an exaggerated concern with dirt even though this is consciously thought of as being in the interests of eliminating it. Persons whose sadism inclines them powerfully towards cruelty to animals or children but whose super-egos will not let them gratify their cruel wishes in reality will become strongly committed to animal- and child-welfare organizations and inevitably find much to secretly gratify their sadism in searching out the cruelties of others and ministering to those who have been subject to it. Campaigners against pornography will find that their concern to protect others from what they regard to be the insidious effects of obscenity will inevitably result in their own exposure to it (without, one notices, any harm to themselves). Their desire to search out what they regard as a social evil is only distinguishable from the desire of the pornophile if we take their own valuation of their motives seriously. But from the point of view of overt behaviour (and, we might add, unconscious wish), their concern to find the obscene is indistinguishable from the appetite for the salacious which they would be the first to condemn in others.

But to return to St Paul. His fanatical hatred of the Christians can only have one meaning from the psychoanalytic point of view; that is, it was just such a reaction-formation designed to allow him to repudiate consciously the very thing with which he must come increasingly in contact in executing his duties. Eventually, as he—or, rather, his hallucination of the voice of Christ—put it, it was hard to kick against the pricks.[21] Like my acquaintance when he dropped the shell on his foot, Paul on the road to Damascus became unable to maintain the repression against his unconscious wishes any longer, and in a blinding light of hallucinatory revelation the repressed flooded back into consciousness.

According to his own account,[22] he was struck down in the road by a blinding vision, and heard the voice of Christ asking why he was persecuting him. When he got up, Paul found that he was blind. This blindness must have been hysterical because we learn that it was soon cured by a Christian who 'laid hands' on him. There is some evidence to suggest that throughout his life Paul was an epileptic, and there is no doubt that he had mystical as well as infernal experiences.[23] In the Second Letter to the Corinthians he speaks of having had an affliction which made him feel 'so utterly, unbearably crushed that we despaired of life itself. Why, we felt that we had received the sentence of death'.[24] Freud, in his paper on Dostoevsky, who was also subject to

---

[21] Acts XXVI, v. 14.
[22] Acts IX, vv. 1–19, XXII, vv. 4–16, XXVI, vv. 9–18.
[23] T. Reik, *op. cit.*, p. 271.
[24] II Corinthians I, vv.8–9.

epileptic fits of a hysterical type, notes that such fits correspond to death wishes:

His early death-like attacks can . . . be understood as a father-identification on the part of his ego, which is permitted by the super-ego as a punishment. 'You wanted to kill your father, in order to be your father yourself. Now you *are* your father, but a dead father'—the regular mechanism of hysterical symptoms. And further: 'Now your father is killing *you.*' For the ego the death symptom is a satisfaction in phantasy of the masculine wish and at the same time a masochistic satisfaction; for the super-ego it is a punitive satisfaction—that is, a sadistic satisfaction. Both of them, the ego and super-ego, carry on the role of the father.[25]

I have quoted Freud at length on this because I believe that his general conclusions about such attacks are highly pertinent to the case of Paul's conversion. The experience resulted in a symbolic and hysterical castration in that he became *blind.* Injuries to the eyes are common symbolic equivalents for castration, as is seen in Sophocles' *Oedipus Rex* where Oedipus blinds himself as a self-inflicted punishment for his incest with his mother and his murder of his father. We may give the Pauline equivalents of the latent thoughts attributed by Freud to Dostoevsky in the quotation above as follows: 'You wanted to kill Christians because you wanted to be a Christian yourself (that is, your persecution of them was motivated by your attraction to them). Now you *are* a Christian, but a dead Christian. Now Christ is killing *you.*' Paul, we should recall, had participated in the stoning of Stephen. That stoning had been illegal. To a punctilious Pharisee like Paul this aspect of the affair must have been worrying. His guilt would have been further increased by the Oedipal basis of the hystero-epilepsy that he shared in all probability with Dostoevsky. In the vision Christ took revenge on Paul, who fainted away as if in death. When he came round, he found that he was blind—that is, castrated. The quotation above from Freud shows how this comes about. Two motives are involved. First, Paul is subjected to a symbolically-mitigated castration because the person who has castrated him is his father—that is, Christ identified with God who punishes Paul in this way. This is equivalent to Freud's statement that *for the super-ego the hysterical attack is a punitive satisfaction.* Paul we know had a very strong super-ego and this was the basis of his bigoted Pharisaism. Secondly, Paul is symbolically castrated because he identifies with the dead (that is, castrated) Christ, and so becomes dead and castrated himself. This corresponds to what Freud says about *the attack being a masochistic satisfaction of the ego.*

In short, one may sum up the situation by saying that Paul started out as an obsessional neurotic with strong unconscious attractions to the heretical sect which, contrary to his whole religious education, proclaimed that Christ was the Son of God. Against this seductive blasphemy he reacted by fanatical

[25] *Dostoevsky and Parricide,* XXI, 185.

opposition to it. Eventually, on the road to Damascus, the repressed desires broke through and Paul was converted to what he had previously hated. This conversion required him to gratify his super-ego by allowing it to carry out on him the sentence of death that he had carried out on St Stephen; and also it required that his ego should identify itself in a complementary fashion with the persecuted Christians and become the persecuted victim of the super-ego.

Before we go on to inquire into the nature of the attraction to which St Paul had succumbed and the reason for the irresistible power of the idea of becoming a Christian, let us first pause for a moment to notice something about the Damascus road incident which is like something we have seen before. When examining the monotheism of the Nuer and the Dinka, I remarked that 'prophets' appeared from time to time among them who were 'possessed' by a spirit which spoke through them. Usually these spirits were assumed to be totemic, and usually what they said was unintelligible. In the case of the Dinka masters of the fishing spear, however, we saw that possession by the clan divinity was common, and took the form of hysterical trembling during sacrifices. The reader will recall that this trembling was said to reproduce the twitching of the flesh of the sacrificed animal. Here is a case of members of a monotheistic elite (if you like, the Pharisees of the Dinka) manifesting hysterical attacks which are based, as was St Paul's, on identification with the sacrificed victim (in this case, St Stephen-Christ). But I also showed that the trembling seizures had another latent motivation. They were an identification with the father in a second sense since the obvious erotic significance of trembling in the lower limbs reproduced what the father does with the mother and what the sons wish to do when they see their father 'Flesh' killed before their eyes.[26] Here again, Freud's general principle of hysterical attacks holds true. The masters of the fishing spear provide a punitive satisfaction for the super-ego by identifying with the slain victim—they tremble like the newly-killed flesh. But equally, there is a satisfaction for the ego, because by way of submitting to the identification of itself with the sacrificed totem it achieves the satisfaction of identifying with it in the most erotically-exciting way possible. St Paul's experience was only a very special case of a religious phenomenon common to all monotheisms but most clearly exemplified by the Dinka spear-masters. Most of the Old Testament prophets seem to have been subject to comparable attacks whether induced by fasting and penances or spontaneously. St Paul's experience is only outstanding because the spirit that possessed him was something new. It was the super-ego of course—as we have seen, it always is—but it was the super-ego in a new form; this is why that event on the road to Damascus was of such vast significance for the history of religion.

But what was this thing which St Paul found so irresistibly attractive that

[26] See above p. 106ff.

all his neurotic defence-measures against it totally collapsed on the road to Damascus? The short answer is obviously 'Christ'. He found the person of Christ so profoundly disturbing that he could do nothing but become wholly committed to him for ever after that shattering event. If we could discover what it was about Christ—or, at least, what it was about Paul's idea of Christ —that influenced him in this way we might be able to explain not only the conversion of the most important figure in the early Church and founder of Gentile Christianity, but also the attraction of the religion to all subsequent Christians.

The key obviously lies in St Paul's conception of Christ. If we could understand how St Paul saw him we could probably piece together the unconscious motives underlying his commitment to him. One of the most astonishing things about St Paul's writings is that they do not contain one sentence about the life or teachings of Christ outside of this crucifixion, the last supper, and his ascension. In his letters he shows an extraordinary lack of interest in Christ's birth, youth, his ministry, his family, his sayings, his parables, his miracles, and all the other things which fill the gospels. This cannot be because he did not know about them. On more than one occasion he met the disciples of Christ and had ample opportunity to hear from them first-hand accounts of all these things. Yet he ignores them. Only one thing about Christ seems to matter for Paul. This is that Christ is the Son of God, that Christ died to save the world, and that he rose again and sits on the right hand of God. Not only does Paul ignore the teachings of the Nazarene, he actually traduces them. In place of the tolerant, gentle morality of Jesus, Paul erects the cruel and puritanical ethics of his own morose bigotry. Christ could forgive the prostitute who showed herself capable of love and repentance; Paul recommends that a man who has committed a technical infringement of the law against incest should be 'delivered to Satan'[27]—evidently a euphemism for some form of corporal punishment. Christ, who seems to have ascribed equal rights to men and women in the Kingdom of God, is followed by a narrow-minded misogynist who holds that women should not speak in church and should regard themselves as chattels of their husbands.[28]

If we turn our attention to what Paul *does* say about Christ, as opposed to what he so significantly does not, we find that the central idea of all the epistles is that sin is death but that Christ is life and deliverance. Throughout the sixth and seventh chapters of his letter to the Romans the theme of death equated with sin tolls like a bell:

The end of those things is death . . . the wages of sin is death . . . you have died to the law through the body of Christ . . . While we were living in the flesh, our sinful passions . . . were at work in our members to bear the fruit of death. But now we are discharged from the law, dead to that which held us captive . . . Apart from the law

[27] I Corinthians V, v. 5.
[28] I Corinthians XI, v. 7, Ephesians V, vv. 22-3.

sin lies dead . . . I was once apart from the law, but when the commandment came,
sin revived and I died; the very commandment which promised life proved to be
death to me. For sin . . . deceived me . . . and killed me. Did that which is good bring
death to me? . . . It was sin, working death in me . . . Wretched man that I am, who
will deliver me from this body of death?[29]

Paul, we will recall, 'died' on the road to Damascus perhaps very much as
Dostoevsky described himself as 'dying' in his epileptic fits. Paul was thrown
down unconscious, blinded and symbolically castrated by Christ. Later Paul
rationalized this mystical experience in terms of his theological exposition of
the central truth of Christianity. This was that, in dying on the cross, Christ
had died for all men because all men were identified with him in the Church
as Paul had been identified with him in his hystero-epilepsy on the road to
Damascus. The notion of hysterical identification is the psychological reality
underlying the theological fiction of the 'Mystical Body of Christ'. This is an
idea elaborated in the course of the epistles which holds that all Christians
participate in the Church as organs do in a body: 'so we, though many, are
one body in Christ'.[30] This mystical unity comes about because Paul, in a
manner entirely in accordance with his dictatorial self-righteousness, assumes
that all other Christians ought to participate in the experience of conversion
with which he has been favoured: 'I have been crucified with Christ; it is no
longer I who live, but Christ who lives in me.'[31] In other words, if all identify with Christ as Paul has done, all will die with Christ and all will rise with
him so that all will be one with him. Hence the Church is his mystical body.

Death in Pauline theology is punishment for sin. It is the punishment which
he symbolically underwent on the road to Damascus. However, having
undergone the experience of death, albeit vicariously, by identifying with
the dead and crucified Christ, the guilt is assuaged. In psychoanalytic terms,
once the super-ego has had its sadistic satisfaction in persecuting the ego by
castrating it, the ego can have the masochistic pleasure of identifying itself
with the super-ego represented as a castrated son—that is, Christ. Once this
identification is achieved there is no more need to feel the guilt of sin because
the ego has been punished by virtue of its identification with the castrated son.

This explains another Pauline theological notion, that of original sin. If
Christ is to be identified with as the son who is castrated by the father, it is
clear that the individual must first feel himself to be guilty of the crime for
which the son is castrated. This fundamental and ineradicable crime is the
son's incestuous desire for the mother which is, as we have seen, the root of
all anti-social tendencies in a species whose altruism has been a late acquisition
in evolutionary terms and whose basic instinctual drives do not predispose it
towards selflessness. The individual must feel this latent and universal guilt if

[29] Romans VI, vv. 21–3, VII, vv. 1–24.
[30] Romans XII, v. 5.
[31] Galations II, v. 20.

he is to be able to make the identification with Christ which the doctrine of the Mystical Body and the whole Pauline soteriology presupposes.

We are now in a position to answer the question as to what might have been the irresistible attraction which Christ held for St Paul. The answer is that it was the attraction of hysterical identification and vicarious solution of a neurotic conflict which pressed heavily on the troubled mind of Paul, the obsessional neurotic and professional fanatic. The latent logic of the conversion runs like this: 'I, Paul, am a weak man totally terrorized by my conscience (or super-ego) which, because I am a Jew, is cast in the mould of an omnipotent father-God. I hear about the followers of Jesus of Nazareth who claimed to be the Son of God. This is blasphemy; but my ever-watchful super-ego will not allow me to tolerate that because its cruel oppression tempts me to it so much myself. Therefore I must persecute these heretics. However, I know that this Nazarene, this Jesus, was cruelly put to death. He deserved that because he blasphemed against God. Yet I am also tempted to blaspheme against God. If he died, he suffered the fate which by rights should have been mine as well. This makes me feel like the Nazarene; but I cannot identify with him unless I can show that I am only doing so to the extent that he was punished for my sin. Yet if he was punished for my sin, I am free of it, at least in so far as I am he and he is myself. So if I identify myself completely with him I simultaneously punish myself and release myself from the guilt of sin.'

So must have run the latent logic of Paul's conversion. It followed the same general lines as any case of possession by the divinity in a monotheistic religion, and closely parallels the psychopathology of the trembling hysteria in Dinka masters of the fishing spear. The only material difference was that whereas they were filled with the spirit of Flesh on witnessing the sacrifice of an animal dedicated to their totem, St Paul was filled with the spirit of Christ after witnessing the martyrdom of a man dedicated to the Son of God, who had himself been sacrificed in expiation for sin.

Paul's soteriology, his doctrine of salvation through identification with Christ who sacrifices himself for man's sin, has obvious pre-Christian parallels. Theodor Reik and others have drawn attention to the extraordinary similarly between Christianity according to St Paul and the cults of Osiris, Adonis, Attis, Zagreus, Dionysus, and Bacchus.[32] In all these, the god in question died and was reborn in different ways; and it was the identification of the devotees with the god which ensured them salvation. In the case of another mystery religion, Mithraism, the initiate was literally washed in the blood of a sacrificial bull and received a series of new names, the culmination of which was 'Father'. Christ, according to St Paul, was a sacrificial lamb who died, like the bull of Mithras, to cleanse men in his blood. Like Osiris, he was resurrected, and like Dionysus was consumed by his followers in a ritual

[32] *Op. cit.*, p. 271.

meal. However, perhaps the closest parallel is with Orphism. Reik points out that

A comparison between the Orphic theology and the Christology of St Paul shows remarkable resemblance. According to Orphism, Zagreus, the young son of Zeus, is torn to pieces and killed by the Titans. Zeus calls him back to life and takes him to Heaven . . . The Orphic communion had the following elements: the human soul suffers from an inherited sin, but can be delivered from it by obtaining divine life. New birth is achieved through communion with the dying Dionysus or Zagreus. For Orphism, as for Paulinism, the aim is to deliver the souls from the burden of the flesh and to bring them into contact with God. Compare those essential features of Orphic belief with Paul's doctrine. Christ died in order to free mankind from the Adamic sin. Deliverance is attained by men through dying and being born again with Him. The body is the seat of sin. In being born again sin is destroyed in the body. The centre of the mystery was to become similar to a god.[33]

I have already commented on the totemic nature of much of the polytheistic mystery-religions, decked out as they were with bull-roarers, white-clay, animal fetishism, esoteric dramas and churunga-like cult-objects. The most solemn moment of such rites is the totem-meal, the sacrament by means of which the initiates most graphically express their identification with the god. In Pauline Christianity this element, too, becomes of first importance. Before Paul, the essential ritual expression of being a Christian appears to have been baptism, which was a once-and-for-all affair. But with St Paul, the Christian communion as we know it comes into prominence as the most solemn and important rite; and one which is, furthermore, repeated throughout the life of the Christian. St Paul's theological interpretation of this rite springs from the same delusional source as his other theological notions, especially those relating to salvation. According to Genesis XVII, circumcision is a covenant between God and man and the blood shed therein is spoken of as 'the blood of the covenant'.[34] Hence Christ's words at the Last Supper really mean 'I am the sacrificial victim whose blood is shed for you to seal a new covenant with God.'[35] This connection of the Old Testament notion of the covenant with the crucifixion appears to be a Pauline idea; and it arises out of the unconscious equation already found in Paul's conversion which identifies castration (=circumcision in old covenant) with crucifixion and death (in the new covenant).

These quasi-totemic elements in Pauline theology do not contradict the basic obsessional ideas underlying his conversion. On the contrary, they were an inevitable consequence of them. It is, of course, possible as Reik has suggested that St Paul had an unconscious hankering after the heathen son-god

[33] *Ibid.*, pp. 273-4.

[34] Of course, Genesis is right. The blood shed in circumcision does seal the covenant, if by that we mean the relation between the ego and the super-ego.

[35] H. Lietzmann, *Messe und Herrenmahl*, p. 220.

cults. But if he did, he had it for precisely the same reasons that he had a hankering after Christianity: because he wanted to resolve his unconscious conflicts by introducing a castrated son-god into his neurosis. Tarachow[36] has suggested that St Paul's elevation of the Son, and his identification with Christ mark an unconscious, passive homosexual surrender, especially since Paul appears to have had difficulty in differentiating between God and Christ. Putting the matter succinctly, one might say that, in so far as Paul's conversion was a punitive satisfaction of the super-ego, it was an episode in his obsessional neurosis, and was psychologically comparable to the preponderant element of punitive monotheism which we have found in Judaism. However, to the extent that his conversion was a masochistic satisfaction of the passive (and homosexual) trends in his ego, it can be seen as a paranoid episode analogous to a reapparance of the Atenism of Moses and the Egyptian tradition of monotheism. Like Akhenaten, who was feminized by his pituitary disorder, or like Schreber, who believed himself to be undergoing emasculation by the 'rays of God', Paul was symbolically castrated and made to play a passive role *vis à vis* Christ on the road to Damascus. His conversion came about through a vision at high noon, a hallucination in which he saw *a light brighter than the sun* and *heard the voice of Christ*.[37] Hallucinations—and, above all, *voices*—although rare in obsessional neurosis, are among the principal symptoms of paranoia. The content of Paul's hallucination could hardly have been more 'Atenist' in the sense that it was *solar* and featured Christ as Son of a good and loving God. Furthermore, we should recall that Paul, before his conversion, was a persecutor of the Christians. By becoming one of them he effectively exchanged persecuting *for being persecuted*, and it is common knowledge that delusions of persecution (often crystallized around a core of reality) are important symptoms of paranoia. As Tarachow has pointed out,[38] Paul was a man with extensive masochistic strivings who gloried in shipwrecks, floggings, stonings, and punishments, culminating in his martyrdom in Rome. (In this he resembled Christ, who also contrived to have himself persecuted; and the fact that thousands of his early followers imitated him in this is not without significance.) I might also add, in conclusion, that megalomanic elements are not missing since Paul was later to claim to have been raised to the 'third heaven' in a mystical apotheosis,[39] and, by virtue of the doctrine of the Mystical Body of Christ, clearly identified himself with Christ and, to that extent, with God himself.

The nature of Paul's conversion had profound consequences for all later Christians. We have already seen that it could be expected to further the

[36] S. Tarachow, 'St Paul and Early Christianity', reported in *The Psychoanalytic Quarterly*, XXI, 462–3, 1952. I am indebted to Prof. Werner Muensterberger for bringing this material to my attention.

[37] Acts XVI, v. 13.

[38] *Op. cit.*, p. 463.

[39] II Corinthians XII, v. 2.

autonomous development of what I have called 'Atenism' in Christianity. We saw above that Christ's own conception of the Deity was markedly Atenistic, and that this was the basis of his identification of himself with God as his Messiah. In introducing Christ as a separate personality in the previously austere monotheism of Judaism, St Paul was effectively furthering the breakdown of the unified conception of God and of the group super-ego which, as we have seen, was the major feature of Judaism and the reason why it was such an absolute and highly developed monotheism. Traditionally, it contained both the punitive, censorious God of pastoral monotheism and the loving, splendid, God derived from the imperialistic phase of the evolution of a great polytheism. Now, with St Paul's conversion and his development of soteriological doctrines hingeing on the sacrifice of Christ, that great synthesis began to crack, and slowly the punitive Deity of pastoral monotheism began to become the Father, and the regal Deity of the Atenist monotheism became the Son.

This process of dissolution of the Jewish synthesis—effectively a case of the return of the repressed—can be seen beginning in St Paul's Christology. We have already seen that St Paul quotes the same psalm that I quoted above[40] when talking about Christ as Messiah, and which is in all probability a coronation anthem of the Hebrew monarchy.[41] Throughout the letter to the Hebrews he stresses Christ's role as 'high priest after the order of Melchizedek, king of Salem'.[42] Originally, king and high priest were one, as this biblical quotation suggests; and we have seen that this situation reflects a more fundamental reality in polytheism in which originally the gods were deified kings, the primal-father-as-hero-of-agriculture. In drawing the analogy between Christ and Melchizedek, Paul was effectively saying that Christ was a regal Deity whose true descent traced him back to a pagan polytheism rather than to Hebrew pastoral monotheism. Christ's soteriological mission in saving the world from sin and redeeming man from the otherwise inevitable wrath of God the Father further emphasized the loving aspect of the Diety derived ultimately from Atenism. God now not only smiled on man and provided for his natural wants, he alleviated his supernatural wants as well, and saved him from death and the punishment of sin with which the divinity had traditionally been equated by the punitive monotheism of the pastoral tradition. The goodness of God now knew no bounds, and God himself came down to earth and taught man the gospel of salvation, sealing that salvation with his blood. Then, elevated to heaven, and at the right hand of the Father, he ruled as Christ the King and origin of grace, merit, benevolence, and salvation, a veritable Pharaoh in heaven. It is hardly surprising that in a mosaic in the second-century Vatican Cemetery Christ is shown as Helios driving the chariot of the sun. If Rome had been colonized by Egyptians rather than Greeks he would doubtless have been shown as Re or the Aten.

[40] Page 150.   [41] Hebrews V, v. 5.
[42] Hebrews V, v. 10, VI, v. 20, VII, vv. 1–17.

The subsequent history of Christianity (especially on the Vatican Hill) shows that the parallel with Egypt is pertinent even if chronology and politics distorted it considerably. We shall see that the Christian re-embodiment of Atenism was taken up in the capital of the Empire and that highly-placed Romans did do much to further and establish the religion, and that new dynasties of Christian Pharaohs established themselves first as secular emperors and then as sacerdotal ones. But this is to anticipate. For the moment, let us merely observe that although Christianity, like the original Atenism, did in all probability originate far away from the imperial power and in an existing monotheism, it soon became inextricably bound up with geopolitical imperialism and moved its centre to the city on which all roads converged.

Up to this point I have discussed Christianity very much as if it were simply an out-growth of Judaism and nothing more. While this may be true of the Pauline era and perhaps even for a little after that, it is clear that as time went by Christianity became more and more an autonomous religion no longer closely connected with Judaism which, as Freud remarked, was from this time on something of a fossil.[43] As it did so, it began to evolve characteristic features that we should now examine. However, there was no abrupt break with Jewish tradition, only a gradual development away from it and a steady elaboration of the essential elements which St Paul had introduced. Paul's doctrine of salvation, based as it was on his own pathological experiences, became the orthodox soteriology of Christianity as a whole. It now became accepted dogma that Christ died in recompense for the sins of all men and that through him all men could be saved. The 'Good News' of the gospel was a formally-rationalized equivalent of Paul's experience of conversion. What for him had been a means of off-loading some of his immense Oedipal guilt onto an ego-ideal who was a castrated son-figure and obedient servant of the super-ego became, in theological terms, a doctrine of salvation that said that man had been redeemed by the sacrificial death of Christ which had justified all the members of the Mystical Body before God. In psychological terms, the 'Good News' of the gospel was the tidings that man was now, at least in phantasy, free from Oedipal guilt because a son of God had borne it and paid the penalty in his stead. This idea was to have profound and long-lasting consequences, not the least of which was to begin to shift emphasis from the traditional Jewish soteriological rite of baptism (which, the reader will recall, was practised by St John) to the eminently Christian redeptive rite of Communion. Visions and hysterical seizures of the Pauline type are obviously not possible for all men—fortunately there are many whose psychopathology is not as severe as that of Paul. However, his interpretation of the Last Supper made it ideally pre-adapted to become a religious observance by means of which all could share in his experience on the road to Damascus by quite literally becoming one with the crucified Christ. As Christianity evolved, the

[43] *Moses and Monotheism*, XXIII, 88.

literal identification of the crucified Christ with the bread of the Communion became more and more emphasized until in the later Middle Ages church paintings could be seen which showed the body of Christ being fed into a meat-mincer and consecrated Hosts emerging from it. Canonically, the process reached its climax in 1215 when the dogma of transubstantiation was defined by the Fourth Lateran Council. This was followed in 1263 by the famous miracle at Bolsena. A priest beset with doubts about the Real Presence had seen the Host begin to drip blood when he broke it. The miracle, which caused a sensation at the time, was carefully investigated by St Bonaventura and St Thomas Aquinas at the instigation of Pope Urban IV, and proclaimed authentic. It was largely responsible for the institution of the Feast of Corpus Christi, and to this day its authenticity is an obligatory belief for all Catholics. The reason for this vast development in the ritual and soteriological significance of the Mass lies in the fact that it was for the Christian church as a whole the means by which it could participate in the redemptive experience that is the centre of the Pauline conception of Christianity. It was the outward and visible sign of an inward and invisible psychological process of identification with the castrated son-god, which from St Paul to the present day remains the central element in the psychology of Christianity.

But this idea contained one very great danger. This was that the redemptive role of Christ would overshadow the punitive role of the Father and that the God of Atenism would supervene over that of the Hebrew nomads. In fact, there was every likelihood that this would happen because the economic and social basis of punitive monotheism was not to be found in Roman or medieval Europe. There were no pastoral tribes to maintain naturally such a belief merely by way of practising their economy. The vengeful God of the Old Testament was a literary relic, only preserved by the Judaic tradition in Christianity and by the obsessional trends in mass and individual psychology which underpinned it. Yet in the early centuries of Christianity that Judaic tradition was very strong and the Pharisaic and obsessional stamp that St Paul had given to the religion was still very much in evidence. This is why the principal religious developments of the first three centuries after his death hinge on the fierce controversies which surrounded the theological definition of the nature of Christ and his relationship with the Father.

It is clear that once it had been accepted that Christ was God, belief in the God of the Old Testament—the Father-God, in other words—might be threatened. This is precisely what began to happen, especially among the Gnostics, who greatly reduced the significance of the Old Testament God. Atenism was returning strongly from the unconscious in the new religious climate of the first three centuries A.D., and it threatened to totally overcome the old Hebraic synthesis and eradicate what I have called punitive monotheism altogether. In fact, this is exactly what it succeeded in doing in the long run; but in the short term, Christianity was to resort to typically-obsessional means to counteract it.

The danger, as I pointed out at the beginning of this chapter, was of a complete breakdown in the Judaic synthesis and—which is much more important—in the mass obsessional neurosis which underlay it. As long as the collective super-ego could be maintained, invested with both sides of the ambivalence that the ego feels towards it—namely, fear and love—all was well. But once this compromise began to disintegrate the possibility of a dissolution of the obsessional neurosis was very real. Catholic Christianity was just such a process of dissolution of the Judaic obsessional neurosis; but it was a dissolution which had to encounter severe resistance, both within individuals and within the religion at large. The first attempt to prevent it was made by Jesus' original Jewish followers when they sought to limit access to the new sect to the circumcised alone. They failed; and the destruction of Jerusalem by the Romans brought to an end any hope of Jewish control being maintained over Christianity. The second great attempt to protect the traditional synthesis of the two aspects of God was made in the struggle against the Gnostics and other heretics who threatened it. Here again, the attempt was unsuccessful even though in the short run the heretics seemed to have been defeated. But it was a pyrrhic victory. Deep down, nothing could prevent the continuation of the process of dissolution and the gradual appearance of increasingly paranoid and psychotic traits.

The method used to try to overcome this intractable process of dissolution was the erection of elaborate dogmatic formulas which would safeguard the old compromise between Atenist and pastoral Deities. As Theodor Reik so correctly pointed out, 'dogma is a compulsive effort to overcome religious doubt'.[44] It is, in fact, a typical reaction-formation, characterized by a high degree of intellectualization and at least some attempt at rational plausibility. This is the means by which the Christian Church chose to try to overcome the conflicts caused by the introduction of the Son-God into the otherwise austere-monotheistic religious tradition of Judaism. Never before in history had theological controversies occasioned such bloody conflicts. A Latin historian of the fourth century, Ammianus Marcellinus, remarked that 'no wild beasts are such enemies to mankind as are most of the Christians in their deadly hatred of one another'. That hatred was to continue virtually unabated—and sometimes severely exacerbated—for the next sixteen centuries; but in the third and fourth what is notable about it is not its unspeakable cruelty or the appalling barbarity of the followers of him who recommended all men to love one another, but rather the fact that such conflicts centred on the finer points of theology. Reik is undoubtedly correct when he says that Christological controversies of the first four centuries were misleading trivia which were in reality distorted expressions of the most basic unconscious conflict of Christianity—the rivalry between the Father and the Son.

This was the rivalry between two quite different religious systems and their

---

[44] *Dogma and Compulsion*, p. 50.

characteristic psychopathologies. On the one hand stood the Father, in other words, the super-ego, whose worship comprised the collective obsessional neurosis of Judaism, with its characteristic introjection of aggressive feelings. On the other stood the Son, that is, the ego, whose megalomanic self-aggrandisement was symptomatic of the collective paranoia that we call Christianity. Because it greatly de-emphasized the punitive nature of God, and the introjection of aggression which goes with it, Christianity enabled Christians to begin to project their aggression into the outside world, and, in particular, enabled them to indulge in the paranoid hatred of those whom they believed were their enemies which is so typical of this pychosis. The early theological controversies and the bloodshed which they entailed were the first expressions of the psychotic suspicion and hatred which Christians down the centuries have directed towards those whom they imagined were conspiring against them. As Atenism returned, so did the bigoted intolerance of Akhenaten for all religions except his own, and the foundations were laid for the great institutions of Christian religious intolerance, such as the Inquisition, the Index, the witch-hunts and the Crusades.

Nevertheless, when Christianity became the official religion of the Roman Empire, a powerful political and institutional motive was found for restoring peace. Most of the great theological controversies about the nature of the Christian God were settled when the emperor Theodosius imposed the so-called Nicene Creed on his subjects. This document (most of which actually dates from the Second Ecumenical Council held in Constantinople in 381) will repay our close study since it expresses the orthodox Christian resolution to the problem of the relationship between God the Father, the God of the Old Testament, and God the Son, the Atenist Deity of the New.

It begins with what appears to be an unconditional assertion of the singularity and primacy of God the Father:

I believe in one God the Father almighty, creator of heaven and earth; maker of all things visible and invisible.

This appears to say that God is one, is omnipotent and, by implication at least, omniscient and omnipresent by virtue of being the creator of all things. It also emphasizes his paternal quality. No Jew—or Dinka, or Nuer, for that matter—would object to this. However, the creed continues:

And in one Lord Jesus Christ, the only begotten Son of God; born of his Father before all worlds . . .

This clearly implies the subordination of Christ to God the Father and, what is more, emphasizes the sexual aspect of their relation because it insists in a way which is quite inappropriate to an omniscient, omnipotent, and omnipresent, non-anthropomorphic Deity that Christ is *begotten* and *born* (in the

Latin: *filium Dei unigenitum et ex patre natum ante omnia saecula*). But, having implied this filial subordination of Christ, the next series of statements goes on to assert not Christ's subordination, but his equality with God:

God of God, Light of Light, True God of True God; begotten, not made, one in substance with the Father, through whom all things were made.

The severe confusion which this series of statements introduces is clear to anyone who reads them with a rational mind; but it would be wrong to dismiss them as merely the outcome of erroneous reasoning or weak logic. Psychoanalysis is habituated to seeing in such manifestly-absurd assertions evidence of unconscious wishes which cannot be made to conform with reality but which are expressed as if they were rational and intelligible in order to fulfil important unconscious needs. This is true of all dogmas, sacred or secular, but it is especially true of this part of the Nicene Creed. It asserts that Christ is subordinate to the Father but is one in substance with him—that is, *identical* with him. True, it repeats the earlier statement that he is *begotten* and opposes this to being made: '*genitum non factum*', presumably to deny that Christ is a creature; but then it also goes on to say '*per quem omnia facta sunt*' ('through whom all things were made'), which can be taken to mean that all things were made through Christ, and which clearly contradicts the opening claims that it is God the Father who is creator of all things.

In short, the Nicene Creed does not solve the problem of the relationship of the Son to the Father. It only confuses it further, and seems to assert that one should simultaneously hold that there is only one God, and that there are two. Actually, the situation is even worse than this because later in the creed a third Deity is introduced, the Holy Spirit, who, we are told, 'together with the Father and the Son is adored and glorified'. He is defined as 'Lord and Giver of Life' in the Nicene Creed and makes three appearances in the New Testament: at the conception of Christ, at his baptism by John, and at Pentecost. In each case he is associated with birth, or rather with *begetting*. The Holy Spirit begets Christ by the Virgin Mary who conceives through the ear.[45] Christ's baptism is a rite of rebirth from God, who claims his paternity, using the words of Psalm 2 mentioned above.[46] On Whit Sunday the Holy Ghost begets the apostles as the earthly sons of God. In Catholic liturgy the Holy Spirit is referred to as *digitus dextrae patris*. Róheim draws attention to the phallic significance of the finger and hand, and to the fact that Ishtar, who was a dove-goddess, also appears as a hand.[47] Among the Egyptians the dove has the reputation of killing its father and mating with its mother. Jones points out that the dove which represents the Holy Ghost at the conception

[45] Ernest Jones, 'The Madonna's Conception Through the Ear', in *Essays in Applied Phychoanalysis*, Vol. II, 266ff.
[46] See above, p. 150.
[47] *Animism, Magic and the Divine King*, p. 157.

of Christ is evidently a phallic symbol.[48] This explains the Holy Ghost's association with paternity and conception, but it leaves us with the problem of having to explain why a third form of the Deity is needed in Christianity. I cannot accept Jones' conclusion that the Holy Ghost represents a female deity and so completes the series 'Father' and 'Son' with the term 'Mother'. This does not seem to follow from the evidence he adduces (which is essentially what I have reproduced above), and seems to me to raise more problems than it can possibly solve. My own solution to the problem of the third person of the trinity is much simpler and far more obviously in accordance with the facts. If God the Father represents the punitive, feared aspects of the God of Judaism inherited by Christianity, and if Christ represents the Son-God who corresponds to the Atenist conception of a beneficent saviour-god, then the Holy Spirit, who seems to be something of an afterthought even in the Nicene Creed, represents the residual attributes of the original Judaic Deity. These residual attributes are actually those of the pastoral monotheism and are comparable to those of the God of the Nuer and Dinka. Besides being a paternal and punitive agency (that is, the super-ego), the God of the primitive pastoralists also has the attributes of being a *spirit* (that is, a quasi-meteorological presence which permeates everywhere) which, in certain circumstances, might possess people. The persons possessed by this spirit are called 'prophets'. According to the words of the Nicene Creed, it was the Holy Spirit who 'spoke through the prophets (*'qui locutus est per prophetas'*). Finally, the Holy Spirit is the *third* person of the Holy Trinity, and we know that the number 'three' always has phallic significance.[49] Here the attribute of being the third—that is, the most eminently *phallic*—person of the trinity is fused with being the possessor-spirit, so that the third person is the inseminating agency of the Deity.

With the formulation of the Nicene Creed and the establishment of imperial authority over the Church, the bitter conflicts over the nature of the Christian Deity—or rather, *Deities*—reached some sort of provisional solution. As we have seen, it was a compromise. It could hardly have been otherwise. As a compromise and an attempted synthesis of different and even contradictory notions of God it was bound to be unstable; but as a dogmatic solution it succeeded, and remained the definitive, official solution of the problem. What it meant effectively was that the unified Judaic conception of God, compounded as it was of ancient Hebrew pastoral monotheism and Atenism, underwent a decomposition in the course of which it broke down into three elements each of which was defined in dogmatic terms as equal and consubstantial with the others. The first of these was God the Father, in fact the punitive paternal authority of pastoral monotheism who, in a non-pastoral economic ambiance, declined in importance. The second was God the Son—Christ—who was a new Aten who had undergone the fate of the

---

[48] 'A Study of the Holy Ghost', *op. cit.*, p. 365.
[49] Freud, *Introductory Lectures on Psychoanalysis*, XV, 163.

male gods of polytheism out of which the Aten developed, and been castrated and killed, resurrected and assumed into heaven. In a religion which
had now become that of a great empire, his importance increased. Finally
came the Holy Spirit, the Deity who took on all the residual attributes left
over from the old Hebrew pastoral God. Inevitably he remained a somewhat
shadowy and unimportant figure, as befitted his origin. By means of an
ambiguous, logically fallacious, and conceptually-confused dogmatic definition these three Gods were said to be One, and failure to accept this obvious
absurdity was punished by the severest means. The result was that doctrinally
the religion had reached a solution of sorts to its inner conflict, but there was
no guarantee that in other respects Christianity would be able to ward off the
tendencies within it towards dissolution of the synthesis that produced a
largely-obsessional outcome in Judaism. On the contrary, the tendency to
separate out the persons of the Deity (notwithstanding the casuistry that
attempted to unify them) is a psychological trait characteristic of paranoia.
Schreber's God underwent a comparable process of splitting, first into two,
and then into dozens of different parts. 'A process of decomposition of this
kind,' says Freud,

is very characteristic of paranoia. Paranoia decomposes just as hysteria condenses. Or
rather, paranoia resolves once more into their elements the products of the conden-
sations and identifications which are effected in the unconscious.[50]

In the case of heretical sects such as the Gnostics, obsessional counter-
tendencies such as those revealed in the tortuous logic of the Nicene Creed
were largely absent, and Marcion, one of the greatest gnostic teachers, came
very close to the true state of affairs when he taught that there were two Gods,
a punitive, jealous, and angry God portrayed in the Old Testament, and a
supreme, forgiving, and benevolent God portrayed in the New. The latter
God sent his son to save mankind, but servants of the former God (the Jews)
killed him. However, their action was the undoing of the Old Testament God,
and led to the freeing of men from the legalistic requirements of the Jewish
law, which was now replaced by a simple trust in divine providence.

In Marcion's gnostic heresy the psychological forces which were making
for the dissolution of the Judaic synthesis between pastoral monotheism and
Atenism were given a clear expression in terms of a theological delusion.
That delusion was successfully countered by dogmatic instruments such as the
Nicene Creed, which sought to cling to the old obsessional insistence on monotheism. But, as we have seen, this was only a formal and superficial measure
of defence. In terms of its fundamental psychology, Christian monotheism
was irremediably compromised. Marcion's heresy lay in revealing the fact.

On the religious level, a move from obsessional and neurotic mechanisms

[50] 'Psychoanalytic Notes on an Autobiographical Account of a Case of Paranoia',
XII, 49.

towards narcissistic and psychotic ones meant increasing tendencies to polytheism. We have already seen that the first, and most important manifestation of this was in the doctrine of the Trinity. This, in itself, had clear precedents in ancient Egyptian polytheism, where gods were often grouped in threes, the most important being the son-mother-father trinity of Horus, Isis, and Osiris. Despite the dogmatic definitions of the councils, pre-Protestant Christianity does not deserve to be regarded as a true monotheism; and as time went by its claims in this respect became more and more hollow. Increasingly, it became a Christian polytheism in which the gods and goddesses of Graeco-Roman and Egyptian polytheism staged a spectacular return from the repressed. Each one of the different strata of religious belief which characterize polytheism reappears in a peculiarly Christian form. The oldest, and perhaps most fundamental of these, that of animistic deities, returns as the angelic hierarchies. According to the Pseudo-Dionysius,[51] all things, both animate and inanimate, participate in the Divine Being. In psychological terms, we might say that they are subject to the omnipotence of the thoughts of God. This includes those animate but immaterial beings who constitute the heavenly hierarchies and who do the will of God with regard to his creatures. But these animistic agencies of command and control of the world are also accessible to human prayer. Men could, through the grace of God, attempt to influence those spiritual forces in various ways and thereby satisfy their long-lost desire to see their most impossible wishes come true. Miracles—that is, satisfaction of such wishes in contravention of reality—abound. If they are not the work of the angelic agencies, they are produced by the saints. Here, the return of polytheism is too obvious to be missed by anyone. Many saints in the calendar are only thinly-disguised Christian versions of pagan deities who have been baptized by canonization but whose attributes and origins are still discernible as pre-Christian. Their cults are modelled on the polytheistic rites of the pagan deities. They have their festival days; they receive the appropriate offerings (in the case of one South Italian saint, these are clay models of the male genitals which are brought to the church for blessing by the women of the town; and in a village in the Abruzzi live vipers are offered to St Dominic). They are prayed to and have vows made to them in the same superstituous (i.e. animistic) manner familiar to us from traditional polytheism. Like the deities of ancient Greece and Egypt, the saints of pre-Protestant Christianity are expected to do what their worshippers expect, and run the risk of their anger if they fail. It is believed that the saints can be manipulated by the correct prayers and ritual observances, and that they in their turn can animistically manipulate destiny so that what is demanded of them can be achieved. Hence, one of the main qualifications for canonization becomes the working of miracles. No saint can be admitted to that élite spiritual status until he has shown what he can do for suffering humanity.

---

[51] Dionysius the Areopagite, *The Celestial Hierarchies*, p. 32.

Such regulations reveal the true animistic basis of the cult of saints. They are the polytheistic deities returned from the repressed and given a subordinate status beneath the principal trinity of Christian Deities.

In an austere monotheism like Judaism prayer was a matter of moral and spiritual self-abasement before the awesome splendour of the Deity. The Hebrew prophets constantly reiterate that what God demands is not sacrifices of the blood of animals (that is, ritual observances) but frank confession and true worship from the heart. Righteousness in his worshippers is more pleasing to him than the smell of burnt offerings. In pre-Protestant Christianity prayer becomes essentially what it is among the polytheists: a matter of the repetition of magical spells with which to influence and gain the goodwill of the deities. Repetition by rote becomes more valuable than sincere feeling. Saying the *Ave Maria* or the *Pater Noster* a hundred times is seen as more efficacious than saying it once. Whereas the Jewish prophets taught that the intention is all-important, in Catholic and Orthodox Christianity it is the form of the words which matters. In this way prayer approaches the condition of being little more than a magical spell. Along with this tendency, amulets, charms, talismans, and magical objects of all kinds reappear as sacred medals, relics of saints, wood from the True Cross, and even, in one case, the foreskin of Christ. These material objects are believed to have magical properties which will benefit those who touch, revere, or possess them. In medieval Europe the cult of relics, holy medallions, and other such objects achieved a degree of development only rivalled by the ancient Egyptians with their ubiquitous scarabs and spell-inscribed amulets.

The animistic omnipotence of thoughts therefore attains a return from the repressed in early and medieval Christianity closely comparable to that seen in ancient polytheisms. In the angelic hierarchies animism becomes institutionalized in the way in which I have described, and it is even possible that, as Wallis Budge observes, the spiritual presences mentioned in the ancient Egyptian Pyramid Texts constitute the origins of the Christian angelic hosts.[52] The saints, too, become subject to the general animistic atmosphere of polytheism, although they undoubtedly belong to the stratum of polytheistic deities *per se* rather than to that of animistic residues. When discussing polytheism in terms of this geological analogy, I argued that it was likely that the first anthropomorphic deities were the Earth-Mother goddesses who originated in that distant epoch when women invented agriculture and provided the occasion for the coming of the new religious and economic order. It is significant that in Christianity this priority of the Mother-Goddess is reflected in the primacy of the Virgin in the hierarchy of saints.

The psychological process which transforms an obscure Jewish carpenter's wife who seems to have conceived out of wedlock into a universally-worshipped Queen of Heaven whose attributes include eternal virginity,

[52] *From Fetish to God in Ancient Egypt*, p. 336.

motherhood of God, fullness of grace, and immaculate virtue is a not-uninteresting one. It is unintelligible unless we take note of the extent and importance of the return of the repressed in pre-Protestant Christianity. Significantly, it was at Ephesus that an early ecumenical council attributed to her the most efficacious and glorious name that she was to possess—that of 'theotokos', 'Mother of God'. As Freud points out,[53] Ephesus had always been an important centre of the Great Goddess cult in classical times, and it was the famous temple of Diana (Artemis) at Ephesus which Herostratus burnt down 'so that history should not forget his name'. Here, Mary is alleged to have lived with the apostle John, and it was here in Freud's own time that the famous German visionary and hysteric, Anne Catherine Emmerich, redis-covered the house of the Virgin. Accounts of the Council of Ephesus leave little doubt that the bishops, who were beseiged by the populace, would have been lynched if they had come to any lesser conclusion than to attribute to Mary the dignity of 'Mother of God'. The incredible scenes of festivity and joy which greeted the decision reflect the supreme importance which the Ephesians attached to having a cult of the Great Virgin Mother. Once Mary acquired this title she rapidly added all the other attributes of the Great Goddess. She was Diana-Artemis-Athena-Isis-Aphrodite-Ishtar returned from Polytheism (or, more accurately, at least in places like Ephesus, continued into Christianity under another name). If goddesses come first in the evolution of the polytheistic pantheons as I have suggested, the pre-eminence of the Blessed Virgin Mary among the saints can be partly accounted for as a late return to this situation; and if the presence of such female goddesses is what is perhaps most distinctive of polytheism, then Catholicism and Orthodox Christianity bear the unmistakable signs of being quasi-polytheisms as much as they do those of being near-monotheisms. What is exceptional about Mary's process of canonization—or, rather, *deification*—is that it continued right up to modern times, and in an increasingly regressive way restored to her more and more of the lost attributes of the original Mother-Goddess. Had the last of the great Tridentine popes, Pius XII, lived, there is every reason to suppose that Mary, who in 1950 had been proclaimed bodily assumed into heaven, like Christ, would have also been proclaimed *Co-redemptrix* and therefore virtually part of the Trinity. (The cessation of this tendency to deify the Virgin is probably one of the most fundamental symp-toms of the decline of the Catholic Church in the modern world and evidence that its inherent nature has undergone irreversible changes which will render its continued existence problematic in the extreme and its role in history played out.) Jones' assumption that the mother ought to be the third person of the Trinity, although not in accordance with the facts of early Christianity, would probably have been fulfilled if Pius XII had lived a little longer; then

53 'Great is Diana of the Ephesians', XII, 342ff.

the Christian—or at least Catholic—Trinity would have been very close to the Horus-Osiris-Isis pattern of ancient Egyptian polytheism.

As far as the later, male deities of this stratum of polytheistic belief is concerned, it is clear that most male saints play their role. The halo of the saints, not to mention the crown of the martyrs, seems to be a regal attribute which accords with the belief that the saints will reign with Christ in the heavenly kingdom. The careful preservation of their bodies and of relics associated with them is another respect in which they resemble the deified kings of ancient Egyptian and other polytheisms. The beatitude which they enjoy is only a very-much-revised version of the beatitude of the Pharaohs of the Pyramid Texts, who went about having their way with men and women, cannibalizing whom they pleased and indulging to the full the pleasure of their instincts. The beatific vision of the saints is only an aesthetically and morally-improved variation on the theme of enjoying after death all that one was not able to enjoy during one's lifetime.

Above all, Christ's own position in the Christian pantheon as incarnate Son of God reveals the polytheism underlying the religion up to the Reformation, and even beyond. We have already seen how the chief gods of the polytheistic pantheons can be regarded as deified kings, and how kings can be seen as incarnate deities. Osiris, we will recall, was the first and greatest king of Egypt. He was also, for many, the first and greatest of the gods. Divine kings are the gods incarnate in polytheism because they represent the return of the primal father to the earth and his re-establishment as the paternal authority of the primal horde of agriculture—the kingdom. Christ, too, has a kingdom; he, too, is a king. He is the incarnation of the Deity just as each divine king of the Shilluk is the reincarnation of *Nyikang*,[54] or as each Pharaoh reincarnates Horus in his lifetime and becomes Osiris on his death.

As far as the temporal power of such divine kings, or royal divinities, is concerned, we can perhaps see it in the case of Christianity reflected not in the earthly career of Christ himself, but in the aspirations of his vicars, the popes. They acquired the title of the chief priest of ancient Rome, *pontifex maximus*, and, in the course of time, an impressive temporal jurisdiction over the Papal States. The inability of any temporal power to achieve universal dominion of the ancient Roman sort during the Dark and Middle Ages resulted in the popes getting what territory they could and indulging their quasi-polytheistic but frustrated imperialism in a doctrine of spiritual supremacy and legal dominion over all. In the reign of Innocent III—the pope who proclaimed the dogma of trans-substantiation—papal power reached its apogee; and in that of his successor, Innocent IV, the claims of the papacy to *universalis potestas* ('world dominion') were canonically defined. In men like Innocent III the Pharaohs of the XVIIIth Dynasty would have found much to admire. The ritual regalism of the court, the sacerdotal functions of the

[54] See above, pp. 67, 71.

Sovereign Pontiff, and his legal and religious dominion over the whole known world would have seemed most familiar to them, as might even some of the very details of their religious belief. The popes inherited a tradition of political imperialism from the Roman Empire, and one of religious imperialism from Egypt via Judaism. Their power never coincided with an Augustan period of their own; they came too late for the Roman one and too early for the golden age of imperialism in modern Europe. But even if imperialistic monotheism and aspirations to world dominion were only derived realities in medieval Catholicism, they were realities nevertheless and reproduced in mimic fashion much of the polytheistic imperialism out of which they grew.

Even the totemic, theriomorphic characteristics of divine kings such as the Pharaoh-as-Sphinx[55] are not lacking in Christianity. Christ, in Christian iconography, is typically spoken of as 'the Lamb of God', and, like all divine kings, is an incarnation of the totem-father. In so far as the Mass is a version of Orphic-Dionysian-Osirian totem rituals, polytheistic totemism can be seen as present in the religion precisely where it was present in ancient Greek or Egyptian religion: namely, in the mystery cult. To some extent the Mass becomes an animistic-magical conjuring trick designed to obtain what supplicants want of their God (for example, requiem and votive Masses); but it is much more the equivalent of the mysteries, during which, as we have seen, initiates undergo ritual purgation (Confession), spiritual enlightenment (Gospel, Homily), and finally, union with the Deity through the totem meal (Communion). In so far as the inner psychological meaning of all this was rediscovered by St Paul, the Mass is a uniquely Christian thing, but in so far as St Paul's experience in particular and Christian ritual in general stands on a common foundation with that of the mystery religions, the Mass was a return of the repressed in a double sense: first, as a return of the pagan mysteries, and second, as a return of the totemism which those mysteries themselves perpetuated within polytheism.

This leads us to the remaining aspect of polytheism which can be found transmuted into Christian tradition. In my earlier discussion of polytheism I said that the thunder-gods of the polytheistic panthions like Zeus and Jupiter were late additions of pastoral and monotheistic origin. In Christianity these deities are contained in the first and third persons of the Trinity. St Thomas Aquinas was of the opinion that ringing the bells of churches could avert lightning, which strongly suggests that in the mind of the angelic doctor, God had some of the meteorological attributes of Zeus or the Nuer 'kwoth'. I have already argued that pastoral monotheistic elements make up the persons of the Father and the Holy Spirit, and as we have seen, Christ can be regarded as the equivalent of the divine monarch who becomes the imperial divinity and, ultimately, the Aten. Thus, the persons of the Trinity, plus the

[55] See above, pp. 60, 67.

Virgin Mary, the saints, martyrs, and angelic hierarchies, make up a pantheon which in no major respect fails to correspond to that of a classic polytheism.

Finally, it is worth pointing out that this process of 'the return of the repressed' was not limited to the sacred sphere but seems to have overflowed into the purely secular. Classical paganism returns to other aspects of culture besides the religious during the period that we call the Renaissance. The latter is usually regarded as the beginning of modern times rather than the culmination of the Middle Ages, but there is a sense in which the Renaissance is indeed the final outcome of what went before. This is the extent to which it is a return of the repressed elements of classical civilization which were overlaid, but not destroyed, by medieval Christendom. As classical polytheism reasserted itself in the religion, so classical culture in general seems to have returned to the surface and, in this sense, to be reborn.

But however important the return of the repressed may have been in pre-Protestant Christianity, it would be a grave mistake to imagine that it was the only important psychological feature of the religion. On the contrary, there was another which was of equal, or perhaps even of greater importance. This second psychological component is what I have called the 'renunciation of instinct'. The fact that this enters into the situation and exists alongside the return of the repressed should not surprise us in the least. In every previous stage in the evolution of world-religion that we have examined in the course of this book both the return of the repressed and the renunciation of instinct have been present and have been the two principal evolutionary mechanisms. In the case of totemism, the renunciation of instinct was represented by the institution of inhibitions on incest and parricide that enabled hominids to maintain a social structure adapted to hunting. The return of the repressed was represented by the return of the primal father as the conscience of the sons and the totem of the clan. In polytheism, renunciations and inhibitions of instinctual gratification were required by the establishment of an agricultural economy and the rational administration of land and agricultural products that it demanded. The return of the repressed was associated in this case with a reappearance of the old primal horde social structures in the new agricultural communities and the re-emergence of the primal father, not now in the guise of a totem, but in that of divine king. Finally, in monotheism, a renunciation of instinctual gratification was obtained by the suppression of aggressive drives against the totem-father, which economic dependence on domestic animals required, and an accompanying intellectualization and abstraction of the idea of God. Here the totemic basis of the monotheist psychology and the return to an economy based on animal protein corresponded to the return of the repressed. In early and medieval Christianity, polytheism returned from the repressed in the manner I have already suggested, but a notable instinctual renunciation also occurred—indeed, as the perspicacious reader will already have realized from the evidence of this brief summary, the two things seem to go together. A consideration of why this is so will have to be postponed until the last chapter, but for the present let us return to the question of Christianity and enquire into the nature of the renunciation of instinct which was peculiar to it.

The renunciation of instinctual gratification represented by Christianity is enshrined in the moral precepts of the Sermon on the Mount and the epistles of St Paul. The essence of these teachings, which is that one should love others as much, or more, than one loves oneself, is pure altruism. Of course, all renunciations of instinct are likely to be instances of altruism in a species which lacks the instinctive altruism of other animals as ours does. But different religious ethics differ in the degree of altruism demanded. In totemism, altruism is limited to what is necessary to make a hunting economy work, and no more. In monotheism, altruism reaches higher development, especially in the more advanced monotheisms like Judaism. In the latter case, a level of altruistic behaviour is demanded that is not expected of Australian aborigines. Far higher standards of submission to paternal authority within the family and state, stricter controls on sexual activity, and more extensive social limitations on egoism typify the higher monotheisms. But even these high standards are exceeded by Christianity, which demands *total* altruism. This is why the more precepts of Christianity are so simple by contrast to the elaborate laws of Judaism. 'Love they neighbour as thyself' really *is* the Law and the Prophets of Christianity and St Paul could say that there remain Faith, Hope, and Charity, but the greatest is undoubtedly Charity—that is, Altruism. It is interesting to see both Christ and the founder of scientific sociology, Edmund O. Wilson, giving the same definition of altruism. Christ says: 'Greater love hath no man than this, that he lay down his life for his friend.' Wilson says: 'When a person (or animal) increases the fitness of another at the expense of his own fitness, he can be said to have performed an act of altruism.'[56] The essence of Christian ethics is a demand for unlimited altruism in this sense, and for total love of one's neighbour, even one's enemies. Of course, it contains a paradox which is of the first significance. This is, that by acting altruistically individuals may promote the fitness of others who are much less altruistic than themselves, with the result that overall altruism declines. In all other animals who have evolved altruistic behaviour the altruism in question is largely instinctual and therefore under genetic control, so that an equilibrium can easily be reached by means of which selective forces establish just the right amount of self-sacrifice to maintain a viable system with a stable level of altruism. In the human animal altruism is, as we have seen, much more a question of psychological determinants (mainly the super-ego), and so equilibriation of the level of altruism is not so simple. But let us return to Christianity, and solely retain from this brief digression the observation that Christianity calls for a high and perhaps self-defeating level

[56] E. O. Wilson, *Sociobiology*, p. 117.

of altruism, and that the instinctual renunciation represented by the teachings of the founders of the religion was one of perfect selflessness.

Put another way, one could say that it was an ideal of perfect *masochism*. To promote the fitness of another at one's own expense is clearly to injure one's own fitness, at least in the short run. To love others—even enemies—as much, or more, than oneself is clearly to mortify one's narcissism and egoism and to divert it to the love of others who may well be much less worthy of it. Or, at least, so it would seem. Yet here we encounter a paradox: I have said that Christianity was notably altruistic, that is, masochistic, yet earlier I was arguing that in Christianity narcissism was enhanced, rather than reduced.

The apparent contradiction here reflects an exactly similar position in paranoia. In that case, narcissistic regression and a general increase in the libido directed towards the ego are obviously present—indeed, as we have seen, these are the principal pathological aspects of any psychosis. Yet masochistic suffering is also found in psychotics, perhaps especially in paranoiacs. Speaking of Schreber, Freud says:

He believed that he was dead and decomposing, that he was suffering from the plague; he asserted that his body was being handled in all kinds of revolting ways; and, as he himself declares to this day, he went through worse horrors than any one could have imagined, and all on behalf of a holy purpose.[57]

The mention of a 'holy purpose' should alert us, if we were not sufficiently aware of it already, to a close parallel with the situation as we find it in Christianity. Here, too, the masochistic suffering is for a sacred end, and is vindicated in part by its moral value.

In a discussion of moral masochism, Freud remarks that there is a difference between *masochism of the ego* and *sadism of the super-ego*.[58] Although both may look superficially alike in that in both cases the super-ego punishes the ego to an intense degree, nevertheless a fundamental difference exists between them. Essentially it is the same difference as that between pastoral monotheism and Christianity for, in the former case, we have a sadistic super-ego (punitive God), while in the latter we have a masochistic ego (as Freud says, 'the true masochist always turns the other cheek whenever there is a chance of receiving a blow').[59] This cheek-turning propensity of the masochist reveals the essential difference. The person with the sadistic super-ego (the pastoral monotheist) does not go looking for punishment, he just accepts it when it comes as the will of God, and submits, morosely (we will recall that pastoral monotheists are subject to depression to an unusual degree). The masochist (Christian), on the other hand, positively looks for opportunities to be humiliated,

[57] 'Psychoanalytic Notes on an Autobiographical Account of a Case of Paranoia', XII, 13–14.
[58] 'The Economic Problem of Masochism', XIX, 169.
[59] *Ibid.*, XIX, 165.

and unconsciously enjoys them—or, at least, uses them to ease the burden of an unconscious sense of guilt.

In the case of Schreber, these humiliations took on a sexual tinge, as suggested in the quotation above where it mentions his body 'being handled in all kinds of revolting ways', and in his discussion of moral masochism Freud concludes that the unconscious sense of guilt that occasions it is only a desexualized version of an unconscious desire to be beaten by the father. Here, moral and erotogenic masochism coincide, since in both cases pleasure is derived from maltreatment of the body. Finally, the third form of masochism isolated by Freud, the *feminine*, also becomes relevant, since submission to sexual assault at the hands of the father casts the ego in a passive, feminine sexual role. In Schreber's case, this resulted in his complete emasculation: 'He took up a feminine attitude towards God; he felt that he was God's wife.'[60]

That such considerations may be relevant to Christianity is suggested by the following remarks of St Paul.

Do you not know that he who joins himself to a prostitute becomes one body with her? . . . But he who is united to the Lord becomes one spirit with him . . . Do you not know that your body is the temple of the Holy Spirit within you.[61]

As the Church is subject to Christ, so let wives be subject to their husbands. Husbands love your wives as Christ loved the Church.[62]

It is by no means self-evident that he who joins himself to a prostitute becomes one body with her, and if this is St Paul's idea of an illustrative metaphor, it is notable that it is a metaphor which is based on the further metaphor that sees a man and a woman having sexual intercourse as constituting one body. If we reverse the order of the metaphors, they correspond to the second analogy which he draws: namely, that Christ is to his followers as a husband is to his wife, and now the quotation reads: 'Do you not know that he who is united to the Lord becomes one with him as a prostitute does with him who has intercourse with her (i.e. sexually, and in the feminine role)?' Through symbolism like this the Church—*Mater Ecclesia*—becomes the bride of Christ, and those who participate in that mystical body become by implication brides as well. The symbolic death and castration which St Paul underwent at the hand of God on the road to Damascus are hysterical equivalents of the passive subjugation to the super-ego which is the essence of moral masochism, and which is itself based on phantasies of incestuous and homosexual self-prostitution to the father.[63]

The same remarks might apply to the appalling suffering and the psychic

---

[60] Freud, 'Psychoanalytic Notes on a Case of Paranoia', XII, 32.

[61] I Corinthians VI, vv. 16–17.

[62] Ephesians V, vv. 24–5.

[63] For a masterly analysis of the part played by homosexual passivity to the father in obsessional neurosis, and its impact on world-history, see Freud and Bullitt, *Woodrow Wilson*.

emasculation to which Schreber had to submit. In both cases the masochistic suffering was more than balanced by the unconscious sexual—indeed, *homo-sexual*—pleasure which that suffering occasioned. In so far as a feminine, passive, and homosexual enjoyment of the sadism of the super-ego is a gratification of the masochistic ego, we can certainly say that Christianity, although more narcissistic in certain respects than Judaism, was also the more masochistic. Thus the high degree of altruism demanded by Christianity reflects the intense masochism on which the religion is founded. It is hardly surprising that the gospel of supreme altruism was first taught by a man whose masochism led him to undergo voluntarily a protracted and agonizing death, or that it was first preached by followers whose chief concern seems to have been to have themselves persecuted and tortured as extensively and elaborately as possible. Those who gratified their moral pride by telling themselves that they were undergoing conversion to an ethical system of absolute and perfect altruism were in reality being seduced into a form of indulgence in the perverse joys of masochism and the hidden delights of unconscious homosexual eroticism. Like Schreber, they suffered terrible agonies; yet, like him, they suffered all for a holy purpose: for the love of the Father, and in his chastisements they felt his thrilling touch.

Yet one question of the greatest importance remains left over from our consideration of Christian altruism, and that is this: Why did it occur? We know that the instinctual renunciation represented by totemism occurred because of the economic consequences of guilt following parricide and attempted incest. In the case of polytheism and monotheism the renunciation in question had enormous adaptive consequences in making new economies possible. But what economy did Christianity make possible? And what motivated its incredibly altruistic ideals in the first place?

Let us answer the second question first, and begin by looking back over the cases so far considered. One thing will strike us immediately. This is that if we ask why the renunciation of instinct came about *in the first place*, the answer always is that it did so *because it carried a gratification for someone*. In the case of totemism, that gratification was the parricidal and incestuous satis-faction which bands of young hominid hunters experienced when they actu-ally attacked their true fathers and appropriated their true mothers and sisters. It was the guilt and remorse that followed this gratification that produced the renunciation and made greater altruism possible through the totemic and incest taboos. The renunciation was therefore obtained as a result of a prior gratification. Once totemism was established, this situation continued in a symbolic way in that initiations and other ceremonies provided mitigated gratifications of the very instincts which totemism was set up to control. Similarly, with polytheism, it was the gratification of the desire of the more masculine women to be as men and have a penis that, as I showed, must have led to the discovery of agriculture. As a consequence, it also led to patterns of child-rearing which instilled into children greater capacity for the deferment of gratification, that was to be the principal renunciation demanded by agriculture. In monotheism, it was again a feminine gratification, but this time that of more feminine women who wanted to treat young animals as babies, which made possible the initial discovery of domestication and which brought about as a consequence, the suppression of aggression against animals which was to be the psychological basis of pastoralism and monotheism alike. Throughout, there appears to be a clear pattern of instinctual gratification followed by consequences involving renunciations or repressions which lead to economically profitable results and which in turn guarantee the persistence of the instinctual renunciations in question. So much is clear from the cases of totemism, polytheism, and monotheism. But what of Christianity? Where does it fit into this otherwise elegant and satisfying pattern?

If we examine the question of the origin of the renunciation in a previous instinctual gratification, Christianity does seem to fit into this pattern in the following way: In totemism, the gratification was that of *men acting as men* (that is, motivated by lust for females and in competition against other men—the fathers); in the case of polytheism, it was a question of *women acting as men* (that is, planting their seed in Mother Earth); in that of monotheism, *women acting as women* (mothering animals); and finally, I have already established that the homosexual basis of Christian ethical masochism is a question of *men acting as women*. In short, the answer to the question of what instinct altruistic self-repression like that demanded by the Sermon on the Mount can possibly be expected to gratify is that it can be expected to gratify a masochistic homosexual tendency found in men who have a masochistic ego and a negative resolution of the Oedipus complex. Put in these terms, Christianity fits into the pattern previously established for totemism, polytheism, and monotheism in an exact and satisfactory way. Now we see that, whereas totemism and hunting are based on a *positive Oedipal resolution in men*, polytheism and agriculture are based on a *negative Oedipal resolution in women*; and, just as pastoralism and monotheism are dependent on a *positive resolution in women*, so Christianity and any economic corollary it might have is apparently a question of a *negative resolution in men*.

Now let us turn to the second question, that of the success of the renunciations embodied in the Christian ethic. If we ask why the renunciations on which totemism, polytheism, or monotheism relied were maintained against the tendency of human beings to seek to escape from them, the answer must be that these religious systems supported economies whose adaptive value far outweighed the psychological cost in terms of human happiness which the instinctual renunciations in question demanded. If this general principle is correct it should apply to Christianity just as well as it does to the other cases which we have examined.

The economy characteristic of early and medieval Christianity is what we can call genuine agriculture (mixed farming). Now, of course, ancient Egypt and ancient Greece were agricultural economies in this sense; but the point

I made about polytheism is that it originated in, and owed its early success to an economy which was based on cultivation, originally carried on by women, and which existed before the domestication of animals. Monotheism arose in societies which were strictly speaking agricultural, in the sense that plants are usually cultivated to a considerable extent (usually by women). But again, pastoralism *per se* was what was relevant to the development of monotheistic deities, and so one could say that herding is the typical economic corollary of monotheism, just as the cultivation of plants is that of polytheism. One does not *have* to grow vegetable crops on the side in order to be a pastoral mono-theist but, as I have shown, one *must* keep domesticated animals; this is why, as we saw in an earlier chapter, a strong positive correlation exists between the extent of the economic dependence on herding and the extent of the monotheism. Similarly, one does not *have* to keep domestic farm animals to be a polytheist, although it helps in the sense that they can do useful work in the agricultural economy; however, as I have shown, one *must* practise the cultivation of domesticated plants in order to give rise to the psychological processes which maintain the system of polytheism. Furthermore, it is clear that both cultivation and pastoralism so defined would not exist were it not for the original psychological changes which gave rise to them and to their associated forms of religion.

As far as early and medieval Christianity is concerned, the implication of these observations must be that one *must* practise both the cultivation of crops *and* the keeping of herds to maintain the religious system. We have already seen that the essence of Christianity is that it contains within it both the God of Hebrew pastoral monotheism and the God of Atenist monotheism. There-fore one would expect—especially in view of the tremendous return of repressed polytheism which characterized early and medieval Christianity—that the religion would correlate with an economy that was a mixture of both pastoralism and cultivation, and this, at least in the senses in which I have understood these terms, is precisely what it was. We may conclude that, far from upsetting the generalizations so far established, pre-Protestant Chris-tianity fits in exactly where it should; and that in terms of renunciations that maintain themselves because of their economic significance, Christianity was a mixture of those of the two preceding stages in religious evolution. As such, it corresponded to an economy that was also a fusion of the two.

However, the reader may still have doubts about this situation. One of these may be that the explanation advanced above for the relationship be-tween the medieval agrarian economy and pre-Protestant Christianity is not a causal one like those I established between monotheism and pastoralism, or polytheism and cultivation. In the latter cases the religious ethic supported the system of production by enshrining psychological values which made it possible. The phallic mother-goddesses who appear to have been the earlier manifestations of polytheism enshrined psychological values which made possible an economy which in all probability relied on female agricultural expertise (at least in its initial stages), and, as we have seen, may also have featured genuine matriarchy. The vengeful sky-God of monotheism maintained the moral force which held in check the animal blood-lust of men and so made pastoralism possible. But did early Christianity make possible the first appearance of what I have termed true agriculture? By no means. Clearly, an economy of the medieval type was an inevitable development both of cultivation and pastoralism, and nearly all such economies followed this course independently of Christianity. Not merely in ancient Egypt and Greece, but in many other parts of the world, domestication of animals followed the domestication of plants to produce full-scale agrarian economies. Christianity in its early and medieval stages may have contained the right psychological propensities for such an economy, but it was not responsible for the original appearance of that form of production.

This is doubtless the reason why pre-Protestant Christianity came to resemble the religions of the agricultural economies it had succeeded to so closely. It is also the key to understanding the impressive return of the repressed which we have seen taking place throughout the first fifteen centuries of the Church. It is clear that the major facilitating factor was the fact that Christianity grew up for the most part in lands which had been polytheistic and agrarian before, such as the Near East, Italy, Greece, and Egypt. Polytheism returned so strongly because the economic basis of early Christianity was practically the same as that of late polytheism and because the places in which it underwent its crucial early evolution were saturated with Graeco-Roman and Egyptian polytheism. Thus, in so far as Christianity was the outcome of a breakdown of Jewish monotheism into its respective pastoral monotheistic and polytheistic parts, the economy to which it gave rise is exactly what we should have expected, even in its characteristic of being a repetition of the later economy of polytheism. In early and medieval Christianity God the Father came to play a role analogous to that played by quasi-monotheistic sky-gods like Zeus in the pantheons of late—that is, agrarian—polytheism. Christianity only differed in respect of the strength and quality of the monotheism which it had absorbed into itself.

Yet a difficulty still remains, and it is one to which we must resolutely face up. It is simply that, considered as a renunciation of instinct, Christianity seems to have been more than just a mixture of the renunciations achieved by the foregoing polytheisms and monotheisms. Although it indubitably contained such a mixture and equated in the Middle Ages at least with the agrarian economy that one would predict on that basis, it also featured advances in instinctual renunciation over and above what can be obtained by simply summing up monotheism and polytheism. Hebrew pastoral monotheism plus Egyptian imperialistic polytheism does not necessarily equal the Sermon on the Mount. Undoubtedly, there is an original element in Christianiaty not found in either. This original feature appears to be the perfect altruism enshrined in the gospels and the epistles and which goes far beyond anything necessary for the maintenance of a mixed pastoral-agricultural economy—as can be easily proved by the observation that in many parts of the world such economies have evolved without the need for Christian ethics. Perhaps the advance in instinctual renunciation implied in Christianity does not have any economic significance over and above that already suggested. Perhaps the trend established by the previous cases cannot be continued. Perhaps even though totemism, polytheism, and monotheism all equated with distinctive forms of economic life, the higher Christian ethic does not. Certainly, anyone who studied the early history of Christianity could be forgiven for believing that this was true. It is clear that those who held most faithfully to the precepts of the Sermon on the Mount could hardly have been expected to have any economic significance at all. If one sells all one has and gives it to the poor the economic effect is likely to be some redistribution of income, but no change in production. On the contrary, paying wages for no work—which is what such charity really means—is likely to undermine any existing system of production rather than to establish a new one. Furthermore, the masochistic ethic of Christianity did not end with charity to the poor. It led to Christians willingly giving up their lives in the persecutions and, once they were over, resorting to the most extreme mortifications obtainable by sitting on pillars for thirty or forty years like St Simon Stylites, or living alone in desert hermitages like other early ascetics. Those who carried mortification of their bodies to such extreme lengths could have no economic impact whatsoever, especially when perfection was interpreted as a hatred of life itself which caused those who pursued it to try to escape from the world into wildernesses or onto the tops of high pillars. In the careers of the early ascetics the masochistic factor in Christianity seems to have totally triumphed.

Yet it would be wrong to think that the ethical ideals of Christianity were to have no economic significance whatever. If the explanation of the origins of economic systems advanced in this book is correct one would most certainly expect them to have some effect; and, in so far as Christianity's instinctual renunciations were so much more comprehensive than those of other religions, one would expect them to have a proportionately greater significance. This is because repression is directly linked to economic effort. Cultivation is a more effective and successful mode of economic life than hunting because it demands greater instinctual renunciations and therefore makes possible more elaborate economic adaptations, specifically in the matter of restraining immediate consumption in the interests of future production. Pastoralism, by inhibiting the killing of animals to satisfy immediate hunger, does much the same. If Christianity makes so much greater instinctual renunciation necessary one might conclude, if one had the courage to stand by the theory implied in these observations, that Christianity must have given rise to an economy which is even more successful and highly adapted than those which preceded it. This is exactly what we find.

In so far as the early history of Christianity was dominated by the factor of the return of the repressed—and we have already seen how important this was—it corresponded with an economy which was comprised of elements of animal husbandry and agriculture. As I argued in the first part of this chapter, the economic ethic present in Christianity, in so far as it represented a return of classical religion, was the same as that of late antiquity and featured elements of pastoral monotheism and agricultural polytheism. However, in so far as Christianity featured unique advances in rationality not already found in Judaism or Graeco-Roman polytheism, it gave rise to a distinctive form of economic life that was wholly determined by those advances. The economic form in question is what we know as capitalism.

The precocious advance in instinctual renunciation enshrined in the ethical teaching of Christ and endorsed by St Paul was for a long while more-or-less wholly encapsulated within the religion, unable to influence economic life in any significant way. The mechanism of this encapsulation was religious asceticism. I have already remarked that originally the absolute altruism of Christianity could only be expressed in the way in which Christ had defined its ideal: as laying down one's life for one's friends. The long centuries of persecution saw countless Christians crucified, burned, decapitated, torn to pieces by wild animals, stoned, strangled, flogged to death in the galleys, worked to death in the mines. When the persecutions finished the strongly masochistic tone which Christianity had acquired persisted. The early anchorites and ascetics did what they could to persecute themselves in order to show that they were as good as the martyrs. In time, however, the epoch of the persecutions became more remote and the life of the ascetic less severe. It was softened initially by the very unconscious forces which had produced it. The unconscious homosexual element in Christian masochism tended to make anchorites come together in ascetic communities out of which the first monastic orders evolved. The idea appears to have occurred first to St Anthony, an Egyptian of the third century, in whose psychopathology sexual elements seem to have played a very obvious role—at least if the evidence of tradition is to be believed. His disciple, St Pachomius, founded the first monastic community. In the West, fully evolved monasticism begins with St Benedict in the sixth century.

Throughout this period and right up to the thirteenth-century monasticism served to encapsulate the ideal of renunciation contained in Christianity and provided an environment in which those whose masochism was sufficiently developed to make them despise the normal comforts of life could find institutions in which they could pursue perfection in common with others of like mind. Nevertheless, and as is perhaps only to be expected, a noticeable trend towards mitigation and softening of the masochistic rule is seen throughout this period. This was constantly countered by recurrent reforms which aimed to restore the original severity; but however much this may have occurred, and however much it may have succeeded in maintaining the fanatical masochism of the members of monastic orders, there is nevertheless discernible an apparently irreversible trend towards closer and closer involvement in the world and its works.

The reasons for this are not difficult to understand. Partly they spring from the tendency to mitigation and softening already mentioned, but perhaps more importantly the tendency to become involved with the secular world is a result of the ethical ideal itself. As the age of martyrs receded into ancient history and Christianity became established as a state religion, the masochistic ideals of the first few centuries of its existence became less marked and what that masochism was based on, namely, a subordination of the ego to the super-ego tinged with strong elements of passive homosexuality, came to the fore. Of course, it could not do so in any overtly genital way; the prudery of Christianity ensured that. But there was every reason why it should be expressed in a sublimated—that is, *de-sexualized*—form; and that is exactly what occurred. Masochistic asceticism gradually became more and more associated with charitable and humanitarian works. The anchorites of the fourth century, who lived alone and expected alms from others, gradually became replaced by communities of monks who farmed land, distributed alms to the poor, housed travellers, ran hospitals, and engaged in many other works of mercy.

A new and most significant departure occurred during the reign of Innocent III. At the very moment when the Catholic Church was reaching the height of its power, proclaiming the dogma of transubstantiation and extending the legal and political influence of the supreme pontiff, its ideal of ascetic existence decisively broke out of the confines of traditional monasticism and gave rise to the orders of mendicant friars; the Augustinian Hermits, Carmelites, Dominicans, and Franciscans. None of these orders gave up the monastic, masochistic ideal—on the contrary, in their simple mode of life and emphasis on asceticism they actually outstripped most of the existing monastic orders. What was different about them was that their members broke out from the isolation of closed monastic communities and either wandered through the countryside ministering to the people or set up houses in poor quarters of towns and cities for the same purpose.

Of the four original orders established in the thirteenth century, the Dominicans and Franciscans were most important. The former were founded by St Dominic for the purpose of preaching and combating heresy—a task which soon led to the acquisition of inquisitorial functions in which the more sadistic members of the order obviously delighted. The reputation for savage cruelty, which we have seen Christians had already earned by the fourth century, was to be fully deserved by the events of the thirteenth and subsequent centuries. Even today, the involvement of Christian churches in terrorist wars in Africa and Northern Ireland seems to continue a hallowed tradition.

Yet perhaps the best possible example of the way in which Christian sado-masochism expressed itself in asceticism and, in the thirteenth century, began to come out into the world at large, is provided, not by St Dominic, but by his contemporary, St Francis of Assisi. He seems to have been one of the most austere and authentic ascetics possible, as is revealed by the following, doubt-less genuine anecdote: Francis was on a journey with a brother in winter. The brother asked Francis in what lay perfect joy, to which he replied:

When we have come to St Mary of the Angels, soaked as we are with rain, and frozen with cold, and dying of hunger, and shall have knocked, if then the porter comes in a rage and asks angrily, 'Who are you?' and we reply, 'We are two of your brethren,' and he answers, 'You lie. You are two lewd fellows who go up and down corrupting the world and stealing alms from the poor. Get you gone from here!'; and he will not open to us but leaves us out in the snow and the rain, in cold and hunger—then, if we should bear abuse and cruelty and dismissal patiently, without disturbance and without murmuring, write O Brother Leo, that is perfect joy.[1]

—or, in other words, perfect masochism.

But an analysis of Francis reveals very considerable sadism directed in his case, not against heretics as it was in that of St Dominic, but against his father and the wealthy bourgeois circles to which he belonged.[2] In his youth, he reported an incestuous dream of the most obvious sort in which he was in his father's shop being married to his mother.[3] When he first began to beg, he did so in French, the native tongue of his mother;[4] and later, in one of his not infrequent delusions, he decided to go and evangelize France which, as one of his most enlightened and perspicacious biographers has realized, was an in-dulgence of a childhood erotic phantasy.[5] The most famous incident in his whole life, his repudiation of his long-suffering father (from whom he stole money to further his religious obsession) springs from one source and one source only—namely, his desire to hurt and humiliate him in public.[6] When Francis stripped off his clothes in front of the people of Assisi and handed them over to his father while announcing that he was wedded to 'Lady Poverty' we see a phenomenon exactly like that seen in delinquent middle-class adolescents who repudiate their parents in order to join a colony of other drop-outs. Oedipal rivalry and guilt at an affluent existence are the major factors in both cases. This is why the Franciscan movement drew its members

[1] E. Raymond, *In the Steps of St Francis*, pp. 191–2.

[2] The difference between the two is doubtless to be found in St Dominic's considerable intellectual ability (which must have made doubt of dogma a great temptation) and St Francis' notably-limited intelligence, which predisposed him to more emotional and hysterical reactions to his ambivalence.

[3] *Ibid.*, p. 20.

[4] *Ibid.*, p. 38.

[5] *Ibid.*, p. 179.

[6] *Ibid.*, p. 48ff.

from the social élite of thirteenth-century Italy. An order dedicated to poverty would not appeal to peasants who had lived all their lives in the most
crushing, dehumanizing conditions of want that one could imagine. But it
did appeal to the rebellious children of the pampered aristocracy and wealthy
bourgeoisie, who could simultaneously hurt their parents and salve bad consciences about their affluence by following the hysteric from Assisi. The list of
members reads like a selection from the *Who's Who* of the thirteenth century:
Francis' first disciples were Bernard of Quintavalle, a wealthy magistrate;
Peter Cataneo, a learned (and well-paid) jurisconsult; Angelo Tancredi, a
knight; Rufino and Clare, children of the noble house of Scefi. Later came
Giacoma, a Roman patrician lady; Orlando, Lord of Chiusi; Giovanni da
Vellita, Lord of Grecchio; Lady Colomba of Monte Rainero; King Louis of
France; John, King of Jerusalem; Aiton II, King of Armenia; not to mention
prominent intellectuals like Roger Bacon and poets like Dante.[7] This alone
might be enough to suggest that with the Franciscans asceticism was degene-
rating and had become little more than the final self-indulgence of a corrupt,
declining, and luxurious feudal aristocracy. Even the founder shows signs of a
degeneration of the ascetic ideal when, dying, he is fussed over by a rich
Roman lady who feeds him on marzipan and who is addressed as 'Brother' so
that her presence might not infringe the Rule.[8] In the light of St Francis'
incestuous fixation on his mother, his cruel treatment of his father, and his
movement's parasitic dependence on those who worked for their living, the
words which his masochistic fantasy put into the mouth of the doorkeeper
of St Mary of the Angels do not seem so untrue. In his unconscious he *did*
see himself as a lewd fellow who went up and down corrupting the world and
stealing alms from the poor; and his unconscious was right.

Perhaps one could put it another way and say that in the sadistic pleasure
which the Dominicans took in torturing heretics, or in which St Francis and
his followers took in crucifying their fathers, one can see Christian sado-
masochism impinging more and more on society itself. In the charitable
works which these same orders undertook one can see Christian homosexuality sublimated in correcting some of the evils of the world; and in the
career of a pope like Innocent III one can see Christianity actually beginning
to dominate the world much more than ever before. No wonder then that
both Francis and Dominic—but Francis especially—were canonized in record
time. They were enrolled among the saints because they had served the
Church so well on earth, and had undertaken the crucial transformation of
the Christian ethic in the later medieval world. Nevertheless, what they did
would be of little significance if it had not been for what followed after them;
and the stage in the secularization of the Christian ethic which they mark
would be of no significance had it not been followed in the sixteenth century
by an immeasurably greater event and by an incomparably more important

[7] *Ibid.*, pp. 144–5.
[8] *Ibid.*, p. 342.

figure. The event in question was the Protestant Reformation, and the man, Martin Luther.

What happened to St Paul on the road to Damascus happened to Luther on the road to Erfurt.[9] He appears to have had a vision during a thunderstorm and to have been narrowly missed by lightning. Something in him made him pronounce a vow 'before the rest of him knew what he was saying'.[10] This vow was that he should become a monk. The parallel with St Paul's experience is even closer if we notice that in Luther's mind the incident in the thunderstorm seems to have been associated with a slightly earlier one, also on the road to Erfurt, in which he had accidently run a sword through his thigh, severed an artery, and nearly bled to death. 'The incident is puzzling in the extreme,' says Friedenthal, 'people do not go round playing with drawn swords.'[11] Perhaps not; but from what we know of the psychology of parapraxis[12] such 'accidental' self-mutilations become comprehensible as expressions of unconscious hostility against the self. When the self-inflicted wound is as close to the genitals as this one was one suspects tendencies to self-castration may be present. What was in St Paul a symbolic and hysterical equivalent of castration appears to have been close to the real thing in Luther: Paul was blind and unconscious for a while, but Luther severed an artery in the region of the genitals and very nearly died. Other parallels between the two must have been clear to Luther's superiors, one of whom presented him to the nuns of the convent of Muhlhausen as a 'second Paul'.[13]

Yet there is also some similarity with St Francis of Assisi. Luther's father did not approve of his entering the monastery at Erfurt. Like the father of St Francis, he seems to have been a relatively prosperous, self-made man who doubtless planned an advantageous marriage for his son. But Luther had his way, and in due course entered the house of the Augustinian Hermits at Erfurt—an order which we have already noticed was founded at the same time and along similar lines to that of St Francis. In time, Luther's father gave his grudging approval and attended his son's first Mass. During it, Luther had the sensation of being alone with God and of speaking to him directly, a feeling which seems to have made him want to run away.[14] Afterwards, a quarrel broke out between Luther and his father, who suggested that this son's conversion-experience in the thunderstorm might have been the work of the Devil. This remark struck him like a thunderbolt. 'You . . . hit me so cleverly and fittingly that in my whole life I have hardly heard a word that resounded in me more forcibly and stuck in me more firmly,' said Luther later.[15]

[9] R. Friedenthal, *Luther*, p. 27.
[10] E. Erikson, *Young Man Luther*, p. 90 (author's italics suppressed).
[11] *Op. cit.*, p. 27.
[12] Freud, *The Psychopathology of Everyday Life*, VI, 162ff.
[13] Friedenthal, *op. cit.*, p. 46.
[14] Erikson, *op. cit.*, p. 139.   [15] *Ibid.*, p. 140, Friedenthal, *op. cit.*, p. 47.

This appears to have been the cause of another celebrated incident in which Luther is said to have 'become possessed' during Conventual Mass in the choir at Erfurt. The attack occurred immediately after the reading of Mark IX, v. 17: 'And one of the crowd answered him, "Teacher, I brought my son to you, for he has a dumb spirit and whenever it seizes him, it dashes him down; and he foams and grinds his teeth and becomes rigid." '[16] On hearing these words, Luther fell to the ground, raving and roaring in a loud voice '*Ich bin's nit!*' or possibly '*Non sum!*' As Erikson points out,[17] the German expression is best translated as 'It isn't me!' the Latin one as 'I am *not*!' Either way, the meaning is clear. The gospel reading that day had concerned a man whose son was possessed by a devil which made him mute and subjected him to epileptoid attacks like those to which Luther was prone.[18] In this hysterical attack Luther was identifying with the man's son, both because of the epileptic attacks and because he, too, was a mute by virtue of living in a monastery where there were strict limitations on speech, where much communication went on by means of signs, and in which all inessential and frivolous talk was excluded. (Such restrictions must have been especially mortifying to a man who later in his life described himself as *homo verbosatus*.) But most important of all, he, too, was possessed by a devil—or at least, that is what his father had said in those words which had struck him so deeply. His impassioned denial, '*Ich bin's nit!*' or '*Non sum!*' is a repudiation of what his father alleged, and what he clearly more than half believed himself. It was an attempt to prevent the second thunderbolt that had struck him undoing the work of the first; for in both instances the voice of the Father had been heard. In the first, that during the thunderstorm on the road to Erfurt, God had revealed himself as he does to the Nuer and Dinka and other peoples with vengeful sky-gods. He was Zeus and Yahweh, Hurler of thunderbolts, Terrorizer of mankind, the sadistic force of conscience which in an earlier incident near the same place had made him nearly kill and castrate himself. In the second incident God had spoken as the earthly father with whom he felt confronted as he celebrated his first Mass. His father's words, suggesting that Luther's experience in the thunderstorm had been the work of the Devil, set up a neurotic conflict within the young monk's mind which was to be the direct cause of the Reformation. In the fit in the choir Luther vehemently denied that he was the son possessed by a devil which had inspired him to enter the dumb world of the Augustinian Hermits, but later, when Luther wrote his work on the nullity of monastic vows and had himself repudiated the monastic life, he was acting as if the second word of God, that of his father, had been the more effective one. Later, he openly confessed that his father had been right.

But that realization took time; it did not break through into consciousness

---

[16] RSV (Catholic Ed.).
[17] Erikson, *op. cit.*, p. 46.
[18] Friedenthal, *op. cit.*, p. 46.

while he was at Erfurt. Only somewhat later, when he had been transferred to the Augustinian house at Wittenberg in order to carry out his teaching duties at the university there did it fully penetrate, and even then only in the delusional guise of a theological insight. Nevertheless, it was to be the most important insight Luther ever had, was to cause him to be able to act on the command implied in his father's reproaches about his entering the monastery, and was to be the instigating cause of the Reformation. But just as the circumstances of his previous crucial psychological experiences had been of the utmost importance—the thunderstorm coinciding with the place on the road to Erfurt where he nearly killed himself, the fit in the choir occurring during the gospel describing the son possessed by a dumb spirit—just as those events had been in large part induced by the circumstances in which they had occurred, so the experience which Luther rated as the most important in his whole life can only be understood if we take account of the fact that it happened in the privy of the monastery of Wittenberg.[19] This transcendental experience was the realization of the the necessity of justification by faith, and it struck him 'like a flash of lightning'.[20] Presumably detained in the privy for long periods by his chronic constipation, he had been ruminating on the terrifying justice of God when, in the utter darkness of the monks' privy, 'the gate of paradise' opened to him and he saw Christ in limpid celestial light.[21] Then everything became clear to him: *Faith is not a human act but the grace of God. Man is justified by this faith, predestined by God.*

This was in fact not a new realization at all. Actually, it was orthodox Catholic theology to insist that faith is a gift of God and that, in so far as God knows all, he knows (and thereby pre-ordains) who shall be damned and who shall be saved. But traditionally, Catholic theology had also emphasized individual works and human volition as an essential part of the process of salvation. What Luther's doctrine of justification by faith really did was to put a heavy emphasis on the divine side of the process of salvation and on the purely passive role of the individual: one could only have faith and be justified by it if God gave it as his free and gratuitous gift.

Luther's dogma of justification by faith is a theological rationalization of a passive attitude to his father. It was motivated by a desire to find a reason for obeying his father and leaving the monastery. By showing that works like living the life of a mendicant monk were worthless in securing salvation, he was justifying by faith his unconscious desire to obey his father and leave the monastery, just as years later he said that he married because his father had wanted him to do so as a young man.[22] Acts of charity, labours of mercy, the

---

[19] N. O. Brown, *Life Against Death*, p. 202.

[20] Friedenthal, *op. cit.*, p. 121.

[21] I like to think that this vision was accompanied by an ecstatically-gratifying motion of the bowels (cf. the Wolf Man's feeling that a veil was lifted from the world when he had an enema (Freud, XVII, 75)).

[22] Erikson, *op. cit.*, p. 230.

practice of piety—all these things were worthless and were the trickery of the Devil. He became convinced that his father was right. His decision to become a monk *had* been a diabolical inspiration. Within the monasteries of the Augustinians he *did* live like a man possessed by a dumb spirit. But that meant that all monks were minions of the Devil. All practices of the monastic life were the worship of Satan—indeed, all piety of the traditional sort was the work of the Devil, and the pope, the head of the Church on earth, was Anti-Christ. Hence justification could not come through the Church with its emphasis on works—that is, on the outward show of piety—it had to come from God through the faith which he gave the individual. In short, his theo-logical notion about justification was the conscious realization of his con-viction that his father had been right all along, that going into the monastery to save his soul by the practice of good works, such as those to which the mendicant orders were dedicated, was a snare of the Devil, and that the only true piety came from within by faith rather than by works that could be outwardly evaluated as 'good'. Thus, when an ecclesiastical entrepreneur by the name of Tetzel came round Germany hawking indulgences to raise money for the building of St Peter's Rome, Luther found a brilliant opportunity to express his contempt for such means of salvation. He did so in the *Ninety-Five Theses* and started the Reformation.

But the idea of justification by faith did more than allow him to find a reason for accepting the will of his father in the matter of leaving the monas-tery. It was also a general statement of Luther's passive and dependent attitude to his father expressed in the manifest content of a passivity towards God. Using the frank sexual imagery of which he was so fond, Luther once re-marked that 'conscience is that place where we and God have to live together as man and wife'. His life-long chronic constipation, his habitual use of excre-mental and scatological symbolism, and the fact that he was in the privy straining his bowels when the great enlightenment came, are all related to his passivity to his father by means of the unconscious link between anal eroti-cism and *sadism of the super-ego*.

In discussing St Paul's great religious experience, I made the distinction, first drawn by Freud, between sadism of the super-ego and masochism of the ego. I pointed out that, whereas the former corresponds to punitive mono-theism, the latter corresponds to Christianity, or, as we should more accu-rately put it, to the Atenist, paranoid monotheism that was predominant in Christianity up to the time of the Reformation. Luther did not entirely renounce the paranoid, Atenist element in Christianity, but he did greatly reduce its scope and dramatically re-emphasized the punitive monotheism which Christianity had inherited from Judaism. Luther restored that mono-theism by insisting on justification by faith. With the Reformation, the old thunder-God of the Hebrew pastoralists was staging a return from the re-pressed and confronting the polytheistic-animistic tendencies which seemed to supervene completely during the later Middle Ages and the Renaissance.

Luther's insistence on justification by faith was a Protestant equivalent of the Old Testament prophets' insistence on righteousness in place of sacrifice, a sincere love of God in place of a purely ritual practice of the religion. With this idea Luther completely repudiated all the quasi-polytheistic cults which had appeared in Catholicism. He dispensed with relics, holy medallions and such-like magical charms of Christianity. He despised the reverence in which the saints and the Virgin were held, and taught the worthlessness of Masses for the dead, and the sale of indulgences. Above all, he attacked the sacred kingship of the popes and divested Christ of many of his benevolent, Atenist attributes. He perceived Christ as 'a strict and wrathful judge',[23] and says that words like 'justice of God' struck him like thunderbolts.[24] God had once again become the awesome judge and vengeful punisher of mankind. With Luther, the God of the pastoralists had returned in a flash of lightning on the road to Erfurt. His doctrine of justification by faith—the central theological idea of the Reformation—was a return of the punitive monotheism that Catholicism had increasingly suppressed during its fifteen-odd centuries of increasingly polytheistic development. It meant the end of all magical and ritual means of salvation. Now, entry to the kingdom of God was restricted to those who had the inward graces of salvation rather than the outward marks of ritual observance. Morality had once again taken over from magic; the 'omnipotence of thoughts' had given way to the omnipotence of the super-ego.

In the light of this it is not surprising to learn that in the nineteenth century a Dinka became a famous Protestant evangelist in England,[25] or that Luther was approached by rabbis as a potential convert to Judaism. In many respects the new secular asceticism of Protestantism was superficially similar to the more puritanical types of Judaism; and there is a sense in which Protestantism made Jews of everyone. Certainly, there can be no doubt that, represented as a purging of polytheistic-animistic elements, Luther's Reformation was a major advance in instinctual renunciation, and, like all such renunciations, was carried out at the command of the super-ego.

In Luther personally, and in Protestantism collectively, the renunciation of the animism and polytheism of Catholicism was enforced by a new and powerful return of the punitive super-ego of pastoral monotheism. The dogma of justification by faith stresses the extreme passivity of the individual before God, or, conversely, the extreme and irresistible power of God over the individual. The collective super-ego of Christianity which, during the first fifteen centuries of its development had become increasingly benevolent and had found its punitive role being taken over by the auto-punitive, masochistic trends of the ego, now once again became omnipotently sadistic. The moral masochism and self-punishment of Catholicism had expressed itself as traditional asceticism which, as we have seen, bears close comparison with

[23] Erikson, op. cit., p. 67.
[24] Brown, op. cit, p. 202.
[25] G. Lienhardt, Divinity and Experience, p. 105.

the masochistic torments of paranoiacs such as Schreber. Justification by faith put an end to such traditional asceticism and, by implication, to paranoid masochism as well. In place of the masochism of the paranoid ego, Luther established the sadism of the obsessional super-ego. This manifested itself not in the self-torments of the paranoiac, but in the anal eroticism of the obsessional.

To be quite accurate, anal eroticism is not a characteristic exclusive to obsessional neurosis. On the contrary, it is an important factor in paranoia. Schreber comments on it at length, and recounts in detail the ecstasies which accompanied the 'miracle' of evacuation:

The need for evacuation, like all else that has to do with my body, is evoked by a miracle . . . When . . . I actually succeed in evacuating . . . the process is always accompanied by the generation of an exceedingly strong feeling of spiritual voluptuousness . . . the relief from the pressure caused by the presence of the faeces in the intestines produces a sense of intense well-being in the nerves of voluptuousness . . .[26]

This feeling of intense well-being, even voluptuousness, is understood by psychoanalysis to be derived from the anal period of childhood and to reappear in paranoia as a result of a process of regression. In childhood, before the libido becomes focused on the genitals, it is associated with other regions of the body, such as the mouth and the anus. In the case of the oral region, a certain element of libidinal gratification remains for ever afterwards associated with it and may express itself as a pleasure in kissing or sucking. In the case of the anal region, libidinal pleasure is derived in childhood from the filling and evacuation of the bowel. Schreber's enjoyment of these functions is exactly comparable to that of the young child, and the fact that it is here reported by an adult should alert us to the possibility that anal eroticism can live on in the unconscious long after childhood is passed.

In adults, and again in the case of Schreber, such anal erotic propensities are associated with masochism and with passive homosexuality. The anus is the obvious male equivalent of the female vagina, and so can easily become associated with passive and homosexual libidinal trends. The connection with masochism comes about via the idea of being feminized—that is, *castrated*—by the father. Freud found that:

If one has an opportunity of studying cases in which the masochistic phantasies have been especially richly elaborated, one quickly discovers that they place the subject in a characteristically-female situation; they signify, that is, being castrated, or being copulated with, or giving birth to a baby.[27]

We have already explored the place of phantasies of feminization and castration in the Atenist—that is, paranoid—tradition in Christianity. We have

---

[26] Freud, 'Psychoanalytic Notes upon an Autobiographical Account of a Case of Paranoia', XII, 26–7.

[27] 'The Economic Problem of Masochism', XIX, 162.

already seen that the founder of Atenism, Akhenaten himself, was feminized by his pituitary disorder and is suspected of having been homosexual. We saw how Christ's masochism expressed itself, and we may note in passing that he, and nearly everyone else who followed him into the religious life in pre-Reformation Christianity, made himself a eunuch for the sake of the Kingdom of Heaven.[28] St Paul, we saw, was blinded by Christ, and Freud, a few lines after the quotation above, refers to blinding as a frequent phantasy equivalent of castration. We have seen that Christian altruism in general can be understood as generalized masochism, and how Christian asceticism was a regularized form of self-punishment. In the case of St Francis of Assisi we had a vivid example of how self-inflicted pain could come to be nothing less than 'perfect joy'.

Pre-Reformation Christian asceticism was comparable to the feminine masochism found in paranoia and in sado-masochistic perversions to the extent that its effects were emasculating and produced a passivity and submissiveness which were feminine in character. To the extent that it was completely divorced from sexuality we may term it 'moral masochism', but should follow Freud in observing that both forms are based on what he termed primary, erotogenic masochism.[29]

The dogma of justification by faith put an end to traditional Christian asceticism (justification by works). Psychologically, it also put an end to masochism. In place of the masochism of the ego, which we find in paranoia, we have the sadism of the super-ego, which we find in obsessional neurosis. But it did not put an end to the anal eroticism indistinguishable from the passive homosexual trends which we have seen to be an integral part of Christian religion. Luther may have abolished good works as the path to salvation, but he did not abandon Christian moral principles. The precepts of the Sermon on the Mount and the Epistles of St Paul still remained in force. Traditional Christian altruism was in large part retained, and although Luther personally and Protestantism in general avoided the more extreme sadomasochistic excesses of Catholic asceticism, the religion nevertheless retained a passive homosexual trend. It also retained the main outlines of Christ's paranoid monotheism in the dogma of the Trinity, the Incarnation, and numerous other beliefs. But the Atenist aspect of Christianity, so strongly developed in Catholicism, did undergo a marked reduction. Part of this reduction involved the repression of the passive homosexual, sado-masochistic trend and its replacement by obsessional tendencies. The ego which enjoyed emasculation by the Father was now replaced by the omnipotent super-ego—in other words, the Father—which utterly dominates and terrorizes the ego. The anal eroticism of passive homosexuality remained, but was reduced in significance and firmly repressed. From now on, anal, submissive, and feminine tendencies could only be expressed by Protestants in an indirect and

[28] Matthew XIX, v. 12.
[29] Freud, *op. cit.*, XIX, 162.

disguised manner. Rather than being regressively indulged as in paranoia, anal eroticism had now to be repressed and sublimated as in obsessional neurosis.

As Luther crouched in the gloom of the privy in the Augustinian house at Wittenberg trying to open his bowels and ruminating on the theology of salvation, a solution occurred to him which was both personally satisfying to his latent passive homosexuality and historically of the first significance in bringing about the Reformation. Both psychologically and historically, it was comparable to the experience of St Paul on the road to Damascus. The difference is that Luther's great spiritual enlightenment occurred in two stages. First, he was converted to traditional monastic asceticism by the thunder-God he met on the road to Erfurt; but later, we have seen that God spoke to him again through the voice of the man whom he really represented—Luther's father—and caused him to have to undergo a second experience of conversion during which he became convinced that his father's command to leave the monastery was the will of God. Added together, the two experiences, that in the thunderstorm on the road to Erfurt and that in the privy at Wittenberg, summed up to much the same sort of passive subordination to the super-ego that had occurred in St Paul. Both men adopted a feminine, submissive attitude to the Father which is reflected in their use of similar matrimonial metaphors to describe the relationship between a man and God. Both had passive homosexual tendencies, and both underwent neurotic experiences of conversion which were of the greatest historical importance. But Luther differed from St Paul in firmly repressing his submissive, feminine and maso-chistic drives. Instead of conceiving of Christ as the perpetually reborn Son-God of the polytheistic mystery cults as St Paul had done, Luther saw him as the punitive sky-God of pastoral monotheists. His passive homosexual libidi-nal tendencies, like his anal eroticism, became strongly repressed and searched for alternative outlets. In Protestants as a whole, and perhaps most especially in the followers of Calvin, substitute-gratifications of, and reaction-formations against, anal eroticism and the passive homosexual trends which it represented became crystalized in what is known to psychoanalysis as the *anal character*. This, in turn, was to give rise to the form of economic life which we call capitalism.

If we consult Freud's paper entitled 'Character and Anal Eroticism' we find him saying that:

The people I am about to describe are noteworthy for a regular combination of the three following characteristics. They are especially *orderly, parsimonious* and *obstinate*.[30]

It is hard at first to see how orderliness, parsimony, and obstinacy could be related to a form of economic life, but we should remember that we are looking for *substitute-gratifications*. Freud explained the first characteristic as a

[30] IX, 169.

reaction-formation against anal eroticism to the extent that defecation produces disorder ('Dirt is matter in the wrong place'). We have already seen that reaction-formations can be—and indeed often are—substitute-gratifications, and it is easy to see how an obsessive interest in cleanliness and orderliness can mask an interest in the exact opposite. The third characteristic that he mentions—obstinacy—seems to be a straightforward substitute-gratification because retention of the faeces, as in Luther's constipation, is pleasurable to the anal zone. What is more, it can be used by young children to arouse anxiety in the parents.[31] Parsimony seems to be something of a mixture of both retentive obstinacy and orderliness, but immediately suggests a possible economic significance. This is greatly reinforced when we learn that:

The connections between the complexes of interest in money and of defecation, which seem so dissimilar, appear to be the most extensive of all.[32]

According to Theodor Reik, the Aztecs used to call gold 'the feces of the gods', and in Melanesia, according to Róheim, shell money is called 'excrement of the sea'. In colloquial German, defecation is called 'a golden deal', 'to lay golden eggs', 'to lay in stock', or even 'devaluing'. The anus is a 'gold-mine', diarrhoea is a 'rain of gold', and a person with haemorrhoids has a 'golden vein'. The W.C. is called 'gold-mill', 'office', 'bank', or 'stock-exchange'. The chamber-pot is a 'piggy-bank', toilet paper is a 'treasury bill', an 'invoice' or 'securities'. Conversely, a person in financial difficulties on the London Stock Market is referred to as 'constipated', whereas in the American colloquialism he is 'up shit-street'. Officials of the Federal Bank in Germany are called *Dukatenscheisser* (that is, 'ducat-shitters'), and someone who cannot pay his debts is said to be 'up to his neck in shit'. In English, a miser is 'tight-arsed', whereas the rich are said to be 'filthy with money'.[33] Such examples can be multiplied almost limitlessly. What they all have in common is the overwhelming certainty they give to Freud's assertion that, in the unconscious, excrement equals gold, and all that has to do with defecation has much to do with money, and conversely.

With this realization, it suddenly becomes clear that all the characteristics of the form of economic life that we know as capitalism can be shown to be substitute-gratifications of, and reaction-formations against, anal-eroticism. The accumulation of capital on which capitalism depends can be shown to be

[31] Salvador Dali, who did not submit to toilet-training until he was past eight years old, reports the ultimate refinement with regard to creating anxiety in the parents. He insisted on defecating on the carpet, in cupboards, or wherever it would cause most consternation, but very occasionally he would secretly do so in the W.C. Unable to find that day's offering, for long afterwards no one in the house could open a drawer, or look under a chair without apprehension about what they might find. (S. Dali, *The Unspeakable Confessions of Salvador Dali*, p. 28.)

[32] Freud, *op. cit.*, IX, 173.

[33] E. Borneman (Ed.), *The Psychoanalysis of Money*, pp. 48–50.

based on unconscious symbolic equations which explain the origin of the propensity to save money and invest it. For the paradox of capitalism is that while money is something that should be spent, which exists ultimately only to be spent, it can nevertheless produce more money (interest) if it is not spent. Yet a conscious and rational desire not to spend money will inevitably be countered by powerful (and unconscious) instinctual demands that it should be spent. However, if such an unconscious instinctual demand can come to the service of the desire to save money, then the results are likely to be impressive and much more successful than if only conscious, rational intention can be called upon. The Freudian insight into anal eroticism explains how the accumulation of capital can be more gratifying—at least to anal erotics—than the spending of it; and this is precisely what any psychological theory of capitalism which takes the demands of instinct seriously must explain. It must explain why instinctual gratification does not always result in the immediate expenditure of money but rather results, in certain circumstances, in its conservation and accumulation. The theory of anal eroticism shows how instinctual drives, which always seek discharge and satisfaction, can come to the service of a form of economic life which demands great self-restraint, parsimony, and postponement of gratification. In short, it explains the pleasures of miserliness.

This is important because the followers of Luther, and, even more so those of Calvin, did not set out to become rich for rational and conscious reasons. On the contrary, the Protestants set out, not to be miserly in order to become wealthy, but to be miserly in order to save their souls. Wealth came to them as an embarrassment, yet, because of their miserliness and devotion to hard work, come to them it did. Their unintended capitalism originated in the fact that their interest in accumulating money was unconscious. It was unconscious because it was a substitute-gratification of the equally unconscious desire to indulge in the forbidden pleasures of anal eroticism. Because of the unconscious equation of money with excrement we can see that Protestants were not only anal erotics but also *money erotics*, and that their money eroticism is the unconscious origin of their capitalism. Certainly, there can be no doubt that anyone who is highly parsimonious would be very much at home in a capitalist economy. So would the individual who tends to excessive orderliness and punctilious attention to detail. It is evident that not only is this an aid to parsimoniousness (especially where double-entry bookkeeping and other office routines are essential), but that it is also the psychological basis on which the bureaucratic administrative structures of modern capitalist economies are built. Excessive attention to detail and laborious formalism in administrative matters, obstinacy in pursuing one's self-interest, orderliness, restraint, and meanness in one's everyday life, inability to tolerate interference, miserliness with money—all these anal personality traits, which in other environments would put their possessor at a disadvantage, are powerfully reinforced by capitalism and rewarded with economic success. Just as the individual who could divert his parricidal sadism onto animals was rewarded with the success of the hunter under totemism, and he who could postpone oral gratification and sublimate his incestuous libido in agriculture was put at an advantage in polytheism, so he who could entirely suppress his sadistic and libidinal drives but gratify them in the perverse manner peculiar to capitalism would thrive under Protestantism. The psychological mechanism is analogous in each case; it is only in the increasing strength and comprehensiveness of the inhibitions that they differ.

In short, the dogma of justification by faith had an effect on Protestants as a whole exactly similar to that which it had on Luther in particular. It provided a manifest and conscious justification for a latent and unconscious assertion of the sadism of the super-ego, which now became omnipotent once again, and found its collective representation in the reassertion of punitive monotheism within Christianity. The sadism of the super-ego now overwhelmed the masochism of the ego and caused it to repress its submissive, feminine gratification of its homosexuality. The erotic corollary of that feminine masochism—anal eroticism—was also repressed but returned as the obstinate and well-ordered parsimony in money matters which made many Protestants into proto-capitalists. Now, if individuals pursued perfection they were not expected to do so in terms of 'good works' of the type practised by traditional ascetics. On the contrary, now that one was saved by faith—that is, by an inward disposition of trust in God—the outward observances of one's life were of no significance. Or, rather, they were of no necessary *positive* significance. Luther was fond of pointing out that even if one were to meet St Peter himself one could not be sure that he was one of the elect. Outward sanctity, which means personal effort at acquiring holiness, could be a cover for all manner of pride, dishonesty, and sinfulness. However, one could determine negative qualities which were quite incompatible with the life of grace, and proved that a person was definitely not among the elect. All obviously sinful and vicious dispositions of persons fell under this heading. The result was that a person would continue to live a normal secular existence in any occupation which was not self-evidently depraved, criminal, or at variance with Christian ethics, and assume that if he were one of the elect God had predestined him to live such a life and pursue such an occupation. Indeed, occupation was of especially importance because, more than anything else, it implied work, and the value of work as far as the Protestant soul was concerned was that it was the secular equivalent of monastic asceticism. It was a form of masochism which was not stigmatized as mere 'good works', but which, because work implies labour, self-discipline, effort, and postponement of pleasure and relaxation, was highly regarded as an ethically valuable way of pursuing one's salvation. It is indicative of the attitude of Protestants that Calvin should have instigated the setting up of a cloth industry in Geneva to provide work for the unemployed and that when this failed he supported a similar idea to produce watches.

But the paradox of the Protestant ethic was that hard, highly-motivated, and masochistically-intensified labour almost invariably produces gain for the worker, usually in pecuniary terms. In these conditions parsimony had scope for gratification far beyond anything in traditional monasticism. Sober, hard-working, and righteously-inclined Protestants would be bound to become richer; and, if they gratified the tendencies to parsimony in the anal character-type which was their ideal and their norm, the only possible result was that they would accumulate the vast money surpluses without which the capi-talist economy could not have evolved or even begun. A reaction-formation in so far as its currency was hard, shining, without odour, and gratifying to receive in social exchange (by contrast to excrement, which is soft, muddy, malodourous, and disgusting to oneself and to others), parsimony in eco-nomic terms also became a substitute-gratification for the erotic pleasures of retention of excrement which the obsessional nature of the Protestant (and especially the Puritan) religious ethic inevitably condemned.

Finally, one might also point out that the work-ethic of Protestantism is itself not unconnected with the subject of anal eroticism. Jones has shown that in the unconscious the act of defecation is symbolized by the carrying out of morally obligatory activities (that is, those which remind us of how we had to part with our faeces against our will as children), and also by tasks which are intrinsically tedious or disagreeable (and which originate in the same situa-tion).[34] In the scale of values of Protestantism, especially of the more extreme, Puritan type, work which is tedious and unpleasant but carried out for reasons of moral obligation to God or man is particularly meritorious. Here the latent element—the desire to repeat actions which remind one of the pleasures of defecation—is exactly complementary to the conscious intention —the pursuit of asceticism in the secular life—and both derive from the regressive propensity to the enjoyment of anal eroticism.

In general, we may say that capitalism of the classical, Western type can be expected to appear when anal eroticism is repressed but allowed to reappear in the distorted guise of substitute-gratifications and reaction-formations typical of the anal character. We may further conclude that such an outcome is likely wherever a cultural tradition of marked passive homosexual and masochistic tendency is repressed in the interests of an assertion of the sadism of the super-ego. This occurred in Christianity when Luther re-emphasized punitive monotheism at the expense of Atenism. The degree to which anal eroticism is likely to express itself as the anal character type is directly pro-portional to the extent of the tension between the repressed anal drives and the repressing, active one. In Protestant Christianity this tension was at a maximum, especially in the more extreme—that is, more obsessional—Cal-vinist and Puritan forms. For this reason Calvinism and Puritanism correlate with classical capitalism even more than Lutheranism does.

---

[34] Jones, *Papers on Psychoanalysis*, p. 684.

But clearly, this tension between paranoid masochism and introjected sadism is present in all religions that unite paranoid and obsessional forms of monotheism. In the case of Judaism, both forms of monotheism were present, even if the punitive, obsessional monotheism was dominant; and even though the tension between the two was less than it was in Protestantism, it was still sufficient to cause the Jews to acquire a propensity for capitalism which they have shown right down to the present day. Furthermore, the similarity that writers such as Sombart have noticed between Jewish and Japanese character suggests that success in capitalism may be related to psychological constants which are not limited to the Western, Judaeo-Christian tradition. Ineed, there is even a sense in which primitive pastoralists such as the Nuer and Dinka can be called embryonic capitalists, even though their religion only shows the presence of the punitive super-ego and is lacking in evidence of masochism of the ego. The pastoralist 'invests' in his cattle, which are his 'capital', and lives off the 'interest', the blood and milk which they produce. There is a sense in which capitalism is the equivalent of pastoralism in a non-herding, money economy.

I mentioned earlier that, whereas hunting and totemism could be shown to be the outcome of a positive Oedipal resolution in men, agriculture could be supposed to be that of a negative Oedipal resolution in women.[35] Similarly, we have seen that pastoralism, understood as the domestication of animals, was invented by women with a positive (maternal) Oedipal resolution. Now we can see that, as I suggested earlier, capitalism and Protestantism fit in exactly where they should since, being the result of the repression of passive homosexual trends, they can be seen to originate in a *negative Oedipal orientation in men*.

There remains one characteristic of Luther and of Protestantism that we must examine before bringing this chapter to a close. This is the notable place of the Devil in the psychology of both.

The great age of belief in devils and demonic possession in Europe coincides with the age of Protestantism and runs roughly from 1450 to 1750.[36] Ernest Jones points out that the Devil as we know him is a predominantly Christian idea, but that where the idea can be seen developing among the Jews it coincides with the tendency to see God as benevolent.[37] A clue to why this should be so is provided by his observation that 'like Zeus and Odin, he [the Devil] had special power over the weather'.[38] Zeus and Odin, like the Nuer 'kwoth', were hurlers of thunderbolts and, as we have seen, represent the feared, punitive super-ego. As Atenist ideas of God as a benevolent agency supervened among the Jews, the negative, feared aspects of the old thunder-God tended to be invested in the person of the Devil; but this tendency never

---

[35] See above, p. 184.
[36] E. Jones, *On the Nightmare*, p. 57.
[37] *Ibid.*, pp. 156–7.   [38] *Ibid.*, p. 161.

went very far. At the end of the Middle Ages however, it underwent an enormous development in Europe, and for the next three hundred years both Catholics and Protestants—but especially Protestants—were obsessed with the Devil, demonic possessions, witchcraft, werewolves, vampires, *incubi*, and *succubi*. The Bible of witch-hunters, the *Malleus Maleficarum*, was published three years after Luther's birth and became one of the most famous and widely consulted books of the age.

In Luther himself, preoccupation with the Devil and his works dates from his father's words following his entry into the Erfurt monastery. As we have seen, the very same 'something within him' which made him vow to be a monk—that is, his super-ego manifested as thunder-God—later made him renounce his vocation when it manifested itself as the reproach of his father. The idea that his entry into the monastery had been the Devil's work grew to such huge proportions that Luther ended his days believing that everything about the Catholic religion was demonic. 'The Devil is Lord of the world,' says Luther:

Everything is full of devils, in the courts of princes, in houses, in streets, in the fields, in water, in wood, in fire . . . The Devil lets his own do many good works, pray, fast, build churches, establish Masses and Holy Days, and behave as if he were quite holy and pious . . . Men of holy works are Satan's captive servants, no matter how much they appear outwardly to surpass others in good works and in strictness and holiness of life.[39]

But it did not end there. Luther's unconscious was not content to allow his father's accusation of the demonic origin of traditional piety of the sort Luther tried to achieve in the monastery at Erfurt to be limited to that alone. It extended the reproach to the very moral force in which Luther had come to believe as a substitute for the Church. Even conscience, the touchstone of the Protestant morality and the authority which could oppose popes and councils, was under the Devil's sway:

Conscience is a beast and bad devil. Hence the poets invented the Erinnyes and Furies, that is to say, hellish devils which avenged wrong-doing . . . Conscience stands in the cruel service of the Devil; a man must learn to find consolation even against his own conscience.[40]

That phrase, 'consolation even against his own conscience', strongly suggests some attempt at resolution of the obsessional religious neurosis which, as we have seen, rests on the projection of the super-ego as God. It suggests that Luther wanted a consolation against God—that is, autonomy of his ego from the restrictions enforced upon it by the super-ego. He plainly recognized

[39] Cited by Brown, *op. cit.*, pp. 211–13.
[40] *Ibid.*, p. 213.

that often it is impossible to tell whether one is serving God or the Devil when trying to follow one's conscience.

This equation of the Devil with the conscience suggests that in his unconscious Luther was taking his father's reproach to its logical conclusion. He was coming to see not merely his original attempt at monastic asceticism but each and every attempt he made to become holy as diabolically inspired. From this it was but a short step to seeing God as the Devil. Already he had come to fear and even hate Christ, in spite of his superiors' patient arguments, as 'one who came to punish'.[41]

Psychoanalytic studies of cases of demonic possession show that the Devil represents the father, not as he is loved and respected, but as he is hated and despised by the other side of the ambivalence which is always present.[42] We have already encountered this hating ambivalence in our discussion of the punitive monotheism of the pastoralists, and in that case we saw that all of it was turned back against the ego so that it was not the father who was hated and despised, but the self for hating and despising him. We also saw that sadism of the super-ego was the main element in the force of conscience in general and in the obsessional neurosis which underlay Jewish monotheism in particular. In protestantism, the sadism of the super-ego was once again predominant, but passive, masochistic libido was repressed, giving rise to the anal character.

This is the explanation of the marked anal-sadistic characteristic of Luther's demonology. Apart from some frightening poltergeistic manifestations, the main physical characteristic of Luther's Devil is that he is covered in excrement and is best repelled by his own weapon—the fart. As Brown points out, 'Luther's most general word for the assaults of the Devil is the homely German verb *bescheissen*.'[43] If a fart would not do, Luther recommended defecating in one's pants and hanging them round the neck of the Devil. He used to threaten Satan with being 'thrown into my anus, where he belongs'. Clearly, the anal aspects of Luther's Devil can be accounted for by reference to the same anal erotic connotations of masochistic homosexual self-prostitution to the father which explain the greatest moment in Luther's life having taken place in a privy. But the fact that the Devil is overtly anal in his appearance and is even consciously threatened with being made to sodomize Luther shows that in his unconscious the father before whom he was so passive and feminine was both the Devil *and* God. It should not surprise us to find him praying—albeit in jest—'*Sancte Sathana, ora pro me*' (Holy Satan, pray for me).[44] The real difference between the treatment of God and the Devil in Luther's delusions was that the anal erotic aspects of his relation to the latter were not repressed. The Devil could be as anal and excremental as

[41] Erikson, *op. cit.*, p. 143.
[42] Freud, *A Seventeenth Century Demonological Neurosis*, XIX, 73ff.
[43] *Op. cit.*, p. 208.
[44] Erikson, *op. cit.*, p. 238.

he wished—he represented the father who was hated. But the father who was loved could not be reviled, even though the anal erotic attachment truly belonged to him. For the purposes of protest against the sadism of the super-ego, God had to become the Devil, and passive, anal erotic attachments to him had to be transformed into excremental repulsiveness.

The significance of the obsession with the Devil seen in late medieval Europe and in the mind of Luther is that it signals a breaking-down of the more extreme moral masochism of Christianity and a turning-back against the father (now represented as Devil rather than God) of all the hatred and hostility which had previously been directed against the self for feeling those very emotions against him. The late medieval and Protestant preoccupation with diabolism is evidence that the masochistic trends in European religion were undergoing dissolution and that soon its very psychological basis would be undermined. This is exactly what was to happen during the Enlighten-ment and subsequent epochs, but initially this breakdown of the masochistic mechanism of Christianity was revealed by the appearance of a demonic anti-God, one endowed with many of the attributes of the old punitive sky-God, but hated and vilified rather than feared and respected. This is why Christ was hated by Luther. In his mind the second person of the Trinity was well on the way to becoming the Devil; he was the feared judge who would soon not be feared at all but would be subject to the same negative emotions as those which had been turned back against the ego in establishing his fearsome authority over it in the first place. One of Luther's monastic preceptors seems to have hit the nail on the head when he told him that 'God does not hate you, you hate him.'[45] The breakthrough of the ambivalence is clear in the following confession of Luther's:

I am unable to pray without at the same time cursing. If I am prompted to say 'Hallowed be thy Name,' I must add 'Cursed, damned, outraged be the name of papists.' If I am prompted to say, 'Thy kingdom come,' I must perforce add, 'Cursed, damned destroyed by the papacy.'[46]

This chronic conscious ambivalence about God was inevitably reflected in intellectual doubts about religion and in failures in his faith. In 1527, a mere ten years after he published the *Ninety-Five Theses*, he was having to repeated-ly ask his friends to reassure him about his central theological tenet, the dogma of justification by faith. Finding his prayers could not help him, he once asked someone to recite the *Paternoster* in his ear with 'a ringing voice'. In the case of Luther, and that of the first few generations of his Protestant followers, these doubts were not to prove of sufficient strength to overwhelm the dogmatic reaction-formations which Christianity had set up against them in the years leading up to and following the Council of Nicaea. But eventually, it was

[45] *Ibid*, p. 54.
[46] *Ibid.*, p. 240.

inevitable that they should; and it was a matter of psychological and historical necessity that Protestantism, which began as a reaction-formation to the paganizing tendencies of late medieval Catholicism, should itself evolve as an increasingly secularized religion, and one which would finally secularize itself out of existence altogether.

Summing up, we may say that what was effectively happening during the Reformation was that a reaction was setting in to the paranoid tendencies which had gained the upper hand in Christianity up to that time. This reaction was obsessional, and, as I have already pointed out, seemed in some ways to hark back to Judaism. Yet it was a reaction not unconnected with the inner logic of the paranoid process in Christianity.

In the beginning, Christianity, like an individual psychosis, was dominated by what are termed 'regressive' symptoms. These are the symptoms of the essential pathological process, the withdrawal of libido from objects and its regression to narcissism. In Christianity, as in individual cases of paranoia, two of the most important of these are megalomania (narcissistic hypercathexis of the ego) and End-of-the-World fantasies (chronic object-loss). We have already seen how important these symptoms were in the psychopathology of Christ, and in so far as every Christian identified with him and shared his belief in the imminent end of the world, every Christian manifested these regressive symptoms. Yet the movement as a whole generated its own regressive features, which have clear parallels in individual psychopathology. As we have just seen, early Christianity was typified by extreme asceticism which resulted in the anchorite reducing his contact with the world to such an extent that he lived a solitary existence, immured in a hermitage, or chained to the top of a pillar. This state of affairs is an exact parallel to the narcissistic withdrawal seen in cases of psychosis.

Yet, as we know, this psychotic withdrawal, this ethic of world-rejection, became mitigated, and gradually an enhanced involvement with the world developed. This is, again, an exact parallel with the situation found in cases of individual paranoia. A second class of symptoms, distinguished from the regressive, is termed the 'restitutional'. These are symptoms which develop as attempts at recovery, after the initial, regressive phase. Typical of these are 'world-reconstruction' phantasies, hallucinations, and, in paranoia, delusions of persecution. As in the case of regressive symptoms, the parallel between individual and collective restitutional symptoms is sometimes startlingly close. In at least one well-authenticated case we have evidence of what can only be called a 'mass-hallucination'.

Let me digress for a moment to draw my reader's attention to the remarkable similarities between the hallucinations of paranoiacs like Schreber and the famous 'Miracle of the Sun' at Fatima. After a series of apparitions to some young children by the Virgin Mary (again a parallel with psychotic symbolism, which, like Catholicism, frequently regresses to the matriarchal in religion), a huge crowd, numbering thousands, gathered to witness the final appearance on 13th October, 1917. It was raining heavily, but then the rain suddenly stopped, and the sun appeared in a clearing in the clouds. Many eye-witnesses said that *they could look at the sun without blinking*, and nearly all saw the sun 'dance in the sky'. (Susceptibility to this miracle seems to have varied in proportion to how far the witnesses were Portuguese and Catholic. An Anglo-Saxon Protestant who was present saw virtually nothing.) Schreber claimed that, even after his illness, he could look at the sun without being dazzled,[47] and in the course of it reported many visions comparable to the Fatima prodigy (which, as if to give it the stamp of Pontifical approval, was later seen by Pope Pius XII in the Vatican Gardens). Such examples could be multiplied, but let us return from this brief digression to the history of Christianity.

As solitary anchoritism gave way to the early monastic communities, and as these eventually gave rise to the orders of mendicant friars, one can see a phantasy of world-reconstruction slowly supervening over one of world-rejection. In the group, as in the individual, such phantasies are attempts to re-establishing contact with reality and reacquiring lost objects of the libido. Usually, such restitutional symptoms are unsuccessful attempts at recovery, and lead nowhere. But, in the case of Luther, the outcome was different. He was a mendicant friar, and, as such, one involved in what was at the time the most elaborate attempt which had been made at world-acceptance by the ascetic élite. Luther, and those who followed him, represent such a decisive step in world-acceptance and libidinal restitution that they largely cured themselves of the psychopathology of Catholicism and substituted an obsessional neurosis for what up till then had been a paranoid psychosis with obsessional complications. For if we compare Protestantism with Catholicism we see that the psychopathology of the founder and of the religion as a whole is dominated by the super-ego, the punitive thunder-God whom Luther met on the road to Erfurt. As we have seen, punitive monotheism correlates strongly with obsessional tendencies, and Luther's promotion of this aspect of Christianity could only lead to a diminution in its regressive, paranoid element. Hence, by contrast to Catholicism, which is a collective paranoia with obsessional complications, Protestantism is a collective obsessional neurosis with paranoid complications. In the latter respect it is much like Judaism, but it differs from it in the extent to which it proved impossible to maintain the punitive element, which, as we have seen, tended to turn into hatred of God disguised as hatred of the Devil. But Protestantism was like Judaism in its Oedipal orientation, which was predominantly positive, as opposed to that of Catholicism, which was predominantly negative. This explains why Protestants did not insist on clerical celibacy and why they did not extol the virtues of virginity as Catholics did. Although full of the bigoted hypocrisy in matters of sex which is typical of the Judaeo-Christian

---

[47] Freud, XII, 80–1.

tradition in general, Protestants revealed their more normal and positive Oedipal orientation as much in their avoidance of ascetic communities of persons of the same sex as in the example of their founder, who signalled the triumph of the positive element in his Oedipal resolution by repudiating his monastic vows and marrying a nun. Such evidence of a positive outcome of the Oedipus complex was an inevitable result of Luther's reaffirmation of the omnipotence of the Father-God, as opposed to the masochistic submissiveness of Christ, the Son-God. Where the super-ego is all-powerful a man will accept it as his own ideal ego and will identify with the father. Only where it is lacking are we likely to find the feminine, masochistic ego-identity which was the ideal of pre-Reformation Christianity. It is true that later in his life Luther shows unmistakeable signs of paranoid tendencies which suggest that as he grew older his positive Oedipal orientation weakened and the negative reasserted itself. But by that time the Reformation was launched, justification by faith was established, and the leadership of Protestantism could pass to others who, like Calvin, manifested psychopathologies more consistent with the original inspiration of its founder.

5

RESOLUTION AND RECOVERY

We have reached a stage in our analysis where it would be advisable to pause and review the significance of our progress and to try to summarize our findings. It would not surprise me at all if the reader had almost totally forgotten that man is our subject, and the psychoanalysis of his culture the principal aim of this book. The last chapter was so completely devoted to particular historical events and to particular persons that he probably discounts their having any universal significance whatsoever. After all, even though space restricted me to only one or two examples of polytheism and monotheism, at least they were examples of forms of religion which are fairly typical. Catholicism and Protestantism are not typical examples in this sense. On the contrary, they are discrete religious phenomena without obvious parallels anywhere else in the world. Furthermore, the reader will probably feel that the consideration of such specific instances of religion will not in any way fit the analogy I have drawn between the psychological development of the human race as a whole and that of the individual human being in particular. He will probably have concluded by now that this was a purely literary conceit, which I have now had to abandon in the face of the intractable facts, and that all that I have said so far about the possibility of equating certain trends in the evolution of world-religion with psychological factors found in individuals is of no further significance, and cannot be made to yield any more meaningful insights. I can hardly blame him for holding this view when I recall that I have had to subject him to a lengthy account of the development of Christianity, interspersed with a few cases of individual psychopathology. Yet I must confess that I am unwilling to abandon something which seems to have been so useful up to now. As we shall see in a moment, Freud himself entertained the view that the psychological evolution of the human race as a whole had certain affinities with that of individual human beings; and since my earlier remarks give every reason for suspecting that this analogy is more than just a literary artefact and hides some deeper causal connections, it seems unfortunate in the extreme to have to abandon it now. Consequently, I propose not to do so—or, at least, I propose to try to see what significance it may have in the light of the findings of the last chapter and those of this. So let us take a rest for a moment from the detailed analysis of our patient's neurosis and try to come to some overall view of what has been going on.

I concluded my remarks on monotheism by saying that in terms of the individual analogy it amounted to an obsessional neurosis of the sort which can be seen beginning in individuals in the course of the period of latency. I argued that nowhere was this obsessional neurosis more clearly seen than among the Jews, whose particular compound form of monotheism predisposed them to an especially comprehensive and dogmatic version of it. As we saw, Christianity developed out of this unique monotheism; partly at least because of the inner tensions which characterized it, and which were bound to set up deep and long-lasting reverberations throughout the history of any religion which developed out of it. If Judaism is the equivalent of man's original obsessional neurosis, and if the period of human development to which it corresponds might be termed man's 'latency', then it is clear that what follows it must correspond to the next stage in individual psychological development—puberty and adolescence.

To this suggestion the reader's reaction is almost certain to be utter disbelief. He is probably now quite sure that I have gone too far, and is certain that there can be no connection between such an individual and physically-determined phenomenon as adolescence and the history of Christianity. But let me remind him that we are speaking only of psychological developments, and here, contrary to appearances, there is much to be said about Christianity and adolescence.

In the first place, one of the major psychological factors in puberty and adolescence is the return of the repressed, just as it is in Christianity. The recommencement of the physiological maturation of the sex organs, interrupted by latency at about the age of five, brings with it a return of the psychological concomitants of infantile sexual development. The marked increase in libido seen in young adolescents triggers off a rapidly-recapitulated version of child psycho-sexual development. The animal phobias of early childhood become the animal enthusiasms of adolescence, (especially in girls where they often become compounded with a substitute-gratification for reawakened penis-envy in the form of horse and riding manias). Masturbation stages a spectacular return from the repressed, as do the more or less conscious Oedipal conflicts which accompanied it in childhood and which, now become transmuted into adolescent irritability and opposition to parental authority. In short, the return of the repressed, albeit in a somewhat distorted form, is the outstanding psychological phenomenon of adolescence, and if the evidence of the last chapter is anything to go by, so is it also of Christianity which, in its recapitulation of polytheism in Catholicism and monotheism in Protestantism, comprised within itself just about every characteristic of the previous stages in the evolution of religion.

But the similarities do not end there. Writing of puberty, Anna Freud says:

Alternating with instinctual excesses and irruptions from the id and other, apparently contradictory, attitudes, there is sometimes in adolescence an antagonism towards the instincts which far surpasses in intensity anything in the way of repression which we are accustomed to see under normal conditions, or in more or less severe cases of neurosis. In the mode of its manifestation and the width of its range it is less akin to the symptoms of pronounced neurotic disease than to the asceticism of religious fanatics.[1]

We have already seen that the other main factor in the evolution of Christianity, apart from the return of the repressed, is what I have termed the renunciation of instinct. In this respect adolescence also resembles Christianity. We have already seen that the fanatical asceticism of which Anna Freud speaks in connection with adolescence is the key element in the advance in instinctual renunciation represented by Christianity. The demand for complete altruism means thorough-going repression of many aspects of the egoistic and libidinal instincts. For the Christian, merely looking at a woman is equivalent to fornication with her; and sin can be committed by thought alone. Renunciation of the ego-instincts goes as far as lifelong self-starvation in the ascetic saints; and fasting, like celibacy, becomes a norm of the religion. In adolescence, the fasting of the ascetics is reproduced in disturbances like *anorexia nervosa*; and a similar repression of the life instincts is attempted, often seen alternating, as it did in Christianity, with indulgence in forbidden pleasure. In the adolescent, these alternations, if they occur, take place within the same person; in Catholic Christianity, the ascetic reaction took place within the monastery or convent, the indulgent phase outside it. In adolescence, marked tendencies to homosexuality are often present and originate in a recapitulation of the negative Oedipal orientation which precedes the emergence of the positive one. In Christianity, I have already indicated the homosexuality which was latently present as the inevitable accompaniment of its high ethical ideals. It is also notable that idealism, often of the most ludicrously-unrealistic kind, is a common feature in adolescence and is usually accompanied by a foolishly-charitable attitude to the human race already familiar to us from Christianity.

Finally, Anna Freud mentions one other characteristic of adolescence which is not without a parallel in Christianity.[2] This is the tendency to *intellectualization*, and is also something of a reaction-formation. The notable development in intelligence and interest in abstract problems found in many adolescents is produced by the severe inner conflicts to which their condition predisposes them. By thinking over its instinctual conflicts in some suitably distorted form, the adolescent ego seeks to deal with them. Such thinking is compulsive and often quite sterile in objective terms, but it does provide a suitably-abstracted expression of that to which the adolescent cannot otherwise face up. Anna Freud remarks that:

Closer examination shows that the subjects in which they are principally interested are

---

[1] *The Ego and the Mechanisms of Defence*, p. 167.
[2] *Ibid.*, p. 172ff.

the very same as have given rise to the conflicts between the different psychic institutions.[3]

Here again, the parallel with Christianity is exact. In the religious equivalent, intellectualization expresses itself as an overriding concern with dogmatic doctrinal definitions and with the elaboration of systematic theology. We have already seen that the Nicene Creed and other dogmatic instruments of Christianity are concerned with conflicts between the different psychic institutions of the mind represented by the Father (super-ego), and the Son (ego). Certainly, there can be no doubt that the asceticism of Catholic Christianity led many to sublimate their frustrated instincts in intellectual speculations which, like those of adolescents, are only notable to us today for their unreality, elaborated nonsensicality, and prodigious, but misapplied, intelligence. Anyone who reads the works of St Thomas Aquinas, St Augustine, or any of the other great Catholic theologians, is immediately struck by the huge intellectual stature of the men who produced them. But he also cannot help being struck by the supreme ludicrousness of finding such great minds exercising themselves in the service of a collective delusion which many lesser minds, both in their own day and now, could easily have shown to be a tissue of fantasy and a web of dreams. Such delusional systematization has a clear parallel in paranoia, but let us neglect this aspect of the situation for a moment, and conclude that scholastic theology seems to be an exercise in the intellectualization of instinctual conflict familiar to us from the psychoanalysis of adolescents.

If we pursue the parallel between Christianity and adolescence we should expect to find that Protestantism corresponds to the later period of adolescence, while Catholicism corresponds to the earlier. The later period is the time during which the adolescent shows a marked disillusionment with the parents, whose over-valued image, retained up till now from childhood, comes more and more under the eye of rational criticism. Ambivalences which previously were strenuously repressed and formed the basis of the neurotic reactions of puberty and early adolescence now give way to consciously-perceived, conflicting emotions which make the adolescent love his parents at one moment and hate them implacably at the next. Such extreme alternations of mood are the exact parallel of Luther's diabolism and his outbursts against God. Like the maturing adolescent, Luther is an iconoclastic individualist. He asserts his own opinions in the face of the emperor and the pope, and—again like the adolescent—gets away with it. He manifests all the reckless effrontery of youth when he contradicts ecumenical councils, the church fathers, and even Holy Writ, calling the Letter of St James a 'right strawy epistle' merely because he does not happen to agree with it. His vehement hatred of anyone who did not share his views, and his vitriolic attacks on those who dared to oppose him make Luther very much the 'angry young man' of Christian

[3] *Ibid.*, p. 176.

history. Infuriatingly illogical, cruelly selfish, brutishly bad-mannered, yet heroically independent and utterly sincere, Luther is a monstrously-magnified adolescent; he represents in world-history the emerging ego of man still struggling to gain its independence from the neurotic forces which oppose it.

Protestantism as a whole played a role in history exactly analogous to that played in the evolution of the individual by the period of late adolescence. Protestantism, and the Protestant emphasis on individual conscience and personal moral and religious responsibility, did much to free Western man from the traditional authority of sacred and secular father-figures. The Protestant doctrine of the priesthood of all believers signalled a revolt against the sacred paternal authority of the pope and of priestly religion in general; and what began as a purely religious protest against priests went on in the course of later centuries to become a political and social revolt against the persons of princes and kings. Protestant religious individualism gave rise to modern political individualism; and the Reformers' respect for individual moral conscience paved the way for the political and social emancipation of the masses. In time, Luther's obstinate insistence on his right to his own religious and moral views became the collective insistence of the West on the inalienable rights of the individual man and woman. The history of the last five hundred years has been one of the debunking of myths, the pulling-down of ancient, sacred authorities, and the gradual emancipation of the individual in religious, moral, political, and social terms. This process was given a tremendous initial impetus by Luther because Luther confronted those ancient authorities and sacred myths on their own ground and at their most essential focus—the collective super-ego, which is the essence of society and which we commonly call 'religion'. Yet, psychologically, each and every individual repeats, or should repeat, just such a process of individual emancipation from the super-ego during the later phase of adolescence. This is the time when, bodily maturity being complete, the ego should come fully into its own, and when it should assert itself against, and achieve some measure of equality with, the super-ego. There is one sense in which the whole process of 'modernization' or 'secularization' reflects little more than the gradual loosening of the obsessional psychological restraints of the super-ego and their gradual replacement by controls of the ego. Hence, rational law comes to dominate irrational taboo, secular authority supervenes over sacred, the claims of merit and competence assert themselves over hereditary right and privilege, rational justification becomes preferable to appeals to tradition, critical respect to blind obedience, democracy to despotism. All of these antitheses reflect the opposition of ego to super-ego, and the gradual triumph of the latter. There is much more that must be said about this process in later pages, but for the present let us merely observe that Protestantism, in so far as it represented the partial freeing of the ego from the old irrational domination of the collective super-ego, played a part in cultural history exactly comparable to that played by late adolescence in that of the individual.

The spread of Protestantism, like the spread of Gentile Christianity long before, was affected by many complex factors. Political circumstances in Germany at the time exerted a strong influence and made many princes wish to see Protestant churches established in their territories as an excuse to confiscate land and revenues from Rome, and as a means to exert their independence of the Emperor. But deeper forces were also at work, as is shown by the way in which the ancient boundaries of the Roman Empire reappear as the dividing line between the Protestant and Catholic worlds. Here, the major factor must have been the dependence of Catholicism on classical polytheism. In all those lands that had once been long-standing parts of the Roman Empire and which had not fallen to Islam, Catholicism stood firm. But in the parts of Europe which had either never been within the Roman Empire, or had only been a part of it for a short while, such a polytheistic foundation was lacking and Protestantism rapidly took hold.

Initially, the Protestant vanguard could draw on individuals who in the previous century would have gone into monasteries and convents to pursue the life of perfection away from the world. Following Luther, they left their monastic houses (or never entered them) and began to pursue the ascetic life as otherwise normal members of the community. To the extent that they collectively shared the omnipotent and sadistic super-ego which Luther had introduced into Christianity through his insistence on justification by faith, they also would tend to manifest evidence of anal character traits because of the repression under which traditional Christian passive and masochistic trends had fallen. As we have seen in the previous chapter, those passive homosexual tendencies find their erotic expression partly in anal eroticism, and it was this anal erotic proclivity of traditional Christian masochism which Protestants most inhibited, but which nevertheless expressed itself in the form of the reaction-formations and substitute-gratifications which constitute the anal character.

It is probable that parents with anal personality-types pass on their character tendency more easily to their children than do others. The reason for this is the crucial importance of toilet-training in the development of the anal personality. Among the Australian aborigines obsessional personality disorders do occur—although they are rare—but anal eroticism seldom if ever enters into the clinical picture. The reason for this is easy to see. The Australian aborigines are so uninhibited about defecation that it would be hard for anyone to form a reaction-formation against anal eroticism, particularly in early childhood. But if a child's parents show marked negative reactions to excrement while he is still passing through the anal-sadistic phase and create in him a proclivity to repress his anal eroticism even more strenuously than is normal, the chances of the child developing the reaction-formations and substitute-gratifications typical of the anal character in later life are vastly enhanced. As far as the populations of Protestant lands were concerned, Luther's Reformation brought the obsessional ethic of Protestantism out into the open as a psychological reality which began to influence the lives of generations of children long before they were old enough to say the words 'justification by faith', let alone to understand them. What we know of medieval norms of toilet-training suggests that it occurred rather later and was much less strict than it was to become in modern times.[4]

The net effect of all this was to produce generations of Protestants who had the anal personalities that were suitable for building the modern industrial economy. They were hard-working, independent, sober, easily disciplined, readily bureaucratized, fully socialized. Working for meagre rewards, saving all that was not necessary for unavoidable consumption, totally dedicated to their condition in life, completely convinced of the need to postpone gratification, these Protestant generations achieved a level of economic growth and collective prosperity unknown before. Once established, the economic system tended to become self-sustaining; and workers found that they could not eat unless they approximated to it, while entrepreneurs found that without acknowledging at least its basic ideals of orderliness, parsimoniousness, and self-sufficiency, they could not succeed in it. A whole literature and a richly diversified culture arose to sustain and reinforce it so that, even when its original religious inspiration began to wane, it could still continue to achieve its goals and could still manage to maintain the obsessional ideals on which it was based. In the eighteenth century Adam Smith produced a completely secularized version of the economic ethic of Protestantism. Weisskopf remarks that:

The ethical importance of work remained a main tenet in the value system of capitalism through the eighteenth and nineteenth centuries . . . Capital accumulation, saving, parsimony, industry and profit-making were treated as ethical duties in *The Wealth of Nations*.[5]

Weisskopf claims that it is the ethical value attached to work by the religious tradition of the Protestant West that caused Ricardo, Smith, and Marx to choose labour as the only basis of economic value, despite the insuperable theoretical and practical problems to which such an absurd idea gave rise.[6] Today, work still remains a fetish of Western man. I doubt very much whether anyone could explain to an Australian aborigine why people in the West become indignant when they have no work to do, and regard a job as their right even when they are fed, housed, and clothed by the state when unemployed. He would probably conclude that Westerners were masochists, and would not be far from the truth. But to be absolutely accurate he would have to say that Westerners *had been* masochists who adopted the work-ethic of Protestantism as a substitute-gratification for a more simple and extreme form of masochism—traditional Christian asceticism.

[4] Fromm quoted by Borneman, *The Psychoanalysis of Money*, p. 6.
[5] W. Weisskopf, *The Psychology of Economics*, pp. 27, 32.
[6] *Ibid.*, p. 27.

But the effects of Protestantism have not been limited to the economy. In art, literature, and especially music, its effects have been profound. In painting, the Reformation coincides with a new concern with rationality and orderliness expressed by the discovery of scientific perspective. From the sixteenth century onwards, realism becomes the major aim of painting, especially in the Protestant parts of Europe. In literature, the Protestant concern with conscience and moral introspection (justification by faith) lays the foundations for the modern novel, which in our own century reaches its supreme culmination in the obsessional auto-analytic masterpiece of Proust, but which begins with such Protestant epics as *Pilgrim's Progress* and *Paradise Lost*.

The origins of Western rationality in music lie, like those of rationality in economic and administrative matters, in the monasteries. Modern Western musical intervals evolved out of the chants of the monks; the development of the tempered scale, and of harmonic chords that enable intervals to be combined with one another with calculable and regular results is the supreme achievement of an obsessional concern with rational ordering.[7] Above all, the ascetic and abstract nature of music has meant that, of all art forms, it is the one that has been most highly developed in the West, and has been well regarded by even the most puritanical Protestants.

The relationship between Protestantism and modern science is equally close. R. K. Merton has documented the influence of Puritanism on the development of early English science.[8] The greatest scientist of them all, Isaac Newton, was an extreme case of the Protestant anal personality-type and is an example of how such a neurotic disposition can produce unparalleled mathematical genius—not to mention incomparable obstinacy and egotism.[9] In the case of Newton, an anal character-type was a valuable pre-disposition in an intellectual field where orderliness, exactness, and theoretical parsimony are institutionalized and regarded as essential in any piece of research. But perhaps even more important than this—at least as far as results, rather than the method of science is concerned—was the fact that the Protestant Reform greatly aided the emancipation of the mind from the restricting influence of classical tradition and ecclesiastical dogmatism.

The fundamental reason why the Protestant Reformation produced a great advance in scientific knowledge as well as in economic development was that advances in instinctual renunciation usually result in greater adaptation to reality. To understand why this is so we need to recall Freud's two primary principles of mental functioning: the reality principle and the pleasure principle.[10] The pleasure principle is what dominates the id, and is what would solely preoccupy the organism if it lacked perception of the outside

---

[7] M. Weber, *The Rational and Social Foundations of Music.*
[8] *Society, Technology and Science in Seventeenth Century England.*
[9] F. E. Manuel, *A Portrait of Isaac Newton.*
[10] Freud, 'Formulations on the Two Principles of Mental Functioning', XII, 215.

world. The existence of an objective reality outside the organism causes it to take account of this reality and to moderate the pleasure principle in the interests of survival. This is the main task of the ego. Any advance in instinctual renunciation is obviously a set-back for the pleasure-principle and therefore (by definition) an advance for the reality principle. When the instinctual renunciation is greater, the supremacy of the reality principle must also become greater; and this, in psychological terms, is what we mean by science. Freud makes precisely this point when he says that:

Science is . . . the most complete renunciation of the pleasure principle of which our mental activity is capable.[11]

Thus, from purely psychological deductions, we could have predicted that not only would the secularization of the Christian ideal of altruism produce a major economic advance, but that it would also be bound to produce a major scientific one. The fact that this has happened, and that it has happened most in those countries which became Protestant, and which also showed the most tendency to develop capitalism, bears out the prediction that scientific advance is psychologically closely linked with instinctual renunciation. In the Middle Ages the Queen of the Sciences was theology for the simple reason that, in a culture where ascetics pursued a separate life in monastic isolation, wish-fulfilment and the dominant animistic attitude strongly discouraged any far-reaching advances in the interests of the reality principle. Considered solely as a return to polytheism, Catholic Christianity was a victory for the pleasure principle, and showed a marked regression in terms of rationality. Both instinctual renunciation and dominance of the reality principle were less than they had been in the founders of Christianity; and although renunciation was maintained within the monastic communities, the scope for the development of science seems to have been limited, doubtless because of the pervading animism. Nevertheless, it is important to notice that what scientific understanding and intellectual culture there was found a safe home in the monasteries of the Middle Ages; and the example of Mendel, albeit a modern one, should warn us against dismissing the possibility of scientific endeavour within an ascetic order. But even so, it is clear that in Catholic Christianity most intellectual work was done in the service of the pleasure principle and of theology, rather than in that of the reality principle and science. As long as phantasy and regression to the omnipotence of thoughts played such a major part in European religion, science with its uncompromising realism and tendency to unmask mysteries, was inevitably seen as a threat to religion and as a snare of the Devil. When a more consistently obsessional and non-animistic attitude became dominant in Protestantism this situation changed. Luther, it is true, was still medieval enough to distrust scientific researches and abominated Copernicus (as, for that matter, he did capitalism), but his

[11] 'A Special Type of Choice of Object Made by Men', XI, 165.

fearless stand in favour of a more rational and less magical type of religion could not possibly fail to be the prelude to an epoch of rapid scientific discovery.

Yet Luther's distrust of science is something more than a vestige of medievalism. It reveals the tension between science and religion, and touches on the most profound element of the Reformation, namely, the fact that it represented the beginning of the end of religious belief and the start of man's final recovery from the collective neurosis from which he had suffered since that fatal day when the first hominid felt guilt at committing parricide and began to develop inhibitions about incest.

The early Protestants regarded science as the revelation of God's wonders and an aid to human endeavour, as Merton shows.[12] But very quickly, scientific research began to find things which dealt body-blows to the religious conception of the universe and of man's place within it. Even as the Reformation was happening, Copernicus was advancing a theory which put the sun, and not the earth, at the centre of the universe. As Freud pointed out, this was the first of the great setbacks to man's narcissism which science was to entail. 'The central position of the earth,' says Freud,

. . . was a token to him of the dominating part played by it in the universe and appeared to fit in very well with his inclination to regard himself as lord of the world.[13]

The second setback was a biological rather than a cosmological one. Now, thanks to Darwin, man learnt that he was much more a part of nature and the world of animals than he had previously thought. Besides being compromising to man's narcissistic pride in himself as a being inherently superior to animals, the theory of evolution put a considerable strain on the accepted religious conception of man. Not only did it contradict Holy Writ on the issue of man's creation, the theory of evolution also had the temerity to suggest that natural selection, rather than divine providence, was responsible for the animal and vegetable creation. True, intelligent religious thinkers could get round this by pushing God's intervention in the world further and further back, both in time and in the causal processes which maintain the structure of the world—something which had already begun to happen when Newton showed that the solar system, once put in motion, would go on working everlastingly. All that was needed was to assume that God was responsible, not for the creation *ex nihilo* of each and every species, but merely for the principle of evolution. However, this was far from a happy solution because it necessarily attributed to God the responsibility for a most non-providential and seemingly cruel law of natural selection.

Finally, came the last, and greatest, setback both to man's narcissism and to

[12] *Op. cit.*   [13] *A Difficulty in the Path of Psychoanalysis*, XVII, 140.

religion. This was the psychological one.[14] Freud's discovery of the unconscious and of the way in which it influenced man showed that mentally man was not even the master in his own house. He had unconscious thought-processes which were unknown to him and often contrary to those of which he was aware. Psychoanalysis demonstrated that man possessed instinctual drives which he could only in part control by the exercise of his will and which, if abused by his consciousness, could take the most frightening and weird revenge on him. Man's narcissism—that is, his love of his own self—suffered a great diminution with this discovery, but so too did his commitment to religion. Now it began to become clear that religion itself was not all that it seemed to be. Objections to religious belief originating in cosmological or biological discoveries are one thing; cosmology and biology are, after all, peripheral to the central issues of religion, which are ethics and morals, prayer and ritual, faith, hope, and charity. But what if science began to trespass on these same central issues, and began to show that moral behaviour and ethical theories have psychological causes quite distinct from those of which people are usually conscious? What if psychoanalysis began to demonstrate that prayer and ritual had certain revealing similarities with the compulsive behaviour of obsessional neurotics? Supposing faith turned out, on closer scrutiny, to be a reaction and defence-measure against doubt, hope a vestige of psychological infantilism, and charity only a very hypocritical sort of selfishness? It is clear that in these circumstances religion is in even more serious trouble than man's narcissism. 'Probably very few people,' writes Freud, 'could have realized the momentous significance for science and life of the recognition of unconscious mental processes.'[15]

But the facts are clear to anyone who has the sense to see them: psychoanalysis, in so far as it is an extension of the reality principle in mental life, spells the end of the self-delusions on which both man's narcissism and his religion are based. Man—or rather his conscious ego, for this is the part of him which is responsible for these delusions—can no longer pretend that he is free to do as he pleases and to regard himself as an autonomous being, above the dictates of natural laws and free of the inner determinisms which control the rest of nature. With the coming of psychoanalysis, he has had to admit that this is not so, that there are within him powerful forces which it is not in his competence to ignore, that deep within him there are unknown factors which set close limits on what he may think and do, and that, even when he believes he is unconstrained, the hidden hand of the unconscious intervenes in his affairs and pursues its interests whether he should wish to recognize it or not. It has brought him, in short, the last and most significant revelation, namely, objective knowledge about himself and the causes of his behaviour.

Luther was right to be apprehensive about science, just as he was right to be apprehensive about capitalism. Both of them in their own way were to

[14] *Ibid.*, XVII, 141.
[15] *Ibid.*, XVII, p. 143.

undermine and ultimately to destroy religion; capitalism by increasing consumption far beyond anything compatible with the ascetic ideals of the Reformation, and science by gradually unmasking the phantasies on which all religions are based. Yet Luther bears the full responsibility for all that happened subsequently. He was the one who broke with the regressive narcissism of the Middle Ages; it was he who confronted the obsessional neurosis of religion on its own ground; it was he who began to hate God and, in his unconscious and in the guise of a demonic delusion, to begin to demolish the image of God as a credible being. With Luther, the idea of God reached its penultimate stage and was made ready for the final revelation.

This final revelation of the true nature of God was to be made by Freud, but Luther's conception prepared the way much more than anything else. In the first place, Luther had a deep consciousness of sin. This is, of course, typical of obsessionals, but the important point is that it is essentially a true consciousness. The obsessional whose hypersensitive conscience may give the impression of over-reacting to what are only peccadillos is in fact giving distorted expression to a deeper and truer consciousness of guilt, that originating in the Oedipal conflicts which are the root of the neurosis. Luther gave religious expression to this in an unforgettable way through his dogma of justification by faith. This presupposed that man could only be saved by the free act of God and could do nothing in himself to merit salvation. It assumed that God is totally good and that man is totally bad, so that even his desire for salvation is, in so far as it is his own, sinful. When praying, Luther recommended that one should first of all ask God to give one the good intention necessary, for one could not generate it oneself. This implicit recognition of the totally-culpable nature of man is not far from the Freudian realization of the force of the unconscious and the role of the instincts in mental life. Freud, too, maintained that everything which man thinks, wills, and does is sinful—if by that we mean that it is dominated by self-interest, aimed at satisfying abysmal aggressive, libidinal, and egoistic drives, and intended to secure pleasure whenever and wherever possible. Luther went a long way towards this view with his realization that man is by nature totally sinful, and that acts of charity, and mortifications which seem to make for holiness on the surface, are only the creations of human vanity and sin, and that all outward show of goodness can only be the work of the Devil.

Secondly, Luther's preoccupation with the Devil provided the expression of negative ambivalences which Freud was later to uncover in everyone and which was to be the beginning of the realization of the other side of God, the dark side which had remained permanently turned away before, but which Freud more than anyone else was to reveal. As far as the individual was concerned, Luther's realization of the dogma of justification by faith meant that in his dealings with God all that man could rely on ultimately was his conscience—and even that was not infallible. If priests and Masses, indulgences and mortifications, could not absolve one from guilt, and if the religious institutions which peddled these wares were the work of Satan, then the individual was thrown back onto his own resources and onto the goodwill which God would give him and which Immanuel Kant was later to secularize into a principle of moral philosophy called the Categorical Imperative. This identification of the moral authority of God with one's own conscience went a long way towards Freud's final revelation of God as the super-ego. By making moral introspection of the sort later rationalized by philosophers like Kant into a necessary part of religion Luther was preparing the way for the free-association introspections of psychoanalysis. By recognizing the need for sexual gratification of the body and the wrong-headedness of extreme ascetic mortifications, Luther was already well on the way to the recognition of the demands of the instincts which Freud was to embody in a definitive theory of human nature some four centuries later.

We might sum up the situation by saying that if Luther and Protestantism represent the later adolescence of Western man, Freud and psychoanalysis represent final maturity. With Freud, the neurosis is finally resolved and the truth revealed. According to a comparison between the history of the individual and that of the race suggested in *Totem and Taboo*:

> The animistic phase would correspond to narcissism both chronologically and in its content; the religious phase would correspond to the stage of object-choice of which the characteristic is a child's attachment to his parents; while the scientific phase would have an exact counterpart in the stage at which an individual has reached maturity, has renounced the pleasure principle, adjusted himself to reality and turned to the external world for the object of his desires.[16]

This quotation is of the first importance, not merely because in it we find Freud conscribing to the analogy which exists between the individual's psychological development and certain aspects of human history, and which has been so elaborately developed in this book, but much more because it contains the assertion that psychoanalysis is itself a notable advance in instinctual renunciation, and therefore by implication something comparable to previous advances in the evolution of world-religion. I have already expanded on the circumstantial similarities between psychoanalysis and Protestantism, but this quotation seems to establish a more formal similarity in that it suggests that psychoanalysis is a stage in the evolution of religion comparable to the attainment of maturity in the individual rather in the way in which Protestantism is comparable to late adolescence. Yet if we understand it in this way it immediately throws up an apparent paradox which suggests either that we are incorrect in representing psychoanalysis like this, or that my characterization of the advance in renunciation of instinct achieved by Protestantism was mistaken. The paradox is this: If the advance in instinctual renunciation made by Christianity was one of complete altruism and renunciation of all pleasure, no further advance is possible, and so there could have

[16] XIII, 90.

been nothing to renounce on gaining maturity with the coming of psycho-analysis.

In order to resolve this difficulty we must re-examine more carefully what we have meant when in the past we have spoken of stages in the evolution of religion as being typified by a renunciation of instinct. The renunciations of Protestantism, and in particular of Puritanism, appear to be no more than those of Christ and St Paul, but were an advance over Catholicism in the sense that they were applied to the whole religious community rather than to just a part of it as had been the case where monastic asceticism existed. In that respect Protestantism represented an undoubted advance. But renuncia-tions of instinct in the service of altruism, although extreme, are not the only instinctual renunciations one can be called upon to make. Protestantism made a major new renunciation of instinct when it eradicated the animism and poly-theism which had crept into Catholicism. The instinct gratified by these re-gressive features of medieval religion had been man's narcissism, as my earlier discussion of animism showed. In this respect psychoanalysis is clearly a further advance in renunciation over Protestantism because, as we have just seen, Freud describes it as corresponding to the phase in the individual's life when he 'has renounced the pleasure principle' and 'adjusted to the external world'. My remarks earlier about the impact of psychoanalytic discoveries on man's narcissism and the pleasure principle leave little doubt that this is correct.

But what of altruism? We shall see in a moment that altruism of the kind represented by the Sermon on the Mount is not a feature of the psycho-analytic system of values, no matter how much some seem to have wished it were. In any case, Protestantism actually reduced altruism in so far as it put an end to indiscriminate charity ('good works'), and came to see poverty as evidence of lack of grace, rather than the outcome of injustice or hardship. No one would, I think, want to claim that Protestants were in the mass more altruistic than the Catholic ascetic communities. No one could be more altruistic than St Francis of Assisi, whatever the hypocrisy on which that altruism was erected might be. Yet we must be more circumspect if we are not to be led astray. Earlier, I said that an ethic of total altruism, like that of St Francis or Christ, was an ideal of total masochism. So much is undeniable. But we must recall that psychoanalysis finds that masochism is intensely gratifying to masochists—'perfect joy' in the words of St Francis—and that this is why they practice it. Perfect altruists like Christ and St Francis might practice absolute renunciation of their aggressive and libidinal drives as far as other men are concerned, but they practice no such renunciations with regard to themselves. St Francis' hysterical nature, represented above all in the hysterical identification with Christ, which gave him the stigmata of the crucifixion, is understood by psychoanalysis to be, like all cases of hysteria, an eroticization of the whole body. As such, his stigmatization was masochistic-ally highly gratifying to him—'perfect joy', no less. When we include in the picture of the hidden gratification of St Francis' altruism all the sadism gratified by his persecution of his father and all the joys of self-righteousness that come with thinking oneself—especially if one never does think oneself—holier than others, the balance sheet of renunciation and gratification evens up and, like all well-drawn-up balance sheets, tallies exactly. And so it is with all ascetic saints. Judging from the case of Schreber, paranoid psychotics with megalomanic phantasies of world-redemption such as Christ must have lived in an almost perpetual state of unconscious erotic enchantment with themselves (cf. Schreber's 'miraculous' defecations).

But to return to the problem. Let us take it as established that, although the ideally-altruistic ethics of Christianity do involve considerable renunciation of instinct, they also include indirect, perverse, and unconscious gratifications which increase in equal proportion to the original renunciations. My reason for making this point is to try to show that Protestantism was an advance in instinctual renunciation in terms of these inner and much-less obvious gratifications. The dogma of justification by faith, and the Protestant emphasis on predestination, meant that inner, hypocritical gratifications of holiness and asceticism were greatly reduced. Of course, it is possible that relatively few Protestants—like very few Catholics, for that matter—ever lived out their religion to the full and with total commitment. But the insincere and the backsliding are not relevant to this discussion; what matters is that the ideal Protestant had fewer opportunities for gratification of his pride, narcissism, and sado-masochism than the ideal Catholic ascetic. This was because justification by faith meant that he could never be sure that he was one of the elect—only God could know that—and if he were among the sheep, rather than the goats, it was by no virtue of his own that he had achieved salvation. The true Protestant could not feel that anything was perfect joy save the possession of divine grace, and of that he could never be sure. Certainty of salvation was sin and presumption on the will of God—it meant certain perdition. Thus in Protestantism the absence of the more spectacular asceticisms and the more-mindless charity of the Middle Ages is not indicative of any reduction in instinctual renunciation. On the contrary, these things are symptoms of a deeper ethical renunciation, one which even goes as far as renouncing the certainty of salvation and all those little hypocrisies which add up to the great satisfactions of righteousness.

It is clear that if psychoanalysis can also be called an advance in rationality over Protestantism it is an advance of precisely this sort. Psychoanalysis, as the quotation from Freud on page 223 reveals, aims to free man from the last of his self-delusions. As such, it is a triumph of the reality principle, and hence a renunciation of those narcissistic instincts which obtain their pleasure from wish-fulfilment. Even if Protestantism had dispensed with all the magic and most of the ritual of animistic-polytheistic Christianity, it still retained God, the greatest phantasy of all. Even if it made do without the magic of relics, indulgences, penances, and priestly offices, it still could not get by without divine providence or the notion of predestination. True, the sacraments had been reduced from seven to two; but the central mysteries of the Christian faith, the incarnation, the Trinity, Heaven, Hell, and the Last Judgement, all remained largely untouched by the Reformers. Psychoanalysis and the scientific world-view of which it is a part dispatched the lot and substituted rigorous adherence to the reality principle in place of the wish-fulfilments of man's narcissistic need for God. Psychoanalysis made the greatest renunciation of all in the religious sphere by showing that religion is itself an infantilism and a neurosis, that religious belief is a capitulation to the pleasure principle, and that the practice of religion is a flight into neurotic illness—albeit one whose numerous adherents disguise its fundamentally-pathological nature. The revelations of the inner workings of the mind leave man with not one of his hypocritical righteous satisfactions, and show him that the concept of the soul is a day-dream which, like any dream, fulfils a wish and hides its latent meaning under a misleading manifest idea.

In terms of its renunciations of the narcissistic instincts, psychoanalysis obviously goes as far as anything can; and this is why Freud, as we noted above, called it the third and greatest blow which man's collective narcissism had received. But what of the other instincts? Psychoanalysis is not usually identified with a renunciation of all instinct; so how can it be called a comprehensive advance in instinctual renunciation over Protestantism, or even Catholicism or monotheism? In order to answer this objection, let us go back to a consideration of altruism.

Earlier, when discussing altruism, I pointed out that perfect altruism was the same thing as complete anti-egoism and that, in psychological terms, anti-egoism means masochism. To love one's enemies is to love the punishment they give one, which is a perverse and masochistic gratification. So much is clear. Protestantism, with its different attitude to the poor and needy, reduced charity somewhat, but it would be wrong to argue from this that Protestants were less altruistic as a result. They still accepted the Sermon on the Mount and all the recommendations of St Paul regarding the moral primacy of love for one's fellow man. What occurred within Protestantism with regard to altruism was exactly like what happened with regard to asceticism. It became rationalized and intensified through the renunciation of its hidden and hypocritical gratifications. For the Catholic who pursued perfection, all that mattered was that one should become unencumbered of worldly goods. But such charity contained an evident paradox: If all the rich go and sell all they have and give it to the poor, the poor become the nouveau riche and all that the charity of the previously rich has achieved is to place the souls of its recipients in jeopardy. Protestant altruism contained no such paradox. Because of justification by faith, it despised such outward shows of spectacular charity (and one only has to recall the case of St Francis to see with what good reason), and took seriously the question of the effect of charity on those who received it. The altruism demanded by the Sermon on the Mount was now interpreted as a need to become completely at the disposal of God, and to subjugate all one's egoism, not by spectacular acts of self-mortification, but by an inner passivity towards God which made a Protestant accept his station in life as that to which divine providence had called him. Charity now became a means of helping others to do the same, rather than an end in itself which discouraged its recipients from trying to help themselves. Of course, this Protestant altruism had its own form of masochism and its own hidden, anal gratifications. But the important point is that they were gratifications that followed from the renunciation of traditional asceticism and all the hypocrisy it entailed. With Protestantism, the irresponsible, negative altruism of Catholicism is transformed into an ethic which expects of everyone, not merely the élite, a contribution to the well-being of all by the pursuit of a useful trade or occupation (and, as such, was ultimately to become the rationale of the market economy).

Freud's attitude to the altruistic ideal of Christianity is not hard to discover. In *Civilization and Its Discontents* he tells us expressly that

The commandment, 'Love they neighbour as thyself' is . . . an excellent example of the unpsychological proceedings of the cultural super-ego. The commandment is impossible to fulfill; such an enormous inflation of love can only lower its value, not get rid of the difficulty. Civilization pays no attention at all to this; it merely admonishes us that the harder it is to obey the precept the more meritorious it is to do so. But anyone who followed such a precept in presentday civilization only puts himself at a disadvantage *vis à vis* the person who disregards it.[17]

With regard to altruism, psychoanalysis stands in relation to Protestantism just as it does on the issue of narcissistic wish-fulfilment. It is its logical extension. Protestantism distinguished between the outward show of altruistic self-sacrifice and the inward realities. By making man reliant on grace and incapable of goodness in himself, Protestantism recognized that man could not be naturally altruistic. If he did love his neighbour as himself, it was only because God gave the grace to do so, and that could be given without sensational marriages to Lady Poverty. The Protestant would have regarded St Francis' life of itinerant begging as completely contrary to the Sermon on the Mount; and would have held that Francis should have patiently served God in the station in life to which he had been called and should have pursued the less glamorous, but more difficult, goal of true charity while trying to run a substantial business. After all, if inward grace is what matters, outward shows of poverty and concern with others are liable to be highly deceptive. Finally, the good Protestant would probably have noticed, and not without reason, that such altruism is counter-productive if the ascetics it produces have to go round the countryside begging—that is, living by the altruism of others. The Freudian attitude to altruism is only an extension of this. As in the case of Protestant attitudes to charity, there is indeed a renunciation of instinct

[17] XXI, 143.

involved. It is a renunciation of the perverse joys—the 'perfect joy'—to be found in futile altruism of the Franciscan type. Furthermore, like the Protestant advance in the rationalization of Christian altruism, which it itself advances on, psychoanalysis is mindful of the effects of altruism, and we find Freud giving voice to the fundamental principle governing altruism which I mentioned above. This holds that altruism always declines if the more altruistic allow the less altruistic to prosper at their expense. Freud's argument is that there can be no point in loving my neighbour if that love only gives him an opportunity to be more sadistic to me than he might have been otherwise. 'Love thy neighbour as thy neighbour loves thee'[18] is perfectly rational altruism, but it is hardly what Christ meant. Like the Protestant who will not hand out charity merely to subsidize laziness and ineptitude, Freud will not allow us to practice altruism if its only result is to put us at a disadvantage to those less altruistic than ourselves. Such a disadvantageous situation vis-à-vis the recipient of one's altruism was doubtless highly gratifying to Christian masochists, but to those who have renounced such self-indulgence this irresponsible charity is not evidence of moral perfection, but of moral stupidity. In insisting on introducing the reality principle into the calculus of altruistic behaviour, Freud is carrying out the most radical renunciation possible and repudiating completely the moral sentimentality which characterizes the Sermon on the Mount in particular, and Christian ethics in general. In the Freudian attitude of realism towards other men there is no room for the sublimated homosexuality which pervades Christianity. Altruistic behaviour becomes a rational and non-masochistic affair in which one gives up something to someone in return for some real and tangible benefit. Renunciation of self-interest for the sake of the reality principle, rather than for hidden masochistic gratification of the pleasure principle, is a much more difficult thing to achieve, and makes the psychoanalytic criterion of altruism a vast advance in instinctual renunciation over that of Christianity.

So much for the ego instincts; but what of the libido? Surely, here we shall find that psychoanalysis shows up as a definite regression in terms of instinctual renunciation.

There can be no doubt that each previous stage in the evolution of religion discussed above has corresponded to an increasing repression of sexuality. Speaking of his own times, in which the Puritan ethic was still very effective in matters of sex, Freud says:

Present-day civilization makes it plain that it will only permit sexual relationships on the basis of a solitary, indissoluble bond between one man and one woman, and that it does not like sexuality as a source of pleasure in its own right and is only prepared to tolerate it because there is so far no substitute for it as a means of propagating the human race.[19]

[18] Freud, ibid., XXI, 110.
[19] Ibid., XXI, 105.

This quotation strongly gives the impression that the only remaining renunciation of instinct would be total celibacy; but the mention of that word should remind us that a difficulty also exists here as far as Protestantism is concerned. If I am correct in claiming that Protestantism was an advance in instinctual renunciation over Catholicism, then it, too, seems to be an exception in the sphere of sexual ethics. But here again, things are not as simple as they appear to be. When Luther left the monastery and married an ex-nun, what he did was exactly in accordance with the dogma of justification by faith, no matter what the unconscious motivation may have been. Luther's attitude to the sexual needs of the body—which was that they were the creation of God and had to be given their due—was only a logical continuation of the repudiation of the more absurd aspects of masochistic asceticism. His own experience had convinced him that celibacy does not necessarily make a man more chaste. He knew only too well that the celibate monk could become obsessed with sexuality merely by trying to suppress it from his thoughts; and he knew that he could do nothing about the physical concomitants of sexuality, such as erections and emissions. That monks should marry was an obvious advance in the pursuit of genuine chastity, once it had been conceded that celibacy is self-defeating.

The Freudian attitude to sexuality is only a continuation of this trend of thinking to the point where it realizes that the pursuit of chastity is itself an illusion, and that the reality principle decrees that man should recognize that his sexual instinct is much less tractable than the Sermon on the Mount imagines. This triumph of the reality principle over the pleasure principle is, in this sense, the greatest renunciation of instinct possible; and the fact that it involves giving the pleasure principle full recognition in the field of sexuality only follows as a consequence. Freud did not believe that our sexual instincts deserved more gratification because he had bowed to urgent promptings of the pleasure principle. On the contrary, he believed, like Luther, that sexuality had to be given its due gratification because realism dictated that this was the only way in which to avoid the alternatives of neurosis or perversion. Those who hold that psychoanalysis gives grounds for totally unfettered gratification of each and every instinctual need have missed the point completely. Nothing could be further from the truth.

These examples are sufficient to show that psychoanalysis does indeed represent an advance in instinctual renunciation over Protestantism. However, this advance is entirely in the service of the reality principle and, as a consequence of this, in practice results in less repression and in a greater recognition of the demands of the instincts.

Considerations such as these lead us to the realization that each and every advance in renunciation of instinct is also *a limitation of the pleasure and an enhancement of the reality principle*. This is why renunciations of instinct often coincide with economic advances. An advanced economy is one which is intrinsically better adapted to existing conditions than any other available at the time. Adaptation to existing conditions is alternative phraseology for 'enhancement of the reality principle'; it is clear that none of the economic developments discussed above as consequential on a renunciation of instinct would have survived to maintain the renunciations in question if the economy they produced had not been in reality superior to the other possibilities.

At this point the reader may well be struck by what seems, at first sight, an odd implication of this characterization of psychoanalysis as an advance in rationality comparable to that of world-religions like monotheism or totemism, or recent developments like Protestantism or Catholicism. The implication unquestionably present in what I have just said is that psychoanalysis ought to correspond to a new economic system and, presumably, to one which is as different from and as advanced over capitalism as the latter is over the economies which preceded it. One would also expect from this that psychoanalysis would have its own distinctive *weltanschauung* comparable to those of the religions mentioned in previous chapters of this book. Furthermore the reader will probably recall that Freud expressly denied that his new approach to the mind could have any distinctive *weltanschauung* apart from that which it shares with all sciences.[20] But let me reassure him. No one is claiming that psychoanalysis is going to be a new religion in the way in which Protestantism or totemism have been religions. The point I am making is that psychoanalysis represents the last stage—the resolution—of the collective neurosis that we call religion, and that, as such it succeeds religion in much the same way that normality and recovery follow a long and complicated illness. As far as the economic impact of this advance in rationality is concerned, I can only say that, formally, it differs from previous cases analyzed in this book because a normal[21] erotic adjustment—which is what psychoanalysis aims to achieve—is not consistent with any particular repression of the perversion whose sublimation could be employed in a new mode of economic life. However, and notwithstanding such an observation, I have no doubt that in practice psychoanalysis, with its greater realism about human beings and their motivation, may help to promote a more realistic attitude to economic systems, and may help to dispel the moral sentimentalism and counterproductive altruism which pervades much so-called 'progressive' economic thought. I suspect that a psychoanalytic critique of the modern economy would result in the vindication of market forces against bureaucratic control for the simple reason that free markets respond to the real wants of the population, as opposed to planned economies, which can only reflect the fantasies of a ruling élite.

Another aspect of the progressive triumph of the reality principle in each and every stage in the evolution of religion is a purely psychological one that I have mentioned before. This is that such advances in rationality always

[20] *New Introductory Lectures*, XXXV, 'The Question of a Weltanschauung', XXII, 158ff.

[21] Freud, 'Libidinal Types', XXI, 219.

promote psychological realism and bring the image of the divinity one step closer to the truth. In animism there is no divinity in heaven for the simple reason that it was during the sojourn of our gelada-like, seed-eating ancestors upon the earth that the one and only authentic incarnation of God took place. Then, he walked the earth as the fearsome primal father, omnipotent, omniscient, and omnipresent within the horde over which he extended his tyranny. With the transition to a fully-fledged hunting economy, the primal hordes were gradually replaced by fraternal hunting bands, and God was driven out of the garden of Eden, not because he had eaten any apple, but because his sons had tasted flesh and liked it. Now for the first time he appeared in heaven; he became part of the religious system as the totem animal—his strangest, and most primitive representation. From now on, each stage in the evolution of religion would carry his religious image closer and closer to the truth, and would uncover the symbolic wrappings in which he had been hidden. In polytheism, he went through a transitional stage in which he appeared as a divine king following the epoch of the great phallic mother-goddesses, rather as in the mind of the individual the animal phobias of early childhood give way to the crystallization of the super-ego that begins with the phallic mother, who is then succeeded by her castrator—the true bearer of the phallus, the father. With the coming of pastoralism, the complex transitional divinities of polytheism are rationalized into the single omniscient, omnipotent, and omnipresent God of monotheism. Shorn of anthropomorphic attributes, the Deity becomes the punitive father, the religious image of the force of conscience. After a further transitional interlude represented by Catholicism, during which a son-Diety is introduced who signals the beginning of the end of the undisputed rule of the punitive super-ego, Protestantism makes a further great step forward in rationalizing the idea of God by making him equivalent in practical terms to the conscience of the individual. Finally, psychoanalysis makes the last step and equates God with the super-ego in the unconscious of the individual and with the primal father in the forgotten history of the race. The evolutionary series 'Feared Animal—Sole Deity—Individual Conscience—Super-ego' represents a process of advancing rationalization and steadily increasing psychological realism regarding the nature of the figure who stands at the centre of all religious systems. It is the historical and religious equivalent of what takes place in every normal individual between early childhood and maturity.

What occurs in the culture with the coming of psychoanalysis is analogous to what occurs in the individual with the coming of maturity. Psychoanalysis does not mean the complete breakdown of culture, which admittedly is based on instinctual repression, anymore than the achievement of maturity means for the individual the complete demolition of the personality structure he has acquired during childhood. For the individual, maturity ought to mean that the ego has become master in its own house and has established the reality principle as the main arbiter of its action. The head-on collisions between the newly awakened instinctual demands of the id and the newly reinforced repressions of the super-ego which are typical of adolescence should gradually be resolved by the submission of both parties to the arbitration of the ego, which has at its disposal the means of testing reality. This should result in a recognition of the just demands of both instinctual gratification and of instinctual renunciation judged by the criterion of reality, rather than by blind emotional responses left over from childhood.

Similarly, psychoanalysis aims to advance the reality principle and to make the various departments of the mind submit to rational control rather than continue to fight with one another in conflicts which can never be resolved. Like the achievement of maturity in the individual, it is not to be equated with the total undoing of all inhibitions:

For analysis does not undo the *effects* of repression. The instincts which were formerly suppressed remain suppressed; but the same effect is produced in a different way. Analysis replaces the process of repression, which is an automatic and excessive one, by a temperate and purposeful control on the part of the higher agencies of the mind. In a word *analysis replaces repression by condemnation*.[22]

The process of the replacement of blind repression by conscious and reasonable renunciation is the outcome of the tremendous advance in rationality represented by psychoanalysis over all previous moral and psychological progress. It is the ultimate embodiment of the reality principle in morality; it marks the final achievement of realism, reason and truth in the assessment of human conduct. For the culture as a whole, it represents the state of ideal, rational maturity which psychoanalysis aims to provide for the successfully analyzed individual.

Yet it would be quite wrong to imagine that such a transition to normality and maturity in Western society is either easy or automatic. On the contrary, powerful pathological forces seem to be working against it, which must make the eventual achievement of such a desirable state by no means inevitable.

If religion in general corresponds to individual childhood and adolescence, we might immediately—and, I think, correctly—conclude that vestiges of religious belief were a chief obstacle to progress in this respect. We might also assume—again, probably rightly—that in the West traditional religious belief is in full decline, and that the substitution of tolerance and 'ecumenicism' for the traditional Christian attitude of bigoted intolerance in matters of religion signals, as Spengler so perceptively saw, not a new-found strength for compromise, but a debilitating weakness. Yet if traditional religion is weak, and likely to weaken progressively, the prognosis with regard to other forms of social psychopathology is not so encouraging. In fact, far from disappearing, the underlying mass-psychopathology of Christianity is still strongly present, masquerading under the name of socialism.

[22] Freud, *Analysis of a Phobia in a Five-Year Old Boy*, X, 145.

It is a matter of common knowledge that Saint Simon, the inventor of socialism, originally called it 'New Christianity', and regarded it essentially as the Sermon on the Mount, shorn of all supernatural elements. As such, modern socialism enshrines the values of altruism found in the New Testament, but translated into a wholly materialist and worldly equivalent of traditional Christian moral masochism. The need to turn the other cheek becomes a commitment to disarmament and passivism; love for one's enemies becomes concern for the well-being of criminals and foreigners and defence of the rights of all those who threaten the state (without equal regard for those who defend it); traditional Christian humility becomes an emphasis on a levelled-down equality with a positive hatred of excellence and superiority of any kind; Christian charity becomes Welfare, and ideals of Christian generosity the basis for policies of punitive taxation. Finally, the Kingdom of God appears as the totalitarian state, and Divine Revelation becomes its dogmas. Socialism might then, logically, be expected to reveal an underlying psychopathology comparable to that of pre-Protestant Christianity, which I characterized as a collective paranoia. This is exactly what we find.

The reader may have been struck by the notable omission of any mention of paranoid delusions in my discussion of Christian paranoia. Such delusions are, after all, a characteristic of the disease; and he will probably wonder why I did not refer to them earlier when I mentioned the other symptoms of paranoia in Christianity. The answer to this question is that I wanted to reserve the whole matter until the present, and that, in any case, paranoid delusions were not to be expected early on. The reason for this is that such delusions, like world-reconstruction phantasies and hallucinations, are restitutional symptoms—that is, attempts at recovery—which appear after the initial pathological processes have begun ('regressive symptoms'). In Christianity the latter were end-of-the-world delusions, an ethic of world-rejection, and megalomanic identification with the Deity. All of these appear in the founder, and are an outstanding feature of the first centuries. World-reconstruction fantasies also appear early, but do not become translated into action until the monastic communities, and then the mendicant friars, set out to remodel and improve the world of their times. At much the same period as this restitutional symptom was manifesting itself in Christianity, the delusions typical of paranoia begin in earnest. They constitute the most abhorrent chapter in the whole blood-stained history of Christianity, and are the most discreditable feature in a religion notable for the grotesque and horrifying forms of its pathology. I refer to the monumental, and typically Christian delusion of persecution enshrined in what we call *anti-Semitism*.[23]

[23] The paranoid characteristics of Christian anti-Semitism have been noticed by authors such as R. Loewenstein, *Christians & Jews*, and E. Simmel (Ed.), *Anti-Semitism*, and others. But all these analysts make the elementary error of mistaking a single symptom for the whole disease. If anti-Semitism is a paranoid delusion this can only be because it is part of a larger paranoia.

In discussing Schreber's feelings of persecution, Freud points out that the chief object of these delusions, the psychiatrist, Dr Flechsig, was previously highly—indeed, warmly—regarded by his patient.[24] It is characteristic of paranoia that, as an attempt at resecuring the libidinal contacts with the out-side world, which regressive symptoms such as megalomania put in jeopardy, homosexual libidinal attachments, like Schreber's to Dr Flechsig, become re-emphasized, but subject to a typically paranoid reversal. The unconscious idea, 'I love him' becomes 'he hates me'; the paranoiac is able thereby to defend himself against such a latent attachment while at the same time remain-ing preoccupied with it.[25] In this way, a negative Oedipal libidinal orienta-tion seeks to assert itself against a regression to narcissism. An exactly anal-ogous process occurs in the collective paranoia which we call Christianity.

Regarded from the viewpoint of reason and historical truth, Christian anti-Semitism is unintelligible. After all, Christ was a Jew, and so was St Paul, and all the apostles. Originally, the Christian community worshipped in the Temple, and even when the new religion opened its doors to Gentiles, the Jewish tradition still retained much of its force. Even today, the majority of the Christian Bible consists of Jewish books; and even though the Jews may be regarded as having rejected the Messiah, both Judaism and Christianity purport to worship the same God. In short, we might say that, initially, Christians and Jews had the closest possible relationship, and that throughout their history Christians have had the best possible reasons to revere, respect, and look sympathetically on the Chosen People, whose recalcitrance in rejecting Christ should never have become a reason for hating them. The relations between Jews and Christians were originally just like those between Flechsig and Schreber. Yet, again like Schreber, Christians came in due course of time to hate and detest those to whom they once owed so much, and began to make them the subjects of elaborate delusions of persecution.

According to one of the most objective, scholarly, and complete accounts of anti-Semitism which we possess,

... shortly before the year 1000, vague rumours began to agitate Christendom. At the instigation of the Jews, the 'Prince of Babylon' had caused the destruction of the Holy Sepulcher; he had also launched countless persecutions against the Christians of the Holy Land and had caused the patriarch of Jerusalem to be beheaded.[26]

Such rumours were not without their antecedents. As early as the fourth century we find Church Fathers such as Gregory of Nyssa calling the Jews:

Murderers of the Lord, assassins of the prophets, rebels and detesters of God, they outrage the Law, resist grace, repudiate the faith of the fathers. Companions of the

[24] 'Psychoanalytic Notes upon an Autobiographical Account of a Case of Paranoia', XII, 41ff.

[25] Freud, ibid., XII, 63ff.

[26] L. Poliakov, The History of Anti-Semitism, Volume I, p. 36.

devil, race of vipers, informers, calumniators, darkeners of the mind, pharisaic leaven, Sanhedrin of demons, accursed, detested, lapidators, enemies of all that is beautiful . . ..[27]

But it was from the time of the Crusades that 'the destiny of the Jews . . . was henceforth to be singular and unique in Europe'.[28] Their uniqueness and singularity lay in being the object of elaborate delusions of persecution which maintained that there was a world-wide conspiracy of Jews to overthrow Christendom, to murder Christian children, to profane the Host, and to commit other fantastic acts whose only common denominator appears to be their similarity to the 'soul-murder' and other lunatic persecutions imagined by Schreber.[29] Even canonized saints, like St Bernardino of Siena, founder of the Society of the Holy Name of Jesus, held that Jews conspired against Christians to 'extort . . . their worldly goods by public usuries', and to 'seek to deprive them of health and life'.[30] The result was that throughout the later Middle Ages Jews were subjected to the most horrifying violence and discrimination at the hands of Christians. The practice of Christianity and the hatred of the Jews became so closely identified with one another that Erasmus could observe that 'if it is the part of a good Christian to detest the Jews, then we are all good Christians'.[31]

It would be a great mistake to imagine that such hatred was merely the manifestation of ethnic prejudice. 'It is often assumed,' says Norman Cohn:

that all ethnic prejudice is very much of a kind—that, for instance, hatred of Negroes must have precisely the same emotional roots as hatred of Jews; yet the assumption is certainly mistaken . . . however Whites may see Negroes, they can hardly see them as hidden, manipulating 'elders'. The fantasy of an infinitely powerful, world-dominating conspiracy does not in fact get projected onto Negroes . . . It is a different matter with the Jews.[32]

The delusional character of Christian anti-Semitism is nowhere more revealingly illustrated than in the observation that 'if the Jew had not existed, it would have been necessary to invent him'.[33] From the second half of the fourteenth century anti-Semitism:

seems to feed on itself, irrespective of whether or not Jews inhabited a given territory. If the Jew no longer dwelt there, he was invented; and if the Christian population came into less and less conflict with Jews in daily life, it was increasingly obsessed by

[27] *Ibid.*, p. 25.
[28] *Ibid.*, p. 41.
[29] Freud, *op. cit.*, XII, 14, *passim*.
[30] Poliakov, *op. cit.*, p. 147.
[31] *Ibid.*, p. 123.
[32] N. Cohn, *Warrant for Genoicide*, pp. 262–3.
[33] Poliakov, *op. cit.*, p. 154.

their image, which if found in reading, saw on monuments, and contemplated at plays and spectacles.[34]

As in the case of Schreber, once established, the delusional system became self-perpetuating; and the less it drew its inspiration from reality, the more it could give itself up to phantasy.

If my hypothesis is correct, and if Christian anti-Semitism really does play the part of delusions of persecution in a mass paranoia identifiable with pre-Reformation Christianity, we should expect to find a different situation existing after the Reformation, and, indeed, in any circumstances in which Christian paranoia was not strongly developed. The evidence of history confirms this expectation overwhelmingly, provided that we exclude nineteenth- and twentieth-century anti-Semitism, which we shall consider in a moment. It is noteworthy that among rulers of the later, Christian, Roman Empire, only Julian the Apostate was really friendly to the Jews, even going so far as to consider re-establishing them in Palestine and rebuilding the Temple. Such benevolence towards the Chosen People would have been unthinkable in the Christian emperors who preceded and followed him. In the case of both Islam and Protestantism, our hypothesis would not lead us to expect to find much evidence of anti-Semitism, because both these are obsessional, rather than paranoid, forms of monotheism. This is precisely what we do find. Under Islam, Jews and Judaism were tolerated with what one historian of anti-Semitism has called 'a remarkable broadmindedness',[35] and the same author observes that 'Calvinistic doctrine was characterized by a marked benevolence' towards the Jews.[36] At the beginning of the seventeenth century some Puritans even went so far as to become circumcized converts to Judaism —the clearest possible proof that one could hope to find of the antithesis of anti-Semitism. Luther, admittedly, was markedly anti-Semitic, but this was only true of his later years, when his psychopathology became much more paranoid and psychotic from every point of view. Lest I should be accused of bending Luther's case to fit my argument, let me quote from a wholly independent source:

... Luther was not always the enemy of the Jews. At the Zenith of his activity, during the heroic period when this rebellious monk, sustained and justified by his faith, defied pope and emperor and for some time attained the dizzy peaks of total freedom, he had a very different attitude towards the Jews. Apparently he hoped for some time to convert and rally to his cause the people of the Bible. This hope caused him to publish in 1523 a pamphlet with the significant title: *Jesus Christ was born a Jew* ... The author sympathizes with the Jews and mocks their enemies: '. . . The Jews are the blood relatives, the cousins and brothers of Our Lord; if his blood and flesh could be boasted

---

[34] *Ibid.*, p. 123.
[35] Poliakov, *op. cit.*, Volume II, p. 41.
[36] *Op. cit.*, Volume I, p. 204.

of, the Jews belong to Jesus Christ much more than we do. Hence I beg my dear Papists to call me a Jew, when they are tired of calling me a heretic . . .[37]

The time has come to recall the reader's attention to the reason for this brief excursion into the paranoid delusions of Christianity. He will remember that I was discussing socialism, and arguing that, as a clear descendant of Christian attitudes, and of pre-Reformation ones in particular, it might well be found to reflect a comparable underlying psychopathology. If this view is correct, then the conclusion to be drawn from the foregoing discussion of anti-Semitism is clear: Anti-Semitism, or some closely comparable form of paranoid delusion, should be a principal feature of socialism (all the more because Saint Simon's abandonment of the supernatural elements of Christianity almost certainly would entail, from the psychopathological point of view, a diminution in regressive features (such as megalomanic identification with the Deity, world-rejection, etc.), and an enhancement of the restitutional ones, of which one of the most important is the delusion of persecution). It is therefore with some satisfaction about the reliability of our findings that we note that the chief prophet of modern socialism, Karl Marx, was, despite being a Jew himself, virulently anti-Semitic, and that, at least initially, anti-Semitism and anti-Capitalism were one and the same thing, as the following quotation from Marx suggests:

. . . in ridding itself of *huckstering* and *money*, and thus from real and practical Judaism, our age would emancipate itself . . . We discern in Judaism, therefore, a universal *anti-social* element of the *present time*, whose historical development, zealously aided in its harmful aspects by the Jews, has now attained its culminating point . . . The Jews have emancipated themselves in so far as the Christians have become Jews . . . What was, in itself, the basis of Jewish religion? Practical need, egoism. The monotheism of the Jews is, therefore, in reality, a polytheism of the numerous needs of man, a polytheism which makes even the lavatory an object of divine regulation . . . Money is the jealous God of Israel, beside which no other God may exist. Money degrades all the Gods of mankind and turns them into commodities . . . The bill of exchange is the real God of the Jew . . . Christianity issued from Judaism. It has now been re-absorbed into Judaism . . . It was only then that Judaism could attain universal domination . . .[38]

This 'universal domination' of Judaism was, as the quotation above clearly says, the domination of money and of the profit-motive. Hence Marx's anti-Semitism led naturally to anti-Capitalism; and a paranoid delusion that the Jews were plotting the downfall of the human race was replaced by its more generalized equivalent: the notion that an international class of capitalists was plotting the exploitation and enslavement of all mankind. The fact that Marx thought that Christianity had been re-absorbed into Judaism to the extent that Christians, too, were now capitalists, meant that anti-Semitic hatred

[37] *Ibid.*, pp. 221–2.
[38] Marx, *Judenfrage*, quoted in Poliakov, *op. cit.*, Volume III, pp. 422–3.

could logically no longer be limited to the Chosen People, but must be broadened to cover all capitalists, all 'Jews', all worshippers of the supreme God 'Money'. Now, instead of the Jews, it is the Bourgeoisie, the Entrepreneurs, the Capitalist-Roaders, the Imperialists, or Counter-Revolutionary Cliques who are believed to be part of a world-wide conspiracy against the Proletariat. But behind the sociological labels, and beneath the topical masks, there lurks the still-recognizable features of the detested, traditional enemy of the West, the Jew. Viewed, both from the point of view of depth psychology, and of its historical antecedents, the Marxist-Leninist stance against capitalism is only a disguised, secularized, generalized, and hygienically-internationalized detestation of the Jews; it is a Jew's own anti-Semitism. As such, it is, both in Marx and in the present day, just as paranoid and delusional as it ever was. In socialist literature the capitalist, like his modern corporate equivalent, the multi-national company, is caricatured and distorted just as the Jew was in traditional anti-Semitic propaganda. Like the Jew, he is hated, but, again like his Semitic forerunner, he is hated because he is feared; and he is feared because he is thought to intend harm and to have the means to inflict it. Yet, just as any rational Christian in medieval Europe might have noticed, far from hurting anyone, the Jews around him did useful and valuable work, so the rational critic of modern societies must admit that, far from enslaving or exploiting anyone, capitalism has produced the greatest increase in general wealth and welfare ever seen, and that the proletariat under capitalism has prospered incomparably more than it has under Marxist-Leninism. But such a paradox is exactly what we should expect if we recall that, in socialism, we are dealing with an elaborate paranoid delusion, and that conformity with reality is the last thing which we should expect. The fact that Dr Flechsig was one of Schreber's greatest benefactors did not prevent him becoming, in Schreber's view, the chief of his tormentors. The fact that Jews, and their Protestant, capitalist equivalents, have given more to the West than anyone else means that, far from being appreciated by those who have imperfectly freed themselves from traditional Christian paranoia, these benefactors will be hated with a hatred all the more implacable because it is irrational and, ultimately, insane.

Other characteristics of socialism, apart from its delusions of persecution-by-capitalism warrant our notice as comparable restitutional symptoms of paranoia. Perhaps the most obvious of these is its world-reconstruction phantasy. This, again, is only a secularized, de-mystified version of traditional Christian phantasies about the Kingdom of God. Like the delusions concerning the evils of capitalism, it has no foundation in reality, as can be seen by looking at the societies in which thorough-going socialism of the Marxist-Leninist variety has been applied. Perhaps it is only under these 'free', 'democratic', and 'egalitarian' regimes that any truth can be seen in theory that the proletariat is persecuted by a rapacious and cruel ruling class.

If we now turn our attention away from Marxist-Leninist, and other left-wing socialisms to National Socialism (Nazism), and to fascism in general, we once again find paranoid delusions much in evidence. In these cases anti-Semitism does not undergo a metamorphosis into anti-Capitalism, but remains exactly what it always was, except that the more mystical malevolence attributed to the Jews in the Middle Ages has now been replaced by less-overtly magical delusional elaborations. But, just like left-wing socialism, fascism has a world-reconstruction phantasy which is totally at odds with the realities of its effects. World-rejection, narcissistic withdrawal, and end-of-the-world phantasies do not figure at all in these movements. Instead, restitutional features, like delusions of persecution and world-reconstruction dominate their psychopathology. This suggests that these movements are a last, futile attempt to recover from the mass paranoia of pre-Reformation Christianity; and it is perhaps not without significance that, with the partial exception of Germany (where fascism had much to do with the trauma of defeat in 1918, but nevertheless, like German Communism, still had its homeland in the more Catholic states), it is in those parts of Europe which were least affected by the Reformation that socialist and fascist paranoias have been most observed.

Perhaps I might end this final digression into the social psychopathology of Christianity and its latter-day derivatives by pointing out that, in terms of the analogy with individual psychological development that I have pursued throughout this book, it fits in exactly where it should. Unlike phobias and anxiety hysteria, whose collective equivalent is totemism, and also unlike obsessional neurosis, whose collective equivalent is monotheism, paranoia is a mental disorder that occurs only after puberty. This means that it should be associated with post-monotheistic—actually, *post-Judaic*—religion; and this is exactly what we find. Catholicism corresponds to adolescence in individual psychological development because the collective psychopathology of Catholicism—paranoia—is the psychosis which first appears at that time.

My discussion of the evolution of culture and religion raises a number of basic questions which up to now I have left unanswered. My reason for doing this was principally a practical one: I wanted to analyse the material under consideration with as little as possible in the way of polemical digression or theoretical elaboration. Nevertheless, a number of fundamental questions remain to which the reader can rightly expect an answer, however limited that answer may have to be.

The first, and perhaps the most important question is that suggested by one of the central themes of this book: namely, the nature of the parallels between individual and collective psychology. These parallels express themselves in two basic assumptions: First, that religions are closely comparable to individual states of psychopathology; and secondly, that the psychological evolution of mankind as a whole is comparable, in certain respects, to that of the individual.

Let us begin with the first point, the comparison between religion and individual psychopathology. Freud remarked that, from the time of the publication of *Totem and Taboo*:

I have never doubted that religious phenomena are only to be understood on the pattern of the individual neurotic symptoms familiar to us—as the return of long since-forgotten, important events in the primaeval history of the human family—and that they have to thank precisely this origin for their compulsive character and that, accordingly, they are effective on human beings by force of the historical truth of their content.[39]

Commenting on the nature of this 'historical truth', Freud says that:

We have learnt from the psychoanalyses of individuals that their earliest impressions . . . produce at some time or another effects of a compulsive character without themselves being consciously remembered. We believe we have a right to make the same assumption about the earliest experiences of the whole of humanity.[40]

In other words, Freud maintains that *the compulsive aspects of individual and social psychology are based on similar unconscious processes*. In the course of this book I have tried to add more evidence to that adduced by Freud and others to prove the truth of this assertion. Throughout, I have treated the various types of compulsive social behaviour (religion) as if they were cases of individual psychopathology. Hence I treated totemism as a collective anxiety hysteria (animal phobia), pastoral, Jewish, and Protestant monotheism as mass-obsessional neuroses, and Catholicism and Atenism as cultural paranoias. Similarly, we might just as easily regard animal phobias as private totemism, obsessional neuroses as personal monotheisms, and paranoias such as Schreber's as individual Atenisms. Indeed, as we have seen, Atenism in its origin *was* an individual paranoia, but the fact that it was the paranoia of an absolute ruler meant that it could become the delusional system of an entire empire—in short, a *religion*.

This particular case illustrates well a general principle that is inherent in all I have tried to achieve in this book, namely, that *from the point of view of latent content, there is no way of distinguishing between individual psychopathology and its collective equivalents, such as religion*. Thus, if analysis of cases of paranoia reveal it to be based on a denial of unconscious homosexual trends we should be able to show that analysis of collective paranoias reveals the same phenomenon. I believe that I have succeeded in doing this in the course of my inquiry into the latent, passive-homosexual content of pre-Reformation Christianity. Again, this should mean that symptoms of individual psychopathology should find their collective equivalent. As I have tried to show,

[39] *Moses and Monotheism*, XXIII, 58.
[40] *Ibid*., XXIII, 129–30.

mass delusions of persecution, even mass hallucinations, can be found in collective paranoias such as Catholicism.

If we now address ourselves to the problem of why this remarkable resemblance between individual neuroses and religion should exist, I believe that we are in a position to give an answer. First, we can take it as a matter of general principle that the unconscious psychological processes that determine individual psychopathology also operate in shared psychopathologies. There is no such thing as a 'group mind', or 'collective consciousness', or 'social system' that produces social psychological states which are qualitatively different from those of individual psychology. The belief that such collective equivalents of consciousness or unconsciousness exist gives rise to unsuperable theoretical and empirical difficulties and involves the postulation of mental forces which cannot be located in any actual brain, and which are to that extent, occult.[41]

A second reason why collective psychopathology must resemble that of the individual lies in the purely conventional considerations which determine whether we call something 'religion' or 'madness'. If one man believes that he is the Son of God and all others deny it, then he is not the Son of God but an insane megalomanic. If millions accept his claim then he is not mad but divine, not a megalomanic, but a messiah. The underlying psychological process will be found to be identical in both the madman and the messiah, but the fact that the latter is believed by others makes all the difference as far as the classification of his condition is concerned. Indeed, there is a sense in which popular acceptance does change the reality, because, once accepted by others as a messiah, the individual concerned is to that extent a genuine messiah and no longer entirely in a world of his own. His followers have entered it with him and in part have made it real. Those who in recent years have criticized the notion of mental illness as being an arbitrary category of social definition have entirely missed the point. It is not madness, but sanity which is the arbitrary social category, as is proved by the fact that paranoid delusions, like anti-Semitism, can be regarded as perfectly sane if enough of the population believes in them.

This issue leads directly to the third reason why individual and collective psychopathologies are equivalent, and that is the observation that collective neuroses, like religion, function in social terms as an alternative to individual neurosis. If an individual can find a neurosis which already exists and whose manifest content is already fully elaborated by others of similar disposition to himself he will naturally identify with such a movement and will make its psychopathology his own. This is all the more likely if the collective neurosis in question has the weight of tradition and the prestige of the present behind it. Neurotic illness always carries the danger of isolation, social rejection and

---

[41] For a fuller consideration of this point in the context of Durkheim's theory of the *Conscience collective* see my *Levi-Strauss*, pp. 267.

loss of esteem and dignity; an alternative which runs none of these risks but, on the contrary, promises the individual positive merit in the eyes of his fellow men is certain to exert strong attraction on those who can make their latent psychopathology conform to the manifest content of a collective neurosis. Considerations such as these mean that, as a matter of inevitability, neurosis must increase as religion declines.

However, it would be wrong to assume that collective psychopathologies are merely the sum of the individual neuroses for which they function as alternatives. On the contrary, the great collective neuroses and psychoses exist autonomously as collective phenomena that persist over generations and which possess an evolutionary continuity not directly attributable to the individuals who make them up. This is why the psychoanalysis of religions and mass movements cannot be limited to the analysis of individuals alone. For instance, if one wants to understand anti-Semitism, one cannot merely analyze anti-Semites. This, as at least one other analyst of anti-Semitism has realized,[42] may tell one why a particular individual is paranoid, but it cannot necessarily tell one why his paranoia fastens on the Jews in preference to, say, the Gypsies. Here, elements of cultural determinism enter in and mean that religious neuroses must be studied in their totality and not merely by reference to the individual participants. The collective neurosis reveals a structure and a content exactly comparable to that of typical individual neuroses because it obeys the same unconscious logic and evolves along lines determined by the same psychological laws. But these laws do not produce collective psycho-pathologies such as religions by adding individual neuroses; rather, they do so by virtue of the assumed correspondence, clearly stated in the quotations from Freud on page 240 above, between the psychological history of the individual and that of the human race.

This is an analogy which has been elaborately developed in the course of this book. As we saw, it was introduced into psychoanalysis by Freud, and already had a long history behind it before he took it up. The whole argument, both in Freud's work and here (few, if any, other authors seem to have used it, and most modern analysts have specifically repudiated it) assumes that the human race, like each and every individual, passed through a phase of primal narcissism, through an Oedipal crisis, and then through subsequent phases leading ultimately to something comparable to psychological maturity.

We have seen in the course of this book what empirical material I have been able to find to give substance to this idea, but it is clear that, theoretically, the great collective neuroses which I have described all rest on the belief that collective and individual history are homologous, and that if whole groups manifest compulsive or neurotic behaviour it is because whole groups—even the entire human race—experienced collective traumas which were subject to collective repression and which resulted in collective neurotic symptoms.

---

[42] F. Simmel, *Anti-Semitism*, p. 12.

Yet how is this correspondence between individual and collective psychological evolution to be explained? Is it merely accidental, or are there definite causes? I believe that the material contained in this book enables us to give a clear and exact answer to that question. It is quite simply this: Both in the individual and the species similar patterns of psychological evolution emerge because both the species collectively and the individual individually had to undergo similar traumatic experiences and react to those experiences similarly in order to acquire the psychological structures typical of cultural man. As a species and as individuals we do not appear to be genetically predisposed to altruism, incest-avoidance, respect for authority, or concern for the welfare of others. Therefore, both as a species and as individuals, we have had to undergo a traumatizing experience—the Oedipal crisis—which could create in us the psychological mechanisms of inhibition and instinctual renunciation necessary for the acquisition of those attributes of civilization and culture which have become adaptively necessary for us, and the secret of our evolutionary success. In other words, both collective and individual psychological history run along similar lines because both the species and its individual members had to go through the primal trauma which Freud first described in *Totem and Taboo*. As we saw, once it had happened for the species as a whole and man had acquired the rudiments of culture, it had to go on happening for individuals so that in their personal psychological development they could recapitulate the collective psychological evolution of the race. At first, initiation ceremonies achieved this but, later, patterns of child-rearing changed to bring the trauma earlier and to make the psychological development of the child resemble even more closely that of the species as a whole. In short, psychological ontogeny recapitulates psychological phylogeny because it was adaptively necessary for it to do so and because the Oedipus complex, which was the secret of the species' leap to culture, had to continue to be the foundation of its civilization. Since the Oedipus complex is a *developmental* phenomenon, it was necessary that what preceded it and what succeeded it should also be roughly homologous, and so the exact correspondence between the maturing of the individual and that of the species results.

In the earliest cultural epoch, that of totemism, the Oedipal trauma in individuals had to resemble that of early man fairly closely, and took on the animal-phobic form in which the father is first perceived in the child's unconscious. This is the simplest and most primitive father-image, one which is purely terrifying and a simple crystallization of the father as a feared (but once loved) animal. Later, with the coming of agriculture, the importance of initiation declined because the Oedipal trauma now occurred earlier in childhood. The super-ego began to undergo a primitive elaboration in which to the totem-father was added the ithyphallic (that is, uncastrated) mother. This was because the mother had now become a force for inhibition and instinctual renunciation through early weaning and the beginnings of toilet-training and more extensive control of childhood sexuality. After the domestication of animals and the coming of pastoralism, the father-image fully crystallizes and the super-ego reaches its full development, either in the normal positive form (punitive monotheism), or the abnormal, negative one (Atenism). The extensive inhibition of parricidal, aggressive drives demanded by pastoralism necessitates the instilling of a punitive and fully-developed super-ego in pastoralists, and so, once again personal development recapitulates that of the group. Finally, post-monotheistic religions like Christianity reproduce the post-latency development of individuals because they feature divinities evolved after pastoral monotheisms begin to regress in an agricultural and non-pastoral setting. But here again necessity demands that individuals should possess super-egos conformable to their culture. Finally, when scientific and technological progress demand that religion should give way before rational criticism, the super-ego gives ground to the mature ego.

Thus the analogy which I have exploited throughout this book, namely, that the psychological progress of the human race has resembled that of an individual, in fact reveals the exact-opposite process: the fact that individual human development has had to recapitulate that of the species as a whole.

These observations explain why religion has loomed so large in a book purportedly devoted to the psychoanalysis of culture. The reason for this should now be clear: it is simply that, in a species not genetically programmed for altruism and elaborate social behaviour, psychological and social mechanisms have had to be developed to inhibit and control the natural anti-social and aggressive drives of individuals. Of these mechanisms, the super-ego is by far the most important, and it is through its mediation that most others have their effect. As I have tried to demonstrate, religion is, psychologically speaking, little more than the collective elaboration of the super-ego and evolved out of the first means of instilling it in individuals (initiation ceremonies). Throughout history it has been the principal focus of the social aspects of the personality and in culture as a whole it has played the central role. Thus the psychoanalysis of culture cannot but be the psychoanalysis of religion also, and both must ultimately be the psychoanalysis of the collective neurosis on which all culture and religion depend.

The relation between stages of individual psychological development and the analysis of the evolution of culture undertaken in this book is represented diagrammatically on page 246. The reader will see that I have set out my findings under three headings. The centre column, headed 'religion', is merely a list of the seven stages in the evolution of religion that we have considered. Of course, these are not the only types of world-religion, and three of them, Catholicism, Protestantism, and psychoanalysis are really not forms of world-religion at all. Nevertheless, the first four are. The sequence Animism—Totemism—Polytheism—Monotheism represents an evolutionary development of general types of religion which I believe to have occurred in that order, *had* to occur in that order, and in many different parts of the world *did* occur in that order. Nevertheless, some societies remained stalled at the totemic stage, although no surviving human beings could possibly have failed to make the transition from animism to totemism. Many found their religious evolution coming to an end with polytheism; only among nomadic pastoralists and a few exceptional polytheists (like the Egyptians of the eighteenth dynasty) was a transition to monotheism fully made. Furthermore, regressions occurred, and many polytheisms remained at different stages of evolution within polytheism, or underwent disintegration in which some elements supervened over others. I have not discussed all these possibilities. In this book I have limited myself to one or two representative examples of polytheism, totemism, and monotheism. These examples were chosen for their relevance to later parts of the book and for convenience of reference, rather than for any other reason. This means that I have neglected all Eastern religions and many primitive religions which would otherwise have called for inclusion. With Catholicism and Protestantism, I have brought into consideration religions that are specific historical entities rather than general types. As a matter of fact, Catholicism (in which I include Orthodoxy for most purposes) does have some close parallels elsewhere, but, even so, it is by no means a general type and does not represent an inevitable and common evolutionary step after monotheism. On the contrary, it represents one of many possible lines of evolution out of the basic Animism—Totemism—Polytheism—Monotheism stem. Finally, as I have shown, Protestantism gives rise to psychoanalysis which is not a religion at all, but remains in important respects formally comparable to one.

In the first column of Table 2 (p. 246) I have listed the economies which correlate with each of the religions in question. It is important to realize that these correlations are *genetic*—that is, that they specify the form of economic life which developed with the religion *in the first place*. The only exceptions to this are Catholicism, which, for reasons already explained, corresponded to an already existing economy, and psychoanalysis which is not a religion at all and which, again for reasons already stated, is not likely to engender a distinctive form of economic life.

In the second column of the table I have listed the Oedipal orientation of the originators of the form of economic life, where relevant. As we have already seen, this reveals an elegant and complete symmetry. The fourth column draws the analogy with the development of the individual, and the fifth lists the psychopathologies which correspond to the relevant religions.

Each stage in this particular schema of religious evolution is characterized by a renunciation of instinct, but it soon becomes clear that a return of the repressed also invariably occurs. When discussing polytheism I showed in what sense it could be seen as a return of animism. Monotheism could be typified as a return of totemism in a new economic setting; and in discussing the hysteria of the Dinka masters of the fishing spear we saw how moving and powerful that return of totemism from the repressed could be. Catholicism was a case of the overwhelming return of Graeco-Roman and Egyptian

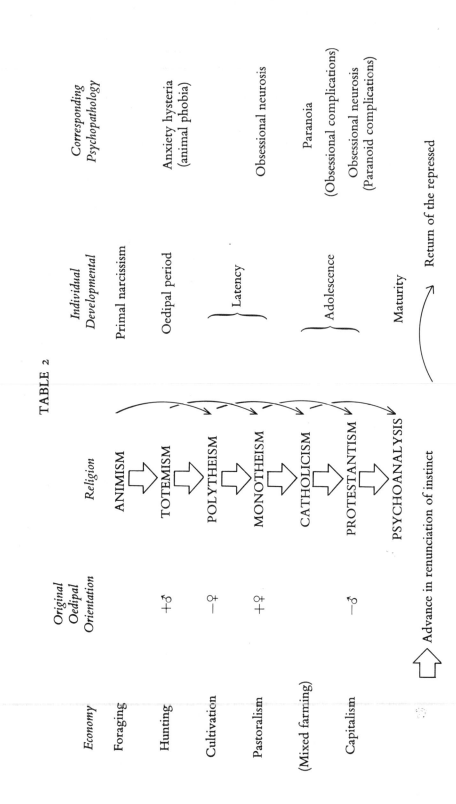

TABLE 2

polytheism; and finally, Protestantism, as I have already explained, was something of a return of the monotheism out of which Christianity originally developed.

If we look at the pattern revealed by these observations of the return of the repressed we notice that it is elegant and consistent: any stage in the evolution of religion represented here shows itself to be a partial return of the religion of the stage before the stage before it. Why is this so? It seems such a clear and consistent tendency that it cannot be dismissed as merely fortuitous. We are strongly inclined to believe that there must be a systematic cause. Furthermore, the way in which the return of the repressed seems to alternate with advances in instinctual renunciation suggests that the two processes are interrelated. That they should be is not at all surprising if we recall that an instinctual renunciation means the suppression of something. The return from the repressed means the re-emergence of something which has been suppressed, but is no longer. Catholicism could not possibly have returned from the repressed in Protestantism because it was Protestantism that succeeded it as an advance in instinctual renunciation and which suppressed all the characteristically-polytheistic elements within it. But with the suppression of what was characteristic of Catholicism it was inevitable that what it had itself suppressed in order to maintain that characteristic identity—namely Jewish monotheism—should now return largely unopposed.

Such an explanation fits every case, and allows us to advance the general principle that when any new advance in instinctual renunciation occurs in religion the repressions maintained by the religion which the new advance supersedes are rendered inoperative. The result is the characteristic pattern of the return of the repressed from the stage before the stage preceding the new advance.

I said a moment ago that this principle applies to every case we have considered, and this ought to mean that it is also true of psychoanalysis—at least in so far as it can be considered a stage in the evolution of religion. The reader need only glance at Table 2 to see the surprising consequence of this: it means that in psychoanalysis we should expect to see a return of Catholicism comparable to the return of polytheism seen in Catholicism itself. His first, and quite understandable, reaction is probably complete disbelief. But let us examine the matter more closely and see what this principle really means where psychoanalysis is concerned.

We have reached the point in our psychoanalysis of man where we are discussing his final arrival at maturity and at some sort of resolution of his neurosis. Such resolutions do not depend entirely on a triumph of the reality principle or a victory for the rational consciousness of the ego. There must also be somewhere along the way an abreaction of disavowed emotions and a return from the repressed of repudiated thoughts and phantasies. So much is normal in any analytic therapy. In adolescence, much the same occurs naturally, except that here the return from the repressed is triggered not by analytic techniques but by the resurgence of instinct associated with puberty. Abreaction of repressed emotions follows inevitably and often takes the form of acting out primal ambivalences towards the parents, for which contemporary conflicts with them only provide the pretext. In the case of man, resolution of the primal ambivalence has developed in a similar, natural way. Like the individual, man experienced a long period of primal narcissism; like him, man was involved in a deep Oedipal crisis; and like every individual, man—or rather his hunting hominid ancestors—repressed the conflict and gradually evolved a punitive super-ego in the course of subsequent adaptive developments. As we have seen, Christianity became the equivalent of adolescence, largely because it featured the return of elements repressed by monotheism, the equivalent of the period of latency. With the Protestant Reformation, the abreaction of long repressed primal ambivalences took a new turn, with a powerful enhancement of the ego made possible by the greater prominence of the reality principle.

But this enhancement of the reality principle brought the process of the return of classical polytheism to a close. It largely excluded the indulgence of magic, animism, and the 'omnipotence of thoughts' on which Catholicism had been based. In so far as psychoanalysis is an ever greater renunciation of instinct than Protestantism, it, too, excludes phantasy and narcissism, but not in the same way. Protestantism did so partly in order to protect its more austerely monotheistic conception of God; but this is a limitation which can hardly be expected to apply to psychoanalysis. Being fully committed to the reality principle, it has no need of such disavowals. On the contrary, it is the nature of psychoanalysis and its commitment to the reality principle that it should make possible the fullest imaginable return of the repressed and the most complete abreaction of latent emotions.

It is in this respect that psychoanalysis is formally comparable to a return of Catholicism. Catholicism has been aptly named, for it really does contain every aspect of religion considered in these pages. In so far as it is a re-embodiment of classical polytheism, it contains all that polytheism did, namely, vestiges of totemism, a great deal of animism and magic, phallic earth-goddesses, and the divine kings who were the male gods of polytheism. In so far as it was an off-shoot of Jewish monotheism, Catholicism also contains both the punitive monotheism of pastoralism and the paranoid, providential monotheism of Egypt. In short, it holds within itself all the major elements of all that went before it: animism, totemism, polytheism, and monotheism. As the last term in the evolution of the sequence of religions studied here and the final exorcism of the idea of God, psychoanalysis is the most complete revelation of what is real in religion and therefore must be something as comprehensive—as *catholic*—in its scope as Catholicism. It corresponds to the ultimate stage in man's emancipation from the past and from the neurosis of religion, and so must also entail a comprehensive abreaction of the ambivalences on which the neurosis was originally built.

In the richness and diversity of its ritual and belief no religion has ever surpassed Catholicism. The reason is clear: Catholicism contained something to gratify every aspect of man's mind. He could call on the saints to satisfy his latent animism; he could attend the totem-feast of the Mass and gratify his Oedipal ambivalences; he could pray to the Virgin in order to sublimate his incestuous love for his mother; he could fear God the Father to gratify his conscience. In its almost inexhaustible religious riches Catholicism could be all things to all men. Only those who wanted to exclude something would be unhappy in it and, as we have seen, this is precisely why Luther abandoned it. He was like the young man who suddenly in his later teens stops being the adolescent equivalent of the polymorphously perverse child and becomes the consistent young adult. At first, such consistency means repression of the more unacceptable excesses of early adolescence, but gradually, as the ego and its sense of reality gain the upper hand, such repressive measures become less necessary. Eventually, much is allowed to return to consciousness because now it can be recognized for what it is and be consciously disavowed rather than remaining repressed. Exactly the same thing (albeit in a more profound and comprehensive way) happens in the course of an analysis and, ideally at least, the final resolution and recovery of the patient is signalled by the return of all the repressed material and the complete abreaction of the emotions involved.

Yet it is inevitable that if psychoanalysis is to succeed in being the final resolution of man's neurosis it will have to shift its main interest away from individual psychotherapy towards education and applied social psychology. Theodor Reik remarks that,

In the discussions held on Wednesday evenings at his home, Freud frequently pointed out that the time will come when the treatment of neurotic and psychotic patients will not be the main aim of psychoanalysis.[43]

At present, psychoanalysis is little more than a specialism in Western medicine. It aims to help neurotics after the harm has been done. At present, it has no idea of preventive psychoanalytic medicine. Yet individual psychotherapy is costly, exhausting to both analyst and analysand, and extremely difficult to carry out properly. Success is by no means assured; and sometimes the analysis, if improperly conducted, can make the patient appreciably worse than he was before he started. It might not be so bad if analysis were easy to learn, and good analysts easy to find. But they are not. According to Wilhelm Reich, Freud, while at the 1922 Berlin Congress of Psychoanalysis, gestured to the one hundred and fifty or so members of the analytic élite who were present and said to him, 'See that crowd? How many do you think can analyze, can *really* analyze?' He answered his own question by raising five fingers.[44]

[43] *Dogma and Compulsion*, p. 7.   [44] *Reich Speaks of Freud*, p. 67.

Despite this, I doubt whether there is a real alternative to classical analysis as far as individual psychotherapy is concerned. So-called 'group therapy' seems to me to be based on incorrect theoretical assumptions and confused therapeutic procedures. But an alternative to individual analytic therapy would exist if it were possible to institute preventive measures. In that event, classical analysis could be reserved for training analysts and those for whom the preventive measures are ineffective. But is such a thing possible? Everybody knows that as far as neurosis is concerned the damage is done in early childhood. Any preventive measures would obviously have to be taken very early and would require the wholehearted co-operation of parents. It is quite possible that if psychoanalysis were to become fully accepted in our culture that in itself would do a great deal to reduce neurosis by making parents better adjusted in themselves and better able to understand and raise their children. Yet such a solution, although desirable, still leaves a heavy responsibility on the shoulders of the parents and may not be effective in the most important cases.

Let us look at the problem from another angle. Essentially, it is no different from that which faced those who were responsible for our neurosis in the first place. In the case of the original totemists the problem was to pass on to their children the psychological inhibitions which they had acquired by parricide and incestuous rape. The solution that they eventually found was what we know as the initiation ceremony. Its aim, as we saw in the first chapter, was to create a neurotic reaction in young men comparable to that acquired by parricidal violence in the parental generation. Only when young men had acquired inhibitions against parricide and incest was society safe and the foundation of the hunting economy assured. Preventive psychoanalysis would have a closely comparable, although opposite aim. It would intend not to cause a neurosis in the young, but to prevent one. Like the initiation, it would aim to make young men acceptable members of society; but unlike aboriginal methods it would not aim to create irrational repressions in them but rather would try to encourage conscious and rational renunciations of the incestuous and parricidal wishes which would have to be renounced if civilized life is to be possible. Individual analysis at puberty might achieve this, but it would be vastly costly and in all probability not particularly effective because of the peculiarities of the adolescent state.

However, acting-out of basic ambivalences and resolution of neurotic conflicts in the young may be possible by symbolic means. We have already seen that in the case of the aboriginal initiations, symbolic acts are capable of being effective substitutes for real conflicts, and there is no reason to believe that they might not do so in a modern psychotherapeutic context. Furthermore, what is true of adolescence might also be true of earlier periods in an individual's life. Among the Australian aborigines initiation takes place at puberty because hardly any significant inhibitions are put on children up to that point. However, it is obvious that in a programme of preventive child-psychotherapy things would have to start very early on because adolescence, although an important turning-point in an individual's life, is only a culmination and recapitulation of something which begins in childhood. Again, however enlightened and non-repressive childhood might become in a Freudian culture, it is inevitable that in order to be able to make the adjustments to reality demanded by a scientific world-view considerable capacity for rationality and instinctual renunciation would have to be demanded of the young. The fact that individuals would have to be able to control their instincts in the interests of the reality principle in their maturity would dictate that they should begin to learn self-control early on in life; and in so far as psychoanalysis represents an advance in rationality beyond any previous cultural ethic, the capacity of the young for instinctual renunciation would have to be correspondingly greater.

Above all, the young would have to be equipped with symbolic means of acting-out their ambivalences and advancing their mastery of themselves. But where would such symbolism come from? If the principal argument of this book is correct, there exists a deep and significant analogy between the history of the individual as reflected in his psychology and that of the entire human race as reflected in its religion. Each and every one of us who makes the transition from birth to maturity successfully recapitulates within himself the entire past of his species and marks in the stages of his psychic development the great turning-points in the history of humanity. As a new-born baby he is living in the state of primal narcissism and, like our distant foraging ancestors, still at one with nature, still, totally preoccupied with feeding, still innocent of inhibition and untouched by neurosis. As a child of three he is developing totemism, lusting like his early hunting ancestors after the flesh of the mother and plotting like them the death of the father. By the age of five the Oedipal crisis is passing and he is in a transitional stage comparable to polytheism in which he is totemist, animist, worshipper of the phallic mother, and monotheist by turns. At the beginning of the period he believed that the mother had a penis of her own just as in the early days of agriculture women symbolically possessed one when they impregnated Mother Earth with the first domesticated seeds. Later the phallic goddess of agriculture was castrated and replaced by the male gods of polytheism, just as the young child eventually sees his mother as castrated and replaced by his father who now becomes the parent with whom he identifies and on whom he builds his superego. When this process is complete, at about six or seven, he is a monotheist who cannot admit that he feels anything but love for the totem-father of his earlier days; the super-ego develops its punitive powers to the full and latency supervenes. As puberty begins, he lives through the early history of Christianity; he becomes a new St Paul, and sublimates his adolescent homosexuality in the ascetic charity of St Francis, or intellectualizes like a latter day Thomas Aquinas. But sometimes he succumbs to the insistent demands of his newly aroused id and becomes a medieval troubadour, obsessed with love and with being loved, the incurable erotic who alternates with the austere ascetic. Later, he relives the Reformation in his egoistic confrontations with his father who ineluctably becomes the Pope and Holy Roman Emperor against whom the tide of history has already turned. Gradually, as the insolent self-assertiveness of adolescence passes and the reality principle gains the upper hand, he is ready to rediscover psychoanalysis and to realize that his ego is secure and can face up to his unconscious without fear. In short, he has recapitulated history to an unprecedented degree and has acted out all the latent emotions and repressed memories of humanity in the course of growing up. In so far as these repressed feelings of the race are also to be found in the unconscious of each and every individual, everyone who expresses them in this way is resolving them in the most comprehensive manner possible.

Education is inevitably a process of absorbing one's culture and making it a part of one's ego. An educational programme which simultaneously promised to give a person a profound grasp of the realities of his culture as well as a deep insight into his mental development could not fail to be a highly effective pedagogical method. By living the past of mankind in the course of his own life the individual would obtain an incomparable understanding of the meaning of history and a unique vision of the forces which have shaped human life since it first evolved. But equally, his knowledge of the past would provide him with a language of unparalleled richness and profundity by means of which he could represent to himself the meaning of his own life and its place in world-history. By being himself he would become the embodiment of those who went before him; by being those who had gone before he would become himself with the greatest authenticity imaginable. No other education could be superior to this; and a civilization based on such a recapitulation of the past within the individual and of the individual within the past would give rise to a general resurgence of culture far exceeding that of the Renaissance.

This is because such an abreaction of individual emotions in terms of those of humanity, and those of humanity in terms of the individual, would inevitably not be limited to childhood and adolescence. It would overflow into every department of life and culture, and I see no reason why, if children should come to express their basic ambivalences in such psycho-historical terms, adults should not do so too. After all, some level of ambivalence and neurosis is normal to humanity and is the unavoidable consequence of civilization. And just as we have seen that among the Australian aborigines adult ceremonial is based on and is the continuation of the initiation ritual, so I would expect to see such an educational system giving rise to an adult culture which would give similar expression to the unconscious and would allow for the abreaction of suppressed emotions and the return of the repressed in a comparable way. The Renaissance was the inevitable outcome of Catholicism because Catholicism, like psychoanalysis although much less so, produced a comprehensive return of the repressed. Psychoanalysis, in doing what Catholicism did, but in doing it so much more completely and effectively, will, if these speculations are correct, produce a general renaissance of culture which will go as far beyond that of the sixteenth and seventeenth centuries as psychoanalysis goes beyond Catholicism in the extent of the return of the repressed to which it will give rise. Given the current decadent state of world culture, this cannot happen too soon.

But however that may be, it is I think clear that if the arguments advanced in this book are in any way to be relied upon they strongly suggest that psychoanalysis is destined to play a role in world-history of the first importance. Certainly, it is my belief that if psychoanalysis ceased to be merely a department of modern medicine and became instead a system of education and the basis of culture the universal neurosis which we call 'civilization' would have been largely resolved and the psychoanalysis of man would have been brought to a provisional, but successful conclusion.

6

BIBLIOGRAPHY
of works cited in the text

Abraham, K., *Selected Papers on Psycho-analysis*, London, 1948.

Albright, W. F., *Archaeology and the Religion of Israel*, Baltimore, 1956.

Aldred, C., *Akhenaten*, London, 1968.

—— 'The End of the Eighteenth Dynasty', *Cambridge Ancient History*, Third Ed., Volume II, Part 2, p. 50ff.

Ashley-Montagu, M. F., *Introduction to Physical Anthropology*, Springfield, 1960.

Badcock, C., *Levi-Strauss*, London, 1975.

Barry, H. et al., 'Relations of Child Training to Subsistence Economy', *American Anthropologist*, 61, 1959.

Bateson, G., *Naven*, Cambridge, 1936.

Borneman, E. (Ed.), *The Psychoanalysis of Money*, New York, 1976.

Breasted, J., *The Development of Religion and Thought in Ancient Egypt*, London, 1912.

—— *The Dawn of Conscience*, New York, 1933.

Brown, N. O., *Life Against Death*, London, 1959.

Budge, E. W., *Egyptian Magic*, London, 1899.

—— *Osiris and the Egyptian Resurrection*, London, 1911.

—— *Tutankhamen, Amenism, Atenism and Egyptian Monotheism*, London, 1923.

—— *From Fetish to God in Ancient Egypt*, London, 1934.

Cohn, N., *Warrant for Genocide*, London, 1967.

Coppleston, F., *A History of Philosophy*, New York, 1962.

Crook, J. H., 'Gelada Baboon Herd Structure and Movement', *Symp. Zool. Soc. London*, 18, 1966.

Dali, S., *Le Mythe Tragique de L'Angelus de Millet*, Paris, 1963.

—— *The Unspeakable Confessions of Salvador Dali*, London, 1976.

Dionysius the Areopagite, *The Celestial Hierarchies*, Fintry, Brook, 1965.

De Beer, G., *Embryoes and Ancestors*, Oxford, 1940.

Edgerton, R. B., *The Individual in Cultural Adaptation*, Berkley, 1971.

Erikson, E. H., *Young Man Luther*, London, 1958.

Evans-Pritchard, E., *Nuer Religion*, Oxford, 1956.

—— 'The Divine Kingship of the Shilluk of the Nilotic Sudan', *Essays in Social Anthropology*, p. 66ff., London, 1962.

Faulkner, R., *The Ancient Egyptian Pyramid Texts*, Oxford, 1969.

Ferenczi, S., *Contributions to Psycho-analysis*, London, 1916.

Fisher, S. and Greenberg, R., *The Scientific Credibility of Freud's Theories and Therapy*, New York, 1977.

Forde, D., *Habitat, Economy and Society*, London, 1970.

Fox, R., 'In the Beginning: Aspects of Hominid Behavioural Evolution', *Man 2*, 1967.

—— (Ed.), *Biosocial Anthropology*, London, 1975.

Frankfort, H., *Kingship and the Gods*, Chicago, 1948.

Frazer, J. G., *The Golden Bough*, London, 1930.

Freud, A., *The Ego and the Mechanisms of Defence*, London, 1937.

Freud, S., *The Psychopathology of Everyday Life*, The Standard Edition of the Complete Psychological Works of Sigmund Freud, London, 1953–74, Volume VI.

—— *Jokes and their Relation to the Unconscious*, *Standard Ed.*, VIII.

—— 'Obsessive Actions and Religious Practices', *Standard Ed.*, IX, 115.

—— 'Character and Anal Erotism', *Standard Ed.*, IX, 167.

—— ' "Civilized" Sexual Morality and Modern Mental Illness', *Standard Ed.*, IX, 177.

—— 'Analysis of a Phobia in a Five-Year-Old Boy', *Standard Ed.*, X, 1.

—— *Leonardo Da Vinci and a Memory of his Childhood*, *Standard Ed.*, XI, 59.

—— 'A Special Type of Choice of Object made by Men', *Standard Ed.*, XI, 163.

—— 'Psycho-Analytic Notes on an Autobiographical Account of a Case of Paranoia (Dementia Paranoides)', *Standard Ed.*, XII, 1.

—— 'Formulations on the Two Principles of Mental Functioning', *Standard Ed.*, XII, 213.

—— 'Great is Diana of the Ephesians', *Standard Ed.*, XII, 342.

—— *Totem and Taboo*, *Standard Ed.*, XIII.

—— 'On Narcissism', *Standard Ed.*, XIV, 67.

—— 'Instincts and their Vicissitudes', *Standard Ed.*, XIV, 109.

—— 'Mourning and Melancholia', *Standard Ed.*, XIV, 237.

—— *Introductory Lectures on Psycho-analysis*, *Standard Ed.*, XV & XVI.

—— 'From the History of an Infantile Neurosis', *Standard Ed.*, XVII, 1.

—— 'On Transformations of Instinct as Exemplified in Anal Erotism', *Standard Ed.*, XVII, 125.

—— 'A Difficulty in the Path of Psycho-analysis', *Standard Ed.*, XVII, 135.

—— 'The Uncanny', *Standard Ed.*, XVII, 217.

—— *Beyond the Pleasure Principle*, *Standard Ed.*, XVIII, 1.

—— *Group Psychology and the Analysis of the Ego*, *Standard Ed.*, XVIII, 65.

—— *The Ego and the Id*, *Standard Ed.*, XIX, 1.

—— 'A Seventeenth-Century Demonological Neurosis', *Standard Ed.*, XIX, 67.

—— 'The Economic Problem of Masochism', *Standard Ed.*, XIX, 155.

—— 'Some Psychical Consequences of the Anatomical Distinction between the Sexes', *Standard Ed.*, XIX, 241.

—— *Inhibitions, Symptoms and Anxiety*, *Standard Ed.*, XX, 75.

—— *The Future of an Illusion*, *Standard Ed.*, XXI, 1.

—— *Civilization and its Discontents*, *Standard Ed.*, XXI, 57.

—— 'Dostoevsky and Parricide', *Standard Ed.*, XXI, 173.

—— 'Libidinal Types', *Standard Ed.*, XXI, 215.

—— *New Introductory Lectures on Psycho-analysis*, *Standard Ed.*, XXII, 1.

—— *Moses and Monotheism*, *Standard Ed.*, XXIII, 1.

—— *An Outline of Psycho-analysis*, *Standard Ed.*, XXIII, 139.

Freud, S. and Bullitt, W. C., *Thomas Woodrow Wilson*, London, 1967.

Friedenthal, R., *Luther*, London, 1970.

Gardiner, A. H., *The Attitude of the Ancient Egyptians to Death and the Dead*, Cambridge, 1935.

Gardiner, M., *The Wolf-man and Sigmund Freud*, London, 1972.

Graves, R., *The White Goddess*, London, 1948.

—— *The Greek Myths*, London, 1955.

Griffiths, J. G., *The Conflict of Horus and Seth*, Liverpool, 1960.

—— *The Origins of Osiris*, Berlin, 1966.

Haldane, J. B. S., *The Causes of Evolution*, London, 1932.

Harrison, J., *Prolegomena to a Study of Greek Religion*, Cambridge, 1903.

—— *Epilegomena to the Study of Greek Religion*, Cambridge, 1921.

—— *Themis*, London, 1963.

James, E. O., *Prehistoric Religion*, London, 1957.

—— *The Cult of the Mother Goddess*, London, 1959.

Johnson, A. R., 'Hebrew Conceptions of Kingship', in S. H. Hooke (Ed.), *Myth, Ritual and Kingship*, Oxford, 1958.

Jolly, C., 'The Seed-Eaters: A New Model of Hominid Differentiations based on a Baboon Analogy', *Man* 5 (1), 1970.

Jones, E., *Papers on Psycho-Analysis*, London, 1923.

—— *On the Nightmare*, London, 1931.

—— *Essays in Applied Psycho-Analysis*, London, 1951.

—— *Sigmund Freud: Life and Work*, London, 1953–7.

Kerényi, C., *Dionysos*, London, 1976.

Kummer, H., *Primate Societies*, Chicago, 1971.

Landtman, G., *The Kiwai Papuans of British New Guinea*, London, 1927.

Lang, A., *Myth, Ritual and Religion*, London, 1899.

Lenski, G. & Lenski, J., *Human Societies*, New York, 1978.

Levin, R. B., 'An Empirical Test of the Female Castration Complex', *Journal of Abnormal Psychology*, 71, 1966.

Licht, H., *Sexual Life in Ancient Greece*, London, 1931.

Lienhardt, G., *Divinity and Experience*, Oxford, 1961.

Lietzmann, H., *Messe und Herrenmahl*, Berlin, 1955.

—— *A History of the Early Church*, London, 1961.

Loewenstein, R. M., *Christians and Jews*, New York, 1951.

Manuel, F. E., *A Portrait of Isaac Newton*, Cambridge, Mass., 1968.

Menninger, K. A., 'Totemic Aspects of Contemporary Attitudes towards Animals', in Wilbur, G. B. and Muensterberger, W., *Psychoanalysis and Culture*, New York, 1967.

Merton, R., *Society, Technology and Science in Seventeenth-Century England*, New York, 1970.

Meyerowitz, E. L. R., *The Divine Kingship in Ghana and Ancient Egypt*, London, 1960.

Nilsson, M. P., *A History of Greek Religion*, Oxford, 1949.

Poirier, F. E., *Fossil Man*, St Louis, 1973.

Plutarch, *De Iside et Osiride*, Edited by J. Gwyn Griffiths, University of Wales, 1970.

Poliakov, L., *A History of Anti-Semitism*, London, 1974.

Pritchard, S., (Ed.), *Ancient Near-Eastern Texts Relating to the Old Testament*, Princeton, 1969.

Raymond, E., *In the Steps of St. Francis*, London, 1938.

Reich, W., *Reich Speaks of Freud*, London, 1972.

Reik, T., *Dogma and Compulsion*, New York, 1951.

—— *Myth and Guilt*, London, 1958.

—— *Ritual*, New York, 1959.

Roback, A. A., *Psychorama*, Cambridge, Mass., 1942.

Róheim, G., *Australian Totemism*, London, 1925.

—— 'The Pointing Bone', *Journal of the Royal Anthropological Institute*, 45, 1925.

—— 'Dying Gods and Puberty Ceremonies', *Journal of the Royal Anthropological Institute*, 49, 1929.

—— *Animism, Magic and the Divine King*, London, 1930.

—— 'Psycho-Analysis of Primitive Cultural Types', *International Journal of Psycho-Analysis*, XIII, 1932.

—— *The Riddle of the Sphinx*, London, 1934.

—— *The Origin and Function of Culture*, New York, 1943.

—— *The Eternal Ones of the Dream*, New York, 1945.

—— *War, Crime and the Covenant*, New York, 1945.

—— (Ed.), *Psychoanalysis and the Social Sciences*, New York, 1947.

—— *Psychoanalysis and Anthropology*, New York, 1950.

—— *Magic and Schizophrenia*, Bloomington, Indiana, 1955.

—— *Children of the Desert*, New York, 1974.

Sachs, H., *Masks of Love and Hate*, Cambridge, 1948.

Schaller, G. and Lowther, G., 'The Relevance of Carnivore Behaviour to the Study of the Early Hominids', *Southwestern Journal of Anthropology*, 25 (4).

Seligman, C. G. & Seligman, B. Z., *Pagan Tribes of the Nilotic Sudan*, London, 1932.

Seligman, C. G., *Egypt and Negro Africa*, London, 1934.

Simmel, E. (Ed.), *Anti-Semitism*, New York, 1946.

Spengler, O., *The Decline of the West*, London, 1961.

Spencer, B. and Gillen, F. S., *The Arunta*, London, 1927.

Strachey, J., 'Preliminary Notes Upon the Problem of Akhenaten', *International Journal of Psychoanalysis*, XX.

Strehlow, T. G. H., *Aranda Traditions*, Melbourne, 1947.

Tarachow, S., 'St Paul and Early Christianity', *The Psychoanalytic Quarterly*, XXI, 1953.

Thomson, G., *Studies in Ancient Greek Society*, London, 1949.

Van Gennep, A., *The Rites of Passage*, London, 1960.

Weber, M., *The Protestant Ethic and the Spirit of Capitalism*, London, 1930.

—— *The Theory of Social and Economic Organization*, New York, 1947.

—— *Ancient Judaism*, Glencoe, 1952.

—— *The Rational and Social Foundations of Music*, Carbondale, Illinois, 1958.

Webster, H., *Primitive Secret Societies*, New York, 1908.

Weisskopf, W., *The Psychology of Economics*, London, 1955.

White, J. M., *Ancient Egypt*, London, 1970.

Wilson, E. O., *Sociobiology*, Cambridge, Mass., 1975.

Wittfogel, K., *Oriental Despotism*, New Haven, 1957.

INDEX